DECADENT CULTURE
in the United States

SUNY series, Studies in the Long Nineteenth Century

Pamela K. Gilbert, editor

DECADENT CULTURE
in the United States

Art and Literature against

the American Grain, 1890–1926

DAVID WEIR

State University of New York Press

Published by

STATE UNIVERSITY OF NEW YORK PRESS, ALBANY

© 2008 State University of New York

For information, contact State University of New York Press,

www.sunypress.edu

Production and book design, Laurie Searl
Marketing, Michael Campochiaro

Library of Congress Cataloging-in-Publication Data
Weir, David, 1947 Apr. 20–
Decadent culture in the United States : art and literature against the
American grain, 1890–1926 / David Weir.
    p. cm. — (SUNY series, studies in the long nineteenth century)
Includes bibliographical references and index.
ISBN 978-0-7914-7277-4 (hardcover : alk. paper)
ISBN 978-0-7914-7278-1 (paperback : alk. paper)
 1. United States—Intellectual life—1865–1918.
 2. United States—Intellectual life—20th century.
 3. Boston (Mass.)—Intellectual life. 4. Chicago (Ill.)—Intellectual life.
 5. San Francisco (Calif.)—Intellectual life.
 6. Degeneration—Social aspects—United States—History.
 7. Decadence in art—History. 8. Art, American—History.
 9. Decadence (Literary movement)—United States—History.
 10. American literature—History and criticism. I. Title.
E169.1.W333 2008
306.4'7097309041—ddc22   2007002072

10 9 8 7 6 5 4 3 2 1

After all, it is not life that is short, it is youth.
—Edgar Saltus

In memory of David Geoffrey Weir (1973–1991)

Contents

Illustrations

Preface

In the final chapter of Joris-Karl Huysmans's À *Rebours* (1884), the decadent hero Des Esseintes despairs of continuing his life of refined corruption and rarefied aesthetic tastes because the kind of society that nurtured such tastes has all but ceased to exist. In its place has arisen a strange new world lorded over by "the jovial bourgeois," who "put[s] his trust in the power of his money and the contagiousness of his stupidity." Moreover, "[t]he result of his rise to power had been the suppression of all intelligence, the negation of all honesty, the destruction of all art."[1] And how best to describe this bourgeois world that is the antithesis of all that the decadent holds dear? "This was the vast bagnio of America transported to the continent of Europe; this was the limitless, unfathomable, immeasurable scurviness of the financier and the self-made man, beaming down like a shameful sun on the idolatrous city, which groveled on its belly, chanting vile songs of praise before the impious tabernacle of the Bank" (203). In Edith Wharton's *Madame de Treymes* (1907) the woman who has married into fin-de-siècle French aristocracy and become estranged from her husband, the decadent Marquis de Malrive, finds relief from her unhappiness in the company of "dear, good, sweet, simple, real Americans."[2] As her American suitor observes, Madame de Malrive (née Fanny Frisbee) "might abhor her husband, her marriage, and the world to which it had introduced her, but she had become a product of that world in its outward expression, and no better proof of the fact was needed than her exotic enjoyment of Americanism" (230). In different ways, then, these two fictional explorations of fin-de-siècle culture set up an extreme opposition of aristocratic, Continental decadence and all things American. Huysmans and Wharton both give credence to one critic's claim that "America is the last place on Earth which one would expect to provide fertile soil for literary Decadence."[3]

The comment is correct, but the metaphor is wrong: decadence does not root itself in "fertile soil" so much as in decaying lands, and America, in the 1890s, was widely perceived to have reached a point of crisis. Paradoxically, when the nation's "manifest destiny" was fulfilled, another, darker destiny loomed: once the frontier reached the Pacific, it ended; the only West left, some thought, was a long twilight of decline. Evidence of America's decay was readily observable in the sickness of its citizens: they were exhausted, they were degenerate, they were neurasthenic. Henry Adams and his brother Brooks analyzed the fin de siècle in different ways but came to the same conclusion: the nation's original energy was nearing maximum dissipation, and in their case, entropy was personal; the Adams family, in fact, was living proof of Max Nordau's theory of degeneration, or so they believed. Clearly, then, by the last decade of the nineteenth century there was decline and degeneracy aplenty in the United States. But decay by itself does not a decadent make; or, more precisely, decay alone is not sufficient to sustain a culture of decadence. What is required, really, is the desire for decay, the wish for degeneracy, the delectation of decline. Huysmans and Wharton are right to wonder whether such a culture is possible among a nation of self-made men and women—"dear, good, sweet, simple, real Americans," as Wharton put it. But as we shall see, the culture of decadence was indeed possible for a few fin-de-siècle Americans who were not so good and sweet, and who were far from simple—quite complex, actually, and not a little unreal.

This sense of unreality is compounded by the near-complete removal of American decadents from the social, political, and cultural life of the nation at large. In Europe, the decadent might well be removed from the social world that had formed him, but, at the same time, he remained connected to his social class. The fictional but prototypical Des Esseintes, isolated from his fellow aristocrats outside of Paris, is still Parisian and aristocratic to the core. In egalitarian America, to separate from society and to claim allegiance to a social class that does not really exist in the United States is to somehow cease to be American. In certain cases, this type of social dissociation was necessary for survival, given the sexual orientation of men such as F. Holland Day in Boston or Henry Blake Fuller in Chicago. That these sensitives could be Theodore Roosevelt's contemporaries is strange to contemplate today, and it is easy to imagine that such men were politically like-minded in their aversion to the vigorous, vainglorious chauvinism Roosevelt represented. But in this case our political imagination would be mistaken: Fuller made public his principled opposition to the imperialist impulses behind the Spanish-American War all right, but Day retreated into the political obscurity of fin-de-siècle Jacobite cults. Whether such cults in the aggregate add up to a unified culture is hard to say, but it is clear that artists as politically divergent as Day and Fuller shared an aesthetic sensibility thoroughly at odds with any number of American traditions, established or emerging: the Puritan heritage, the frontier ethos, sentimental realism, local color. Unlike their more celebrated expatriate precursors (such as Henry James or James Abbott MacNeill Whistler), the American decadents chose not to make their careers in Europe and did not always pursue a vision of high art. By contrast, they "Americanized" their experience of European culture while paradoxically distancing themselves from the national and local traditions that made the Americanization possible. That is, they put American individualism in the service of a culture at odds with America.

The culture of decadence in the United States, historically considered, begs the question of decadence generally and urges careful examination of that question: what, after all, is decadence? As many critics have observed, decadence is hard to define because the concept is so nuanced and polyvalent that the very procedure of definition misses the point.[4] The moment we say "Decadence is," the game is lost: decadence and denotation appear to be opposed. Indeed, before we can even begin to say what *decadence* is, we must first say what decadence *is*. Is it a general cultural condition or an individual mode of behavior? Does *decadence* refer to the state of a particular society at a specific historical moment or to a segment of society at any point in time? Does the appreciation of decadence require a special type of moral, emotional, or psychological sensitivity? Is decadence, simply stated, a sensibility? In aesthetic terms, is decadence mannered and imitative or, as some think, innovative and original? As this last query implies, the meaning of decadence often depends on the cultural disposition of the one offering the definition. As William Blake once said in a different but related context, "this history has been adopted by both parties."[5] Just as the meaning of Blake's mythic narrative of the Fall changes when the perspective shifts from Messiah to Satan, so the meaning of decadence varies depending on the party in power or, less allegorically, on the rhetoric of approval or opprobrium.

The meanings of the noun *decadence* and the adjective *decadent* are intensely problematic, and one must take care to discriminate the various meanings each term has within particular contexts. The starting point is the observation that both noun and adjective are rooted in the word *decay*. What, precisely, is conceived to be in a state of decay, and whether said state is desirable or not are questions that are difficult to answer, but some basic discriminations are fairly easy to make. First, decadence is often used to describe conditions of national or imperial decline. As a historical term, 'decadence' frequently refers to a late period of empire, with the fall of Rome as the paradigm case. Some imagine that Rome fell because of internal weaknesses that resulted, in turn, from social corruption and excessive indulgence in rarefied pleasures. In this view, overcivilization or overrefinement results in a sense of apathy and a feeling of unworthiness that involves the wish for renewal from without—the desire for a fresh infusion of barbarian blood. This is an important meaning of 'decadence' because the late nineteenth century is also an age when different empires begin to unravel; hence both the French and the English imagine that they are experiencing periods of national decline. This idea of decadence, then, attaches primarily to two historical periods: the late Roman Empire and the late nineteenth century, with the former period providing a sort of cultural template for the latter.

A second critical meaning of 'decadence' can be derived from the first. The notion that declining empires or nations are populated by overcivilized weaklings involves the idea of *degeneration*, which may denote something simple like *infertility*, but with the more important connotation that conditions of infertility and impotence are the *result* of excessive, unhealthy pleasures that have replaced the normal, healthy desire to propagate and preserve the species. Hence to be decadent in this sense involves an active antagonism to nature. In the nineteenth century, the German eugenicist Max Nordau argued in his influential book *Degeneration* (published in German in 1892, in French in 1893, in English in 1895) that many of his contemporaries were suffering from a condition of evolutionary atavism; that is, certain members of the human species were "throwbacks" to an earlier period of evolutionary "development." Nordau explains contemporary art almost exclusively in terms of pathological symptoms resulting from atavistic degeneration. The nineteenth-century theory of degeneration can be understood as a biological variation of an older idea of decadence. In this view, the sense of cultural decline that accompanies the loss of imperial power often involves imitative, mannered forms of artistic expression that seem empty and lifeless because of excessive investment in formalistic details: hence the art of a decadent age is unoriginal, derivative, or formulaic. This is one of the more traditional meanings of decadence; it involves the basic organic metaphor that different kinds of art go through ages of youth, maturity, and senescence. Nordau's theory, however, differs from the earlier one in that the kind of decadent art he imagines is not lifeless but alive with degenerate energy. Indeed, the nervous energy of degenerate art cannot be contained by conventional forms, and hence those forms are corrupted or destroyed by the very energy that animates them.

Nordau's energized degeneracy combined with the traditional, negative notion of decadent art as the lifeless index to a sick society suggests another conception of decadence of some importance. This theory proposes that, yes, forms of artistic expression are affected by conditions of historical decline, but they are not mannered and imitative as a result of those conditions. On the contrary, the art that is produced during periods of historical decline is paradoxically innovative and new: decadent art and the art of decadence are far from being the same thing. Art produced under conditions of perceived social or political decadence might very well involve special forms of artistic expression that capture the cultural conditions in operation as the overcivilized city, nation, or empire approaches its end. At such times classical rules of art are abandoned in favor of new and unusual forms of expression. Théophile Gautier described the language of Baudelaire's poetry as "*le style de décadence*" because it seemed to him perfectly suited to articulate the complexity of cultural decline, the anxiety of social decay, and the morality of personal corruption. An important idea here is the concept of literary style modeled on physical decomposition: just as the decaying body comes apart in pieces as it putrefies, so the page gives way to the sentence, the sentence to the phrase, the phrase to the word.[6]

In addition to these four "definitions" (historical decline, physical degeneration, and the negative and positive responses to cultural disintegration), the meaning of 'decadence' takes on new value when the word is used to refer to a set of styles and sensibilities associated with cultural and social transition. In some important senses the decadent style was a predication or an impetus to modernism in literature, while, at the same time, decadent tastes and habits came to signify modes of social behavior that were felt to be progressive or "advanced." The first of these transitional shadings of decadence is fairly well known: European decadents have long been treated as pre- or even protomodernists. The second, social shading of 'decadence' as a transitional term takes the activities of the aesthetes and decadents at the end of the nineteenth century as the preamble to twentieth-century transgressions of social and sexual boundaries.[7] Decadence, so understood, involves the deliberate violation of moral codes of conduct and the inculcation of a sense of sin. One problem with this aspect of decadence is that it validates religious belief and accepted moral categories: only one who *believes* that certain types of behavior are sinful can engage in sinful behavior. For this reason, a decadent lifestyle is simply not possible in a liberated age of relative values, except in the sort of debased, commercial sense captured by the dessert choice on many restaurant menus in America: "Chocolate Decadence." However limited the possibilities of decadence today, understanding nineteenth-century decadence in terms of transition brings together artistic and social meanings into a single construct. Baudelaire, for example, was simultaneously an artist of decadence and a decadent artist; that is, the poetry he wrote and the life he lived were governed, more or less, by a single sensibility that was the product of the transitional age in which he lived. Significantly, for Baudelaire the words *transition* and *décadence* were synonyms.[8]

That there actually were groups of people in the United States who designated themselves "decadent" during the transitional years of the fin de siècle is a fact of cultural history (little known, but a fact nonetheless). Still, decadent culture in the United States differs in important respects from its better-known fin-de-siècle counterparts in France and England. Obviously, the relationship of decadence to empire is complicated by the nature of America as an ascendant, energetic nation, only recently removed from its frontier origins. Likewise, the common formulation, described above, that finds the weak-willed, overcultured decadent awaiting regeneration through a fresh infusion of barbarian blood is complicated in America by the relation of the cultivated class of "native" Anglo-Saxons to the immigrant masses, who were hardly welcomed as a regenerative force. Another complication lies in the relation of decadence to aesthetic sensibility in the aftermath of the Civil War. During

this period many Americans rejected the martial ideals of the war years to follow an aesthetic movement much more populist and domestic than its better-
known British counterpart. Finally, the capitalist, commercial context of
America provides possibilities for the entrance of decadence into popular culture to a degree that simply did not obtain in Europe at the turn of the century.
In short, an examination of decadence in America should help to sharpen our
theoretical understanding of decadence in general by considering variations in
the cultural context in which decadence operates.

In fin-de-siècle America, then, 'decadence' refers at once to a period of historical decline, an aesthetic sensibility, and a cultural movement. In the
1890s, little more than a century after the nation's founding, many Americans
were concerned that the country had already entered a period of decline. The
response to this sense of historical decline—or social decadence—was quite
complex. While most Americans agreed with the politicians and preachers
who urged them to adopt a more vigorous, less aesthetic, less "feminine"
lifestyle, a few welcomed the prospect of social collapse and saw their own removal from the American scene as certification of a superior aesthetic attitude. Strangely, personal degeneration, the individual corollary of some general sense of historical decline and social collapse, was almost a point of pride
among the dudes and dandies of the fin de siècle. Those who cultivated this
paradoxical sensibility recognized and admired the European writers who likewise coupled corruption and refinement. The New York decadents were
largely Francophile and took their inspiration from Baudelaire and Huysmans.
The Boston decadents admired the British most of all and imitated Walter
Pater and Oscar Wilde. The Midwestern decadents combined the tastes of
their East Coast counterparts, but Chicago, surprisingly, was also home to a
small circle of D'Annunzio admirers. In every case, the British and Continental literature that now forms a widely recognized canon of decadence provided
an alternative to the jingoism, sentimentality, and moralism of the 1890s.
Hence, history, aesthetics, and culture form a kind of chain in the American
fin de siècle. The sense of historical decline evokes an aesthetic response that
celebrates the culture of decadence, with 'decadence' here "defined" as the
paradoxically positive valuation of philosophical pessimism, physical degeneration, personal immorality, and social decay. This pattern that links history,
aesthetics, and culture is familiar enough from the history of nineteenth-
century European decadence. What makes the American response different is
the absence of anything like a native tradition of decadent culture to draw upon.
In France, Huysmans was able to write the New Testament of Decadence as *À
Rebours* because *Les Fleurs du mal*, the Old Testament of Decadence, provided
the inspiration.[9] Nineteenth-century Americans, by contrast, had no Baudelaire and, thus, had no choice but to derive their idea of decadence from European models. Inevitably, this means that there is something secondhand about
American decadence, so the traditional, negative meaning of 'decadence' as

"mannered imitation" has some relevance to the American variant. Still, this "decadent decadence" is not without its appeal, given the cultural alternatives on offer in 1890s America.

Against the Grain is a fairly accurate translation of the title of Huysmans's *À Rebours*, and the phrase captures the sense of cultural opposition—or oppositional culture—so important to the idea of decadence. The inspiration for the phrase in my own subtitle comes from Huysmans and not from William Carlos Williams's creative exploration of the "New World" of American literature or from Dwight Macdonald's wry investigation of the effects of mass culture on high culture.[10] Rather, *Against the American Grain* expresses what I take to be a fact of the fin de siècle in the United States: that a number of Americans not only participated in the oppositional culture of Continental decadence but also produced their own version of it. Theirs was an America experienced *à rebours*. The varieties of this decadent culture are most evident, logically enough, in the major metropolitan centers of the country: New York, Boston, Chicago, San Francisco. Hence this book may be read as a kind of cultural geography that seeks to describe how decadence differs from one city to the next. After the introductory chapter "The Problem of American Decadence," chapter 2, "New York: Decadent Connections" examines the links between New York and Europe, as illustrated by Edgar Saltus, Vance Thompson, and James Huneker. Saltus is particularly important to the decadent efflorescence in America, since he wrote not only novels modeled after those of Huysmans and George Moore (the Francophile Irish writer quite popular in the United States) but also an introduction to Schopenhauer's philosophical pessimism and an account of the Roman Decadence. Neither Thompson nor Huneker was a notable creative light, but both had a keen critical sense of contemporary Continental literature, and both did much to introduce a New York audience to European decadents. Chapter 3, "Boston: Decadent Communities" presents groups of men and women who were drawn to decadence partly as a means of revolt against New England tradition and partly as a sort of cultural legitimation of same-sex desires that were socially taboo and legally prohibited. The Boston decadents differ from their aggressively heterosexual counterparts in New York, not only psychologically but also culturally, in that they gave expression to a decadent aesthetic in a wide variety of artistic media: Louise Imogen Guiney in poetry, F. Holland Day in photography, Ethel Reed in book design, and Ralph Adams Cram in architecture. Chapter 4, "Chicago: The Business of Decadence," investigates decadent culture in Chicago, home to the publishing firm of Stone and Kimball, whose house organ, *The Chap-Book*, kept the nation up-to-date on decadent developments in literature. Chicago was also home to Henry Blake Fuller, who turned his highly urbane, aesthetic eye on Chicago's burgeoning business community, recording in his novels some of the same conflicts of class and culture analyzed later, and more famously, by Thorstein Veblen in *The Theory of the Leisure Class* (1899). If chapter 4 describes the dissipation of decadence into the rising middle class, chapter 5 argues for the dissipation of decadence downward into one of the earliest of the many countercultures in "San Francisco: The Seacoast of Decadence." Ambrose Bierce, Gelett Burgess, and George Sterling all contributed to the displacement of decadence by bohemianism, albeit in rather different ways. The death of decadence, however, should not be exaggerated, for the culture makes its reappearance in 1920s America. The final chapter, "The Decadent Revival," shows how writers as various as H. L. Mencken, Kahlil Gibran, and Djuna Barnes, among others, looked at the nineties anew in the twenties. A brief afterword returns to the problem of American decadence announced at the outset and reexamines the topic of cultural dissipation described briefly in chapters 4 and 5. Here I use Kenneth Anger's *Hollywood Babylon*, as well as Anger's own films, to question the place of decadence in American culture—popular culture especially.

This book might very well be the first to devote exclusive attention to decadent culture in the United States. A few older studies, such as Larzer Ziff's *American 1890's* (1966) or Alfred Kazin's *On Native Grounds* (1942; reissued 1982) make reference to some of the same figures I do but place them in different cultural contexts. As the millennium approached at the end of the twentieth century, cultural interest in the prior fin de siècle was widespread, and a number of new studies of decadence emerged from this interest, including Elaine Showalter's *Sexual Anarchy* (1990), Murray Pittock's *Spectrum of Decadence* (1993), Ellis Hanson's *Decadence and Catholicism* (1997), and my own *Decadence and the Making of Modernism* (1995).[11] Curiosity about the prior fin de siècle in the 1990s spurred publication of much primary material formerly unavailable, as in *The Decadent Reader* (1998), which presents previously hard-to-find texts by Huysmans, Mirbeau, Rachilde, and others. Unfortunately, no American writing appears in the collection, and the scarcity of primary texts no doubt accounts for the paucity of critical studies of American decadence. With only a few limited exceptions, critical commentary on decadence in the United States is missing from such otherwise useful studies as *Perennial Decay* (1999), edited by Liz Constable, Dennis Denisoff, and Matthew Potolsky, or Charles Bernheimer's *Decadent Subjects* (2002). As the subtitle of Bernheimer's book suggests—*The Idea of Decadence in Art, Literature, Philosophy, and Culture of the Fin de Siècle in Europe*—the idea of decadence and the idea of America are rarely considered together. My earlier book does include discussion of the American authors James Huneker and Ben Hecht under the rubric "The Decline of Decadence," but, as the rubric implies, the thrust of the discussion is not on their Americaness but on their belatedness. Huneker's novel *Painted Veils* (1920) gets into George C. Schoolfield's encyclopedic *Baedeker of Decadence* (2003) for the same reason; he also mentions, but does not discuss, Hecht, James Branch Cabell, and George Jean Nathan as examples of "the belated American outburst of an imitative decadence."[12]

Schoolfield's assessment of the imitative decadents of the 1920s is apt, but his awareness of the "original" American decadents of the 1890s is nil. Hence, the present study cannot be said to build on a critical tradition specific to American decadence, and the lack of such a tradition, combined with the unfamiliarity of the primary material, means that analysis has to yield to exposition, sometimes extended, in several chapters. In many cases, the books I discuss have been out of print since their original publication. But my purpose is not solely to bring an obscure tradition to light: I hope also to show the relevance of that tradition to more familiar figures—such as Mencken and Barnes—and I suspect readers of this book will find themselves thinking of decadence in connection to some truly canonical authors that I do not discuss (such as William Faulkner and F. Scott Fitzgerald). Even authors and artists who are securely a part of the American grain might very well have the culture of decadence working within them. This possibility exists because decadence dissipated into other areas of American culture after the efflorescence of the 1890s and the brief revival of the 1920s. Perhaps the final paradox of American decadence is simply this: that only by ending could the culture continue.

Acknowledgments

Those who would be decadent have no business at the Cooper Union for the Advancement of Science and Art. The founder of the institution remains a fixture of the long nineteenth century, not the wrong one. Still, enough would-be, latter-day "decadence" survives—especially among the students in the School of Art—that the odd unscrupulous scholar may take occasional advantage. Along these lines three students merit special thanks. Hannah Rawe brought her digital skills to bear on a key image entirely consonant with her diffident disposition. Sascha Braunig provided invaluable research assistance early on; Nina Schwanse did likewise in the later stages of the project. Both of them give reason to hope that the decadent sensibility may not be entirely absent from certain provinces of Canada and California, as Messrs. David Maher and Joseph Mosso, of the Balthazar Institute and the Pastis Foundation, respectively, can confirm.

Dr. Stephen Milner provided something like the original inspiration for this book by inviting me to the University of Bristol—a gorgeous place—for an international conference on decadence. As that inspiration waned the two anonymous readers for the State University of New York Press shored up the writing with their insightful and careful suggestions. Throughout, James Peltz, the director of the press, and his assistant, Allison Lee, were consistently attentive and professional in bringing this project to its degenerate end.

Finally, I remain thankful both to and for my wife, Camille, who continues to do justice to her nineteenth-century name.

Permission to publish material in the collections of the following institutions is gratefully acknowledged:

The Metropolitan Museum of Art, Alfred Stieglitz Collection, 1933, for F. Holland Day's *Portrait of a Man with Book* (accession number 33.43.361), all rights reserved;

The General Research Division, New York Public Library, Astor Lenox and Tilden Foundations for the frontispiece and title page of Ralph Adams Cram's *The Decadent* (1893); and also for Gelett Burgess's "Map of Bohemia" from an 1896 issue of *The Lark*;

The Library of Congress, Prints and Photographs Division, F. Holland Day Collection, for the photograph of Day in medieval costume (reproduction number LC-USZ62-93631) and for Day's *Gainsborough Hat* (LC-USZ62-52468), *Hannah* (LC-USZ62-70400), *Nude Youth with Laurel Wreath and Lyre* (LC-USZ62-63114), *Nude Youth with Laurel Wreath Embracing the Herm of Pan* (LC-USZ62-52927), and *Crucifixion* (LC-USZ62-70385). All other images reproduced herein are from my own collection.

CHAPTER ONE

Introduction: The Problem of American Decadence

However decadence is defined—as cultural decline, physical degeneration, aesthetic imbalance, moral transgression, hedonistic excess, pathological sexuality—the concept seems incompatible with the Puritan, progressive, capitalist values of America. Nineteenth-century Europe, by contrast, provided ample opportunity for social, medical, aesthetic, and moral fulminations against the decadence of the age. In France, the artist Thomas Couture and the critic Désiré Nisard compared their nation to the Roman Empire in decline.[1] Likewise, the German eugenicist Max Nordau took decadent Rome as the paradigm case in making his diagnosis of degenerate Europe. From Nordau's perspective, a major symptom of degeneracy could be found in the artistic irregularities of the late nineteenth century: impressionist artists, for example, painted as they did because their nervous disorders made their eyeballs vibrate.[2] From another perspective, artists and poets departed from earlier, rule-bound styles of art because those styles were simply inadequate to represent civilization in its last hours, with all the attendant psychological unease such a situation involved: hence the critic Théophile Gautier understood the poet Baudelaire to be an artist of decadence, not a decadent artist.[3] In the moral sphere, the combination of Catholic and aristocratic traditions gave the European the advantage in cultivating a life of refined corruption. The Church not only provided in its dogma clear moral categories to violate but also supplied in the sacrament of confession the vehicle to violate them again and again. Add to this the leisure and material resources of the aristocratic class, and a life of Continental decadence becomes a real possibility.

In America, the cultural conditions that produced the possibility of decadence in Europe simply did not exist. What would the poor decadent do in a country that had legislated against aristocratic corruption in favor of democratic idealism? How attractive could capitalism be, really, to one who preferred passivity to progress? And how easy could it be to violate moral codes—to go against the grain—when all morality was viewed as the variable product of the inner light of Protestant conscience? Only by reverting to near-defunct Marxist formulations might one describe American culture—so vigorous, so commercial, so crass—as "decadent." But the Marxist assessment of the decadence of America really belongs to the twentieth century and is hardly an assessment contemporary with Marx himself. In fact, the whole notion of America as a decadent culture is the product of Stalinist-era agitprop that was obliged to promote the superiority of Communist "progress" over Capitalist "decline."[4] Similarly, conservative analyses of historical decline, most famously Oswald Spengler's *Decline of the West* (*Untergang des Abendlandes*, 1918), might have counted America among the nations of the West that were in the process of going under (*Untergang*), but it was hardly the best example of that process.[5] An empire in decline is a far better breeding ground for decadence than an energetic, ascendant nation. In nineteenth-century Europe, conditions of political decline and social disintegration—or the perception of such—called forth the cultural response we now know as decadence. In the United States, that response was not so easy to justify, but surely American ingenuity and resourcefulness count for something: by the end of the century at least some of the nation's hard-working citizens had made themselves into creatures every bit as weak-willed, degenerate, and neurasthenic as their decadent Continental counterparts.

i

Because empire appears to be the necessary precondition of both historical decline and cultural decadence, fin-de-siècle America would seem to be the last place to look for the kinds of dandies, aesthetes, and decadents that populated the clubs of London and the salons of Paris. In Europe, a particular interpretation of history could be combined with a specific identification with a certain social class to produce a unique culture of decadence—unique, that is, to the interpretation of history as decline and the identification with the aristocratic class. To be decadent, then, it was necessary to believe that civilization was nearing its end and to maintain membership in the social class most responsible for that which was most civilized: the refinements of culture at the farthest remove from the barbarities of nature. What was not necessary was that either of these beliefs be true; in fact, decadent culture appears to emerge not so much from the reality of decline or the fact of the aristocracy as from a bourgeois fantasy of both. The examples of Joris-Karl Huysmans and Oscar Wilde help to make this point. Huysmans worked as a clerk for the French Ministry of Information and was about as far from the Faubourg St.-Germaine as it was possible to be; perhaps his own bourgeois removal from the aristocratic class was somehow cognate with his decadent hero's detachment from it, but it is still true that the Duc des Esseintes, whatever his relation to the comte de Montesquieu and other real-life models, is a fictional enactment of a reality largely denied to Huysmans himself. The same is true of Wilde, with the tragic difference that the Irish writer felt the need to enact the fantasy of aristocratic decadence not only in his fiction but also in his life. One of the most striking things about Wilde's *De Profundis*, his excoriation of his life with Lord Alfred Douglas, is how thoroughly at odds the hard-working author and the dilettante aristocrat seem to have been. Time and again, Wilde chides himself for sacrificing his art to the various forms of degradation his association with Bosie entailed.

In Europe, one medium for the bourgeois fantasy of the aristocratic life was aestheticism, and, indeed, in England especially this fantasy was played out almost exclusively among the educated class—meaning educated young men. In the United States, the aesthetic movement had found an audience much more domestic and female than its audience in England. On 31 January 1882, early in his American tour, Oscar Wilde delivered a lecture in Boston on the aesthetic movement with the Paterian title "The English Renaissance," the impact of which was widely felt among New England's intelligentsia.[6] To say that Wilde received an enthusiastic response that evening in Boston in late January 1882 would be a gross understatement. Newspaper accounts of the lecture describe "[c]ertain young men of Harvard" in the audience who behaved like the characters from the operetta *Patience*, Gilbert and Sullivan's lighthearted satire of the aesthetic movement in England. No doubt inspired by recent American performances of that work, they "appear[ed] in 'aesthetic' costume and play[ed] all sorts of pranks. . . . Over a half a hundred young men were there. . . . They filed down the aisle in pairs, arrayed in all the 'aesthetics' that ingenuity could devise. . . . They wore blond wigs and black wigs, wide-floating neckties of every hue and fashion . . . beards and moustaches of startling dyes, knee breeches and black stockings . . . and in every hand the . . . lily or the . . . sunflower. As the gracious youths entered they assumed all sorts of poses and held aloft or looked languishingly down on the flower."[7] The reaction suggests mockery mixed with tribute, with at least a modicum of sympathy. Wilde chided the young men by telling them "that there is more to the movement of aestheticism than kneebreeches and sunflowers."[8] As Richard Ellmann puts it, "It was one of the great moments of his tour, certified as a triumph by no less an authority than the Boston *Evening Transcript* on 2 February" (Ellmann, 193).

The enthusiastic reception of Wilde's lectures, not just in Boston, but throughout the United States (he visited more than a hundred cities in 1882), shows that many Americans were cultivating aesthetic interests well in advance of Wilde's visit. When the advance manager of the tour canvassed booking agents throughout the country to determine the subject matter that most Americans wanted Wilde to expound upon, the overwhelming response was "The Beautiful," rather than, say, "the poetical methods used by Shakespeare" (qtd. in Ellmann, 152). In her study of this celebrated tour, the historian Mary

Blanchard says that Wilde "entered a culture prepared for his visit. The aesthetic revolution was indeed an accomplished fact" in America by the time Wilde arrived (Blanchard, 3). She goes on to argue that this aesthetic revolution was much more populist and domestic than its better-know British counterpart and that it existed to a significant degree as a reaction to the Civil War: "A certain war-weariness induced some Americans to seek alternate modes of self-definition, as new formats—aesthetic style, for one—competed with older categories like the manly soldier in defining manhood. For many, concepts of manhood shifted from the Civil War battlefield to the artistic parlor" (Blanchard, 4). Americans had also turned to the artistic parlor to escape the Puritan church. In an 1884 essay, "Christianity and Aestheticism," the theologian Washington Gladden wrote that "[l]ife was never meant to be so bleak and bare as the Puritans made it. . . . The old Puritan doctrine, that art is sinful, has been roundly repudiated, as it ought to have been."[9] But these notions of aestheticism as a means of either mitigating the severity of Puritan religion or expressing disenchantment with the soldierly ideal of traditional masculinity belong mainly to the 1870s and 1880s.

As America entered the 1890s, many expressed concern that the great national energy that had opened the frontier and settled the continent was on the wane. The historian Frederick Jackson Turner made his reputation by arguing in 1893 that the enlightenment values of liberty and individualism on which the country was founded had been realized most fully on the frontier: it was "the source of American greatness," and the passing of the frontier signaled an inevitable decline.[10] Turner's audience for the original airing of his now-famous "frontier thesis" was limited to a handful of professional historians at a conference held in conjunction with the Columbia Exposition in Chicago. The paper was not especially well received, in part because of competition from the world's fair itself, but also because of Turner's departure from the "germ theory" of American history favored by his colleagues in the profession. The theory held that the institutions and values of American democracy had evolved by adapting European ideas to a new environment. A leader of this school of Darwinian historiography was Herbert Baxter Adams of Johns Hopkins University. Adams explained that it would be "just as improbable that free local institutions should spring up without a germ along American shores as that English wheat should have grown here without planting. Town institutions were propagated in New England by old English and Germanic ideas brought over by Pilgrims and Puritans."[11] Adams and other germ theorists tried to explain America as the product of Old World ideas; Turner focused on the New World circumstances "that modified those ideas in human practice" (Brands, 22). As Turner put it, "The peculiarity of American institutions is the fact that they have been compelled to adapt themselves to the changes of an expanding people, to the changes involved in crossing a continent, in winning a wilderness, and in developing at each area of this progress, out of the primitive economic and political conditions of the frontier, the complexity of city life" (qtd. in Brands, 23). If Americans were more individualistic, energetic, egalitarian, and practical than their European cousins, it was the frontier that had made them so.

Turner was eager to convey his ideas to people outside the narrow circle of his colleagues in the history profession. To this end he gave frequent public lectures and made arrangements with Walter Hines Page, the editor of the *Atlantic Monthly*, to contribute a series of articles explaining the frontier thesis to the common reader. An article from the September 1896 issue of the magazine lays out the double conclusion of Turner's thinking: that life on the frontier had forged the American character and, more important, that the closing of the frontier could not but result in a deterioration of that character—hence the title, "The Problem of the West." First, Turner lays out the main points of his theory:

> The West, at bottom, is a form of society, rather than an area. It is the term applied to the region whose social conditions result from the application of older institutions and ideas to the transforming influences of free land. By this application, a new environment is suddenly entered, freedom of opportunity is opened, the cake of custom is broken, and new activities, new lines of growth, new institutions and new ideals, are brought into existence. The wilderness disappears, the "West" proper passes on to a new frontier, and, in the former area, a new society has emerged from this contact with the backwoods. . . . Decade after decade, West after West, this rebirth of American society has gone on, has left its traces behind it, and has reacted on the East. The history of our political institutions, our democracy, is not a history of imitation, of simple borrowing; it is a history of the evolution and adaptation of organs in response to changed environment, a history of the origin of new political species. In this sense, therefore, the West has been a constructive force of the highest significance in our life.[12]

It is easy to hear in all this the common misconception of Darwin's scientifically neutral "descent with modification" as a form of progressive amelioration, transferred from the biological to the social and political realms (Turner goes so far as to echo the title of Darwin's study in the phrase "origin of new political species"). Against this pseudo-Darwinian "constructive force," however, Turner balances another nineteenth-century scientific theory—the second law of thermodynamics, likewise transposed from natural to sociopolitical terms:

> We are now in a position to see clearly some of the factors involved in the Western problem. For nearly three centuries the dominant fact in American life has been expansion. With the settlement of the Pacific coast and the occupation of the free lands, this movement has come to a check. That these energies of expansion will no longer operate would be a rash prediction; and the demands for

a vigorous foreign policy, for an interoceanic canal, for a revival of our power on
the seas, and for the extension of American influence to outlying islands and ad-
joining countries, are indications that the movement will continue. (Qtd. in
Smith and Dawson, 405–06)

In this passage, Turner anticipates the first great wave of American imperial
expansion that began with the Spanish-American War of 1898 and predicts a
couple of significant events associated with the rise of America's empire. Since
in ancient Rome and modern Britain decadence followed and possibly caused
the collapse of empire, the pursuit of empire might make it possible for America to avoid decadence and its discontents.

Turner's demands for an "interoceanic canal" were not met until the Panama Canal was opened in 1914, but by the end of the 1890s America's power
on the seas had been impressively revived by Commodore Dewey's conquest of
the Philippines. It is hard to say to what extent Turner's ideas actually influ-
enced the events he predicted in 1896, but it is at least worth noting that the
frontier thesis was known to Theodore Roosevelt, who read the 1893 Chicago
address and commented that the historian had put "into shape a good deal of
thought that had been floating around rather loosely" (qtd. in Brands, 24). If
Roosevelt continued to follow the development of Turner's thought in the
popular format of the *Atlantic Monthly*, he would no doubt have been struck by
the conclusion of "The Problem of the West." There Turner speculates about a
possible union of western and southern energies: "The old West, united to the
New South, would produce, not a new sectionalism, but a new Americanism.
It would not mean sectional disunion, as some have speculated, but it might
mean a drastic assertion of national government and imperial expansion
under a popular hero" (qtd. in Smith and Dawson, 406).

ii

With the frontier vanishing, the wholesome energy that had gone into civiliz-
ing the wilderness lacked the outlet that the open spaces provided. Bottled up
in crowded cities, Americans were no longer truly themselves but pitiable
"neurasthenics" who suffered from overcivilization. The New York neurologist
George Miller Beard, who popularized the term *neurasthenia*, diagnosed his
late-nineteenth-century compatriots as pitiful creatures indeed: "pathetic descendant[s] of the iron-willed Americans who had cleared forests, drained
swamps, and subdued a continent."[13] However pathetic they might have been,
fin-de-siècle Americans were not, paradoxically, inferior to their more vigorous ancestors. Quite the contrary, in fact: in Beard's view, neurasthenia, or
"nervous exhaustion," afflicted only those who were most civilized and modern. Indeed, Beard believed that the "primary cause of this development and
very rapid increase of nervousness is *modern civilization*."[14] It stands to reason,

then, that "lack of nerve-force" should be most prevalent and most severe "in the Northern and Eastern portions of the United States" (vi) where civilization is most "intense" (152).

The intensity of modern civilization is distinguished by five factors completely unknown to the ancients and largely unknown to generations prior to the nineteenth century: "steam-power, the periodical press, the telegraph, the sciences, and the mental activity of women" (vi). These factors are not unique to America, of course, so the British and the Europeans also suffer from neurasthenia, though not to the same degree that Americans do: "The greater prevalence of nervousness in America is a complex resultant of a number of influences, the chief of which are dryness of the air, extremes of heat and cold, civil and religious liberty, and the great mental activity made necessary and possible in a new and productive country under such climatic conditions" (vii). Thus neurasthenia was a "distinguished malady" (22) that indicated the superiority of Americans so afflicted. Indeed, neurasthenic Americans were superior not only to their own ancestors but also to peoples of other nations, races, and religions. According to Beard, neurasthenia was "modern, and originally American; and no age, no country, and no form of civilization, not Greece, nor Rome, nor Spain, nor the Netherlands, in the days of their glory, possessed such maladies" (vii–viii).

Beard also argued that neurasthenia attacked only the most "advanced" races, hence the severity of the affliction among the "native" stock of Anglo-Saxon Americans. After all, only those with a "fine organization" are predisposed to the disease. Quite clearly, what Beard calls a "fine organization" is a collection of Anglo-Saxon racial features: "fine, soft hair, delicate skin, nicely chiseled features, small bones, tapering extremities." Those likely to become neurasthenics possess a "superior intellect" because a fine organization is characteristic of "the civilized, the refined, and educated, rather than of the barbarous and low-born and untrained. . . . It is developed, fostered, and perpetuated with the advance of culture and refinement, and the corresponding preponderance of labor of the brain over that of the muscles. . . . It is oftener met with in cities than in the country" (26).

By contrast, those races with "coarse" rather than "fine" features are not susceptible to neurasthenia at all. Beard goes to some lengths to detail the hardiness of the uncivilized, noting, for instance, that "[t]he Indian has less sickness than the white, and is, as a rule, in perfect health and well-developed," despite less-than-ideal living conditions: "bad air, bad water, and bad food do not have any provably injurious effect on his constitution" (183). Not only the Indians, but also the "Southern Negroes" provide Beard with a kind of living laboratory to study the relationship of nervous disease and civilization: "on our own soil, barbarism can be well investigated" (183). Beard studies what he calls "Africa in America"—former slaves living on the islands off the coast of South Carolina, a group "who at no time [has] been brought into relation with our civilization"

(188). This "bit of barbarism at our door-steps" enables Beard to deduce certain key "facts of comparative neurology." In contrast to the educated white citizens of Boston and New York, "[t]here is almost no insanity among these Negroes; there is no functional nervous disease or symptoms among them of any name or phrase; to suggest spinal irritation, or hysteria of the physical form, or hay fever, or nervous dyspepsia among these people, is but to joke" (189). The rude vigor of Indians and Negroes make Beard painfully aware of all that the white races have lost: "All this freedom from nervousness and nervous diseases we have sacrificed for civilization: we cannot, indeed, have civilization and have anything else; as we advance we lose sight and possession of the region through which we have passed" (191). In short, as the historian Tom Lutz puts it, "Beard argued that neurasthenia was caused by the highest levels of civilization and that the epidemic of neurasthenia was proof that America was the highest civilization that had ever existed."[15] Likewise, only the practitioners of the more "advanced" Protestant religions were likely to be affected, since "no Catholic country is very nervous" (126). There was, of course, nervous affliction aplenty in Catholic France, but where the American illness appeared to afflict just about all members of the upper classes, broadly speaking, in Europe the disease, whatever it was called, was confined largely to hypersensitive artists such as the Goncourt brothers.

To imagine that any American could approach the level of cultural sophistication possessed by the Goncourt brothers is strange to contemplate; stranger yet is the notion that *most* Americans did just that. Yet in 1897 the attorney Henry Childs Merwin wrote an essay for the *Atlantic Monthly*, "On Being Civilized Too Much," in which he adjudged the typical American "a creature who is what we call oversophisticated and effete—a being in whom the springs of action are, in greater or lesser degree, paralyzed or perverted by the undue predominance of the intellect."[16] The 1895 English translation of Max Nordau's *Degeneration* found a ready audience in a nation where the masculine values of the founders had so recently foundered. Mayo W. Haseltine, the editor of the New York *Sun,* read Nordau and agreed with the general diagnosis of social decline but disagreed as to its cause. Indeed, Hazeltine's reading of Nordau was challenged by no less an authority than Nordau himself, mainly because the esteemed editor placed too much weight on immorality alone in seeking to account for "the *fin de siècle* malady."[17] According to Nordau, Hazeltine's views differ from his own in three important respects: "Mr. Hazeltine does not believe that this malady is a new manifestation; he does not believe that it is caused by degeneration; and he does not recognize its etiology in the effects of the new inventions, the growth of the great cities, and the ravages of the stimulating poisons, particularly of alcohol; but, rather, in the loss of religious faith" (90).

Nordau faults Hazeltine for failing to see that "delirious tendencies" are at work alongside the "immoral tendencies" that are apparent to both writers. But Nordau does credit Hazeltine for noting analogies between the present age and prior periods of decline, since he "makes religious decay responsible for the disease of this age as well as for the morbid phenomena of the twelfth century and of the time of the Roman empire" (92). Indeed, Nordau places a great deal of emphasis on the historical similitude and repeats his own observation that "[i]n Rome, at the Decline, we find precisely as at the present day, an unraveling of all moral bonds, ferocity in manners, unsparing egotism, sensualism and brutality; we find multitudes whose loathing of life impels them to suicide" (90-91). But Hazeltine's refusal to fully credit the effects of "organic ruin"—that is, degeneration—along with religious ruin prevents him from seeing, in Nordau's estimation, that the malady of the fin de siècle is far worse than any that have gone before: "Our age certainly has individual features in common with other ages, but at no time known to me were there, in addition to the phenomena of mere brutality and lewdness, so many symptoms of organic ruin observable as now" (93).

Despite the general acceptance of his theories in the United States, Nordau's insistence on organic ruin is something that sets him apart from nineteenth-century medical theory in America. Nordau's claims hinge on the bizarre notion that evolution cuts both ways: that some species advance while others—or, at least, certain individual members of a particular species—regress or devolve; these latter are the atavistic "throwbacks" to a more primitive stage of evolution. Hence Nordau is able, in effect, to attribute the ills and anxieties of modern civilization to the presence and activities of degenerate individuals. By contrast, American theorists like Beard and his Philadelphia counterpart S. Weir Mitchell believe that it is modern civilization itself that causes the symptoms in the countrymen they see around them. Significantly, Americans are not degenerate; rather, they are exhausted. In Nordau's Europe, degeneracy is the ruin of civilization; in Beard's and Weir's America, civilization is the ruin of the citizenry, or, at least, that portion of the citizenry charged with doing the "brain-work" that keeps the capitalist economy humming.

S. Weir Mitchell uses the phrase "cerebral exhaustion" to refer to the afflictions of "all classes of men who use the brain severely."[18] The symptoms of an overtaxed brain include "giddiness, dimness of sight, neuralgia of the face or scalp, . . . entire nights of insomnia" (Mitchell, 72). Such symptoms of cerebral exhaustion are most likely to strike "manufacturers and certain classes of railway officials," followed by "merchants in general, brokers, etc.; then less frequently clergymen; still less often lawyers; and more rarely doctors." We are also told that "distressing cases are apt to occur among the overschooled of both sexes" (Mitchell, 63). Lawyers are less susceptible to cerebral exhaustion than are other professional men largely because of "their long summer holiday" (Mitchell, 65). Not surprisingly, the cure for the overworked brain is less work and more leisure, less time indoors and more time outside. Indeed, Mitchell avers early on that nature is the great healer; moreover, nature can strengthen man sufficiently to allow him to indulge in mild vices without suffering the deleterious effects evident in the closed spaces of the city: "The man who lives an outdoor life—who sleeps with the stars visible above him—who wins his bodily sustenance at first hand from the earth and waters—is a being who defies rain and sun, has a strange sense of elastic strength, may drink if he likes, and may smoke all day long, and feel none the worse for it" (Mitchell 7–8). Mitchell strongly advocated "[s]ome such return to the earth" for the purposes of restoring not only the health of individuals but also that of the nation at large.

In an odd complement to Turner's frontier thesis, Mitchell remarks on the earlier benefits of the outdoor life, which gave "vigor and developing power to the colonist of an older race cast on a land like ours" (Mitchell, 8). Strangely, the energies of America's colonists and frontiersmen have the contradictory effect of both preserving and destroying the national welfare:

> A few generations of men living in such fashion [i.e., outdoors, as on the frontier] store up a capital of vitality which accounts largely for the prodigal activity displayed by their descendants, and made possible only by the sturdy contest with Nature which their ancestors have waged. That such life is still led by multitudes of our countrymen is what alone serves to keep up our pristine forces and energy. Are we not merely using the interest on these accumulations of power, but also wastefully spending the capital? (Mitchell, 8)

Fortunately for Mitchell, a sufficiency of Americans continue to live and work in the country to keep the overall effects of the "prodigal activity" of city life in check, at least temporarily. Although Mitchell was writing well before Nordau published his theory of degeneration, his ideas made for a ready fit with that theory, especially as interpreted by Nordau's American followers. Hazeltine, for instance, might have placed more emphasis on the problem of immorality, but he accepted that fin-de-siècle Americans were physically inferior, not only to the soldiers of the Roman legions but also to their own ancestors who had fought the War of Independence. In the end, Hazeltine concluded that a way out of the morass of physical lassitude and moral turpitude might lie in a purifying "return" to the crusading age of medieval violence that America had never, of course, had the chance to experience.[19]

Hazeltine was not alone in celebrating the virtues of medievalism against the ills of fin de siècle America. Many late nineteenth-century Americans cultivated an interest in the Middle Ages by reading the novels of Sir Walter Scott and the criticism of John Ruskin, who helped to spur the Gothic Revival in the United States. Also, the Pre-Raphaelite Brotherhood, which Ruskin had helped to inspire, established a following in America in the mid-1850s and achieved a measure of success at least the equal of its standing in Great Britain.[20] Oscar Wilde's lecture tour of 1882 may have contributed to a resurgence of interest in Pre-Raphaelite art, though it had never really gone out of fashion.

The fascination with the Middle Ages is also evident in Mark Twain's *A Connecticut Yankee in King Arthur's Court* (1889) by way of the satiric reversals that show how utterly different late nineteenth-century America really was from the storied world of medieval romance. But Twain's satire was lost on those who combined their aesthetic interests in Pre-Raphaelitism with an earnest belief that the kind of culture promoted by latter-day medievalists such as Scott and Ruskin was genuinely superior to fin-de-siècle America.

iii

Among those most interested in understanding the social and economic underpinnings of medieval art was Brooks Adams, the youngest of the three brothers descended from two U.S. presidents. "To Adams, medieval character seemed an exhilarating fusion of martial virtue and religious faith, a sharp counterpoint to the sordid commercial ethic of the Gilded Age."[21] The diminished status of the Adams family in the last decade of the nineteenth century also had something to do with the young scion's interest in the problem of historical decline, which he investigated at length in *The Law of Civilization and Decay* (1896). Together with his better-known brother, Henry, Brooks Adams became fairly obsessed with theories of entropy and degeneration, thereby lending scientific support to his ideas of historical and personal decline. Indeed, the Adams brothers felt that their case was representative of a larger, downward-tending dynamic, which, in private, they acknowledged as having particular relevance to their own once-powerful family: "It is now full four generations since John Adams wrote the constitution of Massachusetts. It is time that we perish. The world is tired of us."[22] In 1890, Henry Adams toured the South Seas "and observed the contrast between the healthy nudity of Samoa and the Westernized degeneration of Tahiti." The brothers also took a scientific interest in their own father's decay, with Nordau's *Degeneration* as a guide.[23] Moreover, they understood the applicability of Nordau's theory to themselves and even contemplated a trip to Germany to allow the famous eugenicist to study them in person, since "he seems to have had no degenerates or hysterics of our type—fellows who know all about it but manage to get a world of fun and some pleasure from it."[24]

Personal interest aside, Brooks Adams's investigation of the decay of nations was certainly precipitated by the widespread impression that the United States was in the midst of a period of decline in the 1890s. Adams's explanation for this decline differed from Turner's frontier thesis in that Adams understood America in the broader context of civilization itself, which was regulated by certain immutable laws that produced the same patterns again and again throughout history. Like other nineteenth-century positivists, Adams couched his theory in thermodynamic terms. In 1852, William Thompson, later titled Lord Kelvin, formulated the second law of thermodynamics and identified "a universal tendency in nature to the dissipation of mechanical energy." In 1854, Kelvin's concept of 'dissipation' was further elaborated by Hermann von Helmholtz, who explained that eventually "all energy will . . . be transformed into heat at a uniform temperature," whereupon all natural processes would come to an end. This "heat-death" theory of the universe and the underlying principle of energy dissipation were restated by Rudolf Clasius in 1865 and given the name *entropy*, derived from the Greek word ἐντροπή, meaning transformation.[25] Kelvin's second law of thermodynamics, as elaborated by Hemholtz and renamed by Clasius, underwent a broad cultural diffusion in the late nineteenth century, and Brooks Adams's *Law of Civilization and Decay* is one of the documents of this diffusion. His analysis of civilization's inevitable decay begins by evoking the scientific authority of the second law of thermodynamics: "The theory proposed is based upon the accepted scientific principle that the law of force and energy is of universal application in nature, and that animal life is one of the outlets through which solar energy is dissipated."[26] It follows from "this fundamental proposition" that "as human societies are forms of animal life, these societies must differ among themselves in energy, in proportion as nature has endowed them, more or less abundantly, with energetic material" (ix). An important "manifestation of human energy" is thought, which early on is divided into two simple but "conspicuous" phases: fear and greed. Fear "stimulat[es] the imagination, creates a belief in an invisible world, and ultimately develops a priesthood"; greed, by contrast, "dissipates energy in war and trade" (ix).

Under certain conditions, then, solar energy is dispersed or vented through the medium of human thought in one of three competing forms: imaginative, martial, or economic. One or the other of these three types of thought—motivated by fear, greed, or some mixture of fear and greed—will dominate depending on the degree of consolidation or centralization in any given society. This last point is key because civilization itself hinges on the concept of centralization: Adams's theory purports "to classify a few of the more interesting intellectual phases through which human society must, apparently, pass, in its oscillations between barbarism and civilization, or, what amounts to the same thing, in its movement from a condition of physical dispersion to one of concentration" (viii). The theory is summed up in one of Adams's more scientific-sounding paragraphs:

> Probably the velocity of the social movement of any community is proportionate to its energy and mass, and its centralization is proportionate to its velocity; therefore, as human movement is accelerated, societies centralize. In the earlier stages of concentration, fear appears to be the channel through which energy finds the readiest outlet; accordingly, in primitive and scattered communities, the imagination is vivid, and the mental types produced are religious, military, artistic. As consolidation advances, fear yields to greed, and the economic organism tends to supersede the emotional and martial. (ix)

The objective, "scientific" language does not convey what later becomes evident—that the dominance of economic interests in Adams's own age involves a weakening of both imaginative life and martial temper.

Adams's analysis of the fall of Rome leaves no doubt that ruin is wrought by economic dominance: "The evolution of this centralized society was as logical as every other work of nature. When force reached the stage where it expressed itself exclusively through money, the governing class ceased to be chosen because they were valiant or eloquent, artistic, learned, or devout, and were selected solely because they had the faculty of acquiring and keeping wealth." Paradoxically, the weakness of this governing, "monied class lay in their very power, for they not only killed the producer, but in the strength of their acquisitiveness they failed to propagate themselves" (44). The choice between making babies and making money is one that Adams sees repeated in his own gilded age: "Taking history as a whole, women seem never to have more than moderately appealed to the senses of the economic man. The monied magnate seldom ruins himself for love, and chivalry would have been as foreign to a Roman senator under Diocletian, as it would be now to a Lombard Street banker" (370–71). Just as the Romans of "the third and fourth centuries" were deficient in "the martial and the amatory instincts" (370), the men of the nineteenth century are guilty of a "decisive rejection of the martial and imaginative mind" (324). Adams has the facts to back up the claim that "there has been a marked loss of fecundity among the more costly races" and is concerned that the fate of France awaits the United States: "In 1789 the average French family consisted of 4.2 children. In 1891 it had fallen to 2.1, and, since 1890, the deaths seem to have equaled the births" (350).

The facts most important to Adams's argument, however, concern not the propagation of the species but the production of specie. Practically every civilization he studies is at its height when economic values are based on silver currency. In Rome the purity of the silver denarius is maintained until Nero begins to add copper alloy to the coin, a process of debasement that continues until, by the time of Elagabalus in 220 AD, the denarius "degenerate[s] into a token of base metal" (26). Likewise, the empire of Charlemagne disintegrates as more and more alloy is added to the silver pence (128–29). The fortunes of Venice, Spain, and finally Great Britain rise and fall with the quantity and purity of silver currency, at least until the beginning of the nineteenth century. Adams claims that the victory of Simon Bolivar in Latin America and the defeat of Napoléon in Europe ushered in a new economic age: "From the year 1810, nature has favored the usurious mind, even as she favored it in Rome, from the death of Augustus" (325). What he means is that with the decisive defeats of the Spanish in the New World and the French in the Old World, Great Britain took effective control of the international economy through the introduction of the gold standard, which it had used to finance the war against Napoléon. As James Buchan puts it, "With the defeat of Bonaparte at Waterloo, the gold standard became a legal concept . . . that served the interests of certain classes of society so obediently that those classes came to regard it as natural, perfect, and timeless."[27] The United States adopted the gold standard in 1873, which for Adams is the signal event marking the problems of the age: "When the mints had been closed to silver, the currency being inelastic, the value of money could be manipulated like that of any article limited in quantity, and thus the human race became the subjects of the new aristocracy, which represented the stored energy of mankind" (349). Earlier, we are told that "capital may be considered as stored energy" and that "money alone is capable of being transmuted into any form of activity" (313). Adams's history shows that the type of money that is most flexible and capable of the most rapid transmutations of human energy is silver currency. The adoption of the gold standard in 1873 and the elevation of a handful of bankers to positions of unprecedented power and control indicate, for Adams, that civilization has entered "the last stage of consolidation," in which "the economic, and, perhaps, the scientific intellect is propagated, while the imagination fades, and the emotional, the martial, and the artistic types of manhood decay" (x).

Adams devotes only a few pages at the very end of his treatise to the way art "reflects" the various transformations of solar energy that make up the different martial, imaginative, and economic ages he has described. Nonetheless, he makes the point in the strongest possible terms that imaginative art has been overwhelmed by "the economic taste" (381). The fresco, for example, is nothing more than a cheap substitute for a mosaic devised by some "Florentine banker" who "had his interior painted at about one-quarter the price" (380). Likewise, portrait painting "has usually been considered to portend decay, and rightly, since the presence of the portrait demonstrates the supremacy of wealth . . . for it is a commercial article, sold for a price, and manufactured to suit a patron's taste" (380–81). But Adams is most critical of modern architecture, which has "reflected money . . . since the close of the fifteenth century" (382). Because Adams is dealing in underlying laws of civilization and decay, "what was true of the third century is true of the nineteenth." Like third-century Romans, nineteenth-century Americans favor the type of architecture produced by the economic spirit, "at once ostentatious and parsimonious, . . . a cheap core fantastically adorned" (382). There are, however, differences: "[T]he Romans were never wholly sordid, nor did they ever niggle. When they built a wall, that wall was solid masonry, not painted iron" (382).

For Adams, as for the Boston architect Ralph Adams Cram, the school of American architecture led by Louis H. Sullivan of Chicago represented more than the novel use of iron and steel to engineer the first skyscrapers: Sullivan's work was evidence that America had entered another Age of Iron, for modernity in any form is the antithesis of the Golden Age of medieval art:

No poetry can bloom in the arid modern soil, the drama has died, and the pa-
trons of art are no longer even conscious of shame at profaning the most sacred
of ideals. The ecstatic dream, which some twelfth century monk cut into the
stones of the sanctuary hallowed by the presence of his God, is reproduced to be-
dizen a warehouse; or the plan of an abbey, which Saint Hugh may have conse-
crated, is adapted to a railway station.

  Decade by decade, for some four hundred years, these phenomena have
grown more sharply marked in Europe, and, as consolidation apparently nears its
climax, art seems to presage approaching disintegration. The architecture, the
sculpture, and the coinage of London at the close of the nineteenth century,
when compared to those of the Paris of Saint Louis, recall the Rome of Caracalla
as contrasted with the Athens of Pericles, save that we lack the stream of barbarian blood which made the Middle Age. (383)

The closing reference to "barbarian blood" shows that Adams's scenario of cultural decline includes a component of racial degeneration. Indeed, degeneration and decline combine to produce the larger condition of decadence, even
though the word is not used in this particular passage. Adams does use "disintegration," however, which is a fair substitute for *decadence* in the context he
has devised: "art seems to presage approaching disintegration." The sentence is
ambiguous, implying either that art itself forebodes its own disintegration or
that the state of art in Adams's day is predictive of the disintegration of society. Most likely both meanings underlie Adams's anxiety about the decay of
civilization in his own age, which lacks the organic unity—the integration—
of art and society characteristic of the Middle Ages, or, at least, of the Middle
Ages as John Ruskin and his acolytes understood the era. Another author
might have seen "the close of the nineteenth century" as a particularly ripe
time for art precisely *because* of the conditions Adams describes. To experience decay, to observe decline, to capture the dynamics of social disintegration—might very well require an artist of unusual sensitivity and uncommon
skill. This is one of the larger paradoxes of decadence that Brooks Adams, despite his affinity for degeneration, was in no position to appreciate.

iv

Brooks Adams was far from being alone in his pessimistic views, especially as
concerns the perception of declining birthrates and other markers of racial
decline. The belief was widely held that Americans—that is, the so-called
native stock of Anglo-Saxon Americans—were on the verge of committing
"race suicide," as the future president Theodore Roosevelt put it, soon to be
replaced by masses of vigorous but somehow "inferior" immigrants.[28] So it
was not quite true, as Adams stated at the end of *The Law of Civilization and
Decay*, that America lacked the prospect of a fresh infusion of "barbarian"

blood. Perhaps the analogy never occurred to Adams because, unlike the barbarians who swept through Rome, the immigrant masses, or so Adams and Roosevelt thought, came not to renew but to destroy. The immigrant threat contributed to but did not cause, all by itself, the widespread perception of American weakness. But there was no mistaking that, in the middle of the 1890s, a nostalgia for a more martial and masculine ideal of manhood had set in.

American culture had become too aesthetic, too feminine—so much so that many women were concerned that *they* had become excessively delicate and domestic. An 1896 short story by Edna C. Jackson titled "A Fin de Cycle Incident" tells how a young woman struggles to conform to the daintily feminine ideal her fiancé has of her, which prohibits her from riding her beloved bicycle. The fiancé finally approves of the cycle when the heroine furiously pedals the machine to warn him of a plot against his life. She arrives in the nick of time, explaining breathlessly the necessity of the bloomers she is wearing: "I–I never could have made it with a skirt on" (qtd. in Smith and Dawson, 202). As this story suggests, the 1890s saw increasing interest in outdoor activities and physical exercise. The naturalist John Muir published *The Mountains of California* in 1894 and encouraged Americans to experience the great outdoors for themselves. In 1895 the first professional football game was played in Latrobe, Pennsylvania, which, paradoxically, spurred concern that sport might become "the sole possession of experts and champions," as H. W. Foster wrote in an essay titled "Physical Education vs. Degeneracy." Foster encouraged the adoption of physical education programs in all American schools, with "exercises [and games] specifically designed [to] bring out manliness, as well as the bodily powers" (qtd. in Smith and Dawson, 306).

American concern with physical culture toward the end of the nineteenth century is not always understood as an antidote to the dangers of decadence. In fact, the word *decadence* is rarely used. More often, the active life seems the necessary alternative to either national decline or nervous debility: the former problem a resultant of the vanishing frontier and the latter a product of the stresses of modern civilization. To be decadent one would have to develop an attitude of knowing acceptance of the prospect of collective ruin while also accepting or even relishing personal degeneration. The remedy for the threat of national ruin is the promotion and pursuit of political empire, as Turner had counseled, while the remedy for individual debility is the outdoor life, as S. Weir Mitchell had advised. In this dual context, no better exemplars of active opposition to decline and degeneracy can be found than Theodore Roosevelt and Thomas Wister. Early in the twentieth century, both men stood for everything that decadence was not, because both had become successful through a revival of frontier values, in one form or another. Roosevelt was elected president largely because of the national attention he received when he led the Rough Riders up San Juan Hill in 1898; and Wister had become the best-selling author in America because his novels of the Old West, like *The Virginian* (1902), were based on his firsthand experience working cattle ranches in Wyoming territory. Yet both Roosevelt and Wister had personal histories that included physical debility and cultural decadence. As young men at Harvard during the early 1880s, both Wister and Roosevelt cultivated aesthetic pretensions that have since become identified with decadence. Earlier writers used "Harvard indifference" to refer to "the cult of cleverness, exquisiteness, and boredom at that time, as exemplified by Whistler, Wilde, 'The Green Carnation,' etc. . . . the 'indifference' at Cambridge was partly, at least, an attempt to get into the mode." "Harvard indifference" was also said to include "an honest pose of restraint, calm, understatement, a distaste for exaggeration, expansiveness, [and] a kind of passive resistance to the cult of money."[29]

Wister had gone to Harvard to study music and, like many well-born young men of the time, was a devotee of Richard Wagner. He made the pilgrimage to Bayreuth in 1882, which he recalled as "that first summer of *Parsifal*," and managed an introduction to Franz Liszt, for whom he played one of his college piano compositions, titled *Merlin and Vivien*. Based on the title and the site of performance, the piece seems likely to have been a work of late romanticism inspired by medieval legend—Wagnerian, in short. According to Wister, Liszt approved of the piece and said that the young composer had "un talent prononcé" for music.[30] Nevertheless, Wister's father pressured him to abandon his music career for the law, and in 1885, as Wister puts it, "my health very opportunely broke down" (Wister, *Roosevelt*, 28). Perhaps even more opportunely, Wister was related to S. Weir Mitchell (they were cousins), who prescribed a cure at a cattle ranch in Wyoming. Twenty years later, this type of cure was close to cliché, as implied by the narrator of *Confessions of a Neurasthenic* (1908), who decides to "turn cowboy" in order to recover his "appetite and vigor": "I had frequently read of Yale and Harvard graduates going out and getting a touch of life on the plains; so, as such a life did not seem to be beneath the dignity of cultured people, I would give it a trial."[31] The Western experience does not work out so well for this latter-day neurasthenic, but Wyoming made all the difference for Wister. Going from Wagner to Wyoming in so short a time is a cultural *volte-face* of dizzying dimensions, and, while being a Wagnerite does not, by itself, certify Wister as "decadent," that particular cultural marker, along with his physical weakness and "Harvard indifference," at least put the man on a widely recognized, downward-tending cultural path.

Perhaps even more than Wister, Roosevelt cultivated an aesthetic persona while he was at Harvard and affected a highly dandified appearance. His affectations were such that his friend Wister satirized them in a Harvard musical entertainment as:

> Awful tart,
> And awful smart,
> With waxed mustache and hair in curls:
> Brand-new hat,
> Likewise cravat,
> To call upon the dear little girls.[32]

At the time he entered the New York legislature, Roosevelt had come to be known by a number of less-than-manly epithets, including "Young Squirt," "Weakling," "Jane Dandy," and "Oscar Wilde."[33] The latter epithet was bestowed upon Roosevelt when Wilde arrived in America, which happened to be on the same day that Roosevelt entered the legislature.[34] Roosevelt continued to be satirized as a dude or a dandy throughout the 1880s in the cartoons that appeared in *Puck* and other publications. A reporter at the Republican National Convention of 1884 described Roosevelt as "a rather dudish-looking boy with eye-glasses [who] applauded with the tips of his fingers; he had his hair parted in the middle, banged in front, rolled his *r*'s and pronounced the word *either* with an *i* sound instead of the *e*. He may have ability but he also has an inexhaustible supply of insufferable dudism and conceit, that will some day be fittingly rebuked."[35] After the convention, Roosevelt made a trip to the West—"I think it will build me up," he said.[36] This trip, and others like it, clearly helped to transform Roosevelt's political image. By the twentieth century, Roosevelt was frequently pictured on horseback as a crusading cowboy. It is almost as if Roosevelt had taken George Miller Beard's observations to heart on the relation of statesmanship and horsemanship: "It would appear . . . that the qualities which are necessary to make a good, strong nation are precisely the qualities which make a good horseman, and that he who can ride well makes a good founder of states" (Beard, 35).

In the context of the increasingly vigorous 1890s, to continue the aesthetic preoccupations of the 1870s and 1880s was to go against the American grain and, in fact, to run the risk of decadence. "In literature, even more than in politics, one sees the evil effects of getting far from nature," warned Merwin in his essay "On Being Civilized Too Much": "In a peculiar sense literature is the business and the amusement of persons who are oversophisticated. In fact, to take literature seriously is in itself almost a sign of decadence" (in Smith and Dawson, 314). Not surprisingly, some Americans preferred not to combat the condition of degeneracy they were alleged to exemplify but chose, instead, to take literature seriously indeed and to intensify their aesthetic interests. In fact, it is now clear that the alleged discovery of Continental literature by American modernists such as T. S. Eliot and Ezra Pound was really a revival of literary interests that first emerged in the United States during the 1890s among a segment of an elite, urban class who called themselves "decadents."

In *The Mauve Decade*, Thomas Beer, writing in the mid-1920s, says that the survivors of this first group of Anglophile and Francophile Americans "must have grinned, and . . . groaned aloud, when the new sophisticates of 1916 solemnly disclosed the works of Rimbaud, Laforgue, Vielé-Griffin,"[37] and others whom Beer does not name: Mallarmé, Maeterlinck, Verlaine, and Huysmans. Translations and appreciations of such authors appeared in a variety of short-lived literary magazines in key cities throughout the country. Any study of American decadence would have to highlight such journals as *M'lle New York* in New York City, *The Mahogany Tree* in Boston, *The Chap-Book* in Chicago, and *The Lark* in San Francisco.

Of course, translations of Continental literature and appreciations of the Pre-Raphaelite Brotherhood do not by themselves merit the name of decadence—but in America they do, precisely because these types of aesthetic preoccupations ran so counter to the increasingly muscular—and moral—culture of the 1890s. Symbolism, aestheticism, and decadence formed an alternative to the moral realism recommended by William Dean Howells, who in 1886 had "invite[d] our novelists . . . to concern themselves with the more smiling aspects of life, which are the more American."[38] When this now-famous passage was reworked for his 1891 manifesto *Criticism and Fiction*, however, Howells made it an observation, not an invitation, and he balanced the observation about a fiction "true to our well-to-do actualities" with the wish to restore "the humanitarian impulse" to the art of the novel.[39] But this, too, is remote from the decadent-aesthetic sensibility, which Howells aptly describes as he sketches out his own notions of a morally responsible, realist literature: "The art which . . . disdains the office of teacher is one of the last refuges of the aristocratic spirit which is disappearing from politics and society, and is now seeking to shelter itself in aesthetics. The pride of caste is becoming the pride of taste; but as before, it is averse to the mass of men; it consents to know them only in some conventionalized and artificial guise. It seeks to withdraw itself, to stand aloof; to be distinguished, and not to be identified."[40] Howells adds that "[d]emocracy in literature is the reverse of all this,"[41] and he is right to say so. But "all this" is precisely what the antidemocratic decadents of the fin de siècle demanded—an aristocracy of taste averse to the mass of men.

The cultural decadence of this period, then, is a reaction to the kind of moral culture Howells espoused, but it is also a response to larger cultural, social, and political concerns. Most Americans, like Roosevelt and Wister, saw the necessity of turning away from the feminine, domestic aestheticism that followed the Civil War. Such a shift was felt to be necessary in a very real sense, as America geared up for its first imperial age. But unlike most Americans, small groups and isolated individuals in New York, Boston, Chicago, and even San Francisco rejected the muscular culture the age of empire demanded. To go against the American grain in this way was decadent, all right, and many named themselves as such. And those who called themselves decadent did so by understanding the epithet not as a term of moral opprobrium but as a sign of cultural superiority. The decadents of the American fin de siècle may not have celebrated, exactly, all the decline, degeneration, and disintegration that the likes of Brooks Adams decried, but they did find in decadence something infinitely preferable to the age of empire America had entered.

CHAPTER TWO

New York: Decadent Connections

The decadent tradition first enters America by way of New York City, ushered in by a handful of New Yorkers whose avant-garde appreciations of Continental authors and artists put them in the position of pioneering a new aesthetic in the United States. But it is hardly true that there was anything close to a decadent *cénacle* in New York or a literary movement based on the likes of Verlaine and Huysmans. What is striking about this first incursion of decadence into America is how isolated its few apologists were. The names to conjure with here are Edgar Saltus, James Huneker, and Vance Thompson, only one of whom—Saltus—has any claim to originality, however compromised that claim might have been. Huneker and Thompson were *introducteurs* of foreign literature, chiefly French, or rather, Parisian. But neither Huneker nor Thompson made any original contributions to literature themselves, and, truth to tell, Thompson was a bit of a hack, a claim borne out by his later somewhat middling career. One of the striking things about American decadence that the New York scene illustrates is the odd conjunction of avant-gardism and conventionality. Huneker and Thompson were extraordinarily aware of the latest developments in the various arts, yet they communicated their sense of newness in mannered and cliché-ridden language that is often painful to read, as we shall see. Still, they knew what was new, and they were extremely enthusiastic about it. In fact, the enthusiasm that these New York *introducteurs* generate is completely out of harmony with the sense of weariness and languor customarily associated with decadence. Most likely, Huneker and Thompson got the tone wrong because they were newspapermen in an age of sensational journalism, when a lively style was a professional asset. But they were also out to shock, and one way of doing that was to offer a spirited endorsement of things that most Americans found distasteful at best, immoral at worst.

James Huneker and Vance Thompson are ever so slightly in the second wave of New York decadence, at least as far as their public pronouncements go. The great "original" is Edgar Saltus, but even his originality is derivative of the French authors he so admired. As interesting and versatile a writer as Saltus is, his experiments with decadent literature seem new and daring mainly because of the American context in which they appeared. His novels were introduced to a public attuned to the moral realism of William Dean Howells, who in 1885 had set up his fiction shop in New York City. Perhaps it is not completely fair to treat Howells as the *bête blanc* of the fin de siècle, that is, as the obverse of all things decadent. After all, Howells did attempt to capture a slice of late nineteenth-century artistic sensibility in *The Coast of Bohemia* (1893), and he wrote the introduction to Stuart Merrill's *Pastels in Prose* (1890), a volume of translated prose poems by symbolist and decadent writers. Merrill's book includes a rendering of Mallarmé's "Plainte d'automne," which celebrates "the last authors of the Latin decadence" and finds the "sad voluptuousness" of "the agonizing poetry of the last moments of Rome" all the more delicious because such poetry is so removed from "the infantile Latin of the first Christian prose." Howells' introduction, however, reveals no interest at all in Mallarmé's crepuscular reveries; on the contrary, he reminds the reader that "the noblest prose poetry" is to be found in the English Bible, "the greatest book of all."[1] Howells, then, was about as unlike a decadent writer as it was possible to be, and he was the dominant literary figure in New York and the nation over the last twenty years or so of the nineteenth century. A pretty fair axiom for this period might be: Where Howells is, there decadence is not—and Howells was in New York. So, for that matter, was the old Walt Whitman (although he lived in Camden, New Jersey), not to mention the young Theodore Roosevelt, who was actively remaking himself from an "indifferent" Harvard "dude" into a manly New York politician. Howells, Whitman, and Roosevelt could never provide the cultural milieu most conducive to decadence, which is why Saltus's novels stand out during the period for the oddities they are. But the lack of a decadent milieu also explains why they did not stand for very long.

i

Edgar Saltus may be the one American author of the fin de siècle who most deserves a place in the decadent tradition. Author of dyspeptic novels, historian of the Roman Decadence, and a popularizer of pessimism, Saltus merits the epithet 'decadent' more than most Americans of his age. This is so because he self-consciously pursued a culture of decadence, partly by associating with all the wrong people, including Paul Verlaine in Paris and Oscar Wilde in London. Verlaine's opinion of Saltus is not recorded, but Wilde admired him and called his work "so pessimistic, so poisonous and so perfect."[2] Wilde's assessment hints at the decadent topoi favored by Saltus: pessimism, the Roman Decadence, modern ennui, immorality, eroticism. Not only did Saltus build his work around decadent themes and subject matter, but he also wrote in what has come to be called the "style of decadence," fixing all his exotic erudition and curious interests in jeweled phrases to make a glittering surface disguise for the emptiness within. Possibly Saltus sought to remake himself in the image of a European decadent to counter the solidly American realities he represented. Of Dutch ancestry and merchant stock, Saltus came from money and married more, in the person of the daughter of one of J. P. Morgan's bankers, no less. That the marriage was celebrated in Grace Episcopal Church on Broadway suggests a further, necessary removal from his origins—from the severities of Calvinism so necessary to the accumulation of wealth to the High Church Anglicanism so helpful in displaying it.[3]

In stating that Saltus is all but unknown today but deserves a measure of recognition for his cultural contributions, I am repeating the assessments of earlier critics who have argued for a Saltus revival. Roughly every quarter century someone stumbles upon this forgotten writer and for some reason feels compelled to share the discovery with others. But as H. L. Mencken said of Marie Saltus's biography of her late husband, none of these efforts has yet managed "to resuscitate poor Saltus."[4] Mencken's opinion of Saltus is that he deserves the obscurity from which others seek to rescue him: "The man . . . is simply a silly and hollow trifler—a mass of puerile pretensions and affectations, vain of his unsound knowledge and full of sentimentalities. He began life by hawking the stale ribaldries of Arthur Schopenhauer, already dead twenty years; he departed to realms of bliss chattering the blowsy nonsense of theosophy" (Mencken, 278). By focusing only on the beginning and end points of Saltus's career, Mencken does the author the disservice of ignoring his early success as the author of novels satirizing New York society, such as Mr. Incoul's Misadventure (1887) and The Truth about Tristrem Varick (1888). Mencken also dismisses Saltus's study of Schopenhauer, The Philosophy of Disenchantment (1885), rather too hastily (probably because of Mencken's own preference for Nietzsche). It is true that Saltus spent the last twenty years or so of his career doing hack work for newspapers and trying to repeat his earlier successes. For example, his worst book, The Imperial Orgy (1920), condemned the excesses of the Russian tsars in the same way that his best book, Imperial Purple (1892), celebrated the debauches of the Roman emperors. Altogether, Saltus published some eighteen novels; more than a dozen books of history, biography, or philosophy; and a volume of poetry. He also translated Balzac, Gautier, and Barbey d'Aurevilly. Despite the manifest decline of his creative powers over the last twenty years of his career, it is still hard to reconcile the accomplishments of that career with his reputation today, except that there is really no place in American culture for someone like Saltus—no place, that is, unless we make one, which is precisely what critics of the 1920s were doing before Mencken derailed the effort (see chapter 6).

Before Mencken, the work of making a place for Saltus in American letters was undertaken by Percival Pollard, a widely read critic of some influence in the years leading up to World War I. In one of the few prewar assessments of Saltus's still-emerging oeuvre, Pollard places Saltus squarely within the decadent-aesthetic tradition, a tradition to which Pollard himself evidently belongs. Pollard presents himself as a Paterian: he selects authors for discussion "because they made certain impressions on a mind given somewhat to epicurianism. . . . They gave [Pollard] sensations and ideas that may, possibly, interest you."[5] Although Pollard is more appreciative of Saltus than are most later critics, he begins the tradition of taking the author to task for his erotic and stylistic excesses. He groups Saltus with the "feminist" writers Gabriele D'Annunzio, Pierre Louÿs, and the Englishman Richard Le Gallienne (61) (Pollard calls "feminist" anyone who writes about "erotically minded women" [60]). Although Saltus is compared unfavorably to Louÿs ("The more I read Mr. Saltus the more I wanted to re-read Louÿs" [64]), he scores points for "having had care for literary style" (71). At the same time, Pollard thinks Saltus's "passion for clever phrases" goes too far; while other fin-de-siècle authors of sex stories did not take sufficient care for style, "[i]n the case of Edgar Saltus we had the other extreme; style was too exclusively his preoccupation" (81–82). Pollard then describes what other critics call "the decadent style," though he does not use the term: "Always addicted to the paradox, to the phrase for phrase's sake, to the sentence that glitters but is not gold, this author had been gradually letting go the hold he had on logic, on proportion, and upon the simple enunciation of simple things" (82). Hence, in Pollard's view, by taking "the fine old Art-for-Art's-sake principle" too far Saltus ends up as "the God of phrases" and a "somnambulist of history" (84–85). Still, Pollard singles the author out as virtually the only American writer to devote himself to the cultivation of aesthetic style: "Excepting Saltus, the only approaches to style were made by such men as Pater, Hewlett, Henry Harland and Henry James. Not one of [these] is strictly American" (93–94).

The Saltus efflorescence of the early 1920s aside, Pollard's treatment of Saltus as an artist of excess, combined with Mencken's dismissal of Saltus as the hollow man of the old century, sets the tone for future critical assessments. For critics at midcentury like Alfred Kazin, Saltus is "the only genuine exotic of the day" who fails to keep himself free "from the more bizarre nonsense of the period."[6] While acknowledging that Saltus held some appeal in the 1920s "for other exquisites" who found "his fantastically overstylized books interesting," Kazin follows the cynical Mencken in his judgment of Saltus's lack of substance, the absence of a "moral pattern": "Saltus was something more than a decadent; he was so completely without a core that his fashionable skepticism now seems almost pathological" (66). A decade later, Van Wyck Brooks calls Saltus a "dandy . . . in prose as well as in appearance,"[7] and so continues the tendency of placing the author in the decadent-aesthetic tradition on the basis of his style. At the same time, Brooks connects Saltus to other authors of his time and attempts to position him in American literature: "Saltus expressed a fatalism that was characteristic of the *fin de siècle* and appeared in a dozen forms in such diverse writers as Mark Twain, Henry Adams and Ambrose Bierce" (115). He also suggests that Saltus's novels of New York society anticipate Edith Wharton's, but with certain decadent additions: "[I]n Saltus's vision New York society appeared to be as decadent as the world he had found in Suetonius and pictured elsewhere. It was a kind of fairyland peopled with characters who had not been observed but had rather been dreamed by a mind shaped in France, . . . for which even Gramercy Park at night was 'pervaded with a suggestion of absinthe and vice,' as if Verlaine himself had been reeling through it" (116–17). Despite variations in tone, what these critics have in common is the understanding of Saltus as a solitary and unique figure in American literature. Yes, he is fatalistic like Bierce and Twain; yes, his take on New York society anticipates Edith Wharton's, but by and large the kinds of artistic concerns Saltus expresses are more in harmony with British and Continental trends than with American traditions. He is a Gramercy Park Francophile, a European decadent on native ground.

Harry Levin says as much in what is the most balanced and insightful general introduction to Saltus. In the essay Levin wrote for Spiller and Thorpe's authoritative *Literary History of the United States*, Levin groups Saltus with Ambrose Bierce, Lafcadio Hearn, and James Huneker as one of those writers who made "The Discovery of Bohemia." He is right to understand Saltus not as a disciple of Wilde and the other British decadents but as a true contemporary, one of their peers: "When Saltus is recollected, he is sometimes regarded as an American disciple of Oscar Wilde. . . . Actually he parallels, rather than emulates, the English aesthete, who was his junior by a year."[8] Levin compares Saltus to Wilde on the basis of the separation of art and morality (Saltus is said to have recognized only two types of fiction: "stories which are well written and stories which are not") and on a shared attraction to the exotic/erotic "oriental" world, as represented by two works inspired by the New Testament: Saltus's *Mary Magdalen* and Wilde's *Salome*. Saltus escaped the kind of moral opprobrium visited on Wilde for two reasons: he was not homosexual, and he reserved his most outrageous material for history rather than fiction. As Levin puts it: "Under the guise of historical documentation it was possible to discuss matters still too delicate for fictional handling" (Levin, 1073). Despite Levin's balanced and generally positive critique, Saltus disappeared almost immediately from subsequent literary histories of the period. Significantly, in his book-length study of the American fin de siècle, Larzer Ziff has nothing to say about Saltus at all.[9]

Saltus's disappearance from the canon of American letters may be attributable to the variety of his production. Unlike his famous contemporaries Twain and James, he cannot be identified with a single genre; he was not a humorist and not only a novelist. His sensibility and tastes were more in line with European interests, and he seems to have made a habit of introducing Americans to matters far removed from American life. This wish to educate his countrymen in a foreign culture is something unique to the American variety of decadence. In New York, Saltus, Huneker, and Thompson made a point of introducing French authors to American audiences. In Boston, Ralph Adams Cram, F. Holland Day, and Louise Imogen Guiney concentrated on their British contemporaries. In Chicago, Henry Blake Fuller promoted fin-de-siècle Italian writers, including the decadent Gabriele D'Annunzio. In most cases, the campaign to introduce this type of foreign culture to American audiences took place in newspaper columns, which may account, paradoxically, for the decline of decadence—a type of culture not really suited to popular dissemination in mass media. The paradox may hold, in part, in the case of Edgar Saltus, though his eclipse from American letters had already begun by the time he shifted his literary career to journalism. But the general contradiction holds: Saltus, like others, tried to popularize a culture in the United States that ran completely counter to the cultural interests of most Americans. Instead of local color, like Stuart Merrill he provided French pastels; instead of Emersonian optimism and self-reliance, he counseled Schopenhauerian pessimism and self-annihilation; instead of genteel realism and moral assurances, his writing conveyed artificiality, nihilism, and decadence.

ii

In *The Philosophy of Disenchantment* (1885), Saltus shows a breadth of learning that is impressive for the ease with which he moves among multiple philosophic and literary traditions. He takes the topic of pessimism, or, more precisely, the new "theoretic" or "scientific" pessimism that had developed over the last twenty years, and shows its antecedents in classical philosophy, both Hellenic and Roman (Empedocles, Plato, Epicurus; Seneca, Pliny, Petronius), and in the romantic literature of several countries (Byron, Shelley, Poe; Herder, Schiller, Goethe; De Musset, Leconte de Lisle, Baudelaire). This discussion forms his background chapter "The Genesis of Disenchantment," which is remarkable for the way Saltus relishes the most attention on those figures likely to be least familiar to the general reader. For example, the classical tradition of pessimism has its most detailed exemplar in Hegesias of Alexandria, a disciple of Socrates who "argued that as there was a limit to the knowable, and happiness was a pure illusion, a further prolongation of existence was useless."[10] Saltus says Hegesias delivered this philosophy "with such charm of persuasive grace and eloquence that several of his listeners put his ideas into instant practice"; King

Ptolemy himself was forced to silence the "seductive misanthrope" in order to preserve the city "from the contagion of suicide" (5). Likewise, Saltus takes the Italian poet Giacomo Leopardi as his representative romantic, rather than the more familiar Byron or Shelley. According to Saltus, the solitary Leopardi "watched the incubation of thought very much as others might have noted the progress of a disease" (17). Hence Leopardi is afflicted with the disease of thinking, which makes it easy for Saltus to sum up the Italian's pessimism by taking Descartes's "Cogito, ergo sum" to the logical next step: "I am, therefore I suffer" (19). This identity of being, thinking, and suffering forms the basis of Leopardi's relevance to "the theoretic pessimism of today" and may be reduced to this key formulation: "the sorrows of men and of nations develop in proportion to their intelligence, and the most civilized are in consequence the most unhappy" (33, 21).

"The theoretic pessimism of today" of course descends from Arthur Schopenhauer, and Saltus devotes three considerable chapters to "this Emerson in black" (61), a telling phase that identifies the German philosopher as a kind of counter to the ubiquitous American. Saltus has clearly read and understood not only *Die Welt als Wille und Vorstellung* (The World as Will and Idea), but also several of Schopenhauer's lesser works and a number of commentaries on the philosopher. Saltus understands Schopenhauer, quite rightly, as a major successor of Kant and explains in clear terms how the later philosopher derived the concept of '*Wille*' from Kant's unknowable *noumenon*, the *Ding an sich* or "thing-in-itself" that sensible phenomena conceals from ultimate human apprehension:

> In saying . . . that Schopenhauer is indebted to Kant, it is well to point out that Schopenhauer begins precisely where Kant left off. Kant's great merit consisted in distinguishing the phenomenon from the thing-in-itself, or in other words, in showing the difference between that which seems and that which is. . . . Schopenhauer reëstablished the incomprehensible factor on a fresh basis, christened it "Will," and asserted it to be the creator of all that is, and at once independent, free, and omnipotent; in other words, the interior essence of the world of which Christ crucified is the sublime symbol. (79–80)

This differs from more recent explanations of Schopenhauer's philosophy only with respect to the odd gesture that Saltus makes toward Christianity at the end of the exposition. The author's exposition throughout is measured and reserved, for the most part, and it may be that he was concerned not to alienate the Christian reader in the earlier stages of his presentation.

It is worth noting that Christ is mentioned here only as a "symbol," not as a means of human redemption, which is consistent with Saltus's later skeptical remarks on the value of Christianity, or of any faith, as in this extended summary of Schopenhauer's pessimistic doctrine:

Reduced to its simplest expression, it amounts briefly to this: an unknown principle—an *x*, which no term can translate, but of which Will, taken in the widest sense of Force, is the rendition least inexact—explains the universe. The highest manifestation of Will is man; any obstacle it encounters is pain. Pain is the attendant of life. Man, however, duped by the instinct of love, has nothing better to do than to prolong through his children the sorrowful continuation of unhappy generations. The hope of a future existence in a better world seems to be a consolation, but as hope it rests on faith. Since life is not a benefit, chaos is preferable. Beyond suicide, which is not a philosophic solution, there are but two remedies for the misery of life; one, a palliative, is found in art and disinterested contemplation; the other, a specific, in asceticism and absolute chastity. Were chastity universal, it would drain the source of humanity, and pain would disappear. (121)

These types of summary statements are matched by any number of interpretive comments where Saltus announces Schopenhauer's cultural significance: "[H]e was the first to detect and logically explain that universal nausea which, circulating from one end of Europe to the other, presents those symptoms of melancholy and disillusion which, patent to every observer, are indubitably born of the insufficiencies of modern civilization" (160).

Saltus follows his exposition of Schopenhauer's life and works with a discussion of Schopenhauer's "direct descendant," Eduard Von Hartmann. Saltus understands that Von Hartmann was much more than the popularizer of Schopenhauer's philosophy, which is the way he is often represented in histories of nineteenth-century philosophy. In fact, Von Hartmann extends Schopenhauer's pessimism by introducing the practical possibility of human extinction and by providing not only a rationale for that possibility but also, at least to a degree, the means of annihilation. Saltus says that Von Hartman "tries to reconcile the teaching of Hegel with that of Schopenhauer" by developing a system consisting of "a theory of optimistic evolution . . . counterbalanced by a pessimistic analysis of life." Hence Von Hartmann "concludes that as the world's *progressus* does not tend to either universal or even individual happiness, the great aim of science should be to emancipate man from the love of life, and in this wise lead the world back to chaos" (171–72). (Saltus uses the word *chaos* in the Lucretian sense of the conditions prior to the creation of the cosmos, i.e., nonexistence.) Von Hartmann is said to be "Germany's first thinker," and the publication of *Philosophie des Unbewussten* (The Philosophy of the Unconscious) is termed "the chief philosophical event of the last two decades" (166). Such praise for a book that sees the highest Hegelian reality as the cessation of existence says a great deal about the cultural perspective of Edgar Saltus. Indeed, Saltus's advocacy of the philosophy of pessimism is certified by his personal admiration for Von Hartmann himself, whom Saltus visited in Berlin to seek clarification "over a particular point in this teaching" (170).

Saltus ends his study with an analysis of "the tendency of current literature" to reflect the pessimistic philosophy more systematically represented by the works of Schopenhauer and Von Hartmann. These pages show a familiarity with contemporary European literature that seems quite complete. He admires Henry James for his depiction of disenchantment in *The Portrait of a Lady*; he defends Zola against the charge "that his works are obscene" ("so they are, and so is the life he depicts"); he calls the Goncourt brothers and Alphonse Daudet "those princes of literature" because their fiction is written "with pens pricked in sorrow" (226). The same respect extends to certain authors a generation or so removed from the present: "Stendhal, Balzac, and Flaubert have harped the same note of accentuated despair; Musset has sung songs that would make a statue weep, and Baudelaire seems to have supped sorrow with a long spoon" (227). Baudelaire must have occupied a special place in Saltus's sensibility, for he quotes the poet on several occasions to sum up this or that point about the despairing self. Saltus's reflections on decadent literature lead him to a general conclusion about the temper of his own age that is a tour de force of pessimism and disillusion, which must be quoted at length:

> [T]he moral atmosphere of the present century is charged with three distinct disturbances,—the waning of religious belief, the insatiable demand for intense sensations, and the increasing number of those who live uncompanied, and walk abroad in solitude. That each of these three effects is due to one and the selfsame cause is well-nigh unquestionable. The immense nausea that is spreading through all lands and literature is at work on the simple faith, the contented lives, and joyous good-fellowship of earlier days, and in its results it brings with it the signs and portents of a forthcoming though undetermined upheaval.
>
>   . . . . What its final solution will be is, of course, uncertain. Schopenhauer recommended absolute chastity as the means to the great goal, and Hartmann has vaguely suggested a universal denial of the will to live; more recently, M. Renan has hazarded the supposition that in the advance of science some one might discover a force capable of blowing the planet to atoms, and which, if successfully handled, would, of course, annihilate pain. But these ideas, however practicable or impracticable they may be in the future, are for the moment merely theories; the world is not yet ripe for a supreme quietus, and in the mean time the worth of life may still be questioned.
>
>   . . . . [B]roadly speaking . . . life may be said to be always valuable to the obtuse, often valueless to the sensitive; while to him who commiserates with all mankind, and sympathizes with everything that is, life never appears otherwise than as an immense and terrible affliction. (231–33)

Given the totality of Saltus's pessimism—he does, after all, entertain the idea not only of personal annihilation but also "a sudden quietus" oddly predictive of cold war anxieties of nuclear destruction—the question naturally arises as to how he managed to reconcile his passion for pessimism with his own creative capacities. The question cannot really be answered, but it may be that Saltus was not quite so ardent about his pessimism after all. Indeed, his pessimism seems the product more of diffidence and disillusion than anything else, hence the title term *disenchantment*. If life does not matter, then neither does death. Saltus's first two novels bear the imprint of the kind of diffident, decadent pessimism *The Philosophy of Disenchantment* elaborates. Indeed, the sensitivity requisite for the recognition that life has no value informs *Mr. Incoul's Misadventure*, the first novel, while the delusion that life has value motivates the action of the obtuse hero of the second novel, *The Truth about Tristrem Varick*.

iii

Mr. Incoul's Misadventure combines convention and corruption. The plot is ordinary enough: a younger woman marries an older man for money, not for love. Once they are married, the husband discovers his wife's secret lover and revenges himself by wreaking such social ruin on the lover that he kills himself. Then the husband murders his wife but makes her death look like suicide. These crimes go undetected, and the husband appears unperturbed by what he has done. At the very end the plot perhaps veers toward the unconventional in that there is no confession of the crimes committed, no attempt to draw a moral. All that happens is merely a misadventure on the part of the wronged husband, Mr. Incoul. The novel compares with Balzac's *Eugénie Grandet*, on which part of the plot is based, in the juxtaposition of romantic idealism inspired by love and craven power driven by wealth. Just as the miser Grandet sacrifices his daughter's happiness to his lust for gold, claiming as justification his patriarchal rights, so Incoul destroys his chaste wife and her would-be lover to protect his impeccable reputation. The analogy is not exact, but Saltus's heroine has read Balzac's novel and seeks to pattern her own life after Mlle. Grandet's. Early on she says to Mr. Incoul, "I could not become your wife unless you were willing to make the same agreement with me that Eugénie Grandet's husband made with her[,] to live as though they were not married— as might brother and sister." Saltus's first publication was a study of Balzac (1884), in which the author singled out *Eugénie Grandet* as "a picture of life as it is, and the model of what a novel should be."[11]

Balzac's novel describes the interplay of society's conventions and the world's corruptions, and so does Saltus's. What saves *Mr. Incoul's Misadventure* from becoming a simple imitation of a Balzacian formula is the delicious sense of cosmopolitan decadence that permeates the novel. This quality is unmistakable and unmistakably derived from French sources (Saltus wrote the novel in Paris in early 1887). The title character seems to be one version of Saltus, though not the decadent side. Mr. Incoul is like Saltus in that he comes from old New York money and from Dutch stock. There is a biographical reversal at work in Mr. Incoul's second marriage, since he represents the kind of vast American wealth associated with J. P. Morgan, into whose banking "family" Saltus married. Indeed, Mr. Incoul is compared to the Vanderbilts and the Astors as one of those Americans whom the French are said to regard as "a Vesuvius of gold pieces" (*MIM*, 165). Incoul also follows Saltus in his substitution of European for American education in Paris and Heidelburg (*MIM*, 123). Incoul claims not to be a Puritan because he likes refinement, and yet he believes that "refinement and immorality are incompatible" (*MIM*, 13). In fact he is rather reserved and stiff, as his name, in French, at least, implies (*couler*, "flowing, natural," negated by the prefix *in-*).

The more culturally recondite elements of Saltus's own character are assigned to Mr. Incoul's rival for his wife's affections, one Lenox Leigh, who sees no conflict between immorality and refinement. What Saltus says of Leigh could well be said of Saltus himself:

> He was without beliefs and without prejudices; added to this he was indulgent to the failings of others, or perhaps it would be better to say that he was indifferent. It may be that the worst thing about him was that he was not bad enough; his wickedness, such as there was of it, was purely negative. A poet of the decadence of that period in fact when Rome had begun to weary of debauchery without yet acquiring a taste for virtue, a pre-medieval Epicurean, let us say, could not have pushed a creedless refinement to a greater height than he. (*MIM*, 31)

This passage suggests a taste for the refinements of decadence, but, as the narrative makes clear, Lenox Leigh lacks the means to realize his taste to the fullest degree. Mr. Incoul, by contrast, has the means but not the taste.

This irony emerges most clearly when Mr. Incoul is invited to take over the villa—"servants and all" (*MIM*, 79)—of a French marquis on a visit to Biarritz. The marquis possesses a library and an art collection very like the one in the possession of Des Esseintes in Huysmans's *À Rebours*. Both are surveyed by Mr. Incoul's wife Maida, who looks on in incomprehension at Goya's black paintings, pictures of "women tearing teeth from the mouths of the gibbeted; a confusion of demons and incubes; . . . but best of all, a skeleton leaning with a leer from the tomb and scrawling on it the significant legend, *Nada*, nothing" (*MIM*, 81). Maida then surveys the marquis's bookcases and finds a complete collection of fine editions of French poets, including "the Fleurs du Mal, an unexpurgated copy, and by it were the poems of Baudelaire's decadent descendants, Paul Verlaine and Mallarmé" (*MIM*, 82). This, like the rest of the marquis's collection, is "meaningless to Maida," and there is some high irony in her uncomprehending perusal of the locked bookcase containing a vast store of erotic literature, which Saltus lists in a riot of bizarre erudition:

> In it were Justine and Juliette, by the Marquis de Sade; the works of Piron; the works of Beroalde de Verville; a copy of Mercius; a copy of Thérèse Philosophe; the De Arcanis Amores; Mirabeau's Rideau-levé; Gamaini, by Alfred de Musset and George Sand; Boccaccio; the Heptameron; Paphian Days; Crébillon's Sopha; the Eroika Biblion; the Satyricon of Petronius; an illustrated catalogue of the Naples museum; Voltaire's Pucelle; a work or two of Diderot's; Maiseroy's Deux Amies; the Clouds; the Curée; everything, in fact, from Aristophanes to Zola. (MIM, 82)

The wonder is that Lenox Leigh could take an interest in any woman for whom such a catalog is meaningless, but then most women in the novel exist solely to decorate debauchery.

Such is the case with the Parisian danseuse on which the plot turns. Although Leigh manages to see Maida once or twice after her marriage to Incoul, she makes clear to him that she means to be faithful to her husband. Leigh does not fully accept his mistress's refusal, but he does become involved with a minor star of the Paris ballet named Mirette. The woman is particularly gifted at "that stereotyped form of repartee which is known as the *bagou*" (MIM, 164). For example, when someone asks from whom a rather plain-looking young actress gets her money, Mirette shoots back, "A blind man." And when she is caught lying she says merely, "Lies whiten the teeth" (MIM, 165). One day Mirette is not in to see Lenox Leigh, and he quickly deduces that he has been supplanted by another lover. The new man in the woman's life is Mr. Incoul's servant, Karl, whose seduction of Mirette Mr. Incoul has sponsored with his vast wealth, which Leigh cannot hope to match. This maneuver is the first stage in Mr. Incoul's revenge against the unsuspecting Leigh, who resorts to gambling to keep up with the competition. Leigh is fairly successful at baccarat until the day Mr. Incoul decides to sit down at the table and try his luck. Incoul plants marked cards on his rival and accuses him of cheating, and everyone believes the word of the irreproachable millionaire. Lenox Leigh is a ruined man: he goes to his room, drinks absinthe, and injects morphine, killing himself.

Once again, the conventional ending seems less so because the social disaster is not so much the immediate cause of the man's despair as it is the trigger for a deeper pessimism, which Saltus details over some ten pages of richly allusive prose, ranging from Greek mythology to Buddhist mysticism and Utopian politics, among other topics. The catalog of hopelessness reads partly like a reprise of *The Philosophy of Disenchantment*, partly like a précis of *The Anatomy of Negation*, published the year before *Mr. Incoul's Misadventure*. A prefatory note explains that *The Anatomy of Negation* is intended "to convey a tableau of

anti-theism from Kapila to Leconte de Lisle" (Kapila is an ancient Indian philosopher identified in the opening chapter as "the first serious thinker who
looked up into the archaic skies and declared them to be void") [13] and begins
with the observation that "[t]he sentiment of the immedicable misery of life is
as prominent in the preface of history as on its latest and uncompleted page"
(AN, 11). At the very end of the book Saltus offers the only consolation possible in his dark philosophy: "The best we can do, the best that has ever been
done, is to recognize the implacability of the laws that rule the universe, and
contemplate as calmly as we can the nothingness from which we are come and
into which we shall all disappear" (AN, 223). Between the opening observation and the closing encomium Saltus provides a thorough survey of antitheis-
tic pessimists, some expected (Schopenhauer), some surprising (Jesus).

Likewise, as Lenox Leigh drinks his absinthe and prepares for his suicide, he
runs through a history and rationale for pessimism impressive for both its
breadth and depth, its universality and its psychological intensity:

> He thought of that sage who pitied the gods because their lives were unending,
> and, as he reflected, he remembered that the Thracians greeted birth with lam-
> entations and death with welcoming festivals. He remembered how Plato had
> preached to the happiest people in the world the blessedness of ceaseless sleep;
> how the Buddha, teaching that life was but a right to suffer, had found for the re-
> calcitrant no greater menace than that of an existence renewed through kalpas
> of time. . . .
>
> And, as these things came to him, so, too, did the problem of pain. He re-
> viewed the ravages of that ulcer which has battened on humanity since the
> world began. History uncoiled itself before him in a shudder. In its spasms he saw
> the myriads that have fought and died for dogmas that they did not understand,
> for invented principles of patriotism and religion, for leaders that they had never
> seen, for gods more helpless than themselves.
>
> He saw, too, Nature's cruelty and her snares. The gift to man of appetites,
> which, in the guise of pleasure, veil immedicable pain. Poison in the richest
> flowers, the agony that lurks in the grape. (MIM, 191-92)

The "antitheism" of The Anatomy of Negation appears in comic form when
Leigh imagines the only terms under which he might wish to go on living: "If I
had an ambition it would be a different matter. If I could be a pretty woman up
to thirty, a cardinal up to fifty, and after that the Anti-Christ, it might be
worthwhile" (MIM, 195).

Leigh also despairs of the more realistic, Saltus-like ambition of writing
good novels that never find a mass audience but at least allow their author "to
take immense delight in the reflection that the disapproval of imbeciles is the
surest acknowledgement of talent" (MIM, 195). Because of the scandal Mr.
Incoul has manufactured to ensnare him, Leigh is prevented from putting his

own name to any "successful failures" (*MIM*, 195) he might author. With even the dubious satisfaction of unappreciated art denied him, Lennox Leigh finishes his absinthe, injects an overdose of morphine, and dies a highly synaesthetic, hallucinatory death: "The walls of the room dissolved into cataracts of light and steel. The flooring changed to running crimson, and from that to black, and back to red again" (*MIM*, 201). Oscar Wilde famously conflated Art and Life; in *Mr. Incoul's Misadventure* Edgar Saltus aestheticizes Lenox Leigh's suicide to the point that Art and Death become complementary. Decadence traditionally puts pessimism and aestheticism to the same purpose or, rather, in the service of the same sensibility. In other words, what Saltus calls "disenchantment" is a necessary adjunct to the delectation of highly refined works of art. Indeed, the only virtue available to a decadent hero like Lenox Leigh is elevated taste honed by hopelessness.

iv

The novel that follows *Mr. Incoul's Misadventure* in the Saltus canon is a further exploration of the philosophy of disenchantment but with a different emphasis, this time with an absurdly hopeful hero as its central character. *The Truth about Tristrem Varick* is dedicated to "My Master, The Philosopher of the Unconscious, Eduard von Hartmann." The dedication page also calls the novel an "attempt in ornamental disenchantment."[14] Further, the publisher has chosen a quotation from a review of Saltus's earlier work to introduce the author to the reader: "Mr. Saltus is the prose laureate of pessimism." Hence there can be no question that the novel is meant to be another fictional exercise in the philosophy of pessimism. This notion is borne out by the plot of the novel itself, even though it does not contain any references to Schopenhauer or to Von Hartmann (aside from the dedication page), and there is no polemical exposition of the philosophy of pessimism at all. Rather, the novel takes the reader through the stages of its hopeful hero's thorough and complete disenchantment, as he is betrayed in one way or another by those closest to him—his best friend, his fiancée, and even his own father.

The *Truth about Tristrem Varick* goes against the grain of the grossly moneyed age in which the novel is set by presenting the reader with a hero who gives away a fortune of some 6 million dollars. The revelation of the "true" story behind such bizarre, unconventional behavior begins when Tristrem returns to New York a highly cultured man after a five-year sojourn in Europe and promptly falls in love with a nineteen-year-old opera singer named Viola Raritan. He meets her at a Gramercy Park dinner party given by his childhood friend Royal Weldon, who has married the money attached to the pretty but insipid daughter of a New York financier. As Tristrem, chaste and idealistic like his medieval namesake, politely pursues Viola, his friend Weldon keeps turning up to frustrate the hero's designs, like a doppelgänger in a Hoffmann tale. The reader understands long before Tristrem does that Miss Raritan is Weldon's mistress, or would-be mistress, since there is some doubt about whether the affair has been consummated before Weldon forces himself on the girl and gets her pregnant. Her pregnancy is the reason Viola breaks off her engagement to Tristrem, though Tristrem remains in the dark about this critical fact until, after pursuing her from city to city in Europe (where her mother takes her to have the child), he learns by accident that she has given birth and returned to New York. Tristrem tracks her down and discovers that Weldon is the father of her child, whereupon, acting on impulse, he confronts Weldon alone in his study and murders him with a stiletto. There are no witnesses. When Tristrem goes to tell Viola that he has dispatched the man he believes to be her tormentor, she responds by hissing, "Assassin! . . . I loved him" (228). Tristrem, thoroughly disillusioned—that is, disenchanted—turns himself in to the police, evidently resigned to the gallows.

A subplot of some importance—since it contains the motive *truth* of the title—is the mistaken supposition that Viola breaks off the engagement because she has learned that she and Tristrem had the same father. Tristrem's father believes that his wife had had an affair with one Roanoke Raritan, Viola's father, and disinherits Tristrem when he dies, leaving to his son only a panama hat and a packet of letters he thinks proves his wife's infidelity; his vast fortune is willed to charity. Tristrem's maternal grandfather, however, is outraged that his grandson is left penniless, and, as a savvy man of the world, performs the series of legal maneuvers necessary to void the will and restore the young man's inheritance.[15] Nonetheless, Tristrem believes that he is not his father's son and divests himself of his recently restored fortune, directing it to the charity his father originally designated in the disputed will. Soon afterward, the grandfather assures Tristrem that his father was mistaken in thinking his wife unfaithful and offers an impassioned and credible explanation for Roanoke Raritan's letters to Mrs. Varick. Still, the absurdly honorable Tristrem has no second thoughts about giving away his fortune: "'If he did not wish me to have the money,' he said, 'how could I keep it?'" (148). He takes heart in knowing that he and Viola are not half-siblings after all and so are free to marry; he then begins the Continental quest that ends in utter disenchantment.

In the end, Tristrem's knightly idealism and noble sentiments are so completely dismantled that it is tempting to think that Saltus is satirizing contemporary American fascination with medievalism, as Mark Twain was to do in broader fashion in *A Connecticut Yankee in King Arthur's Court* (1889), published a year after *The Truth about Tristrem Varick*. The eponymous Tristrem does seem to live by some medieval code of honor and is bound not only to quest after the woman he loves but also to defend what he imagines is her virtue. If Saltus means to juxtapose the medieval and the modern, his idea of modernity is drawn from a decadent cultural tradition only recently formed, or in the process of forming, in France and England. Huysmans's *À Rebours* was published in 1884, but Oscar Wilde had not yet written the plays that would make his reputation. This last fact is remarkable because there are passages of the sort of witty, worldly dialogue in *The Truth about Tristrem Varick* that one would swear are patterned after Wilde, yet Saltus is writing well before Wilde. For example, there is this exchange between the debutante Flossy Finch and A. B. Fenwick Chisolm-Jones, a Francophile novelist known familiarly as Alphabet Jones:

> "Do you mean to tell me," Miss Finch asked him across the table, "do you mean to say that you don't believe in platonic affection?"
>
> "I never uttered such a heresy in my life," the novelist replied. "Of course I believe in it; I believe in it thoroughly—between husband and wife."
>
> At this everyone laughed. . . , except Tristrem, who had not heard, and Mrs. Weldon, who had not understood. (37–38)

Given Wilde's admiration of Saltus, there is at least a question here about the direction of influence.

With regard to the French tradition, however, there is no doubt that Saltus is writing with certain decadent precursors in mind. For example, an artist Varick meets in Europe quotes the same lines from Flaubert's *Tentation de Saint Antoine* that Huysmans does in *À Rebours*. Both authors set great store in Flaubert's imagined dialogue between the Sphinx and the Chimera that culminates in the famous lines, "I seek new perfumes, larger flowers, and pleasures unenjoyed" (178). In fact, Saltus's novel contains some fairly direct reference to Huysmans's *À Rebours*, even though the naïve and hopeful Varick could not be more different from the jaded Des Esseintes. When Varick visits Miss Raritan and her mother at their Newport cottage, still in the dark about the true state of affairs between his fiancée and his best friend, he has a dream about being pursued by a monstrous woman, a personification of the terrible revelation that awaits him. The dream passage lifts several key details from Des Esseintes's pox nightmare in chapter 8 of *À Rebours*:

> [B]ehind him was a woman running, and who, as she ran, cast a shadow that was monstrous. In the glimpse that he caught of her he saw that she was bare of foot and that her breast was uncovered. Her skirt was tattered and her hair was loose. He turned again, the face was hideous. The eyes squinted, lustreless and opaque, the nose was squat, the chin retreated, the forehead was seamed with scars, and the mouth, that stretched to the ears, was extended with laughter. As she ran she took her teeth out one by one, replacing them with either hand. And still she laughed, a silent laughter, her thin lips distorted as thought she mocked the world.
>
> . . . and then at once she was upon him, felling him to the ground as a ruffian fells his mistress, her knees were on his arms, he was powerless, dumb with dread, and in his face was the fetor of her breath. Her eyes were no longer lustreless,

they glittered like twin stars, and still she laughed, her naked breast heaving with the convulsions of her mirth. "I am Truth," she bawled, and laughed again. (115, 117–18)

In Huysmans's novel, Des Esseintes is accompanied in his dream by a woman with a "bulldog face, freckled cheeks, irregular teeth projecting under a stub of nose,"[16] very like the features of Varick's dream woman. Shortly afterward in Huysmans's novel the woman loses her teeth, "and, taking a number of clay pipes out of her apron pocket, she proceeded to smash them up and stuff bits of the white stems into her gums" (AR, 90). Saltus also borrows this image, toning it down somewhat. In Des Esseintes's dream the bulldog woman disappears and is replaced by the fantastic figure of the pox, part woman, part plant, "naked but for a pair of green silk stockings" (AR, 91), who overpowers the helpless hero: "An agony of fear set his heart pounding madly, but for the eyes, the woman's awful eyes, had turned a clear, cold blue, quite terrible to see. He made a superhuman effort to free himself from her embrace, but with an irresistible movement she clutched him and held him" (AR, 92). Likewise, in Varick's case the hero is held in thrall by the eyes of the dreamwoman, and overwhelmed, like a woman being raped. This, of course, is the literal truth of what has recently happened: Viola Raritan has been raped by, and, it turns out, impregnated by Varick's duplicitous friend Royal Weldon.

Another fin-de-siècle feature of Saltus's novel is the use of *monologue intérieur*, first introduced into fiction by Eduard Dujardin in 1887 when he serialized his novel *Les Lauriers sont coupés* in *La Revue Indépendent*.[17] The device was quickly imitated by George Moore in *Confessions of a Young Man*, published in 1888, the same year as Saltus's *Tristrem Varick*. Thus it would appear that Saltus shares with Moore the distinction of being the first to employ the interior monologue device in English. In fact, Saltus must have recognized that most readers would find the device unusual, because he provides the explanation that Varick is occasionally given to "monologuing in the fashion that was peculiar to him" (155). A good example of the device occurs early in the novel as Varick walks form the Gramercy Park area to Washington Square, "monologuing" as he goes about past experiences in Europe and more recent ones in New York, having just heard Miss Raritan sing:

She looked like that girl in Munich, the girl that lived over the way, only Mrs. Weldon was prettier and dressed better, much better. Du hast die schönsten Augen. Munich wasn't such a bad place, but what a hope Innsprück was. There was that Victoria Cross fellow; whatever became of him? He drank like a fish; it must have caught him by this time. H'm, he *would* give me the address of his shoemaker. I ought to have taken more from that man in Paris. Odd that the Cenerentola was the last thing I should have heard there. The buffo was good, so was the contralto. *She* sings much better. What a voice! what a voice! Now, which was more perfect, the voice or the girl? Let me see, which is the better fulfilled, the odor of the lily or the lily itself? Tulips I never cared for. . . . That is it, then. I wonder, though—(42)

Interior monologue is today identified more closely with the modernist than with the decadent style, but the use of the device by authors with decadent affinities such as Saltus and Moore shows how closely connected avant-gardism and decadence are. The fragmented style of the interior monologue is aesthetically of a piece with *le style de décadence*, a style that forces attention to the artifice of individual words and phrases at the expense of some imagined organic whole. The alleged stylistic excess that later critics hold against Saltus is here just beginning to make itself felt, mainly by way of the author's often esoteric diction. For example, he writes "appanages" (100) rather than "rights," uses "lupanar" (192) instead of "brothel," mentions "intussusceptions" (192) where he means something like "appearances," and prefers the archaic "glaive" (219) to the modern "sword." And perhaps the reader may be excused for not knowing precisely what it means to be "beset by an insidious duscholia" (77).

v

By traditional criteria Saltus might be termed a decadent writer for his refusal to adhere to the established conventions of the genres in which he worked: his novels are infused with philosophy, and his histories are laced with fictional invention. This last observation certainly applies to *Imperial Purple*, Saltus's impressionistic evocation of the lives of the Caesars. Although Claire Sprague places *Imperial Purple* in the genre of "the magazine essay of the last century,"[18] the book has affinities with less ephemeral types of writing. Saltus evidently intends the work as a serious historical study that can stand as a partial corrective to Edward Gibbon's *The History of the Decline and Fall of the Roman Empire* (1776–1788), the best-known narrative of Roman decadence in the nineteenth century. At one point he chides "the late Mr. Gibbon" for presenting to his readers "not the real Augustus, but the Augustus of legend."[19] But if Saltus intends a more authentic history, that authenticity is the product of a richness of detail that is itself derived from fictional models, Flaubert's *Salammbô* above all. In one of his novels a dilettante author states that he "would rather have written *Salammbô* than have built the Brooklyn Bridge. It was more difficult, and besides it will last longer."[20] A description of a banquet in Augustan Rome is derived equally from "those which Petronius has described . . . so well" and the fantastic fare that appears in Flaubert's novel:

And there, in white ungirdled tunics, the head and neck circled with coils of amaranth—the perfume of which in opening the pores neutralizes the fumes of wine—the guests lay, fanned by boys, whose curly hair they used for napkins. Under the supervision of a butler the courses were served on platters so large that they covered the tables; sows' breasts with Lybian truffles; dormice baked in poppies and honey; peacock-tongues flavored with cinnamon; oysters stewed in garum—a sauce made of the intestines of fish—sea-wolves from the Baltic; sturgeons from Rhodes; fig-peckers from Samos; African snails; pale beans in pink lard; and a yellow pig cooked after the Trojan fashion, from which, when carved, hot sausages fell and live thrushes flew. (37–38)

This Augustan menu seems almost austere in comparison with the banquet that Heliogabalus serves up for his guests as the empire, and Saltus's book, nears its end: "And presently, . . . you were served with camel's heels; combs torn from living cocks; platters of nightingale tongues; ostrich brains, prepared with that garum sauce which the Sybarites invented, and of which the secret is lost; therewith were peas and grains of gold; beans and amber; quail, peppered with pearl dust; lentils and rubies; spiders in jelly; lion's dung, served in pastry" (230–31). Saltus says that "the feasts that Heliogabalus gave outranked" those of Caligula and Vitellius "for sheer splendor" (230). Likewise, Saltus comes close to outstripping his model Flaubert in the floridness of his descriptive passages.

Perhaps it can be said that if Flaubert rewrote Roman history as French fiction, Saltus rewrites French fiction as Roman history. *Imperial Purple* was, after all, written while Saltus was in France, evidently after his divorce from his first wife, and completed in Paris in 1891. His descriptions of various Roman emperors are peppered with French phrases. The young Caligula is said to be "what the French call *charmeur*" (81). Nero is called "a trifle *petit maître*, perhaps, perfuming the soles of his feet" (100); later he becomes "a *poseur* that bored, a beast that disgusted" (103). The young Domitian at table hesitates to dine on "a *ragout à la Sardanapale*, which, he fancied, possibly was *a la Locuste*" (143). The anachronisms of language are of a piece with the occasional comparison of Roman antiquity with the modern world, as when the Rome of Augustus is compared to contemporary London: "The tourist might walk in it, as in the London of to-day, mile after mile, and at whatever point himself, Rome still lay beyond; a Rome quite like London—one that was choked with mystery, with gold and curious crime" (31). Having said this, however, Saltus says more in this double comparison of past and present: "[Rome] compared with Alexandria as London compares with Paris; it had a splendor of its own, but a splendor that could be heightened" (119). Many of the author's comparisons are delightfully arch, as when the recently divorced Saltus observes: "In those days matrimony was not as frequent as it has since become. When it occurred, divorce was its natural consequence" (56). Some Caesars have the distinction of being not only French, or almost so, but also not so different from nineteenth-century gentlemen. Hadrian "was an early Quinet, an early Champollion. . . . And to those in his suite it must have been a sight very unique to see a Caesar who had published his volume of erotic verse, just as you or I might do" (175). Not all of Saltus's anachronisms are so flip; he sometimes analyzes the failings of the Romans in terms appropriated from Marx, as in this explanation of the necessity of the Roman spectacle: "the institution . . . constituted the chief delight of the vestals and of Rome. By means of it a bankrupt became consul and an emperor beloved. It has stayed revolutions, it was the tax of the proletariat on the rich" (117). Saltus ends his chapter on Caligula by offering an economic explanation for the fall of Rome: "She consumed, she did not produce. It was because of that she fell" (92). The observation is interesting because Saltus does not directly ascribe Rome's decline to immorality, perversion, or some other more general type of personal corruption that Puritan or Victorian moralists could so easily summon as the explanation for the eclipse of empire.

Saltus's attitude toward the sensational prurience of the emperors is surprisingly psychologically-minded. His presentation often mixes discretion and delectation; the tone is knowing and sometimes jaded, and he is at his best when describing moral and religious hypocrisy: "As often as not the man who sounds the cymbals to the proprieties and plays the flute to ethereal affection, conceals beneath obsequious cant the stigmata of satisfied vice. It is he who in vichy-water phrases pays to virtue the tribute of sin. On the other hand a tendency toward eroticism is the surest indication of chastity. It is continence that makes the St. Anthony. In the blood of the chaste cantharides abound" (61). This type of psychological analysis sometimes shades into the scientific, as when Saltus understands Messalina in terms of nineteenth-century sexology: "[P]hysically she was a victim of nymphomania, one who today would be put through a course of treatment, instead of being put to death" (85). But more often than not Saltus prefers literary, aesthetic explanations; even in his explanation of hypocrisy, above, the figure of St. Anthony Saltus has in mind is no doubt the fictional character who appears in Flaubert's *Tentation*, rather than the historical personage. The literary, aesthetic nature of imperial perversity is registered again and again, as in this appreciation of Caligula's sadism: "he became a connoisseur in death, an artist in blood, a ruler to whom cruelty was not merely an aid to government but an individual pleasure, and therewith such a perfect lover, such a charming host!" (75). Emperors and vestals alike cultivate the aesthetics of slaughter in the arena: "[A]rtistic death was their chiefest joy" (115). And Saltus acknowledges the aesthetic rewards of contemplating the more lurid exploits of Caligula, Nero, Domitian, Commodus, Caracalla, Heliogabalus: "The lives of all of them are horrible, yet analyze the horrible and you find the sublime" (70).

Saltus has a particular fascination with the transvestitism and even hermaphroditism attributed to the Roman emperors whose lives he recounts. Gender reversal occurs as a kind of structural motif that helps unify the book. The first chapter, in fact, is titled "That Woman," an epithet that refers to Julius Caesar, bestowed on him by Cato, who belonged, Saltus says, "to an earlier day, to an austerer, perhaps to a better one" (13). Hence female attributes are markers of corruption and decline, and what in Julius Caesar is merely an epithet for something potential and implicit becomes in the later emperors an explicit reality. Saltus pictures Caligula for the reader as a woman: "On his wrists were bracelets; about his shoulder was a mantle made bright with gems; beneath it was a tunic, and on his feet were the high white slippers that women wore" (73). Likewise the dissipated Nero becomes: "a bloated beast in a flowered gown, the hair done up in a chignon, the skin covered with eruptions, the eyes circled and yellow; a woman who had hours when she imitated a virgin at bay, others when she was wife, still others when she expected to be a mother, and that woman, a senatorial patent of divinity aiding, was god—Apollo's peer, imperator, chief of the army, pontifix maximus, master of the world" (122). The parallel theme of feminization and corruption reaches its apotheosis in the final chapter of *Imperial Purple* with an account of the androgynous Heliogabalus, who appears first with the face of Bacchus, "the enigmatic beauty of gods and girls—the charm of the dissolute and the wayward heightened by the divine" (224). In describing, or, rather, in not describing the erotic tastes of Heliogabalus, Saltus adopts the attitude of discretion but not of condemnation, and the verbal portrait of this most notorious of emperors is all the more titillating for it. Saltus spends a good two pages writing that the life of Heliogabalus cannot be written and places himself in the company of Lampridus, who said: "I would never have written the life of this Antonin Impurrissumus . . . were it not that he had predecessors" (226–27). Saltus also quotes a remark by Gautier—"The inexpressible does not exist"—and then claims that "even his pen would have balked had he tried it on Heliogabalus" (227). Here, Saltus is thinking of Gautier as the author of that gender-bending novel *Mademoiselle de Maupin* (1835), called here a "notorious romance" (227). Saltus sums up the "difficulty" of writing about Heliogabalus: "It is not merely that he was depraved, for all that lot were; it was that he made depravity a pursuit; and, the purple favoring, carried it not only beyond the limits of the imaginable, but beyond the limits of the real" (229). Having said all this, having expressed so much reservation and reluctance, Saltus then wishes to have been around to *witness* the behavior that is so "inexpressible" that not even Gautier could set it down in words: "It would have been curious to have seen him in that wonderful palace, clothed like a Persian queen, insisting that he should be addressed as Imperatrix, and quite living up to the title" (229).

This sense of curiosity is, of course, one of Walter Pater's aesthetic virtues, and it is a telling confession on Saltus's part. In the end, *Imperial Purple* is none of the things it is so easy to imagine it might have been—an allegory of the corruption of the "Caesars" of Tamany Hall, a fantastic counterargument to the kind of realism and morality urged by William Dean Howells, or even (it is at least thinkable) a cautionary warning about America's own looming age of empire, still a decade away. All of these readings are possible, but none of them rings true. More than anything else, the book seems to express a nostalgic yearning for the great age of decadence represented by Rome in her decline as an alternative to the modernity of the late nineteenth century. In a key passage, Saltus wishes that he could have accompanied Hadrian and, somewhat anachronistically, "dined with him in Paris, eaten oysters in London," and then "to have passed down again through a world still young—a world beautiful, ornate, unutilitarian; a world to which trams, advertisements and telegraph poles had not yet come; a world that still had illusions, myths and mysteries; one in which religion and poetry went hand in hand—a world without newspapers, hypocrisy and cant" (175).

Taken in the aggregate, the works that Edgar Saltus produced in the 1880s and early 1890s comprise a kind of compendium of the decadent sensibility for other American authors whose tastes were not consonant with established or emerging native traditions. Saltus was neither James nor Howells; his novels were not psychological, but philosophical, nor could they be called "realistic," except, again, in a philosophical sense—provided the philosophy is pessimism. Saltus was by turns an American Schopenhauer, an American Flaubert, an American Huysmans, an American Wilde—well before Schopenhauer, Flaubert, Huysmans, or Wilde were known in the United States (the partial exception is Wilde, but he was known as a dandy and wit, not as a decadent writer, for his major works were as yet unpublished in the 1880s). As an American author with affinities to European decadent-aesthetic culture, Saltus had a few contemporaries—Henry Blake Fuller in Chicago, for example— and some successors, but no real precursors. Among the successors, his influence is not always determinable in any specific sense, but it is clear that the Saltus of the 1880s was a one-man avant-garde movement and at least some of the more demonstrative American decadents of the 1890s were following his cultural lead. The most significant of these Saltus successors were James Huneker and Vance Thompson, coeditors of M'lle New York, one of the first of the little magazines dedicated to going against the American grain by promoting a type of culture that was—as Huneker put it—"more Parisian than Paris."21

vi

The few accounts that exist of the brief career of M'lle New York rightly point out its importance to the literary avant-garde in the United States. The magazine was the brainchild of Vance Thompson and James Huneker, both of whom had lived and studied abroad, mainly in Paris, and were well acquainted, often

personally, with most of the key figures of the symbolist and decadent movements: Verlaine, Mallarmé, Huysmans, Maeterlinck, and many others. Both
Thompson and Huneker were journalists; Thompson was drama critic for the
Commercial Advertiser and Huneker wrote for the New York *World* and other
papers, mainly as a music critic, though his interests were extraordinarily
broad and his instinct for modernity in the arts was generally keen. He inter-
viewed Cézanne in 1901 and also wrote about Gauguin, evidently the first
American to do so.[22] He also introduced American newspaper readers to such
decadent authors as Flaubert, Baudelaire, and Huysmans, together with "progressive" figures like Stirner, Nietzsche, and Ibsen. Huneker is one of the few
writers to have played a role in both the original efflorescence of American
decadence in the 1890s and also in its revival in the 1920s (mainly by way of
his sensational novel *Painted Veils*, published in 1920). Vance Thompson also
served as an *introducteur* of Continental decadence with his *French Portraits* of
1899, but his later fame was based on his authorship of two best-selling self-
help books, *Eat and Grow Thin* (1914) and *Drink and Be Sober* (1915). The
last-named volume actually makes an argument in support of Prohibition, so it
is fair to say that Thompson, as least in a social sense, is more antidecadent
than decadent by the 1920s.

Huneker and Thompson met in New York in 1893 when they were both
working as journalists. They discovered in each other a mutual interest in the
very latest developments in music and literature and formed *M'lle New York* as
a means of announcing the "new names" in European culture (*SJ*, 2: 191). Huneker provided short essays about musical developments and also composed
mediocre prose poems, inspired by "the examples of Baudelaire, Mallarmé, and
Huysmans" (*SJ*, 2: 191, 194). Thompson published appreciations of a great
many European writers—"Maeterlinck, Ibsen, Verlaine, Verhaeren, and the
entire lyre of the younger French, Italian, Spanish, and Belgian poets," as Huneker puts it (*SJ*, 2: 191). He adds that Thompson was also responsible for
"wicked attacks on society and government and women" (*SJ*, 2: 189-91).
Eleven issues of *M'lle New York* appeared from August 1895 to April 1896 before publication ceased for lack of funds. The magazine was revived in November 1898, but Thompson and Huneker managed to publish only four issues before it expired for good. Interestingly, the earlier and later incarnations of the
magazine are rather different in tone, the 1895–96 version being more humorous and irreverent than the rather mean-spirited and reactionary issues of the
late nineties.

An issue from October 1895 is remarkable for its wide-ranging essays on
contemporary literature and for the expression of the decadence of the age.
This does not mean, however, that the new literature itself is always an expression of decadence. As often as not, the young European writers singled out for
emphasis in the pages of *M'lle New York* are understood as an enlivening alternative to "the burthen of this sated and indifferent century."[23] This is certainly

the case with a regular feature, "Foreign Letters," this one devoted to Italian writers. An enthusiastic account of D'Annunzio as the "lord of Italian letters today" praises the writer for the way "in which he celebrated—with Roman insolence—the joys of the flesh. The 'Intermezzo di Rime' has Swinburne's impeccable syllabic beauty, Swinburne's abject love for rose-white flesh" (MNY 1:6, [5]). D'Annunzio's appeal seems to inhere in a combination of physical energy and moral daring:

> From him one may expect much—this blond, blue-eyed, square-shouldered, high-browed fellow of thirty-one, in whom there stirs such tremendous Latin energy, in whom there is such artistic zeal, white and strenuous as an electric light.
>
> He chisels words as Flaubert did, as Walter Pater; he has de Maupassant's immense clairvoyance; as well, he has not little of Balzac's power—of Turgenev's power—of questioning souls. No writer of today, unless it be Strindberg, has quite his keen scent of moral anomalies, for the subtle crimes that lurk in the dark corners of the mind. (MNY 1.6, [5])

The closing reference to Strindberg is noteworthy. In his autobiography Huneker emphasizes the important role M'lle New York played in introducing Scandinavian artists and writers: "Edvard Munch, a powerful Norwegian artist, and Strindberg, the Swede, probably had their names printed for the first time in America in the pages of M'lle New York" (SJ, 2: 191). Thompson credits the Columbia University professor Bernard Boyesen for bringing "Scandinavia and the magnificent Norse literature home to a people which was battening on Howells" (MNY 1.6, [5]) and quotes a letter from Boyesen offering his compliments "on your extraordinary acquaintance with contemporary literature" (MNY 1.6, [6]).

What lies behind Thompson's and Boyesen's mutual admiration of Scandinavian authors is the mix of anarchism and egoism that began to emerge in America in the late nineteenth century following the discovery of Max Stirner and Friedrich Nietzsche. In brief, Stirner's egoism was allied to Nietzsche's nihilism, and both were understood to have their cultural embodiment in the plays of Ibsen, a self-proclaimed anarchist. This confused political amalgamation, extended well into the twentieth century by Emma Goldman and other advocates of individualist anarchism, is much in evidence in the pages of M'lle New York. For instance, Thompson labels the Danish writer Georg Brandes an "egoist" and an "anarch" and sums up the author's message as "a plea for independence in thought, hardy self-esteem; for the Nietzschean attitude; and his voice is the voice of one crying, 'Anarch and Autolatrist, I am illustrating Myself'" (MNY 1.6, [6–7]). As the reference to "hardy self-esteem" suggests, the "Nietzchean" attitude Thompson so ardently advocates here may be little more than solid Emersonian self-reliance decked out in contemporary Continental dress. But of course the enthusiastic Emerson strikes the wrong tone for the beleaguered

American "Autolatrist." Hence the reader is urged to emulate the decadent sensibility of Eugenio de Castro, the "extraordinary young poet of Portugal," whose work is reviewed immediately after the excursus on Scandinavian self-reliance. In a poem titled "Sagramor," the title character "cries his woe—the woe of this worn generation, so immensely sad, immensely ignominious, immensely miserable, the woe of sated eyes and nocturnal lips" (*MNY* 1.6, [7]).

In this representative issue of *M'lle New York*, Thompson contributes the literary criticism of new poets such as Eugenio de Castro, and Huneker provides the music criticism, which seems less avant-garde in spirit than Thompson's literary appreciations. For example, Huneker writes "A Brahmsody," which begins, "After Wagner the deluge? No, Johannes Brahms" (*MNY* 1.6, [13]). Huneker also tries to strike the avant-garde note himself with "Frustrate," a bombastic prose poem written from the point of view of desire. The poem begins, "I am the seed called Desire" and ends with this hard-to-read plaint: "Of what avail my travail? Of what avail my countless cruel preparations? O Chance! O Fate! I am one of the accursed silent multitude of the Frustrate!" (*MNY* 1.6, [4]). It is no accident that this poem appears immediately after Thompson's opening excursus on the inferiority of women, replete with "medical" and "scientific" explanations. Thompson's reasoning is that blood lost through menstruation is the physiological cause of female inferiority: "In the man of normal constitution the loss of fifteen ounces of blood produces syncope; the loss of five and a half ounces monthly during a period of twenty-five years would enfeeble him to imbecility" (*MNY* 1.6, [3]). These ideas are justified by the claim that "God alone has the right to be a misanthrope; for man there is only misogyny" (*MNY* 1.6, [i]).

Huneker provides a fuller, fictional treatment of misogyny in "Nosphilia: A Nordau Heroine," a short story that puts Nordau's atavistic ideas into imaginary action. One of Huneker's few commentators calls the story a "parody of Huysmans and decadent fiction,"24 and the parody works, in part, because of a shift in the decadent sensibility from man to woman. Indeed, the male protagonist of the story is a perfectly normal and healthy nineteenth-century gentleman, while his wife reads À *Rebours* and patterns her life after that of Des Esseintes. The story follows Nordau in interpreting Huysman's character not as a decadent but as a "degenerate hero," whom the wife emulates through "costly experiments" (*DSA*, 31). The experiments involve the woman's "passion for odours," though the passion is not marked by the same kind of synaesthetic refinements that Des Esseintes pursues in chapter 10 of À *Rebours*. Rather, the woman substitutes her love of smells for normal sexual love, so the marriage goes unconsummated. The frustrated husband, desperate for some explanation of his wife's behavior, reads Nordau's *Degeneration* (translated into English in 1895, the same year as the story's publication). A passage about "Baudelaire and his passion for perfumes" makes him realize that "[h]is wife was a degenerate. She had a morbid, a horrible love of odours.

She was a nosophile, a thing that divined the world about her by her scent, as does a dog" (*DSA,* 31). (Strictly speaking, a "nosophile" would be a lover of diseases, not a diseased lover along the lines Huneker imagines.)

The story ends when the husband attends the funeral of a friend's mistress and returns home late at night. His "nosophilic" wife picks up the scent of the dead woman on her husband and attacks him in a jealous rage: "[S]he bit into his jugular vein, tearing and rending the flesh like a wild beast, blinded with blood, ferocious and growling" (*DSA,* 32). Even before this final, "predaceous" act, the physical signs of the woman's atavism are evident, at least to the reader schooled in Nordau's theories: "Her eyes were small, and a glance at her ears showed the lobes undetached. . . . And the nose, slightly flattened, was curved beak-wise" (*DSA,* 30). As the story progresses the wife turns feline, then seems doglike, and finally "ape-like" (*DSA,* 32), thereby making her degenerate devolution complete. The new "scientific" authority of Nordau complements Thompson's biological arguments about female inferiority elsewhere in the issue, and Huneker's story makes the point that the same cultural interests (Baudelaire, Huysmans) that mark the male intellect as avant-garde render the female mind dangerously, even murderously, degenerate.

The benighted attitude toward women expressed by Thompson and Huneker during the first run of *M'lle New York* in 1895–96 was only the harbinger of a much broader antiprogressive spirit expressed in the four numbers of 1898. The first issue of the new series, in fact, opens with a political manifesto that reveals an understanding of Nietzsche's ideology that was to be adopted by any number of American moderns early in the next century:

> And *M'lle New York* sees the democratic hatred of the individual that is the chief mark of this drab, commercial civilization. Always democracy has groomed the rough-coated horse. Always democracy has hated the individual; always it has made it its business to castrate the thinkers.
>
> The social good is not the work of the masses, but the work of the few and the superior that a nation counts in history and in the life of humanity. The hypocrisy of liberalism, the ignominy of democracy, the meaner baseness of socialism are futile and discarded modes of thought. Only in an aristocracy—an aristocracy of the sparkling sword and the dominant mind—is there a germ of progress, a desire of ascension.[25]

There is no hint of cultural decadence in this diatribe, but a similar rant from a December 1898 issue suggests that Thompson is following the familiar formula whereby the decadent desires regeneration at the hands of barbarian conquerors: "Today we are ruled by weaklings, rogues, demagogues, vulgarians, shop-keepers—better, I say, the strong man. 'Tis better to be scourged by Atila than to be eaten alive by parasites. *I hear the grinding of the swords, and he shall come.*"[26] Not a lot of literature accompanies this political posturing, and what there is of it is predictably bombastic. An example is "My Country 'Tis of Thee," in which the speaker of the poem warns to "'*Ware the New Christ*" because "He cometh not to save; / Not peace, but blood." The author of this piece is said to be Lingwood Evans, a New Yorker now living in Australia, according to a review of the poet's work in the same issue. Later Huneker called Evans "an Australian rough-neck, writing decadent verse that alternated between the muffled morbidities of Verlaine and the roaring free-verse of Verhaeren." He also revealed the hoax: "Vance Thompson was Lingwood Evans" (*SJ*, 191). The hoax actually helps enforce an observation about *M'lle New York* made by Larzer Ziff: that the magazine "had its say but did not have a literature."[27] But Ziff also observes that "[s]ome twenty years were to pass before capable American writers would catch up with some of the principles of the magazine."[28] The comment refers to aesthetic principles, but it can also apply to political principles: Huneker was conversant in Continental avant-garde literature well before T. S. Eliot was twenty years later, and Thompson was a right-wing Nietzschean far in advance of H. L. Mencken.

The conflict between the cultural and political positions of the second incarnation of *M'lle New York* is characteristic of much of American decadence. Even as the magazine was promoting new and revolutionary foreign literature, it espoused an ideology consonant with the anti-immigrant sentiments of Theodore Roosevelt and other imperialist politicians. When Thompson says that the United States would be better off "ruled by . . . the strong man . . . than to be eaten alive by parasites," he expresses a reactionary ideology that was in the process of undergoing broad acceptance by the American public at the very end of the nineteenth century. The "parasites" he alludes to are almost certainly the immigrant population, massively evident in New York City at the turn of the century. What Thompson apparently wished for was a rejuvenation of American culture through an infusion of foreign influence, not the actual presence of "foreigners" on American soil. The hypocrisy of this position colors Thompson's avant-garde efforts to introduce French authors to an American audience, as in the *French Portraits* of 1899.

vii

Thompson's *French Portraits* is an ambitious effort of cultural diffusion that consists of biographical sketches of a variety of French authors, including generous quotations, mostly in the original French, from their poetry and prose. By subtitling the volume *Appreciations of the Writers of Young France*, Thompson signals that he is not writing as a critic. He finds distasteful "the dull mania of assigning ranks and distributing prizes . . . to men of letters"; instead, he presents himself as a kind of fellow traveler in the "new territory" of literature, populated by those writers who are "extending the frontiers of prose and verse."[29] The avant-garde sentiment is wedded to a decadent sensibility, as it often is: one of the youngest authors of the new literature, Emmanuel Signo-ret, nonetheless lives his life in twilight: "Signoret, impossibly young," is said to be "promenading his pale soul in the autumnal alleys of Versailles" (vii). Thompson does not use 'decadence' here but the sensibility he attributes to the group of writers he has collected includes the oxymoronic quality asso-ciated with the movement: "I have selected those who fought well or failed well" (viii). The book begins with a sketch of Paul Verlaine and his young ad-mirers—those who, like Thompson, "had bought him absinthe"—and con-cludes with an appreciation of Comte Robert de Montesquiou.

Thompson's take on Montesquiou is interesting because he treats the man as a modern version of a decadent Roman poet, rather than as the eccentric, neurasthenic aristocrat that Huysmans has handed down to us in the form of Des Esseintes:

> Always there have been two poetries—the one immediate, contemporary, in touch with the *Zeitgeist*, alive to the problems of the moment and prophetic in the forecasts of human destiny; and the other poetry, which begins by being literature, degenerates at last into sheer trifling, faded eroticism, word-juggling and self-sick analysis. The plant that has borne the hardiest, most splendid flowers, decays soonest; the bravest literature has always the most conspicuous decadence. (225)

Thompson's position here is actually quite shrewd. For him, decadent litera-ture—and Thompson has in mind the conventional idea of decadence as something like "mannered imitation" or "preciousness"—does not arise after a period of greatness; rather, it coexists with greatness and is even an indicator of that greatness: "It is an infinite error to imagine that great artists and their parodists do not exist side by side—that the rose and the dwarf rose may not blow in the same garden. . . . Indeed the strength of a poetical movement is often most notably seen in the crowd of poetasters it drags in its train" (225).

Montesquiou is one of these poetasters, who has "raised literature to the dignity of a sport" (226), by which is meant that the art of verse can be "a game like any other" (226). As evidence of Montesquiou's status as a latter-day Latin poet "of the time of the decadence" (226) Thompson quotes one of the count's poems on the beauty of the dahlia flower, which is:

> Lavé, glacé, sablé, chiné,
> Panaché, recouvert, ombré,
> Onglé, rubanné, marginé,
> Avivé, reflété, marbré,
> Cerné, bordé, friesé, pointé,
> Éclairé, nuancé, carné,
> Frisé, liseré, velouté,
> Granité, strié, cocciné. (228)

Nothing could be more mannered than this, but, nonetheless, Thompson allows a place for Montesquiou's "little songs of the sonorities he hears in *mauve*": "Life would be too sad, were it not for the poets of the blue hortensias, green roses and white peonies—these impassioned lovers of mauve and peacocks and Dresden china" (228–29).

What Thompson fails to see is that he, too, is a "poetaster," and a parodist not of greatness but of decadence. A sense of what an unintended parody of decadence might look like can be gained by a glance at one of Thompson's self-help books, *Eat and Grow Thin* (1914), a harbinger of such fads as the Atkins diet in latter-day America. The book is divided into three parts: the preface by Vance Thompson; "How to Eat and Grow Thin," by Mahdah, a one-named nutritionist of the period; and a list of low-fat recipes, the so-called Mahdah Menus. As different as this book is from the *French Portraits* of fifteen years earlier, Thompson is still playing at the game of putting himself in a position to educate the public, only now aestheticism is wedded to health, not willful sickness or self-destruction: "The idea is to eat enough—as a panther does; and not to eat too much after the manner of a less aesthetic animal."[30] One section of the preface alludes to Thompson's prior life as a corpulent decadent, in which he narrates "the *fabula* of myself" and chides himself for his past excesses: "Too long I had lived in the restaurants of the world—fed too full of Paris . . . , of Vienna, of Rome. The gracilities . . . were slipping away from me, hiding themselves in festoons and furbelows of fat" (25–26). At the end of the section he opines that such a book does not really require a preface but quotes Mahdah herself as saying that "[a] book without a preface is as *inconvénant* as a man without a collar on." Then he adds: "Wherefore I button on this collar (a detachable collar, fortunately—and you can take it off if you wish) and tie round it a mauve necktie" (28). Hence Thompson suggests some slight connection still with the mauve decade of his youth, a minor observation that belies the larger paradox involved in promoting decadent culture in the United States. Like Saltus and Huneker, Thompson believed that, somehow, decadence would be *good* for Americans. As strange as this sounds, Huysmans's novels, Verlaine's poetry, Maeterlinck's plays, and other works of decadent culture were urged upon the American audience as a kind of collection of "self-help" books. The culture of decadence, in other words, might help America to become something other than what it was.

CHAPTER THREE

Boston: Decadent Communities

W hat sets the decadents of Boston apart from those in New York is a true cultural community: disaffected Boston intellectuals and artists met in groups, published journals together, and started their own publishing houses. In New York, by contrast, Edgar Saltus was a fairly isolated figure. Had he remained in Paris and written his books in French, as Stuart Merrill did, Saltus might have gained a measure of recognition today among the ranks of American expatriate authors. Instead, he wrote French decadent novels in English and set them in New York City, thereby ensuring his ultimate obscurity, despite some early celebrity. Likewise, *M'lle New York* was not the product of a decadent *cénacle*; it was, at best, a two-man movement. The "editors" Vance Thompson and James Huneker were, for the most part, the magazine's sole contributors. Hence for all practical purposes there were no little magazines in New York to publish the ideas of like-minded aesthetes and *littérateurs* the way *The Mahogany Tree* and *The Knight Errant* did in Boston, or, more famously, as *The Chap-Book* did in Chicago (and even *The Chap-Book* started out in Boston). The literary scene in New York was also dominated by large commercial publishing houses such as Belford and Clark or Mitchell Kinnerly, the two publishers responsible for most of Saltus's best work. With the partial exception of *Madame Sapphira* (1893), published by F. Tennyson Neely, none of Saltus's books bore the imprint of a specialized, small-press publisher like Copeland and Day of Boston. Of course, the Boston literary world was also dominated by commercial publishing houses, such as the formidable Houghton Mifflin, but this fact only makes the point. In New York there was no real alternative to the commercial press; in Boston there was.

Another component of the cultural scene in Boston that makes decadence there more possible, more logical, than in New York is a fuller sense of tradition. The great Puritan, Unitarian, and Transcendental traditions of New England gave young Bostonians ample fodder for rebellion, whereas, in New York, there was almost no local grain to go against. Herman Melville, New

York's greatest writer (then and now, some would argue), was virtually un-known at the time; besides, he could hardly be identified with New York the way, say, Hawthorne could be identified with New England. More important, many understood the great New England traditions to be thoroughly ex-hausted at the fin de siècle, so that Boston itself now seemed belated, out of date—no longer the cultural center it had been for at least a century. Paradox-ically, the center had shifted to New York by the late 1880s, a shift marked by William Dean Howells's relocation—physically and artistically—to Manhat-tan. And if Howells, the former editor of *The Atlantic* in Boston, represented the literary establishment, so much the better for decadence, or, rather, for the perception that Boston was no longer, culturally, what it had been for so long.

The generation that came of age in the 1890s was somewhat belated in its awareness that Boston was no longer the center of America's power and pres-tige. Twenty years earlier James Russell Lowell and Charles Eliot Norton, not-ing the diminution of their native New England, and taking no interest in the nation at large, turned toward Great Britain for cultural reinforcement "as the immigrant nations began to rival the Anglo-Saxon."[1] This sense of New En-gland's cultural decline is nowhere better captured than by Henry Adams, in his arch third-person autobiography, *The Education of Henry Adams*. Even though Adams was a generation removed from the Boston decadents of the 1890s, his personal narrative of disaffection and deferral not only forms a nec-essary preamble to their story, it also sums up their sensibility. Adams admits to no small degree of confusion over "the conduct of mankind in the *fin-de-siècle*" but takes some ironic comfort in the destructive actions of the an-archists: "Adams disliked the present as much as they did, and his interest in future society was becoming slight, yet he was kept alive by irritation at finding his life so thin and fruitless."[2] Though not so sardonic as Adams, the Boston decadents of the 1890s were likewise removed from the present, and, like him, they figured their disaffection as a kind of illness. As the poet Louise Imogen Guiney put it in 1894, her generation cultivated a "willful sadness" as the only appropriate response to "the sick little end of the century."[3]

i

Although hardly as patrician as his forebears, Henry Adams cannot be grouped with the younger intellectuals of Boston who formed America's first decadent movement. In fact, that movement had largely run its course when *The Education of Henry Adams* was privately published in 1907. What Adams had in common with the younger generation was a deep sense of both personal and historical decline, of living at the end of an age. Adams's attitude toward the age of decadence in which he lived was, however, far more complicated than that of his younger contemporaries. Adams managed to be both magiste-rial and ironic about the lesser America he occupied, whereas many of the young Bostonians at the fin de siècle were almost enthusiastic about the sorry state of the country and quite ardent about their opposition to it. This attitude was expressed by the editors of *The Knight Errant* in 1892 when they announced in the premier issue of the magazine that they were "men against an epoch."[4] Likewise, in the same year, the editors of *The Mahogany Tree*, another Boston literary magazine, summed up their intentions by saying that they too had tried to go against the American grain: "We have tried, of course, to reform the world,—to induce mankind to turn now and then from the mad chase after the Almighty Dollar, and smoke cigarettes and read Oscar Wilde."[5] The antimaterialistic, antimodern editors of *The Mahogany Tree* understood European decadence in almost utopian terms as an alternative to American society. In one amusing fantasy, also from 1892, a decadent man and woman are imagined as the new Adam and Eve, who leave America and "buy an island somewhere in the tropics, furnish it with the implements of the Decadence,—cushions, cigarettes, incense, wine, Turkey carpets, jade bowls, ivory couches, Burne-Jones's pictures, French novels, Oscar Wilde's complete works—and live there the ideal life."[6]

In *The Education of Henry Adams*, the author is very much of the epoch, not against it, however much he may decry the fact and wish he had lived in a different epoch altogether. For Henry Adams, as well as for his brother Brooks, the apogee of Western civilization was the High Middle Ages, and this, too, is something he has in common with the younger generation, or at least those members of the younger generation associated with *The Knight Errant*. As the name of the magazine implies, the journal looked to the Middle Ages for models of modern behavior. The premier issue calls for a new fellowship of aesthetic knights "to war against the Paynims [pagans] of realism in art, to assail the dragon of materialism, and the fierce dragon of mammonism" (*KE*, 1: 1). This modern crusade is said to be more difficult than its medieval counterpart because, unlike the "ancient knights" who "fought man-to-man," the "would-be knight of these barren days may challenge no human opponent, etiquette forbids, rather must he join battle with the world itself . . . in this last night." The battle, naturally, is over beauty, lately discredited, the editors say, as something "childish, unworthy, and—unscientific" (*KE*, 1: 2). The list of contributors to the first volume of *The Knight Errant* reads like a who's who of the Boston movement, for theirs are the names that come up again and again in the context of medievalism, decadentism, aestheticism: Ralph Adams Cram, Bertram Grosvenor Goodhue, Bliss Carman, Bernard Berenson, Richard Hovey, Louise Imogen Guiney, Fred Holland Day.

One of the few studies of this group's activities takes the title *Currents of the Nineties in Boston and London*.[7] In Boston, however, for every cultural current there was a cross-current of some kind that makes characterization of America's first true decadent movement no easy task. Many members of the group were, like their British counterparts, attracted to Theosophy and other mystical, occult developments of the fin de siècle. But it is also true that some of them felt the attractions of traditional religion of the most conventional sort, whether High Church Anglicanism or Roman Catholicism. By the 1890s, the Episcopal ministry was firmly established in Boston, dating back to the rector-ship of Phillips Brooks at Trinity Church in 1869.[8] The Catholic faith had also taken hold with the growth of the immigrant population in the late nineteenth century. Of course, the immigrant nature of the Catholic Church lessened its appeal for the highly Anglophilic Boston group, but no such stigma attached to the Anglican faith. No doubt a highly aesthetic sense of ceremony accounts for the decadents' dual interest in fin-de-siècle cults and traditional faith.

But the aesthetic sensibilities of the Boston decadents were not so uniform as they seem at first glance. Initially, the Boston group appears to be no more than a belated recrudescence of the Pre-Raphaelite Brotherhood, pretty much an American analogue of aesthetic developments in England led by William Morris. In England, the devotion to medievalism that emerged from British romanticism and was codified into artistic doctrine by John Ruskin in *The Stones of Venice* (1851–1853) found political and artistic expression in the left-leaning work of the Pre-Raphaelites and in the socialist ideology of Morris and the arts and crafts movement. In America, and especially in Boston, the influence of Ruskin was perhaps more widespread than it was in England, in part because of Charles Eliot Norton, the Harvard professor whose literary evenings devoted to readings of Dante or to the Pre-Raphaelite poets did much to form the cult of medievalism among young Bostonians. In fact, these influences were deeply registered by Ralph Adams Cram in ways other than the literary. As an architect, Cram became the principal exponent of the Gothic revival in America and went on to design, among other buildings, St. John the Divine in New York City, the largest Gothic cathedral in the world (still under construction, by the way).[9] But the Boston experience of the aesthetic movement includes a pronounced element of High Church Anglicanism that retains more of the conservatism and antimodernism of the late Ruskin and nothing of the progressive ideology of William Morris—this despite the evident artistic influence of Morris. So while it is true that the artists and book designers of Boston took the Pre-Raphaelites and Morris as their models, the American context forced an awareness on the Bostonians largely missing in Britain. Simply put, the weight of materialism seemed so much greater in the United States; hence the impetus to aesthetic escapism was greater, as with the utopian fantasy, above, of an island community of cigarette-smoking, Wilde-reading decadents. The conflict of medievalism and modernity is not, of course, limited to aesthetics; it also informs the group's politics. Unlike the progressive medievalism of the socialist Morris, the Boston decadents took their medievalism much more literally and enter-tained ideas of monarchy as a serious solution to the material and political ills of late nineteenth-century America.

Despite the conflicts and inconsistencies in the group's spiritual, aesthetic, and political preoccupations, their beliefs and tendencies set them apart from ordinary Americans. This much is clear from the group's spiritualist activities. Calling themselves "Visionists," they found a secluded site in the middle of Boston's business district to conduct their spiritual proceedings, about which few specifics are known. A general sense of Visionist interests is, however, suggested by Cram's description of the room where the group met:

> We had our hide-out . . . in Province Court, on the third floor of a disreputably decadent building. . . . The one room was not over-large, but it had an open fireplace, one end was filled by a cushioned divan, and there were bookcases to hold the contributions of the individual Visionists. . . .
>   On the walls, the painter-members had wrought strange and wonderful things: the Lady Isis in her Egyptian glory, symbolic devices of various sorts, mostly Oriental and exotic. . . . In some indefinable way, its place had a mildly profligate connotation, which misrepresented it utterly.[10]

Cram's use of "decadent" in the description of the building calls for comment. The building is so termed because it housed "locksmiths, cobblers, and other modest practitioners of divers sorts of hand labour" (MLA, 91). These types of workers, unlike factory workers, were not part of the Industrial Revolution that led to the machine-age modernity so despised by the Visionist circle, with all its attendant problems, like labor unions. The Visionists and the hand laborers, in other words, were both pre- or even antimodern—hence "decadent."

Clues to the spiritualist activities of the Visionists are provided by some of F. Holland Day's pictorialist photographs. One shows a young man in Turkish costume rubbing a Japanese lacquer box, an activity thought to produce "special emanations" that "made it possible to communicate with the spirit world."[11] Another shows the same young man elegantly robed and holding a sword, a possible representation of some ritual connected with the Order of the Hermetic Students of the Golden Dawn. The Golden Dawn was a secret society notable for the membership of William Butler Yeats, whom Day had met in 1890 (Jussim, 49). The Golden Dawn and other mystical societies of the fin de siècle found much of their inspiration in Madame Blavatsky's Isis Unveiled, published in 1877. Cram's description of the décor of the room where the Visionists met shows Madame Blavatsky's all-pervasive influence to be still active, as does his reference to Herbert Copeland, F. Holland Day's future partner in publishing, officiating at some ceremony while "clothed garishly . . . as Exarch and High Priest of Isis" (MLA, 93). Evidently the members of the Visionist group saw no discontinuity between their esoteric practices and traditional religion, as a letter from Thayer Lincoln, a minor member of the group, shows. The letter recounts the late-night activities of Lincoln, the poet Richard Hovey, and Copeland, the aforementioned "Exarch": "[T]he discussion continued until after two in the morning, when we all adjourned to an all-night restaurant in Dover Street and then went to early Mass at the Cathedral [of the Holy Cross] . . . . When Mass was over, Copeland and I discovered to our dismay that Hovey was sound asleep on his knees."[12] It is worth noting that Cram had already undergone a conversion experience to High Church Anglicanism well before he involved himself with the Visionists.[13] Indeed, Cram is not the only member of the decadent circle of Boston who had turned away from his New England heritage. Most of his associates—or at least those who called themselves "decadents"—were cultivating not only royalism as an alternative to Yankee republicanism but also either High Church Anglicanism or Catholicism as an alternative to Protestantism.

In this latter respect further mention needs to be made of the Catholic poet Louise Imogen Guiney, a kind of missing link between Emily Dickinson and Edna Sainte-Vincent Millay. She was a lifelong friend of Day who was, in the 1890s, his partner in an obsessive, tireless cultivation of the legacy of John Keats. Guiney was a devout Catholic who was responsible for getting a number of American Catholic poets published under the Copeland and Day imprint (Jussim, 63). She also encouraged Day to take up the faith, and though he attended mass with her on a few occasions, he never converted.[14] Day's interest in Catholicism peaked in April 1898, when, with Guiney's help, he made the arrangements for a requiem mass held in Boston to commemorate the recent death of Aubrey Beardsley (Jussim, 91). Guiney was not a regular member of the generally all-male Visionist group, but she was a close associate of several of the regular members and did attend some meetings.

The Visionist group did not limit itself to spiritualist practices and occult investigations. On the contrary, the group was primarily interested in literature and the arts. Occasional meetings were devoted to poetry readings, and some members of the group gained wider recognition for their literary interests through the publication of *The Mahogany Tree*, a forerunner of other little magazines of the period. Like *The Chap-Book* of a few years later, *The Mahogany Tree* was imbued with the "Harvard manner," a contemporary synonym for "decadence." Cram remembers that the journal was "fathered by a cluster of Harvard undergraduates" (*MLA*, 88), and Herbert Copeland, the editor-in-chief, was an undergraduate at Harvard when publication began in January 1892. Cram's biographer Doughlass Shand-Tucci says the origins of the journal are likely due to the influence of the aesthetic circle that formed around George Santayana and Pierre La Rose at Cambridge (Shand-Tucci, 331, 333). This possibility is enhanced because F. Holland Day, who served as the journal's page designer and contributed occasional book reviews, associated with the Santayana group, even though he did not attend Harvard University. A photograph from the late 1880s shows Day seated in the center of a group that includes Santayana, Bernard Berenson, and Louise Guiney (see Shand-Tucci, 174). *The Mahogany Tree* is known today mainly because the journal was the first to publish Willa Cather.[15] This is unfortunate, in a way, because it obscures the journal's true significance as one of the first forums for decadent-aesthetic ideas in the United States. That said, it must also be said that the life of *The Mahogany Tree* was extraordinarily brief—only six months[16]—and the sense of decadence in it was sometimes rather fugitive. Indeed, the alliance with decadence is much more explicit toward the end of the journal's run than at the beginning.

ii

The premier issue of *The Mahogany Tree* states that the taste of "the Editor" (a composite, collective persona) is "decidedly for the romantic. He likes best, of present writers, George Meredith, with a large portion of admiration for Stevenson, and sometimes for Kipling. He does not care so much for Howells." Admiration for Meredith and Stevenson, especially in combination with the tell-tell distaste for Howells, can easily be reconciled with the decadent sensibility, but not so Kipling. The occasional interest in Kipling is likely the result of the group's Anglophilia, a feature that distinguishes the Boston decadents from their New York counterparts, who took their inspiration from Paris rather than London. Still, the editor of *The Mahogany Tree* claims to "read the French magazines, and means to keep track of the best work done abroad." Mainly, the editor counsels aesthetic connoisseurship and a leisurely removal from the hectic pace of American life: he "does not sympathize with the man who always gets up at seven o'clock and never takes a vacation, nor with the woman who is always 'doing' something." He also believes that "the ills of life are dissipated in the smoke that curls up blue and gray from his pipe."[17]

The smoking habits described in *The Mahogany Tree* tend increasingly toward decadence as the journal progresses, and the manly pipe of the premier issue is soon displaced by the more feminine cigarette. The cultural value of the cigarette is detailed in a letter "To the Cigarette Smoker," in which the author of the piece encourages the reader to light up, since the writer is "smoking one . . . as I write":

> What should we do without these little things? They certainly form one of the pleasures of life, these dainty things that we hold between our fingers whose smoke is so comforting, whose cost is so slight. Those people who abuse them so loudly certainly have never tried them, or if they have, they have not the truly artistic, cigarette temperament. Don't you always look down upon men who do not smoke them as rather coarse, unsympathetic beings; who would prefer cabbages to mushrooms, or Crème de Menthe to Chartreuse? (MT 1.16: 248)

One of the attractions of cigarettes is their mildly disreputable reputation; they are said to be "one of the greatest requisites of the villain," who "can never get along without them, nor the 'dude' either" (at this time *dude* is American slang for *dandy*). The writer wonders "that more women don't smoke," since "to do so would be a dainty little 'vice' for them." The prestige of Theosophy is brought to bear on the question of female smokers, "for they have excellent authority for it in Madame Blavatsky, who was a woman not only cultured in the things of the world, but also in the diviner knowledge" (MT 1.16: 249).

In an earlier issue, the "esteemed shade" of Madame Blavatsky herself is petitioned to help defeat pending legislation against cigarette smoking in Boston:

> Oh August Shade of Madame Helena Petrovsky Blavatsky help us! Come with thy troops of elementals; send those elementals into the homes of the lawgivers of Massachusetts and let them bother said lawgivers till they yield. . . . Help us with thy powers and we, the noble army of cigarette smokers, will bless thee for all time, and join the theosophical society forthwith.
>
> The next morning after the above petition was made the proposed law was voted down by a large majority. This is another remarkable instance of the powers of Madame Blavatsky, and shows indisputably that unseen spirits are ever about us and willing to help us, if we only have sufficient faith in them and rely implicitly on their powers to work us good. (MT 1.12: 186)

The tongue-in-cheek tone here should not distract us from the cultural values attached to both Theosophy and cigarette smoking as means of removal from the realities of nineteenth-century American life. Indeed, at least one *Mahogany Tree* piece encourages something stronger than tobacco as a method of escaping the ordinary. In "Smoke," a man and a woman smoke either hashish or opium ("soft, brown paste") in a hookah ("the pipe gurgled"), and both are transported by means of "the faint, sweet smoke . . . above the earth and past the time." Finally, they "float . . . alone in space, a perfect universe" (MT 1.16: 248–49).

In *The Picture of Dorian Gray*, first published in the United States by *Lippincott's Magazine* in July 1890, the decadent hero Lord Henry Wotton calls the cigarette "the perfect type of a perfect pleasure. It is exquisite, and it leaves one unsatisfied."[18] Wilde's endorsement of cigarette smoking has to be one of the reasons behind the Boston group's fascination with the "dainty vice," since Wilde's fame and influence were considerable in 1892, when *The Mahogany Tree* was published. Indeed, the editorial letter "To the Cigarette Smoker" appears in the same issue in which the group's "usual" discussion is said to be "God, Madame Blavatsky, Richard Feverel, Oscar Wilde and the like" (MT 1.16: 250). The high esteem in which the group held Wilde is captured by a brief review of *Lord Saville's Crime and Other Stories* that includes adulatory comments about the essays in *Intentions* (1891), especially "The Decay of Lying." More important, the review gives an account of F. Holland Day's meeting with Wilde when the great man was on his lecture tour of America in 1882 (Day would have been seventeen at the time):

> Regarding Oscar Wilde my friend recounts a rather amusing incident of meeting him during his famous lecture tour in this country. . . . The then preacher of Æstheticism was discovered placidly waiting, with the crowd, in a railway station, for the gates to open. My friend had just bought at the news-stand a new pencil hoping to capture an inspiration for his daily theme [Day had not yet completed his private-school education], during the short journey. Armed with the virgin lead and a slip of spotless paper he approached the Unapproachable, and in the sweetest tones his changing voice could assume requested the Sun's God his autograph. The Great One looked down upon the youth with that sunny smile so often and so cruelly maligned as "incubating" and taking the pencil slowly traced his name in a calligraphy rather the more curious than his appearance. No words escaped the lips of the lilies' apostle. The gates swung open and the throng passed through. For years this slip of paper and the pencil tied with yellow ribbon hung on the wall of my friend's library, who still keeps them, though far from the gaze of the commoner. (*MT* 1.10: 153)

Despite the third-person voice, the eccentricities of style (e.g., "Sun's God his autograph") suggest that the author of the review is Day himself, "employing the indirect method . . . which Victorian literary proprieties demanded" (Jussim, 77). Day may have idolized Wilde more than any other member of the Boston group. He owned a photograph of Wilde taken on the lecture tour of 1882 and may have met Wilde again in 1890.[19] When he formed his publishing house with Herbert Copeland, the firm published several of Wilde's works, including the scandalous *Salome*, which had been banned in Great Britain. In any case, Day was not the only member of the Boston group to revere Wilde, and their collective veneration went a long way to establish the meaning of 'decadence.'

One installment of "Round the Mahogany Tree," a regular feature of the magazine, is devoted exclusively to the question of decadence. "[C]an any of you tell me just what you mean by the *Decadence*, and what a *Decadent* is?" a "self-styled Philistine" asks. Not surprisingly, his interlocutors have trouble coming up with precise definitions. The state of decadence is said to be "blissfully uncertain" and rather "French in its atmosphere." "As to *a* Decadent, he is one who believes in *the* Decadence and lives up to his principles, as far as nature will allow." There is some suggestion as to what these principles might be when the decadent is compared to the bohemian: "he is a more ethereal sort of a person and one who absolutely must live in luxury and idleness to be perfect, but his morals are similar to those of a Bohemian." This last point is clarified: "That is, he has no morals." Moreover, the decadent "must have no conscience and no purpose in life." Instead, the decadent "lies on a window seat in a nest of cushions and 'smokes pink cigarettes and drinks absinthe[,]' . . . arrayed in purple and fine linen" (MT 1: 22: 345). The aforementioned fantasy follows in which we are told what would happen should the decadent, "seeking for a new sensation," find his female counterpart:

> They would buy an island somewhere in the tropics, furnish it with the imple-
> ments of the Decadence,—cushions, cigarettes, incense, wine, Turkey carpets,
> jade bowls, ivory couches, Burne-Jones's pictures, French novels, Oscar Wilde's
> complete works—and live there the ideal life,—the new Adam and Eve, whose
> children would not go wrong at the first touch, because they would have no con-
> sciences and couldn't do wrong. The coming race would be a much more moral
> one than ours, you see, since as there would be no morals, no one could break
> them and be wicked. (MT 1: 22: 346)

Among those persons "who claim to be Decadents" and "are numbered as leaders" are Walter Pater, Oscar Wilde, and "a few others, . . . warring 'against the Paynims of realism and the dragons of materialism'" (MT 1: 22: 346). The quotation is from the opening editorial in the first issue of *The Knight Errant*, whose publication had been favorably noted by the editor in an earlier issue of *The Mahogany Tree*. But the earnest *Knight Errant* turned out to be rather different in tone from *The Mahogany Tree* and made no attempt to match its clever irreverence. Instead, *The Knight Errant* assumed an almost apocalyptic attitude toward the sick little end of the century and concerned itself with a different sort of decadence altogether.

iii

As the discussion with the "Philistine" shows, the principal meaning of 'decadence' in the late issues of *The Mahogany Tree* is positive and cultural; that is, 'decadence' refers to a set of cultural interests (Wilde, Burne-Jones, French novels), as well as to a lifestyle that allows for the leisurely cultivation of those interests (cigarettes, incense, cushions). By contrast, the meaning in the pages of *The Knight Errant* is negative and social; that is, 'decadence' refers to a collection of social concerns (democracy, individualism, commercialism) that call for various cultural correctives (romanticism, medievalism, aestheti-cism). In the first case, there is no discontinuity between culture and society, though it must be said that the kind of society that would make the cultivation of decadent tastes possible is only imagined; in the second case, culture and so-ciety are in conflict because the cultural ideals of the past no longer obtain in present society. Society is decadent because of cultural decline.

This sense of cultural decline and social decadence is captured in an essay by Bertram Grosvenor Goodhue, Cram's partner in his architectural firm. In "The Final Flowering of Age-End Art," Goodhue complains that "[t]his age is not one in which any true art may flourish fairly." "The parching simoon of commercialism" and "the bleak frost of ignorance" combine against the artist, who wistfully longs for the last golden age, "when the meanest monk in a monastery laid stone upon stone, or carved the delicate capitals, with the same unerring truth and fixity of purpose" (*KE* 1: 111). Ruskin's influence is fairly ubiquitous here: the Gothic age is idealized as a time when art was the organic expression of society as a whole, not the fragmented endeavors of isolated individuals. At the same time, art is not "the property of the many" (*KE* 1: 107) because not just anyone is capable of the kind of integrated, organic expression "true art" involves. Hence a principle of individualism asserts itself after all, and Goodhue must resort to some clever rhetoric to get round the problem of the individualistic nature of the artists he admires (Whistler, Burne-Jones, Puvis de Chavanne, "perhaps Manet" [*KE* 1: 108]): "So we have for consideration a number of isolated individuals and small schools who, though they work independently, are striving toward the same end" (*KE* 1: 108). Goodhue holds out the greatest hope for the movement "taking place at present in England," which "seems a sort of Pre-Raphaelite decadence." He refers to William Morris and his followers, plus others who have the capacity to capture the ideal of Ruskin, "that divine thought once a common possession" (*KE* 1: 106), including the Aubrey Beardsley who illustrated the *Morte d'Arthur*. The "combined effort" of such artists "is leading us to something new and glorious, a product of the decadence, perhaps, but nevertheless,—indeed it may be because of this very fact—having a subtler beauty in our eyes" (*KE* 1: 110). Age-end art, in other words, is not without its rewards, and Goodhue closes the essay with that sense of delectation in decline so typical of the decadent sensibility:

> with such honest art and craftsmanship . . . let us content ourselves, and stepping within the angle of the wall, watch the hurrying throng of dusty and besmirched faces press by, knowing that the end of all true artistic expression is the same, though we seem far from the goal. Those who loiter still have for their solace, growing within the shadow of the wall, this pallid flower of the decadence, whose odour and beauty are theirs until the falling of the night. (*KE* 1: 111–12)

Goodhue's essay "has naught to do" with "the socialistic thundering of Mr. Morris," an ideological point that is a key to the distinction between the Boston decadents and their British counterparts. Even Oscar Wilde, in "The Soul of Man under Socialism," flirted with progressive politics, but most of the people associated with *The Knight Errant* held extremely conservative, even reactionary, views. Indeed, Cram gloried in the name "reactionist," and hoped that, "like the word 'Gothic,' the name given in scorn may in a little time be held in honour and reverence" (*KE* 1: 14). Cram's ponderously titled essay, "Concerning the Restoration of Idealism, and the Raising to the Honour Once More of the Imagination," appears in the inaugural issue of *The Knight Errant* and seems intended to serve as the ideological manifesto of the group. As with his partner Goodhue's essay on "age-end" art, the names of Ruskin and Morris figure prominently in Cram's diatribe against "the riot of individualism" that owes its origins to the High Renaissance. Cram's antidemocratic ideology is quite extreme, as in this lengthy but representative passage:

> The general tendency of society for the last two centuries and more has been away from the spiritual and imaginative towards the mental, the intellectual, and now, at last, the hopelessly material. The hero worship of ancient peoples as shown in their various governments, with its spirit of personal devotion and allegiance, has given place to deviant democracy. The social system has changed from the ancient régime where men were not ashamed to acknowledge the superiority of others than themselves, where a noble and honourable lineage gave right of precedence: to a perilous condition of social equality founded itself on a most abstract theory, and failing of its desired result through making inevitable a rigid inequality, the tests of which are purely financial. The conditions of life itself which once were accepted as a means to a clearly visible end, beauty of living and environment, have come to be only such as aid in the struggle for life that has grown now so fierce, in the acquisition of wealth in legal tender and securities, rarely used but hoarded instead, and in the furthering of purely material and enervating bodily comfort. Religion, once the impulse of idealism, the very abiding-place of abstract beauty, the unconquered, immeasurable realm of imagination, has, among many nations, degenerated through Protestantism to Puritanism, and thus to agnosticism and final materialism. (*KE*, 12–13)

Again and again, individualism leads either to the pursuit of materialism or to the enervating experience of its effects: "[T]he decadence visible in so many places is due to one and the same cause, and that cause the forsaking of idealism and the discrediting of the imagination through the immoderate following of individualism" (*KE* 1: 13). In art, individualism and materialism lead to realism.

This three-headed Cerberus of individualism, materialism, and realism has been confronted, in England at least, by a number of men whom Cram lists as his culture heroes, "prophets of the New Life." They include Cardinal Newman, Matthew Arnold, John Ruskin, Dante Rossetti, Edward Burne-Jones, Walter Crane, William Morris, and Walter Pater. This is an odd list, because it includes the political radicals Rossetti, Crane, and Morris along with the conservative figures Newman, Arnold, and Ruskin. If we take Cram's list seriously, we must assume that these disparate figures are listed for different reasons. Newman and Arnold are listed for political reasons, the rest—save Pater—for artistic reasons. Pater stands out because his aesthetics runs directly counter to Ruskin's—*Studies in the History of the Renaissance*, after all, is a deliberate corrective to *The Stones of Venice*. Hence it is probably for modern rather than medieval reasons that Pater is numbered among the "prophets of the New Life." As we are shortly to see in the discussion of F. Holland Day, for the young men of Boston, Pater was no less an exemplar than he was for the young men of London who wished to measure "success in life" by a capacity for intense, lived experience that many understood in terms of same-sex relations. The homosexual nuances of Pater's work aside, his aesthetic philosophy encouraged a radical sense of individualism that is hard to reconcile with Cram's Gothic ideology. Once again, the aesthetic currents of the nineties in Boston are beset by all kinds of political cross-currents.

The writers for *The Knight Errant* hardly spoke with one voice, either aesthetically or politically. In one issue Goodhue might caution against the socialism of William Morris, while in another Morris's admirer Walter Crane would urge the reader to be mindful of Karl Marx and have faith "in labour" (*KE* 42). One of Cram's essays would criticize realism as an aesthetic expression of individualism, only to be followed by an article by Herbert Copeland in which realism was questioned because it was not individualistic enough. Copeland takes the camera obscura as a symbol of the realist novel (because it faithfully reflects reality but also diminishes it) and a crystal ball as a symbol of the romantic novel (because it does not reflect reality as it is but "suggestively, ideally, infinitely" [*KE* 88]). He concludes that the "realistic novel conveys practically the same impression to everyone," whereas the "romantic novel means something different to every one"; in fact, the reader of a romantic novel may find "some meaning that applies to himself alone" (*KE* 92). What these contradictory attitudes have in common is the belief that they are all the products of an age of decadence. Indeed, the coexistence of conflicting systems of thought is one of the features of such an age. And it was Cram's belief that they would continue to coexist until what he called "the Restoration" (of medieval values):

> The two movements will develop side by side, the old régime [i.e., democracy] advancing steadily step by step, and with apparent triumph, confident of ultimate dominion, to its logical culmination; the "Restoration" moving more quietly by its side, gathering strength and power, until at last, when that chaos which is the *reductio ad absurdum* of current individualism, has come, the restored system of idealism shall quietly take its place, to build on the wide ruins of a mistaken civilization, a new life more in harmony with law and justice. (*KE* 15)

The leisurely delight in the refinements of decadence that found expression in *The Mahogany Tree* has here given way to a somewhat anxious faith in the limits of decadence. The belief that one is living at the end of an age confers on the believer a kind of spiteful hope. Such hope also finds its way into Cram's only novel, appropriately titled *The Decadent*.

iv

In his autobiography, Cram understands decadence in at least two ways. There is the sense of decadence as "a crumbling society," which, paradoxically, serves as a basis for youthful optimism: "If the world was indeed decadent, so much louder was the call for crusading" (Cram, 18). This perspective is consistent with the culture campaign of *The Knight Errant* to follow Morris—minus the socialism—back to the "idealism" of medieval society. But Cram also claims— in 1936—that the Decadence of 1892 allowed him and his cronies to "look on ourselves as superior beings. We rather reveled in Oscar Wilde and the bril- liant and epicene drawings of Aubrey Beardsley" (Cram, 18). A taste for Wilde and Beardsley is easy to reconcile with the diffident decadentism of *The Ma- hogany Tree* but harder to harmonize with the crusading aestheticism of *The Knight Errant*. In any case, the youthful, hopeful sense of decadence that Cram remembers from the early 1890s gives way to another sense entirely, which may be uniquely American: decadence becomes indistinguishable from mod- ernity. Cram presents a "periodical" theory of history divided into "intervals of five hundred years." Hence, he argues:

> [O]ur own age—which began with the year fifteen hundred—must come to its end by the year two thousand; and, however ardent and aspiring the individuals that come to birth during the last century or so of the five-hundred year period, they must fail of fruition, since they ride on the sweep of the declining wave. Certainly the record of the elapsed years of the present century would seem to give colour to such a theory, while it would explain the abortive results of so many of those lives that opened with high hopes during the half-century of which I am now recovering the fast-fading memory. (22)

Cram typically follows Ruskin in bewailing "the Renaissance decadence" (66) that ended the Gothic period. In this respect the old curmudgeon of 1936 is consistent with the young crusader of 1892, only the culture clock has been conveniently reset. The present age is scheduled to end in the year 2000, since it evidently failed to do so in 1900. The "riot of individualism" went on far longer than the young Cram expected, as the old Cram makes clear when he writes longingly that "if every protagonist of 'modernistic' art . . . could have been exiled (or rather repatriated) in Venice for six months, society would have been spared much" (64).

In his first and only novel, Cram's idea of decadence was directly inspired by the domestic habits of his friend Day, who was fond of wearing kimonos and other costumes generally not associated with the Puritan heritage of New

England (see figure 1). Indeed, the more outrageous aesthetic qualities of the book derive more from Day than from Cram, whereas the conservative polemics are mostly Cram's. It is as if the diffident decadent tone of *The Mahogany Tree* has been wedded to the crusading spirit of *The Knight Errant* in an effort to come to grips with the burgeoning modernity of Boston and the United States at large. The extensive subtitle of *The Decadent* hints at the problem of the nineteenth century that forms the drama of the novel itself: *Being the Gospel of Inaction: Wherein are Set Forth in Romance Form Certain Reflections Touching the Curious Characteristics of these Ultimate Years, and the Divers Causes Thereof.* The drama, such as it is, involves the conflict between the modern, progressive forces of society, represented by a radical socialist named Malcolm McCann, and the antimodern, reactionary politics of his friend and former disciple, the decadent aesthete Aurelian Blake. The character McCann is likely based in part on the socialist artist Walter Crane, who visited Boston in late October 1891 to promote a traveling exhibition of his work in Boston and other American cities. As Crane explains in his autobiography, he ran afoul of Boston society shortly after his arrival when he accepted an invitation to speak at a "memorial meeting" on the fifth anniversary of the deaths of the Chicago anarchists wrongfully executed in connection with the Haymarket bombing of 1886.[20] When he returned to his hotel after giving the lecture, he found a note from "a very kind Boston lady" warning that his involvement in the Haymarket memorial would "hopelessly ruin [his] social and artistic prospects in America." In fact, the Boston press made such a sensation of the meeting that the publicity helped secure the success of Crane's exhibition (Crane, 366). The success was certified when the staid *Atlantic Monthly* asked him to contribute an article "Why Socialism appeals to Artists." Around this time (October–December 1891), Crane met Cram, Goodhue, and other members of the younger generation associated with *The Knight Errant*, whom he described as "a cultivated group of young men . . . who had been inspired by the recent English revival of painting and book decoration and the higher forms of art generally" (Crane, 371). Although Crane was middle-aged when he met the Boston group, Cram most likely took inspiration from the older socialist when he created the young firebrand McCann to serve as a foil for his own "reactionist" ideology, voiced by the F. Holland Day look-alike Aurelian Blake.

The short novel is divided into three chapters. The first describes McCann's disgust with the modern world as he arrives by train in Boston and then takes a coach to Vita Nuova, Aurelian Blake's mansion in the country. The second contrasts McCann's recollection of his friend's former life as a radical socialist with his present existence as a decadent aesthete. The third and final chapter consists almost entirely of a political debate between McCann and Blake on the relative merits of their differing ideologies. While they are both opposed to the capitalist, materialist society they see all around them,

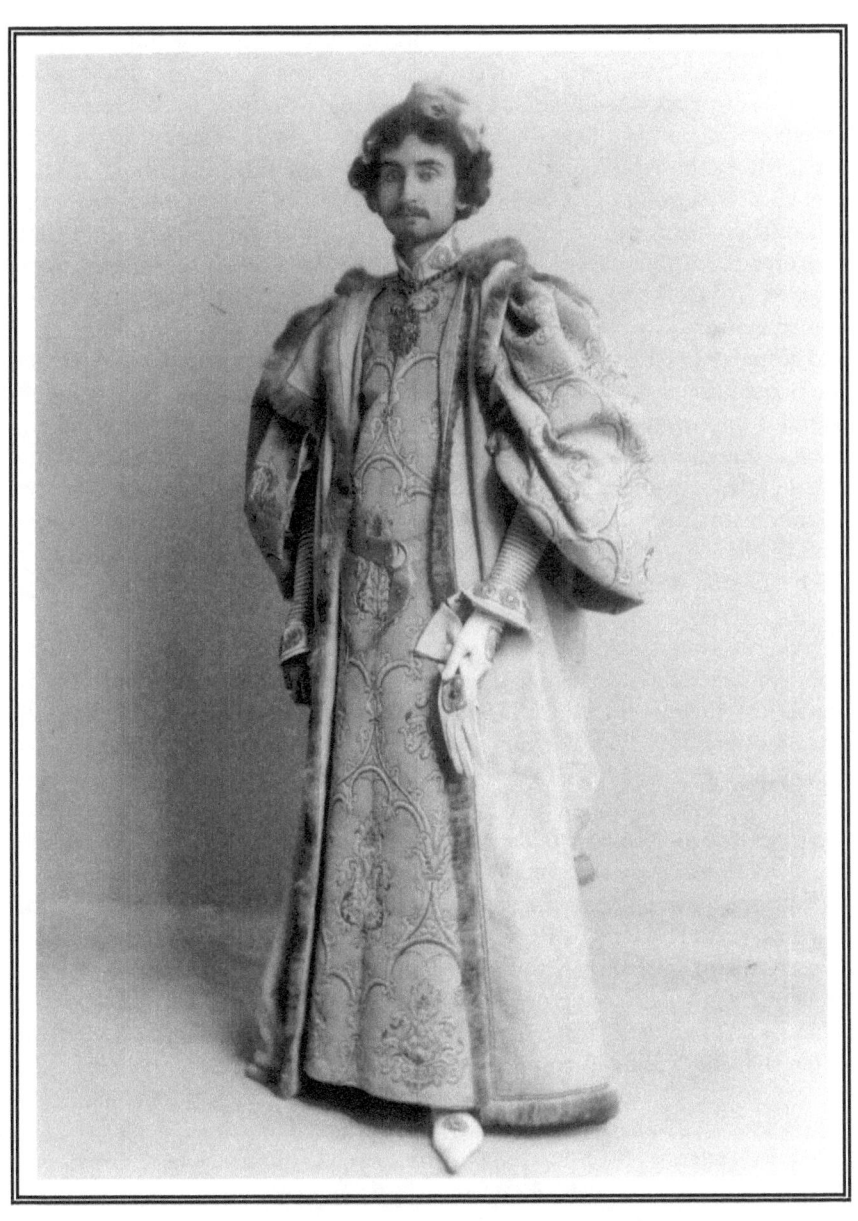

FIGURE 1   F. Holland Day in Medieval Costume (1893)

with its locomotives, factories, and political bosses, they have different strategies for dealing with that society. McCann hopes to organize the workers and usher in a socialist system through political agitation; Blake expects the capitalist system to collapse of its own weaknesses and is content to do nothing until the collapse occurs. After McCann expresses his wish to "destroy the whole system of party and ring rule" in favor of "State Socialism" (19), the aesthete opts instead for "my books of the Elect, my fading pictures, my treasures of a dead civilization" (21).[21] The subtitle also tells us that the novel is set in "these Ultimate Years," meaning not only the final years of the nineteenth century but also the final years of capitalist society. In addition, this odd gospel of inaction is said to be "Set Forth in Romance Form," when, in fact, the novel has none of the formal features of medieval romance. The word romance is important, however, as another verification of the politics of Cram and his circle, who, as we have seen, were medievalists in both an aesthetic and an ideological sense. The antidemocratic ideas of The Decadent, however, go much further than those in The Knight Errant. As the mouthpiece for Cram's ideology, the character Aurelian Blake makes clear that the members of the Boston group advocated a return to royalism and considered themselves Jacobites.

The reactionary ideology of The Knight Errant is nowhere evident in the frontispiece to the book, which looks more like a scene from the utopian decadence imagined by the editor of The Mahogany Tree (see figure 2). Drawn by Cram's business partner, Bertram Grosvenor Goodhue, the frontispiece shows the influence of Aubrey Beardsley and illustrates a scene from the novel in which an androgynous Japanese figure in a kimono attends to the needs of the aforementioned Aurelian Blake, the inert protagonist of The Decadent. The frontispiece probably illustrates a moment in the novel when Blake's friend Eveleth speaks these words through a haze of tobacco and opium smoke: "This is the peace of the land of Proserpina, the faultless content of perfect possession. Philistinism is not without honour, for behold! It has conceived and brought forth—the Decadence" (10). The decadence of which the character speaks is an obvious negation of all things American, as this description of Aurelian Blake's smoking room shows:

> The room was vast and dim, seemingly without bounds, save on that side where the violet flames of a drift-wood fire flickered quiveringly, making a centre, a concentration of dull light; for the rest, a mysterious wilderness of rugs and divans, Indian chairs and hammocks, where silent figures lay darkly, each a primal cause of one of the many thin streams of smoke that curled heavily upward;— smoke from strange and curious pipes from Lahore and Gualior; small sensitive pipes from Japan; here and there the short thick stems of opium-pipes, and by the motionless Mexican hammock a splendid and wonderful hookah with writhing stem. As the thin flames of the dying fire flashed onto some sudden

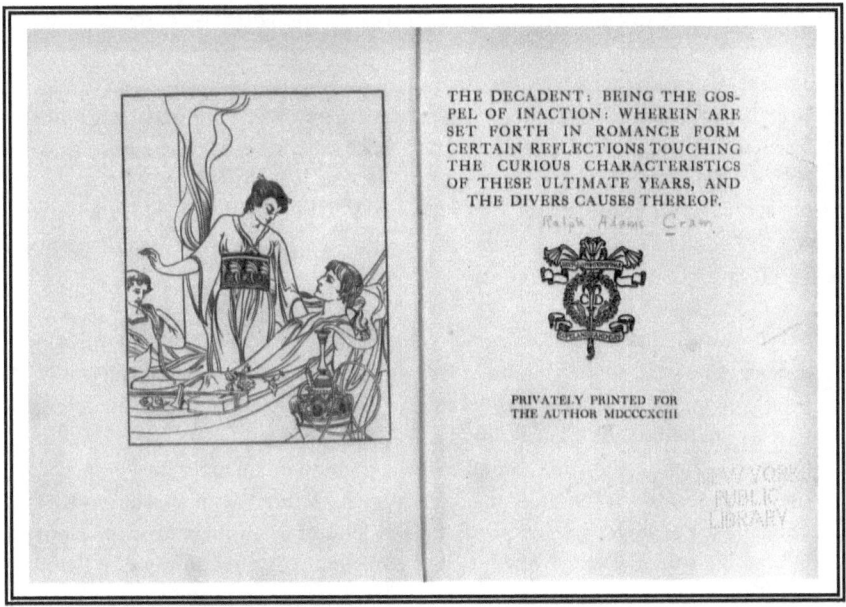

THE DECADENT: BEING THE GOS-
PEL OF INACTION: WHEREIN ARE
SET FORTH IN ROMANCE FORM
CERTAIN REFLECTIONS TOUCHING
THE CURIOUS CHARACTERISTICS
OF THESE ULTIMATE YEARS, AND
THE DIVERS CAUSES THEREOF.

Ralph Adams Cram.

PRIVATELY PRINTED FOR
THE AUTHOR MDCCCXCIII

FIGURE 2 Frontispiece and title page, Ralph Adams Cram, *The Decadent* (1893)

brightness, they revealed details unseen in the general gloom, — a vast and precious missal gorgeous with scarlet and gold and purple illumination, open, on a
carved oak lectern, spoil of some Spanish monastery; the golden gloom of a Gio-
vanni Bellini reft from its home in Venice, and as yet unransomed; the glint of
twisted and gilded glass in an ebony cabinet; great folios and quartos in ancient
bindings of vellum and ivory and old calf-skin, heavily tooled with gold, and
with silver and jewelled medallions and clasps, stacked in heaps in careless indifference; the flash and sparkle of a cabinet of gems, the red splendour of old lacquer; the green mystery of wrought jade. And everywhere a heavy atmosphere
that lay on the chest like a strange yet desirable dream; the warm, sick odour of
tobacco and opium, striving with the perfume of sandal-wood, and of roses that
drooped and fluttered in pieces in the hot air. (10–11)

This passage might be set beside similar descriptions of antiquarian artifacts
and oriental splendors in Huysmans's À *Rebours* or in George Moore's *Confessions of a Young Man*, so relished by the respective heroes of those novels, Des
Esseintes and Edward Dayne. But Cram's decadent novel differs from its precursors in its single-minded aversion to modernity. There is none of Des
Esseintes's ironic aesthetic admiration of the massive beauty of the steam loco-
motive in *The Decadent*. And Aurelian Blake may share Edward Dayne's taste

for Japanese dressing gowns, but unlike Moore's character, he cares only about the art of the past and has no interest in the art of the future.

In fact, Cram's character despairs at the mere possibility of art in an age of materialism: "Individualism begot materialism, and materialism begot realism; and realism is the antithesis of art" (35). The aesthetic doctrine here may be close to Wilde's in "The Decay of Lying," but at least Wilde proposes artistic alternatives to realism; not so Cram. He has Aurelian Blake quote Matthew Arnold's "Dover Beach" to support the claim that civilization "is falling now" and that the age of art is at an end:

> Yes, it is the decadence, the Roman decadence over again. Were Lucian to come among us now he would be quite at ease—no, not that, for in one thing we are utterly changed; so sordid is our decadence, so gross, so contemptibly material, that we are denied the consolations of art vouchsafed to his own land. Even in the days of her death Rome could boast the splendour of a luxuriant literature, the glory of beauty of environment, the supremacy of an art-appreciation that blinded men's eyes to the shadow of the end. But for us, in the meanness of our fall, we have no rags of art wherewith to cover our nakedness. Wagner is dead, and Turner and Rossetti; Burne-Jones and Watts will go soon, and Pater will follow Newman and Arnold. The night is at hand. (33-34)

This mixture of musical, artistic, and literary tastes may chime with the aesthetic interests of the British decadents, but the political context in which those interests operate is quite different in America. Jacobite royalism is a long way from Morris's socialism.

The principal artistic influence on *The Decadent*, however, is not so much Morris as some combination of Pater and Wilde. Aurelian Blake has closeted himself in an aesthetic enclave that makes the reader mindful of the British Decadence for more than one reason, not least because there is not a single female character in the book. As he was preparing Cram's novel for publication, F. Holland Day described the book to a friend in a way that suggests no small degree of unease, on the part of both Day and Herbert Copeland: "[W]e are to print for Cram a book called *The Decadent*. . . . He has tried so very hard to 'do the Oscar' but failed so ignominiously that he will probably not put his name to it, but no persuasion of Herbert's or mine has had the least effect to leave it in M.S. It will appear most 'queer' before Christmas."[22] In fact, Cram chose not to put his name to the book, though probably not because he had failed to "do the Oscar," as Day thought, but, rather, because he had succeeded. It is impossible to know precisely what Day means by "queer" in the letter, but the usage is likely an early instance of the word as a slang term for homosexual. Cram's only reference to *The Decadent* in his biography refers to the book as an "indiscretion" (84), and this, together with the attempt by both Day and Copeland to dissuade Cram from publication, suggests that Cram may have been too candid for comfort about the private activities of the Boston Decadents. Cram's biographer believes *The Decadent* to be "a key marker in . . . New England cultural history" of what Jeffrey Weeks calls "a new community of knowledge, if not of life and feeling, amongst many men with homosexual leanings."[23] In this context, Elaine Showalter is right to describe "the 'decadent' art and literature of the fin-de-siècle" as the record of an emerging identity "around which a subculture [began] to form and to protest . . . [and ultimately] forge its own identity and culture."[24] No doubt because the book hit so close to home, *The Decadent* "stirred a largely negative reaction" within the Boston group. Louise Guiney joined Day in expressing her disdain for the novel and even wrote to Cram that *The Decadent* "stuck in my throat" (Shand-Tucci, 366). Copeland wrote Day from London to express his concern that the first publication of Copeland and Day had gotten the young firm off to a bad start (Shand-Tucci, 368).

Cram's second "indiscretion," *Black Spirits and White: A Book of Ghost Stories*, continued the coded exploration of same-sex relations, though in much more personal terms. At first glance the stories in *Black Spirits and White* seem to have only a tangential relation to the decadent-aesthetic sensibility that Cram explored in *The Decadent* two years earlier. The novel published by Copeland and Day draws on the British strain of the decadent tradition, while the short story collection published by Stone and Kimball adapts the gothic effects of Edgar Allan Poe to the travel-fiction genre popularized by the Chicago writer Henry Blake Fuller, among others (see chapter 4). The collection came out late in 1895 (the *Chap-Book* advertised that it was "available" in November), after Oscar Wilde's conviction for "gross indecency" in May of that year. This fact is noteworthy because the physical format of the book makes explicit visual reference to Wilde, whereas the content of the stories involves some highly coded—and highly anxious—representations of the kind of behavior that landed Wilde in Reading Gaol. *Black Spirits and White* was one of several books published in Stone and Kimball's Carnation series, volumes decorated with stylized images of carnations against a green background on the cover. Unlike the other four books published in this series, *Black Spirits and White* was "issued with green patterned endpapers,"[25] thereby making complete the allusion to the "green carnation," a symbol of homosexual love in general and of Wilde in particular. In "Pen, Pencil, and Poison," another essay from the influential *Intentions* of 1891, Wilde expostulated on "the curious love of green, which in individuals is always the sign of a subtle, artistic temperament, and in nations is said to denote a laxity, if not a decadence, of morals."[26] In *Salome*, the title character is called "Daughter of Sodom" and uses "a little green flower" as a symbol of her seductive power.[27] Also, Aubrey Beardsley's illustrations of the play make stylized images of the carnation blossom a significant part of the visual narrative of Salome's passion. Publishing Cram's ghost stories between boards so heavily decorated with visual symbols of homosexual love just months after Wilde's conviction and imprisonment must have concerned Cram. Again, in his autobiography, published when he was seventy-three years old, Cram refers to *The Decadent* and *Black Spirits and White* as "early indiscretions" that he "perpetrated" in his youth.[28] The tone is humorous and self-denigrating, but the word choice is interesting: crimes are usually said to be "perpetrated," and homosexuality was a crime in the 1890s.

Cram's most recent biographer explains that *Black Spirits and White* is based in part on the author's tour of Europe with one Thomas Henry Randall, a young architecture student whom Cram met in Rome: "Though it may seem improbable, these stories constitute pretty much a record of Cram's and Randall's European travels" (Shand-Tucci, 63). In his autobiography Cram says that Randall "was to play a vital part . . . in my life" (55) as "an evocative and formative influence" (57). The influence Cram has in mind is Randall's Episcopalianism, "of the sound Southern sort, vitalized by Catholic tendencies" (57). The contact with Randall resulted in Cram's conversion from New England Unitarianism to High Church Anglicanism; as Cram puts it, "in due course I received the Anglican Communion of the Catholic Church" (60). *Black Spirits and White* offers evidence of this conversion in that all of the stories are set in Catholic Europe. More important, several make Catholic ritual the modus operandi for the supernatural events the stories recount. In "The White Villa," for example, the narrator experiences a nighttime visitation from the ghost of a woman whose beauty in life earned her the name La Luna di Pesto (the story is set in Paestum or Pesto); the spirit walks the rooms of the white villa on the anniversary of her murder because, as one of the locals explains, "she died unshriven, so was she buried without the pale of the Church."[29] As with several stories, the narrator's experience of horror takes the form of helpless paralysis, while his male companion sleeps peacefully in the same room. The companion is not always named, but when he is, as in "The White Villa," the name is Tom Rendel, obviously derived from Thomas Randall. In most stories, not only is the companion not haunted by the female spirit, but he usually comforts the terrified narrator after the ghostly visitation. In "The White Villa," the aid that Tom Rendell offers has clear homoerotic implications: "He lifted my head and held me in his powerful arms" (76). Shand-Tucci observes of one story that it "seems a literary rendering of what in the old textbooks used to be called homosexual panic" (Shand-Tucci, 66).

This sense of paralyzed panic is most powerful in the first story, "No. 252 Rue M. le Prince." The title refers to an old house willed to the narrator's friend, here named Eugene Marie d'Ardeche, but the house is uninhabitable because of a curse placed on it by one Sar Torrevieja, known as the King of the Sorcerers. The narrator and his friend, along with two other young men, decide to test the theory that the house is haunted by spending the night there. All four inspect the premises and discover some strange rooms but decide to spend the night anyway. Only the narrator experiences anything out of the ordinary; in fact, what he experiences is quite extraordinary. The narrator becomes paralyzed but holds onto consciousness through the following scene, which must be quoted at length:

> Then the end began. In the velvet blackness came two white eyes, milky, opalescent, small, far away,—awful eyes, like a dead dream. More beautiful than I can describe, the flakes of white flame moving from the perimeter inward, disappearing in the center, like a never ending flow of opal water into a circular tunnel. I could not have moved my eyes had I possessed the power: they devoured the fearful, beautiful things that grew slowly, slowly larger, fixed on me, advancing, growing more beautiful, the white flakes of light sweeping more swiftly into the blazing vortices, the awful fascination deepening in its insane intensity as the white vibrating eyes grew nearer, larger.
>
> Like a hideous and implacable engine of death the eyes of the unknown Horror swelled and expanded until they were close before me, enormous, terrible, and I felt a slow, cold, wet breath propelled with mechanical regularity against my face, enveloping me in its fetid mist, in its charnel-house deadliness.
>
> . . . .
>
> Suddenly a wet, icy mouth, like that of a dead cuttle-fish, shapeless, jelly-like, fell over mine. The horror began slowly to draw my life from me, but, as enormous and shuddering folds of palpitating jelly swept sinuously around me, my will came back, my body awoke with the reaction of final fear, and I closed with the nameless death that enfolded me.
>
> . . . . I think I fought for hours, desperately, insanely, in a silence that was more hideous than any sound,—fought until I felt final death at hand, until the memory of all my life rushed over me like a flood, until I no longer had strength to wrench my face from that hellish succubus, until with a last mechanical struggle I fell and yielded to death. (25–26)

This extended passage is typical of the book, in that the pattern of the stories suggests a fear of sexual contact with woman and anxiety over the homoerotic feelings the fear implies. The literary heritage of Poe and the Gothic novel makes possible the coded language Cram employs: supernatural horror is the medium for psychosexual anxiety. Cram's conversion to the High Church may have made it easier for him to relinquish his rationalism and free his imagination to invent supernatural happenings. But given that the agent of this conversion was a young man for whom Cram felt a deep affection, the Catholic conversion comes at the cost of sexual unease.

In the signal first story of the collection, not only is this sense of sexual unease most intense, so is the sense of fin-de-siècle decadentism. The story is set in Paris after all, which allows for the decadent atmospherics that come with "sitting in the queer little garden of the Chien Bleu, drinking vermouth and absinthe" (6). Here, the word *queer* appears in the context of decadent-bohemian behavior, and it is virtually certain that the word is expressive of homoerotic sensibilities. The narrator comments that there is something "queer . . . about the whole affair" (11), remarks on the "queer goings on in the old house" (9), and finds everything all very "queer and fin de siècle" (21). With its green carnation boards and its anxious narratives about the adventures of two young American men on the corrupt Continent, *Black Spirits and White* appears more "queer," even, than *The Decadent*. The book helps to show that, no less than in London or in Paris, decadence in Boston is often "most simply explained" as "a euphemism for 'homosexual.'"[30]

v

Ralph Adams Cram's *The Decadent* was the first publication by the firm of Copeland and Day, whose sense of artistic taste is signaled by their trademark design and the Latin motto it contains: "Sicut Lilium Inter Spinas" (A Lily among the Thorns). The motto suggests the difficulty of sustaining a refined and delicate sense of beauty given the late nineteenth-century conditions under which the practitioners of fine art were forced to operate. When they formed their publishing venture in 1893, Copeland and Day set out to establish a press that would be the equal of Morris's Kelmscott Press in England.[31] Thus there is some irony in that the first book they produced should be *The Decadent*, which has the look and feel of a Kelmscott edition but is filled with antisocialist polemic. Despite their concerns over the book's reception, Copeland and Day obviously selected their friend's work as the press's premier publication because of the affinity the principals felt for British decadence, an affinity certified later on when Copeland and Day took advantage of the International Copyright Act (1891) to form an agreement with Elkin Matthews and John Lane of the Bodley Head and become the American publishers of *The Yellow Book*.[32] (It is probably true that most original editions of *The Yellow Book* in American libraries today are Copeland and Day's rather than Matthews and Lane's.) The business relationship with Matthews and Lane was quite close. Prior to beginning publication of *The Yellow Book* (Copeland and Day's eleventh project), eight of the first ten books published by Copeland and Day came from the British firm's list, including Wilde's *Salome*, which came out in 1894 with Beardsley's famous drawings. The only two independent ventures were Cram's novel, initially advertised as a "revolutionary essay,"[33] and Dante Gabriel Rosetti's sonnet sequence, *The House of Life*, originally published in 1870 and one of the signal works of the Pre-Raphaelite movement. Accordingly, the book was given the full Kelmscott Press treatment, with elaborate interlacing border designs and initial letters for each poem drawn by Bertram Goodhue. As Joe W. Krauss explains in his study of the publishing house, "William Dana Orcutt, who oversaw the printing of the book, went to the

Harvard Library with Day's sample pages to study the Kelmscott volumes there before giving instructions to the compositor. 'It was a turning point for me, for through Fred Day I came to understand William Morris'" (Krauss, 17).

With *The Decadent, The House of Life*, and *Salome*, followed by *The Yellow Book*, the firm of Copeland and Day was well on its way to becoming the most important source in America for decadent-aesthetic literature. To be sure, this was not a type of culture that was altogether consistent with American values. *The Yellow Book*, in particular, stirred some readers to recognize that something unusual was afoot in England that might not be entirely suitable to American tastes. Under the title "A Yellow Impertinence," *The Critic* gave this review of the first number of Copeland and Day's transatlantic publication: "They claim that *The Yellow Book* is the embodiment of the modern spirit. If this be true, then give us the good old-fashioned spirit of *Harpers, The Century*, and *Scribners*, whose aim is to please the intelligent people, and not to attract attention by 'tripping the cockawhoop' in public."[34] The reaction was likely elicited by the writings of decadent sorts like Max Beerbohm and Arthur Symons rather than by the work of established figures like Edmund Gosse and Henry James, who also appeared in the first number. A more tempered response was offered by the *Literary World*, which found the issue "well worth reading," even though "the trait of the serpent, affectation, pervades *The Yellow Book*, as it does all the productions of the recent English school in art, in poetry, and in letters."[35] Although Oscar Wilde was not a contributor to *The Yellow Book*, his name was associated with the publication because so many of the younger writers—like Beerbohm and Symons—were Wilde disciples (or perceived as such), and of course Beardsley was connected to Wilde by way of *Salome*, even though the two men knew each other only slightly. Thus, when Wilde was convicted of "gross indecency" in May 1895 Beardsley immediately lost his position as art editor of *The Yellow Book* (he was succeeded by Ethel Reed, a member of the Boston circle and one of Copeland and Day's designers [Shand-Tucci, 345]). With the Wilde scandal and Beardsley's dismissal, *The Yellow Book* suddenly lost much of its appeal, as *The Critic* noted in a review of the seventh issue: "*The Yellow Book* is shorn of its yellowness; it is nothing now but book."[36] More pointedly, an editorial in *Publishers' Weekly* of 13 April 1895 put Copeland and Day on notice, even before the conclusion of Wilde's trial, that the sort of literature associated with Wilde and his fellows was an offense to American decency:

> We fear that the subtile poison which Mr. Wilde and his followers have helped inject into our literature and art has taken such hold upon a large part of the public that its effects cannot be suddenly shut off and hidden from sight. . . . Publishers should discourage authors who bring these wares to them for publication, and all healthy men and women should be as much ashamed to be in the company of such books as to be in the company of the shameless men and more shameless women they describe.[37]

Significantly, the editorial is titled "The Passing of the Decadent."

Although Copeland and Day continued publication of *The Yellow Book* until July 1896 with the tenth number, the focus of the firm shifted well away from the literature of decadence after the Wilde conviction. With the publication of such books as *An Old Man's Romance: A Tale*, by Christopher Craigie, and *Meadow Grass: Tales of New England Life*, by Alice Brown, the publishers took the firm in a new direction. In truth, even before the Wilde trial Copeland and Day had departed from publishing books that "suggested an aura of English decadence" (Krauss, 23) with Bliss Carman and Richard Hovey's *Songs of Vagabondia* and Charles Knowles Bolton's *On the Wooing of Martha Pitkin: Being a Versified Narrative of the Time of the Regicides in Colonial New England*. The firm also went on to publish such staples of the Victorian canon as Elizabeth Barrett Browning's *Sonnets from the Portuguese*. The death of Robert Louis Stevenson occasioned the publication of a study by Alice Brown and an elegy by Richard Le Gallienne. In short, of the complete list of Copeland and Day publications, numbering 108 items, only about one-fourth can be said to represent decadent-aesthetic culture. These include Cram's novel; Wilde's *Salome*; *The Yellow Book*; several volumes of poetry by members of the Rhymer's Club—Richard Le Gallienne, Lionel Johnson, and, most notably, William Butler Yeats; Douglas Ainslie's translation of Barbey D'Aurevilly's *Of Dandyism and of George Brummel*; and two works by Walter Pater—*A Child in the House* and *Duke Carl of Rosenmold: An Imaginary Portrait*.

vi

Even though the firm of Copeland and Day was hardly devoted to decadence exclusively, the publishing house offers ample evidence of a deep commitment to decadent-aesthetic culture. The fact is important to an understanding of the photographic career of F. Holland Day. Once pigeonholed as a pictorialist interested only in using the camera to imitate the fine art of painting, Day is now understood as a highly individualistic artist not easily identified with a particular school or movement: "Constantly shifting between an aesthetic of symbolist decadence, the refined attributes of pictorialist splendor, and the burgeoning authority of photographic Modernism, Day's activities need new classifications to account for the peculiar web of interrelationships he formed between them."[38] As a pictorialist, Day was in the vanguard of those who thought that photography should be inspired by the tradition of painting. For example, his photograph of the book designer Ethel Reed shows the influence of Gainsborough, hence the portrait is properly titled *The Gainsborough Hat* (figure 3). As this image illustrates, Day is acclaimed as a particularly sensitive photographer of women, and indeed he does seem to have had a gift for getting the personalities of the women he

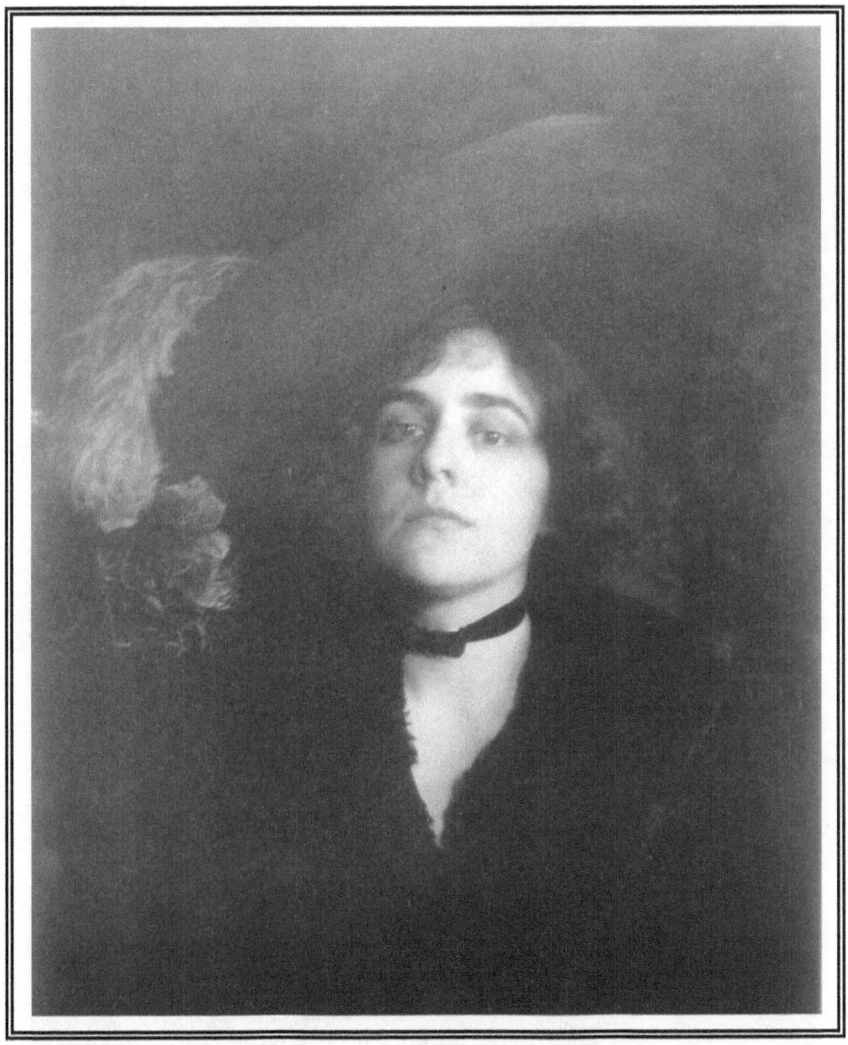

FIGURE 3 F. Holland Day, *The Gainsborough Hat* (1895)

photographed on the plate so that their humanity is allowed to emerge, as in one of Day's early successes, titled *Hannah* (figure 4). This study of pensive New England womanhood, with its compositional debt to Whistler, led to his election in 1895 to the Linked Ring Brotherhood, a London association devoted to the recognition and promotion of art photography (Jussim, 99). The same attention to the psychology of the sitter that shows in *Hannah* is not

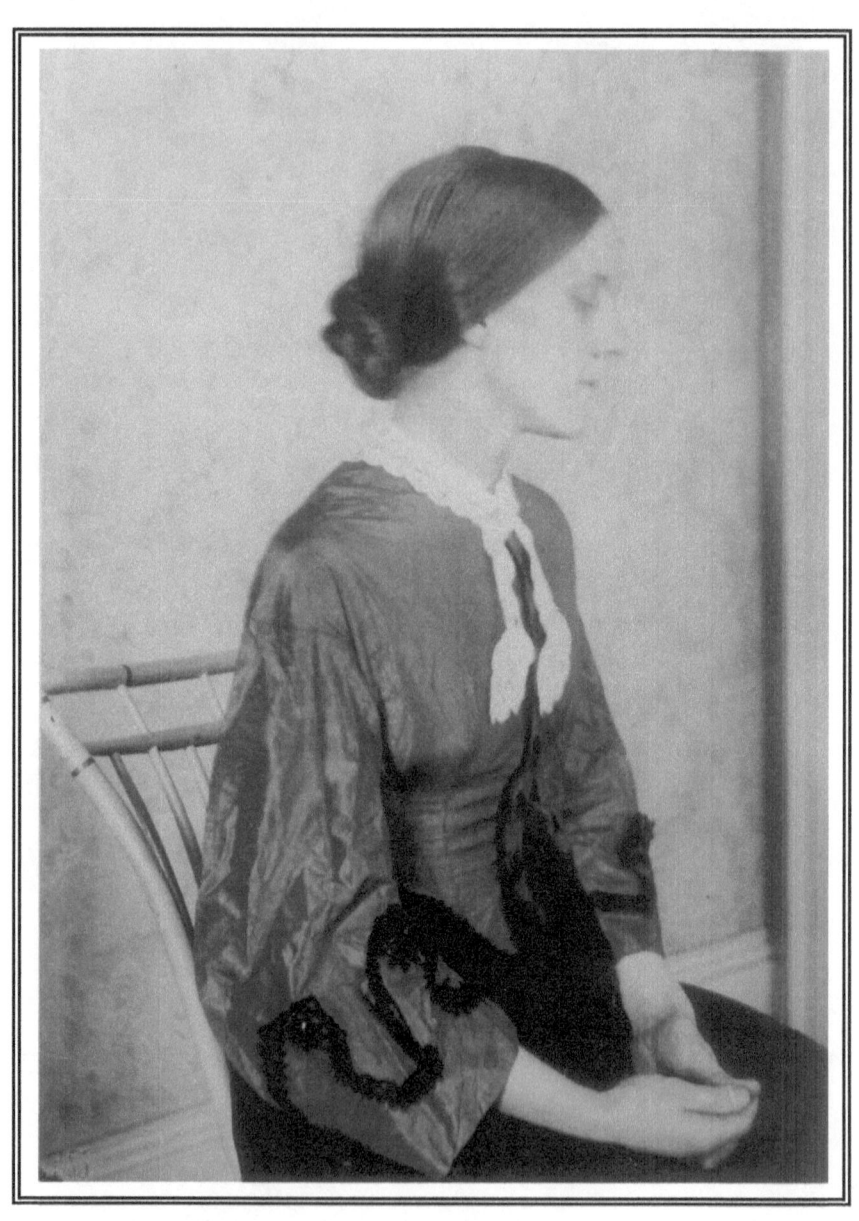

FIGURE 4   F. Holland Day, *Hannah* (1895)

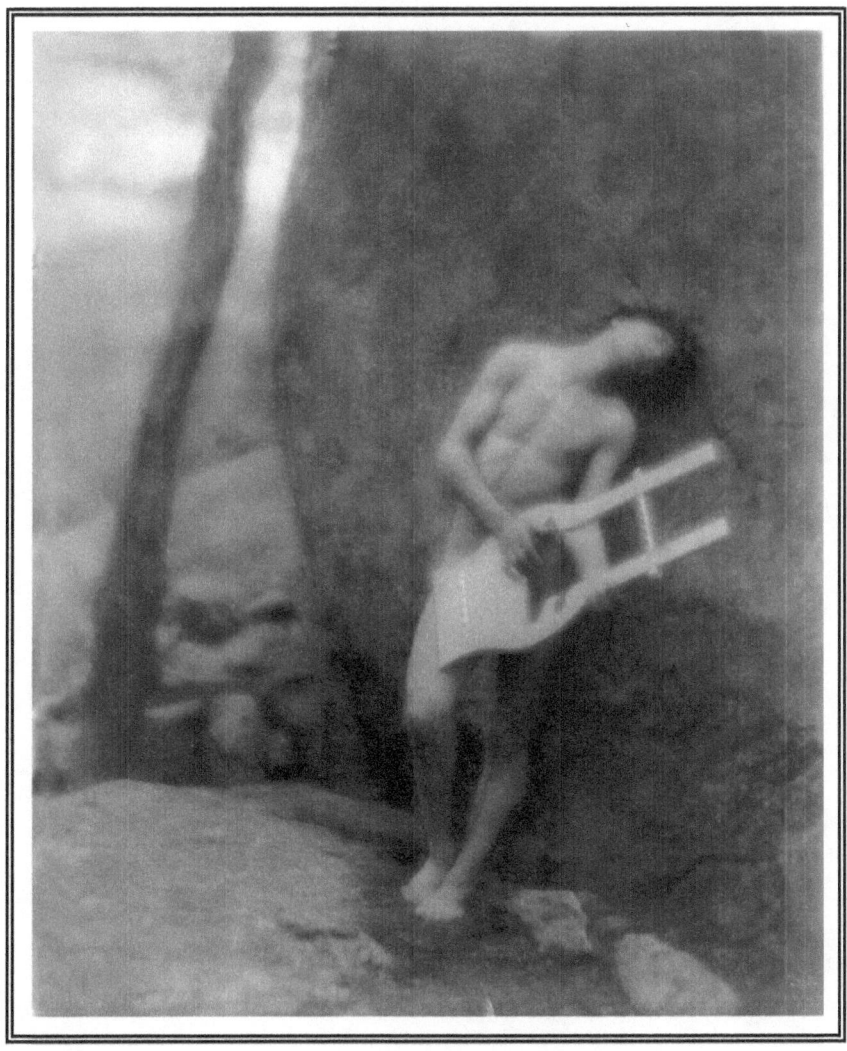

FIGURE 5   F. Holland Day, *Nude Youth with Laurel Wreath and Lyre* (1907)

generally evident in his portraits of men and young boys, whom he insisted on seeing in highly contrived literary or artistic contexts, derived, for example, from some combination of his beloved Keats and symbolist painting (figure 5. *Nude Youth with Laurel Wreath and Lyre*), or from Aubrey Beardsley (figure 6. *Nude Youth with Laurel Wreath Embracing the Herm of Pan*).

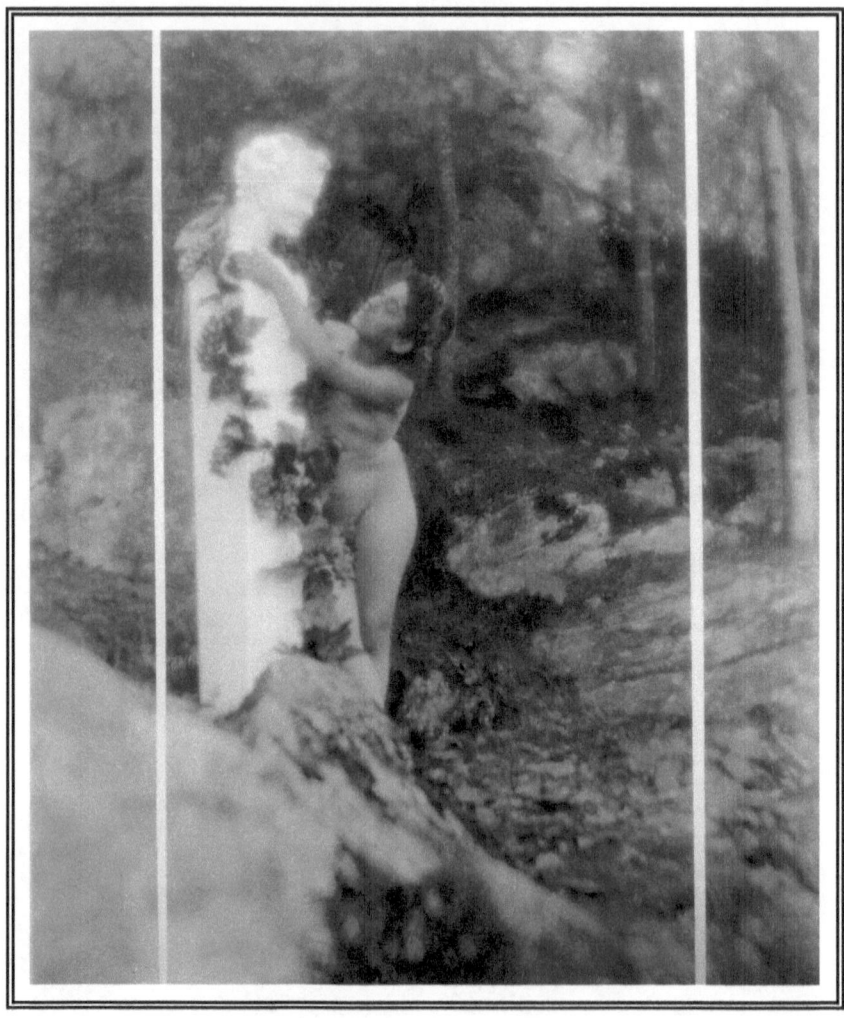

FIGURE 6   F. Holland Day,
Nude Youth with Laurel Wreath Embracing the Herm of Pan (1905)

As these photographs suggest, a large part of Day's complexity lies in the way he took literary inspiration for pictorialist imagery, and the literature that inspired him was largely derived from the decadent-aesthetic tradition. He seems to have been especially devoted to Symbolism, notably the Belgian dramatist Maurice Maeterlinck. Day's interest in Maeterlinck found support in the work of his friend Richard Hovey, whose *Songs of Vagabondia* Day had published in 1894. Hovey had traveled to Europe and gotten to know Verlaine, Mallarmé, and Maeterlinck, eventually becoming Maeterlinck's principal English translator.[39] In 1895 Hovey translated an edition of Maeterlinck's plays and wrote an introduction on "Modern Symbolism and Maurice Maeterlinck." In this essay Hovey set symbolism against morality by arguing that literature "lives for itself and produces no impression of being a masquerade of moralities; but behind every incident, almost behind every phrase, one is aware of a lurking universality, an adumbration of greater things."[40] As Hovey's overheated opinion shows, by the mid-1890s the symbolist aesthetic—with its cultivation of nuance and indirection, its evocation of dream and daydream, its fascination with exoticism and "decadence"—had become mannered and conventional in literature. But those same aesthetic values, when transferred to the medium of pictorialist photography, resulted in genuine artistic innovation. No one before Day managed to achieve the subtle effects of tone that he did, and no one before Day was more committed to resisting the common notion that the camera was simply a recording device for reproducing reality.

In a lecture titled "Is Photography an Art?" Day says that the photographer "no longer speaks the language of chemistry, but that of poetry. He quotes less Hershel than Pater."[41] And, perhaps with Pater's autobiographical story "A Child in the House" in mind, Day goes on to compare the developing photograph to a wakening child: "Slowly, idly, like a waking child, the picture opens its eyes and smiles. It will speak when the artist has paused. But it will remember so well what [the painter] M. Jules Breton [1827–1906] has said of art: 'All must not be said.' Poetry is made of the unknown" (qtd. in Curtis, 300). Those photographers who qualify as poets of the camera do so because they are artists who are not interested in realistic detail, "but simplification of the idea. They have chosen, not the sun-bright hours wherein all is to be seen, but hours neighboring to twilight wherein something is to be guessed. They have found that the indefinite is the road to the infinite."[42] Even though this sort of symbolist mysticism strikes us as aesthetically retrograde now, when Day transferred that aesthetic to the medium of photography the work that he did can only be called innovative. Thus the symbolist tradition in its decadence plays a significant role in the birth of photography as a fine art.

If Day looked to Pater to explain his rationale for photography as a new form of fine art, he also felt his influence in more personal ways. Again, Day was associated with the Santayana circle at Harvard, where Pater was highly revered and profoundly influential on Bernard Berenson and other members of the younger generation. As those who read Pater closely knew, his *Studies in the History of the Renaissance* was a challenge not only to Ruskin's appreciation of Gothic art but also to Victorian norms of social and sexual behavior. This challenge is perhaps most explicit in Pater's essay on Winkelmann, in which the Hellenic ideal of male beauty is put forward as a condition for understanding art itself: "As it is the beauty of man which is to be conceived under one general idea, so I have noticed that those who are observant of beauty only in women, and are moved little or not at all by the beauty of men, seldom have an impartial, vital, inborn instinct for beauty in art. To such persons the beauty of Greek art will ever seem wanting, because its supreme beauty is rather male than female."[43] Thus it stands to reason that the pictorialist who looked to learn more from Pater than from the pioneering photographer Sir John Herschel (1792–1871) should also take the male nude as a subject for art, as Day most certainly did. At the same time, the photographer took care to control the erotic appeal of the male nude by presenting the body within culturally acceptable contexts of art and literature. Day's *Study for Crucifixion* has its sensuousness "explained" explicitly by reference to Michelangelo's sculpture *The Dying Slave* and implicitly by allusion to Pater's essay on Michelangelo. Other male nudes appear in the symbolist role of Orpheus or, more daringly, in *The Herm of Pan* as the photographic equivalent of one of Beardsley's drawings. A photograph of a young man as the martyred Saint Sebastian, however, hints at a darker allegory of homosexual suffering in a Puritan world.

This allegorical interpretation has been made of Day's most controversial series of photographs, which depict Day himself as the crucified Christ. Several versions of *The Crucifixion* show an emaciated Day, who starved himself for weeks in preparation for the shoot, wearing only a loin cloth and hung on a specially constructed cross made of wood imported from the Middle East (see figure 7).[44] Although these photographs make reference to a painting of the crucifixion by Velázquez, a copy of which was owned by Day (Jussim, 124), the pictorialist rationale is not fully adequate to explain the artist's self-immolation on a hilltop just outside his Norwood, Massachusetts, home in 1898. That same year saw the publication of *The Ballad of Reading Gaol*, in which Oscar Wilde alluded to the crucifixion as a metaphor for the hanging of a fictional inmate. The metaphor could not help but suggest that the persecuted Wilde, writing from prison, was also likening himself to the Crucified. As James Crump shows, Day had reason to fear persecution as well for his own curious behavior and ambiguous sexuality in the moral atmosphere of Boston after Wilde's conviction and incarceration. In May 1898, Dr. Francis W. Anthony delivered a lecture at the Essex North Branch of the Massachusetts Medical Society titled "Responsibility in Cases of Sexual Perversion." Dr. Anthony warned of "a band of men . . . of perverted tendencies . . . not far removed"—from Boston, evidently (an allusion to Norwood is not out of the question). He adds that these men "are known to each other as such" and are "bound by ties of secrecy and fear and held together by mutual attraction." Moreover, "[t]his band . . . embraces, not as you might think, the low and vile outcasts of the slums, but men of education and refinement, men gifted in music, art, literature, men of professional life and men of business and affairs."

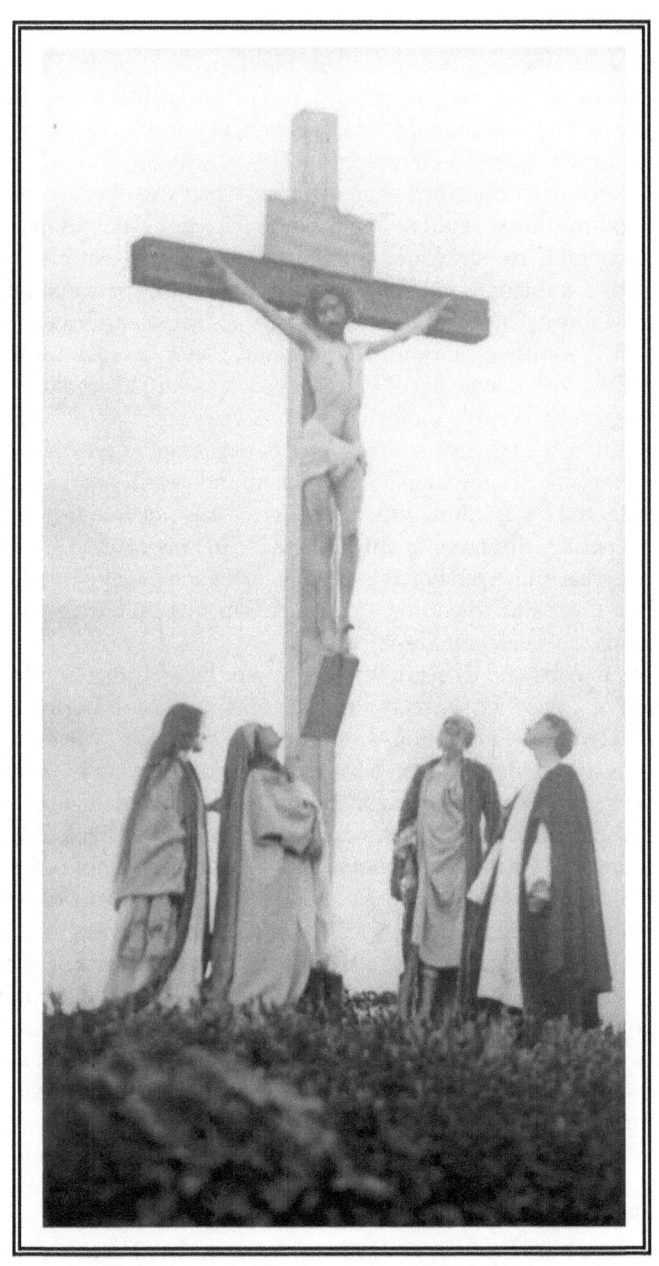

FIGURE 7 F. Holland Day, *Crucifixion* (1898)

These "sexual deviants," the physician concluded, should "be removed from the community to [their] proper place, be it asylum or prison."[45] Dr. Anthony's medical opinion makes credible the interpretation of Day's so-called sacred photographs as an expression of "the historically contingent position of the homosexual in society,"[46] to say the least.

Using Christian iconography as an allegory of private suffering was one way for Day to express his sexuality. The method may not have resulted in work that was acceptable to everyone, but at least it was safe. Another way for a man with Day's ambiguous sexuality to gain a measure of personal satisfaction was through a form of altruism or philantrophy acceptable to Victorian mores. Day was a great admirer of Edward Carpenter, the utopian socialist who advocated "Greek Love" as a means of bettering society, an idea that derives from John Addington Symonds's Victorian tract, *A Problem in Greek Ethics* (1883). There the author uses the term *Greek Love* to designate "a passionate and enthusiastic attachment subsisting between man and youth, recognised by society and protected by opinion, which, though it was not free from sensuality, did not degenerate into mere licentiousness."[47] In this context Day's portrait of a fourteen-year-old Arab boy is especially arresting (see figure 8) and leads us to ask how Day came to photograph the person who, in retrospect, has to be regarded as his most celebrated subject.

The story may be said to begin in 1895, when the architect Stanford White had a statue of a Bacchante erected in the courtyard of the Boston Public Library, completed by the prestigious New York firm of McKim, Mead, and White in 1892. Now in the Metropolitan Museum of Art in New York City, Frederick MacMonnies's fountain ornament in the form of a nude female celebrant of Bacchic enthusiasms caused quite a controversy in fin-de-siècle Boston. The statue was removed for reasons of moral outrage in 1896 but not before a young Syrian immigrant did a sketch of the sculpture. The young artist was one of numerous immigrant children who responded to the atmosphere of moral and cultural improvement provided by the settlement house movement. One of the many counterparts to the famous Hull House run by Jane Addams in Chicago was Boston's Denison House, managed by the social worker Jessie Fremont Beale of the Children's Aid Society.[48] Miss Beale "used her position as librarian [of this society] to enlist the help of the Boston establishment. The wealthy, the artistic, the literary, and the academic were included in her blueprint to bring enlightenment to the poor" (Gibran and Gibran, 38). One of these Denison House volunteers, an art teacher named Florence Pierce, evidently saw the boy's sketch of MacMonnie's *Bacchante* and brought the young Syrian artist to the attention of Miss Beale. Miss Beale, in turn, wrote a letter of introduction to her friend F. Holland Day, recommending that Day take over the child's artistic education; no doubt Day was stimulated to do so by Beale's account of the young man's talent: "A drawing which he made in the cloisters, at the library, of the Bacchante made quite a sensation."[49]

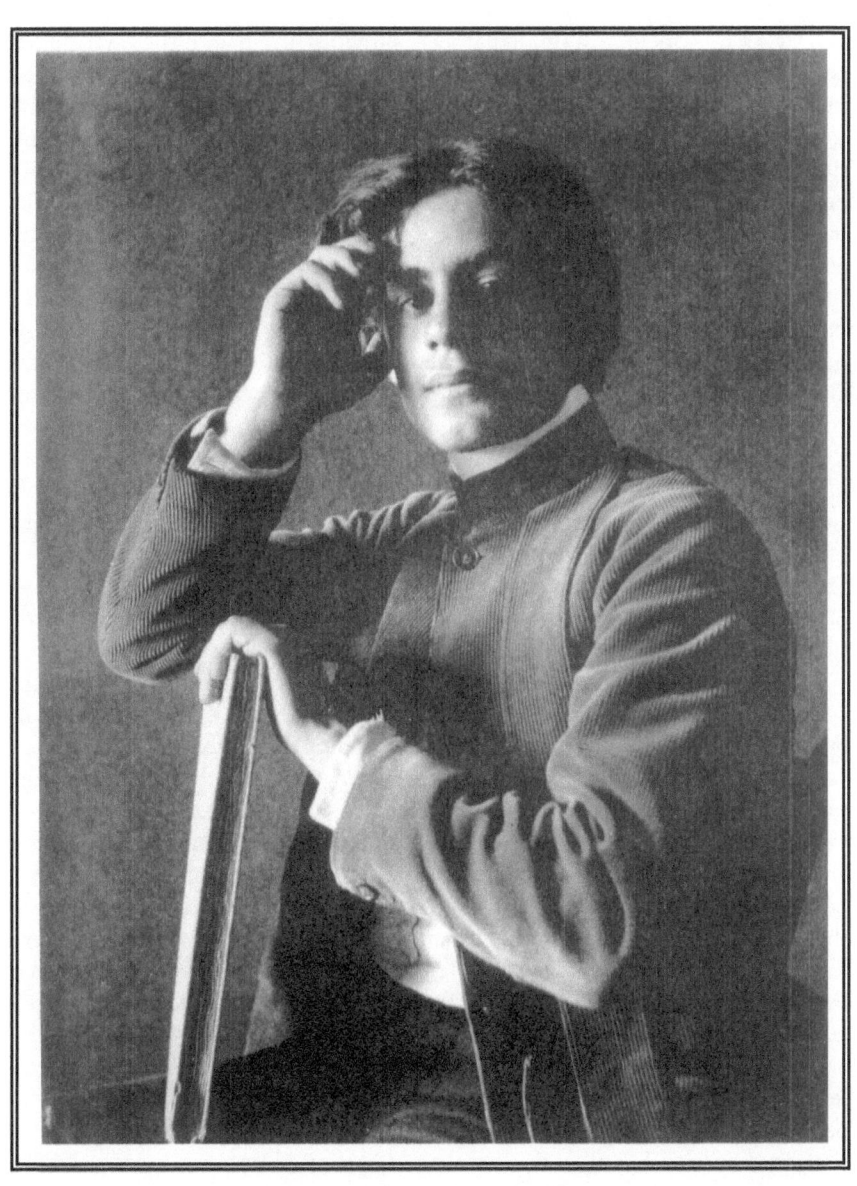

FIGURE 8   F. Holland Day, *Portrait of a Man with Book* (1897)

Day set to work almost immediately to provide the lad with the "artistic education" Miss Beale had recommended he receive. The young man appeared in a variety of "Oriental" costumes in numerous photographs done by Day, the earliest around December 1896, showing that the photographer wasted no time in capturing the image of the young man,[50] who, it turns out, is none other than Kahlil Gibran. Day also wasted no time in tutoring the young Gibran in the fin-de-siècle literature of the decadents and the symbolists that he and his friends were reading and, in Day's case, publishing. Perhaps because of Richard Hovey's interest in Maeterlinck, Day turned to the Belgian writer to further the "artistic education" of the immigrant lad Miss Beale had sent to him. One of Maeterlinck's books that Day read to Gibran and that Gibran eventually learned to read for himself was to have some far-reaching cultural consequences: *The Treasure of the Humble*. Published in 1896 and translated into English in 1897, the work is a compendium of mystical philosophy that might be said to illustrate just how badly things can go awry when the symbolist aesthetic is shifted from the vagaries of poetry and drama to expository prose. A further aesthetic shift occurred, this one from bad to worse, when Gibran published *The Prophet* in 1923. As a recrudescence of fin-de-siècle symbolist thought, Gibran's best-selling collection of aphorisms and mystical insights contributes to the decadent "revival" of the 1920s (see chapter 6).

As Gibran's great fame and Day's near-complete obscurity show, the decadent tradition in the United States is known not so much by its originators as by its imitators. This is true not only of a pop-culture phenomenon such as Kahlil Gibran, but also of a high modernist icon such as T. S. Eliot. As strange as it seems, Gibran's *Prophet* (1923) and Eliot's *Waste Land* (1922) emerged from the same decadent-aesthetic Boston milieu. In many ways, Eliot appears a cultural reincarnation of Ralph Adams Cram, with his Anglicanism, his repressed sexuality, his professionalism, his royalism. The reversion to royalism that Ralph Adams Cram and F. Holland Day entertained seems absurd to us today, but it was not, in a way, so different from the political wishes expressed by others at the time who advocated the cultivation of a martial sensibility as a cure for the weak-willed, neurasthenic, oversophisticated Americans of the 1890s. Both the royalist and the militarist responses to the times express a deep sense of dissatisfaction with American life, a conservative nostalgia for the days before modernity, and an ugly anxiety over the burgeoning immigrant populations in the cities. For all of these reasons, Cram and Day happily accepted the epithet 'decadent' and cultivated an aesthetic, based largely on Ruskin, the Pre-Raphaelite Brotherhood, and the British Decadence (mainly as represented by Oscar Wilde), that was the obverse of both New England tradition and contemporary interest in the realism promoted by William Dean Howells.

The cultivation of the decadent aesthetic went against the grain not only of Howell's realism but also against the anxious American concern to revive both the physical health of individuals and the political health of the nation.

American decadents had no need to find a new frontier, but that is precisely what their more vigorous compatriots set out to do. As we have seen, the widespread belief that America had become too soft and effete in the early 1890s had a great deal to do with the imperialistic campaigns of the late 1890s. Teddy Roosevelt read Brooks Adams's *Law of Civilization and Decay* and then refuted its arguments by charging up San Juan Hill in Cuba, while Commodore Dewey did likewise by wresting the Philippines away from Spain: both returned as national heroes and as proof that America's brief age of neurasthenia was behind it. If nothing else can be said for the Boston decadents of the 1890s, at least they provided an alternative to the imperialistic spirit of the period. At the same time, that alternative was fraught with reactionary ideology no less objectionable for its absurdity. Caught in the cross-currents of the nineties, the Boston decadents are sympathetic figures nonetheless, not least because they dared to go against the grain of the sexual and moral norms of Puritan America at a time when doing so involved no small measure of personal risk.

CHAPTER FOUR

Chicago: The Business of Decadence

The problem of American decadence becomes particularly acute in Chicago, a city that had rapidly emerged in the 1890s as a commercial rival to New York but could not compete with Boston as a cultural center. Still, fortunes were to be made in Chicago, and culture always follows fortune. In Henry Blake Fuller's landmark Chicago novel *The Cliff-Dwellers*, published the year of the Columbia Exposition, the great banking, trading, and railway concerns of the city are compared to the Medici family in Florence, and Chicago itself is said to be poised to produce a latter-day Renaissance in America. Chicago, a character in the novel proclaims, is like "the Florence of the Medicis after the dispersal of the Greek scholars from Constantinople by the Turks." Another character details the analogy: "Our Constantinoples are Berlin and London and the rest—yes, Boston, too; and all their learned exiles are flocking here to instruct us."[1] The comparison is not without irony but also not wholly without truth. Fuller himself, a native son of Chicago, made the grand tour of Europe, sojourned in Boston, and returned to Chicago a cultured man who did what he could to civilize his native city and his nation. Likewise, Herbert Stone, son of the editor of the *Chicago Daily News*, toured Europe, learned French, attended Harvard, and, with his friend Ingalls Kimball, started *The Chap-Book*, the most successful of the little magazines published in American in the 1890s. An American cognate of *The Yellow Book*, *The Chap-Book* was moved from Cambridge to Chicago after the first seven issues, serving as the house organ for Stone and Kimball, a larger publishing venture that, like Copeland and Day in Boston, brought European authors to American audiences.

The presence of *The Chap-Book* in Chicago might be taken to certify the city as the new center of American aesthetic decadence, except that the goals of the magazine were not exclusively artistic; from the start, the magazine was as much a commercial as a cultural concern. Indeed, the widespread success of *The Chap-Book* was likely due more to the business acumen of Ingalls Kimball than to its inherent cultural appeal. At the same time, the realization that decadent-aesthetic culture was not incompatible with business enterprise introduces another meaning of 'decadence' that is now broadly understood to be almost the *only* meaning in the United States. 'Decadence' in this broad, popular sense refers to ostentatious displays of culture to indicate social status. Perhaps it is no accident that Henry Blake Fuller abandoned his efforts to civilize Chicago in the same year that University of Chicago professor Thorstein Veblen explained that culture was nothing more than the means whereby the leisure class was able to make its social status known.

i

The tension between cultural aspiration and commercial ambition became the key concern of the Chicago novelist Henry Blake Fuller in the mid-1890s. In the early 90s, however, Fuller achieved considerable success with two hard-to-classify novels that blend travel writing with decadent aestheticism. The first of these two novels, *The Chevalier of Pensieri-Vani*, was advertised as "an experiment in a new variety of fiction," its author being touted as the artistic equal of British and European writers. "*Style*, if not the man, is, at any rate, the *book*," runs the advertisement, "and style—or rather the lack of it—is what preëminently distinguishes much crude American writing from finished English and Continental work." The newness of the book consists in its form, for it is a type of "idealistic travel-fiction," written in "a series of semi-detached narratives." The combination of experimental form and sophisticated style makes *The Chevalier* "distinctively a ripe product; it is *civilized*—as good as James, to say nothing of Howells." The book is also said to possess a "delicious *timbre*" that is certain to appeal to "the *connoisseur* and lover of genuine literature of the first rank."[2] Although it is hard to say what a "delicious *timbre*" might be, the advertisement nonetheless offers a fair description of the novel. What is most unusual about *The Chevalier* is its experimental structure: each chapter is organized about a city or region of Italy in which various titled characters with comic, allegorical names engage in polite adventures of competitive connoisseurship over paintings by old masters, Etruscan or Roman artifacts, rare books, and so on. The principal characters are the Chevalier of Pensieri-Vani, an ardent antiquarian, and his two friends, the Seigneur of Hors-Concours, whose landed estate is in Piedmonte, and the Prorege (vice-regent) of Arcopia, a fictional region that combines the cultural myth of Arcadia and the political myth of Utopia.

The Prorege of Arcopia is Fuller's vehicle for the expression of a political philosophy that is antidemocratic and antimodern in the extreme. The Prorege believes that "a mild despotism was the only rational and practical form of government" and has particular disdain for America, which he understands as an "example to older countries . . . to serve less as a pattern than as a warning."[3] American democracy and modern industry combine to produce conditions of urban squalor that, in the Prorege's view, require a strong ruler "to save the people from itself" (151). The problem with industrial democracy is due partly to ignorance—"Not ten men in a thousand could think at all" (148)—and partly to the sheer vastness of America: "One refuse-heap could be tolerated; but accumulated thousands produced a New York. A hundred weavers in their own cottages meant peaceful industry and home content; a hundred hundred, massed in one great factory, meant vice and squalor and disorder. Society had never courted failure or bid for misery more ardently than when it had accepted an urban industrialism for a basis" (151). The Prorege is inspired to his extreme views by his wish to mold and shape the sensibilities of the American George W. Occident, a "very ordinary youth from the dark outskirts of Barbaria," that is, the American Midwest. In this as in so much else, Fuller anticipates the cultural prejudices of Thorstein Veblen, who also believed that "modern society [is] only a latter day barbarism."[4] In this instance, the modern barbarian George Occident is "boundlessly wealthy" (36) but hopelessly incompetent in his efforts to procure genuine Italian masterpieces from unscrupulous art dealers. The American is handicapped by "the chains by which art for money's sake had bound him" (140) and requires the services of the Chevalier and the Prorege to ferret out real art from forgeries and second-rate work. Occident is evidently a type inspired by Henry Clay Frick and other turn-of-the-century capitalists who used their vast wealth as a substitute for taste and knowledge. If Occident is a type of the capitalist collector, the Chevalier is the decadent connoisseur.

Fuller does not describe the Chevalier as decadent but provides him with a sensibility consistent with that of the decadent hero. He is said to be "living through other lives and making but a thin blood by dieting on the unnutritious husks of a dead-and-gone past" (97). Such a diet, however, is something to be relished, a type of taste developed by decay. For example, the Chevalier has a love of the town of Orvieto, because it "wears such an aspect of usefulness outlived, and offers such evidence of a long, slow lapse through various stages of mouldering decay" (46). The attractions of decay in the urban setting of old Europe can only be appreciated by someone of special taste, and Orvieto satisfies that taste in multiple ways: "For the connoisseur of the abandoned, the desolate, the Novemberesque, the gone-to-seed, Orvieto has an interest quite its own" (46). The Chevalier would seem to be just such a connoisseur and stands as a contrast to the energetic but misguided Occident even as Italy stands in contrast to America: "The Italian civilization addresses itself primarily to the eye, but after, with immense reaches of depth and breadth, to the intellect. If you prefer a civilization that shall address exclusively the 'moral sense,' I must refer you to New England, with its clapboard schoolhouses and its Cotton Mathers" (43). The removal from morality, especially in regard to art, is another characteristic of the decadent aesthetic that more than one character in the novel upholds and is also upheld by the narrator, who says that "the line between art and morals, as the most advanced of us know, cannot be too rigorously maintained" (65). The

Chevalier also has an aesthetic attachment to Catholicism; his "attitude toward the church was, from the first, one of keen delight tempered by reverent awe, and ended in becoming one of almost personal affection." Here, the object of the Chevalier's affection is not so much the church as the cathedral, "with its sumptuous front so galleried, so gabled, so grandly laden down with its superb array of sculptures and bronzes and vast sheeted spread of richly glittering mosaics" (44).

Although no explicit plot ties the various chapters of the book together, an implicit plot devolves about the Chevalier's relationship to Hors-Concours, Pensieri-Vani's "chief intimate," who shares "his views on marriage, and enjoyed like him, thanks to a standard of morality not strenuously conventional, the pleasures of life, minus its displeasures" (41). The Chevalier's view of marriage is that the idea of matrimony is on its way to becoming as antiquated and "dispensable" as the idea of monarchy. The two men watch the sun set over the Arno at Pisa, and when the Chevalier "silently pressed the Seigneur's arm, or the Seigneur, his, each one knew just what the other meant without any waste of words" (14). This kind of decorous same-sex affection appears throughout the novel and not just between the Chevalier and the Seigneur. The Prorege takes on the young American "Barbarian" as his special patron, in part because "he was extremely partial to young men: one with the right look out of his eyes and the right slope of his shoulders seldom failed of the princely favor" (79). Likewise, another antiquarian "had never been without the power of drawing young men about him" (101). All of this is quite discreetly handled. At the end of the book, however, the implicit theme of homosexual love emerges much closer to the surface when Hors-Concours announces his engagement to a woman. When the Seigneur gives his friend the news, "the dismayed Cavaliere, pierced to the heart, gave him a reproachful glance, murmured the brief yet historical phrase of the great Roman, and muffling himself in the toga of single blessedness sank deserted at the feet of statued Celibacy" (167). The playful, overwrought style aside, there is no mistaking that one man feels betrayed by the other, and the question of celibacy is quite ambiguous. Does Fuller mean that he has lost a partner in celibacy that resistance to matrimony entails, or does he mean that one man has simply lost a partner and, as a result, must now be celibate? The homosexual motif is a constant in Fuller's narrative career; certainly, the delicate, sympathetic, and highly aesthetic shading he gives to same-sex relations must be counted among the features of his work that ally him with the decadent tradition, especially as represented by Walter Pater.

ii

Fuller's second novel, *The Chatelaine of La Trinité* (1892), is a sequel to the more successful and popular *Chevalier of Pensieri-Vani* (1890), as the similarity of the two titles implies. The second novel, however, treats the American fascination with Europe with harsher irony. At the same time, the satire is so completely propelled by the author's misogyny that the tone often shifts from irony to ridicule, with Aurelia West, the wealthy and spoiled debutante from Rochester, the prime target of that ridicule. Briefly, the story is this. Aurelia West is in Europe for no clear purpose, other than to visit friends in Switzerland after enjoying "the distractions in Paris and the diversions of the Riviera" (25). Those friends are Berthe, the Chatelaine of La Trinité (a *chatelaine* is the mistress of a chateau and La Trinité is a place name, so called because three languages—German, French, and Italian—are spoken in the region), and her uncle, known simply as "the Governor." On the train from Paris to Neuchâtel Aurelia makes the acquaintance of an odd collection of opera buffo performers whom she takes to be aristocrats because they present themselves as such: the troupe is led by the Duchess and the improbably named Marquise of Tempo-Rubato. The Duchess turns out not to have an aristocratic name at all—she is none other than Mlle. Pasdenom, whose musical specialty is the déclassé Offenbach. Strangely, Tempo-Rubato turns out to be a real Italian aristocratic, however eccentric (he surprises Miss West by his skill on the trapeze). Embarrassments ensue when Miss West introduces the *faux*-aristocratic Duchess to her friends, who, ironically, have respectable genealogies and might make claims to aristocracy themselves, but do not do so. Mlle. Pasdenom's easy virtue wins the devotion of two aristocratic admirers, Count Fin de Siècle and Baron Zeitgeist (the absurd names sometimes make for amusing allegorical formulations). Initially, the naïve charm of the Chatelaine makes her attractive to the three titled principles, the Count, the Baron, and the Marquise, until Aurelia West goes on a campaign to make her over into an American debutante's idea of what a European lady should be. The concluding irony has the three European men fleeing in the face of the Americanized Chatelaine, who, though not really American, does what Oscar Wilde says all good Americans do when they die—she goes to Paris.

The Chatelaine of La Trinité was not nearly as well-received as Fuller's first romance, nor has it enjoyed the favor of later critics. The alleged problem with the novel is that it does not sustain the mood of nostalgia and romance of *The Chevalier* because of the interference of realism. It is true that the character of Aurelia West is more "realistically drawn" than the "generalized European types" such as Count Fin de Siècle and Baron Zeitgeist, but this does not necessarily make *The Chatelaine* "a badly divided book."[5] On the contrary, the conflict of romance and realism makes the novel all the more interesting as a register of larger conflicts and inconsistencies in American culture, literary and otherwise.

In terms of literary culture, the novel sets the kind of subtle psychological realism associated with Henry James, with its rich social ironies, against the more direct social realism of William Dean Howells and his Midwestern protege Hamlin Garland. The contrasting aesthetics that Fuller himself oscillated between are given over to Count Fin de Siècle, who is the spokesman for the new "scientific" school of fiction, and the Governor, who makes the case for a type of literature that seems "antiquated" to the modern young Parisian. Fin de Siècle explains "the aims, materials, and methods of his art" as the product of "close observation, accurate transcription, nothing more":

> But the observation of his school . . . was more than close; it was searching—yes, it was even remorseless; it spared nothing, since everything served its purpose equally. And when the master transferred the image from his mind's eye, and fixed it on . . . paper, with what cool dexterity, what calm, scientific precision, was the feat accomplished! No passion, . . . no preferences; above all, no fancy. The masters did not aim at romance for this generation; they were preparing historical data for the next. (64)

Despite his Parisian identity, Fin de Siècle's theory of fiction smacks more of Howells than Zola. Once again, the modern point of view, even though it is mouthed by a European, is really American. In contrast to the realist aesthetic, the Governor offers an idea of art that seems truly European, based partly on romanticism and partly on symbolism:

> It seemed to him . . . that the great thing in art was not to know, nor even to feel, but to divine. Observation was good, assuredly; sympathy was better, even indispensable: but what, after all, was to be placed before the exercise of the constructive imagination freely working its own way on to its own end?—an imagination that seized on a word, a gesture, a flower, a flash of color, a simple succession of sounds, and by means of a few humble, external facts called out from within such a multiplicity of correlated fancies as resulted at last in a drama, a fresco, a symphony, a cathedral. The genesis of the work of art was the genesis of the echo; one word is spoken and twenty are evoked in reply. (65–66)

The aesthetic attitude expressed in this passage recalls Huysmans's description of a similar sensibility in À Rebours when Des Esseintes praises Verlaine's capacity "to communicate deliciously vague confidences in a whisper of twilight."[6] What Huysmans's and Fuller's characters share is a taste in language for nuance and indirection, not clarity and precision, for words "guessed at rather than heard" (Huysmans, 171). But such taste belongs to the past and cannot survive the aggressive modernity Chicago embodied.

The Chatelaine was published the year before the Columbia Exposition, which certified Chicago's position as one of America's great centers of industry and progress. In some ways Fuller's novel offers an advance critique of the kind of vigorous and highly American modernity the exposition came to symbolize. Aurelia West is not the only character in the novel who is singled out for her modernity, but hers is the most emphatic and injurious to European tradition: "Indeed, it was the complete modernness of Aurelia West that had first interested the Chatelaine in this young Westerner; had afterward drawn her toward her, and, generally, had laid this poor young mountain maid under a burden of awesome deference from which she was only now emerging" (42–43). Allegorically, what emerges in fact is the complete modernization of the Chatelaine, which is synonymous with her Americanization. And while modernity here has rather limited meanings related to a taste for high fashion and an ability to exploit men, the fashionable, manipulative woman is the harbinger of other forms of modernity that are even more destructive of Old World values, as the final paragraphs of the novel make clear:

> Last summer a wayfarer, descended from the glacial fields above La Trinité, trudged downward through the valley. Some four or five miles below the chateau he passed a group of clever-looking young men, who were occupied with a three-legged instrument constructed of brass and mahogany, and who had left a trail of stakes behind them. Farther on he passed a group of laborers busy on an embankment that had come to dispute the passage with a brawling stream. A mile lower the gaunt form of a great iron truss spanned the river, and from beyond the jutting crag that closed the view came the muffled shriek of a steam-whistle. (176)

The wanderer, disconcerted by all these signs of progress, goes back up the mountain and inquires about the Chatelaine. He is told that she has left for Paris, but the allegory of Americanization is so strong that Paris might as well be Rochester—or Chicago.

iii

Fuller's first two novels are surprising in view of the theories about American art that he was developing at the same time he was writing *The Chevalier*. Both novels suggest that the author has settled into a hybrid but highly aesthetic form that allows him to keep his readers entertained while also making an often amusing critique of American values. But Fuller had not, by any means, settled into a fixed aesthetic program at the time he was writing his first two novels. In an unpublished essay titled "The American School of Fiction," evidently written in 1886 while he was working on his first novel,[7] Fuller explores the artistic problems faced by American novelists who attempt to write in a country lacking the long history and cultural richness of Europe. "The scenic side of life," which the novelist requires as a setting for his or her narrative, is "undeniably . . . in better shape on the other side of the Atlantic than on this," simply because of "the element of age": "In Europe old things are apt to be venerable; in America they are apt to be simply shabby."[8] Hence the American would be wise to travel abroad and find materials for his fiction in Europe. At the same time, because the American is necessarily an outsider he cannot take full artistic advantage of the European scene. This leads to another kind of artistic problem. The artist would do well to opt for the venerable over the shabby, but if he writes too much as an outsider all he can do is practice the "objective" method, which in Fuller's view is inferior to "the subjective method": "in novel-writing it is one thing to take up one's position apart and view as an alien the life and society before us, and another to grasp the full significance and feel the proper relations and relative importance of things, people & actions around us, *of* us, immediately concerning us. Those who can do the former are numerous; those who have shown themselves equal to the latter are few" (250). American novelists, then, are really in a quandary. On the one hand, they require European tradition to supplement the shortcomings of American experience; on the other hand, their removal from that tradition tempts them to the "facility of an objective method" (253).

"The American School of Fiction," as well as Fuller's actual literary career, suggests that the paucity of native materials requires of all would-be American novelists a kind of European apprenticeship, during which they are to learn, paradoxically, what it means to be an American. Fuller says that he "should be disposed to give most praise to the writer who under whatever modifications of environment his people moved, made those people illustrative of his own nationality" (251), a notion that has been taken as "a key to Fuller's own intention in *The Chevalier* and *The Chatelaine*."9 Fuller is aware that "the novelty & charm of Europe" is a temptation ultimately to be overcome in the quest for a national literature of the first rank, and he evidently sees himself, as a young man attempting his first novel, in the same position formerly occupied by William Dean Howells and Henry James, both of whom are praised for working their way through their earlier European stages to become the successful authors of *The Rise of Silas Lapham* and *The Bostonians*. Howells and James are the models here of mature authors who "feel that the proper place for them to be found in & to write about is their own land, and if they are ever to be imbedded in the national literature or to stand out for a comparison with writers of other rank in other literatures, it is more fair & honorable to do [so] on equal terms, & without the adventitious aid of a foreign sojourn and foreign material" (253). Because Fuller himself felt the need to seek the aid of foreign material, he must have understood his sojourn in Europe as somehow necessary but, at the same time, as a stage in his artistic development that would one day lead to an embrace of native material.

The position that Fuller works out for himself in "The American School of Fiction" helps to explain *The Chevalier of Pensieri-Vani* and *The Chatelaine of La Trinité* as romantic exercises on the road to realism that must have involved a level of aversion to the material available to him in his native Chicago. In other words, even though Howells and James are both cited as exemplars for their embrace of native materials, Fuller seems to have turned to James instead of Howells as a partial model when it came time for him to produce his first and second novels. This fact is remarkable in view of Fuller's stated preference for Howells in an unpublished essay that appears to antedate "The American

School of Fiction."[10] In "Howells or James?" Fuller praises the realism of Howells over the "idealism" of James because Howells's art is better suited to the social reality of modern America: "Now we, in these days of democracy, take a very frank and undisguised interest in ourselves; we are a good deal concerned with our own day and generation—in our art as well as elsewhere."[11] To Fuller, "[r]ealism seems coincident with modern democracy, and the advance of one will doubtless be accompanied by the spread of the other" ("H or J," 163). The social world of *The Rise of Silas Lapham*, Fuller finds, is preferable to James's "own particular little garden of exotic culture" ("H or J," 163). Fuller simply trusts Howells more to represent American society as it is: "Who would do it most kindly, most sympathetically—he who deals with the normal earning of money at home, or he who prefers to deal with the exceptional and privileged spending of money abroad? He who lives amongst us and knows us intimately and treats us all with the fullest measure of good will; or he who alienates himself from us, knows us, in general, none too perfectly, and doesn't feel sure but that we are a big mistake, after all?" ("H or J," 163). The publication of *The Bostonians* in 1886 evidently helped to moderate Fuller's extreme opinion of James and led him to the notion that a sojourn in Europe, both literal and literary, was prerequisite to the artistic development of an American novelist. In any event, Fuller's first two novels convey an image of America much closer to the negative one he attributes to James. In both *The Chevalier* and *The Chatelaine* the American characters are "exceptional and privileged," and one can easily come away from either novel thinking that, yes, perhaps America was a big mistake after all.

iv

Fuller left Chicago for another European trip in early 1892 intending to gather material for a third travel romance, this one about Spain, that would follow the general pattern of the two previous novels set in Italy and Switzerland. He returned six months later with only a few notes for a Spanish romance, and the idea was soon abandoned in favor of a novel about Chicago that would provide a more realistic index of the nature of the city than the Columbia Exposition, which was under construction when Fuller returned to his native city. Fuller wrote with approval about the classically inspired style of the buildings designed by Daniel H. Burnham and John W. Root, comparing them to the "great structures" built on "the Palatine hill in the days of the Roman emperors." He went so far as to say that the buildings going up in Jackson Park were evidence "that artistic America is moving along at an equal pace with Industrial America."[12]

Fuller had a different opinion of the real architecture that had been transforming the skyline of Chicago since the first skyscraper was built there in 1885. And he was disappointed when the promise of a classical revival in

architecture implied by the exhibition halls of the Columbia Exposition came
to naught. In 1897 he wrote in the *Atlantic Monthly* that Chicago architecture
"becomes more hideous and preposterous with every year, as we continue to
straggle farther and farther from anything like the slightest artistic understanding."[13] Well before this highly public critique of the Chicago cityscape,
Fuller had investigated what he saw as the human cost of the removal from
"artistic understanding" in *The Cliff Dwellers* (the title refers to those who live
and work in skyscrapers), a novel set in a fictional building called "The Clifton." Fuller's third novel attempts to recapture the initial success he achieved
with *The Chevalier of Pensieri-Vani*, but here he shifts from the mode of travel
romance to the realism favored by Howells and Garland. The characters who
populate the novel are all businessmen and their female consorts, and they
seem to bear out the claims of Veblen's *Theory of the Leisure Class*, published
six years after Fuller's novel.

Any possibility of "artistic understanding" is completely overwhelmed by
material and social ambitions, and the city of Chicago itself becomes an urban
wasteland, a place "of flimsy shanties and back views of sheds and stables; of
grimy, cindered switch yards. . . ; of dingy viaducts and groggy lamp-posts and
dilapidated fences whose scanty remains called to remembrance lotions and
tonics that had long since passed their vogue; of groups of Sunday loungers before saloons, and gangs of unclassifiable foreigners picking up bits of coal along
the tracks" (175). Here, the ugly image of the immigrant poor is only indirectly related to the negation of high culture, but the point is eventually made
quite explicit. When a character asks "Why are things so horrible in this country?" she receives this explanation: "Because there's no standard of manners—
no resident country gentry to provide it. Our own rank country folks have
never had such a check, and this horrible rout of foreign peasantry has just escaped from it. What little culture we have in the country generally we find
principally in a few large cities, and they have become so large that the small
element that works for a bettering is completely swamped" (236). But it is not
just the "foreign peasantry" that swamps the possibility of culture. An even
more invidious, anticultural force is the crassness of Chicago's businessmen.
The protagonist of the novel is a young man only recently arrived from Boston, one George Ogden, who is quite taken aback by the craven nature of the
real estate agent to whom his sister is engaged: "George felt his heart give an
indignant throb. He seemed to see before him the spokesman of a community
where prosperity had drugged patriotism into unconsciousness, and where the
bare scaffoldings of materialism felt themselves quite independent of the
graces and draperies of culture" (50). This theme is sounded in the novel again
and again. A debutante attributes artistic abilities to Ogden and assumes he is
a writer. She puts Fuller's own internal artistic debate between Howells and
James into a phrase when she asks, "Well, what is it—dialect or psychological?" "Business letters," he replies (27).

Business replaces culture at every turn and ultimately comes to replace it entirely. Every real estate man is really a poet, as Fuller's satirical narrator explains: "We of Chicago are sometimes made to bear the reproach that the conditions of our local life draw us toward the sordid and the materialistic. Now, the most vital and typical of our human products is the real estate agent: is he commonly found tied down by earth-bound prose?" (105). The ironic art of real estate, the poetry of property, stands in for culture through most of the novel, and only two characters have any actual connection to the arts, however compromised. One is the opportunistic philanderer Russell Vibert, a tenor who sings for money and uses his voice to seduce the daughter of the wealthy financier Brainard, only to beat and abandon her when she is disowned by her father. The other is Marcus, son of that same financier, who fancies himself an actor but ruins himself gambling in the company of the corrupt Vibert. When his wealthy father refuses to pay his gambling debts, Marcus becomes so enraged that he stabs the old man with a paper cutter. His father lingers for a while but dies when he learns that the son who tried to kill him has killed himself. So much for those who would be artists in Chicago.

As this sketch suggests, there is a surfeit of decline, destruction, and degradation in the novel, but precious little decadence. A number of businessmen are ruined, but there is none of that delectation of decay that so distinguishes *The Chevalier of Pensieri-Vani*. Marriages and families are destroyed, though not by the force of one culture on another, as in *The Chatelaine of La Trinité*. In *The Cliff-Dwellers*, the narrator's explanation for all the disappointment and destruction wrought in the novel is the American affliction of neurasthenia, phased in terms suggestive of the second law of thermodynamics: "Why do we go mad? Why do we kill ourselves? Why is there more insanity and more self-murder to-day than ever before? It is because, under existing conditions, the relief that comes from action is so largely shut off. . . . What so increases and intensifies the agonies of to-day? The fact that society has a closer and denser texture than ever before; its fine-spun meshes bind us and strangle us. Indignation ferments without vent" (295–96). The formulation is consistent with James Miller Beard's analysis of neurasthenia as the product of the pressures of industrial, urban life in America (see chapter 1). And while "the cultural counterpart of the second law of thermodynamics" is generally taken to be degeneration rather than neurasthenia,[14] those two nineteenth-century conditions have many symptoms in common, differing mainly in their presumed etiology—with degeneration due to hereditary afflictions, neurasthenia to environmental pressures.

Still, Fuller's evocation of neurasthenia as one of the root causes of social ruin in *The Cliff-Dwellers* does not distinguish the novel as decadent, certainly not in the positive sense that the travel romances are. In *The Cliff-Dwellers*, the utter absence of aesthetic values that comes with absolute commitment to material gain might qualify as decadence in one way, while the complete abandonment to the aesthetic sensibility in *The Chevalier of Pensieri-Vani* suggests decadence in another sense. The difference is due, in part, to the shift from the Old World setting—with its ruins and antiquities that cultivate aesthetic delectation, to the New—with its shops and gadgets that encourage conspicuous consumption. Somehow, the Old World setting is more conducive to the decorous handling of human relations, same-sex relations in particular. The homosexual theme of *The Cliff-Dwellers* is so far removed from the main action of the novel as to be almost invisible, but it is nonetheless there. The subplot involving Brainard's son, Marcus, and his relationship with the unscrupulous character Vibert, the man who marries Brainard's daughter for her fortune and then deserts her, appears as a darker version of the genial relations of the male characters in *The Chevalier of Pensieri-Vani*. Because Marcus insists on a career as an actor, his father disowns him; as a result, he is drawn to the self-serving Vibert, a singer with artistic ambitions of his own. In Vibert's case, however, art is merely a cover that he uses to ingratiate himself with Chicago's wealthy business class—successfully, in the case of Brainard's daughter.

Early in the novel, Vibert and Marcus become involved in some kind of shady dealings that are never really explained, but it is clear that Vibert has managed to gain control over Marcus through the force of his personality: "The boy . . . seemed to have been fascinated and then dominated by the bigness and the hardihood of the other" (150). The story of Marcus's degradation is not fully narrated, but by the end of the novel it is clear that he has learned to survive in the streets of the Black City by following Vibert's example: "Vibert knew the ropes, and now I know them just as well myself" (268–69). In the climactic scene, Marcus barges into the offices of his father's bank, where his brother Burt has been installed as vice president, and tries to get his father to see the results of favoring one son over another: "I want him to see me. I want him to have a look at the poor devil who has been knocking around from pillar to post for the last two years, who has hidden in dives, and who has been dragged through the slums, and who has been driven from the variety stage, and has served his time more than once" (304). Then comes the sensational scene mentioned above, in which Marcus tries to kill Burt, is restrained by another office worker but, when he is released, stabs his father. The father dies a slow death, and the son hangs himself. The ending of the narrative is less interesting than the plot parallelism that sets Vibert up as the agent of the ruin of both sister and brother, which implies some sort of homosexual attachment between Vibert and Marcus; that is, Vibert succeeds in seducing not only Brainard's daughter but also his son. This reading is all the more compelling when the ending of *The Cliff-Dwellers* is compared to a similar ending in one of Fuller's closet dramas, which quite explicitly concerns same-sex relations. Indeed, the explicit nature of "At Saint Judas's" makes easier the retrospective interpretation of male relations in *The Cliff-Dwellers* as somehow homophilic, if not homosexual. As Kenneth Scambray observes, "[t]he melodrama and violence in 'At Saint Judas's,' much like the ending of *The Cliff-Dwellers*, were Fuller's only means of resolving in his writing his conflict with the values of his society."[15] That the conflict can only be resolved through imaginative self-destruction is, of course, an unfortunate commentary on same-sex relations in the American fin de siècle.

v

"At Saint Judas's" is a one-act drama that appears in *The Puppet Booth: Twelve Plays*, published in 1896. The title of the collection derives from Maurice Maeterlinck's use of the term *marionette* to refer to unrealistic, puppetlike characters in dreamlike Symbolist plays, works never intended for actual performance. Fuller's choice to experiment with symbolist drama after his earlier naturalist novels is not due solely to the fashion for Maeterlinck among late nineteenth-century American *litterateurs*. The vague, indirect discourse of the symbolist drama allowed Fuller to express psychological and personal topics that were simply not suited, for reasons of social convention, to either romance or realism, the genres in which Fuller had previously worked. Fuller's sense that the indirection of the symbolist aesthetic had, paradoxically, allowed him to approach the question of same-sex love more directly than in other artistic forms is expressed in a letter to Charles Eliot Norton of 6 April 1898: "How can a man give himself to the public and hold himself back at the same time?" Fuller went on to explain that the method of Maeterlinck had been "adopted as a species of self-defense," adding further that "one must make his compromise with his own community."[16] The nature of that compromise concerns Fuller's own thoroughly closeted homosexuality, but, in taking on the theme of same-sex relations, Fuller was also addressing a larger social issue in the United States.

The conviction and subsequent imprisonment of Oscar Wilde in May 1895 was a recent reminder that homosexuality was a criminal offense, in America no less than in Great Britain. In addition, at the time Fuller was writing "At Saint Judas's" he would have known about another homosexual "case" much closer to home. In the spring of 1894, a letter carrier in Chicago named Guy T. Olmstead fired several shots at his male lover, William L. Clifford, on a public thoroughfare in the middle of the day, "as part of what he had conceived to be a lovers' suicide pact." A mob descended on Olmstead and prevented him from killing himself after he had wounded Clifford. The attack occurred on 28 March 1894, only a few days after Olmstead had been released from Mercy Hospital, where he had gone to have his testicles removed in an effort to control his "unhealthy" passion for other men.[17] In *Studies in the Psychology of Sex*, the Victorian sexologist Havelock Ellis prints a letter from Olmstead to his doctor at Mercy Hospital, the contents of which offer considerable insight into the social stigma attached to same-sex relations during the American fin de siècle:

Heaven only knows how hard I have tried to make a decent creature out of myself, but my vileness is uncontrollable, and I might as well give up and die. I wonder if the doctors knew that after emasculation it was possible for a man to have erections, commit masturbation, and have the same passion as before. I am ashamed of myself; I hate myself; but I can't help it. I have friends among nice people, play the piano, love music, books, and everything is beautiful and elevating; yet they can't elevate me, because this load of inborn vileness drags me down and prevents my perfect enjoyment of anything. Doctors are the only ones who understand and know my helplessness before this monster.[18]

As Lawrence Senelick observes, Fuller's choice of homophilic relations as subject matter when he wrote *The Puppet-Booth* in November and December 1895, after the Olmstead affair and the Wilde trial, "is probably not coincidental."[19] Nor is it coincidental that in "At Saint Judas's" efforts to sublimate homosexual desires by means of culture ultimately break down.

The play is a closet drama in more than one sense, as one male character emerges completely from the closet to declare his love for another man on that man's wedding day, just as the ceremony is about to be performed. Perhaps as a way of ennobling same-sex love after the squalid details of the Wilde prosecution had become public, Fuller sets the play in medieval times: the two men are knights of an unspecified order who have fought together in unnamed wars. Each man owes his life to the other: the bridegroom has saved his friend from drowning, and the best man has saved the bridegroom from being "hacked [to death] by African sabers."[20] Despite this profound connection, a feeling of unease arises between the bridegroom and the best man while they await the arrival of the bride in the sacristy of the church of St. Judas. As the unlikely, overtly allegorical name of the church implies, the play deals with betrayal. The best man feels betrayed by the bridegroom because of his decision to marry, and because of this, he in turn betrays the bridegroom by manufacturing rumors to slander both parties to the impending marriage with the hope that the union will be forestalled. The action of the play consists almost entirely of a conversation between the two men about the falsity of the slanders—that the bridegroom lacks courage, for example, or that the bride is "untrue" and "impure" (*PB*, 94). The climax of the play comes when the bridegroom finally figures out that the best man is the source of all the rumors. He draws his sword to attack his friend just as the bride arrives for the ceremony but then insists that the best man kill himself, for he has "no other road to redemption" (*PB*, 98). The play closes with the bride and bridegroom at the altar rail, the best man lying "on the floor of the sacristy . . . in a pool of blood"—"while the choirboys and the organ unite in a resounding Gloria" (*PB*, 98).

This summary fails to convey two key points about this strange play: the explicit treatment of the theme of homosexual love and the fantastic scenic devices that, in part, employ aesthetic imagery to convey a strong sense of sexuality. The two men talk about their prior intimacy from the outset, as they wait in the church for the bride. The best man remarks that he first learned of his friend's plans for marriage when he muttered them "[i]n your sleep—your own pillow next to mine" (PB, 89). As the time of the marriage approaches, doubts about the bride's arrival lead the best man to say: "If she were to come, I should not let her have you. She shall not have you. Nobody shall have you" (96). When the bridegroom finally deduces that the best man is the source of the slanders against him—"It is *you* who have insulted my love?"—his accusation is met with this response: "No one loves you more than I" (PB, 97). Throughout, the conversation is punctuated by strange symbolic imagery, as the eight painted windows of the church (listed as "persons" in the text) come to life to dramatize critical moments in the play. For example, just before the best man claims that the bride "has sinned, and sinned—with me" (PB, 95), the seventh window becomes animated: "The SEVENTH WINDOW. The Seven Cardinal Virtues; they change, with a slow but relentless movement of color, of outline, of feature, into the Seven Deadly Sins. This transformation, like all the others, pass unheeded" (95). Then, at the point where the best man insists to his friend, "Nobody shall have you," the stage directions read: "The Deadliest of the Seven Sins hides her face; it is too hideous for contemplation" (96). Finally, when the best man confesses his love in the boldest possible terms—"No one loves you more than I"—Fuller's imagery is equally bold: "The sculptured wreath entwined round the great central column writhes in descending spirals, like a vast serpent" (97). The image is phallic in more than one sense, and quite suggestive of homosexual intercourse. Direct discourse about homosexual love in the dialogue between the two men, combined with the symbolic imagery in the stage directions, makes the play a remarkably daring treatment of a subject that was as forbidden in America as it was in Great Britain, especially after Wilde's recent conviction. The critic Scambray says that Fuller himself was "outraged over Wilde's conviction and wished to defy his society's values with his play," but, at the same time, he tempered his defiance by the idea of the sinfulness of homosexual love and by the insistence on the need for redemption.[21]

The sense of sin in "At Saint Judas's," especially as transmitted through the double filter of medievalism and symbolism, reminds us again that social and aesthetic meanings of decadence often coalesce around notions of same-sex relations. As Senelick notes, Fuller deserves to be more widely recognized as a pioneering author of homosexual themes, "for he shares with Henry James and E. M. Forster an evasive homophilia fascinated by innocents in thrall to European decadence."[22] While this description may be better suited to *The Chevalier of Pensieri-Vani*, the larger point that an American author on native ground who takes up the theme of same-sex love stands less of a chance of lasting recognition than an expatriate like James or a British novelist like Forster is well taken. Indeed, Fuller's two most extensive treatments of same-sex love, "At

Saint Judas's" and *Bertram Cope's Year* (1919; see chapter 6), were all but ig-
nored by the critics and the public. Even *The Chap-Book* took only limited notice of Fuller's symbolist plays, despite having published one of them, "O, That
Way Madness Lies," in the issue of 1 December 1895. In its review of *The
Puppet-Booth*, *The Chap-Book* did nothing more than explain the Maeterlinck
connection: "If you prefer a more modern expression and know the works of
Maurice Maeterlinck you may call [the collection] plays for marionettes."[23] Of
course, there is no mention whatsoever of "At Saint Judas's" and its controversial topic. Already in 1895, *The Chap-Book* was calling the once-popular author
of *The Chevalier of Pensieri-Vani* "old Fuller,"[24] and he never recovered from the
decline in his reputation that set in after his two Chicago novels. Somehow,
Fuller managed the trick of remaining "decadent" but ceasing to be "new," the
two attributes essential to the kind of culture *The Chap-Book* promoted.

vi

The Chap-Book is usually taken as the most successful of the little magazines of
the 1890s, with success here being defined in terms of circulation, reputation,
and imitation. It is often compared to *The Yellow Book* because of certain commonalities of fin-de-siècle literary and artistic culture: both made reference to
Oscar Wilde, and both printed designs by Aubrey Beardsley.[25] The two magazines are also alike in that they served, in varying degrees, as house organs for
larger publishing concerns, the Bodley Head at Oxford in the case of *The Yellow Book* and Stone and Kimball in the case of *The Chap-Book*. This latter
comparison is probably truer for *The Chap-Book* than for *The Yellow Book*,
whose editors were not quite so commercially minded as Herbert Stone and
Ingalls Kimball.[26] The commercial connection to the larger concerns of the
book-publishing business also accounts for some significant differences in the
content of the two magazines. *The Yellow Book* tended to publish and offer
commentary on British authors almost exclusively, whereas *The Chap-Book*
provided its readers with a mix of French, British, and American literature.
The French emphasis is due mainly to Herbert Stone's interest in French culture, which emerged when he toured Europe with his family from 1888 to
1890. At Harvard, which he entered the same year he returned from Europe,
Stone concentrated on French literature. He became sufficiently educated in
the language that he was able to entertain the French novelist Paul Bourget at
a Harvard luncheon when the writer toured America in 1893–94.[27] The
American emphasis emerged from Stone and Kimball's efforts to publish new
American authors, and, as *The Chap-Book* was the house organ for Stone and
Kimball, those authors also appeared in the magazine.[28] The mixture of avant-
garde French authors such as Verlaine and Mallarmé and American realist authors such as Hamlin Garland has the result of emphasizing the avant-garde position of realist literature, but it also suggests the oscillation between "Howells

and James" that marked the career of Henry Blake Fuller. Like Fuller, the editors of *The Chap-Book* tried to have it both ways; but, unlike Fuller, Stone and Kimball seemed far less anxious about the necessity of making artistic choices between American and European perspectives.

The Chap-Book started as the collaborative venture of the two Harvard undergraduate friends, with editorial assistance from the transplanted Canadian poet and critic Bliss Carman, who also had connections to the firm of Copeland and Day in Boston. The Boston context should not lead us to assume that *The Chap-Book* was the product of precisely the same politico-literary ferment that had led to *The Knight Errant* and *The Mahogany Tree*, though the latter magazine did have an influence. From the start *The Chap-Book* was an adjunct to Stone and Kimball, and Stone and Kimball was a Chicago concern. In fact, the company got its start when Herbert Stone wrote a successful guide to the Columbia Exposition. Published in 1893, *Chicago and the World's Fair: A Popular Guide* antedated the *Chap-Book* venture, which began the following year, on 15 May 1894. In fact, prior to beginning *The Chap-Book*, Stone and Kimball had already published a significant number of books.

The first issue of *The Chap-Book* indicates that it was published by Stone and Kimball of "Chicago & Cambridge," and the issue reflects this dual identity to some degree. That is, the issue communicates the Harvard take on the British art for art's sake sensibility, even as it promises a more vernacular, American version of literary art. But more than anything else, the magazine promotes a new, youthful attitude toward literature, which takes as its watchwords *simplicity*, *directness*, and *delight*. These aesthetic principles are articulated early on in "A Bitter Complaint of the Ungentle Reader," a kind of manifesto against interpretation and for unmediated pleasure in poetry. In this irreverent statement, ample satire is directed against the Boston literary establishment:

> The Muse is dying nowadays of over-interpretation. Too many shepherd swains are trying to Get the Most Good out of her. When Caius Scriblerius Bostoniensis prints a lyric about the light of Amatoria's eyes which disperses his melancholy moods, the average public, at least in Boston, cares nothing for it until somebody in lack of employment discovers that as Saint Patrick's snakes were heathen rites, and as Beatrice Portinari was a system of philosophy, so Amatoria's eyes personify the sun-myth! And Caius shoots into his eleventh edition.[29]

Overinterpretation is one of the symptoms of the "super-civilization" in which poets find themselves, an unfortunate fact of the literary marketplace, dominated by "the ascendant New England readeress": "What is meant for literature now, begotten in simpleness and bred in delight, arises as a quarrel between producer and consumer" (CB 1.1: 10, 11). This battle of the books is partly between male poet and female reader, and partly between old consumer and young producer: "Even in a sophisticating age, it is the nature of poets to remain young. Their buyers are always one remove nearer to the sick end of the century, and being themselves tainted with the sense of the importance of the scientific, are in so much disqualified to judge of the miracle, the phenomenon, which poetry is" (CB 1.1: 11). Likewise, a note at the end of the issue asks why the reader of poetry wishes "to torture [herself] with thought. Is it not enough [to] be made glad and happy?" (CB 1.1: 18).

This note also emphasizes Aubrey Beardsley's detachment from morality and his remarkable youth; a self-portrait of Beardsley, complete with halo, accompanies the text. The artist is described as "a person against whom the charge of secreting a moral precipitate in the potion of his art, cannot possibly be laid," someone who is "hardly more than a boy, . . . but he is a wise youth" (CB 1.1: 17). The wisdom of youth is used to account for Iokanaan's "proper desire to die" in Wilde's *Salome* as illustrated by Beardsley. The wish to die, the explanation runs, comes about as a means of escaping "the company of black-caped ladies" (CB 1.1: 17), thereby making *Salome* a kind of allegory of the male poet beset by moralizing New England "readeresses." Beardsley is also said to be at work on some "illustrations of Poe" (CB 1.1: 18), perhaps the first hint of Stone and Kimball's edition of the works of Edgar Allan Poe, originally planned to have illustrations by Beardsley (see figure 9). The book was prominently advertised in future editions of *The Chap-Book*.[30] Hence the pose of artistic detachment from the literary marketplace seems to be exactly that—a pose, and a profitable one.

The mixture of the commercial and the artistic is one of the things that made *The Chap-Book* distinctive, even to the point of advertising the products of rival publishers. Copeland and Day advertised in practically every issue of *The Chap-Book*, and sometimes the line between art and business is completely obscured. An example of this practice is a poem made up of limerick verses about Salome, or, to be more precise, about Copeland and Day's edition of Wilde's *Salome*, with its Beardsley designs. The poem is titled "The Yellow Bookmaker":

> There once was a certain A. B.
> And a Yellow Bookmaker was he.
> His dead black and white
> Was such a delight,
> All Vigo street came out to see. (CB 1.2: 41)

The poem proceeds to offer a doggerel summary of the Salome story and the outrage caused by Wilde's play: "And poor Mrs. Grundy / Was buried on Sunday, / Oscarified such things could be" (CB 1.2: 42). It concludes with another apostrophe to Beardsley and a plug for Copeland and Day:

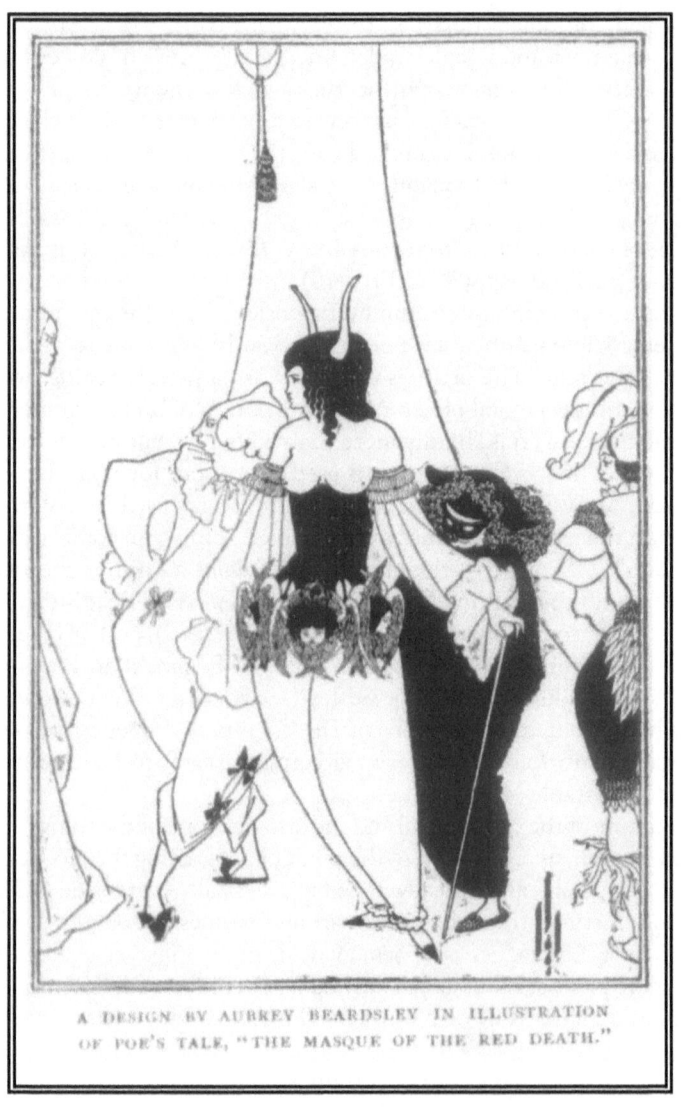

A DESIGN BY AUBREY BEARDSLEY IN ILLUSTRATION
OF POE'S TALE, "THE MASQUE OF THE RED DEATH."

FIGURE 9   Aubrey Beardsley,
design for Stone and Kimball's edition of Poe (1894)

Now this is the tale of A. B.
The grotesque black and white devotee,
The décadent fakir,
The Yellow Bookmaker,
The funny-man over the sea.

P.S. If you're anxious to see
This most up to date Salomee,
Send over the way
To Copeland and Day,
Cornhill, in the hub, dollars three—
And seventy
      five

         cents.

The doggerel endorsement of *Salome* and "The Yellow Bookmaker" is all the more curious in light of a rather scathing review of the second issue of *The Yellow Book* a few months later. The review appears in the issue of 15 August 1894, the first issue of *The Chap-Book* edited out of the Caxton building in Chicago. The move to Chicago must have made it easier for the editors to distance themselves from the more Anglophilic of the Boston litterateurs, in particular Copeland and Day. This much is evident from the near-hostile review that Pierre La Rose gives to Copeland and Day's edition of *The Yellow Book*. The poetry in the issue under review is said to be merely "various and indifferent." Of one poet the reviewer says only that "it is difficult to decide whether or not [he] is overpaid." Another is credited with producing "a pleasant little 'Song,' although on a very slender pipe"; as such, the poem has "all the charm of modest unimportance" (CB 1.7: 163). The prose fiction in the issue is "also various and indifferent," with the exception of a story by Henry James. The art that appears in this issue of *The Yellow Book* is denigrated as "a dreary waste of artlessly messy sketches, with a grotesque oasis of Mr. Aubrey Beardsley" (CB 1.7: 164). Yet even Beardsley, who in the first issue of *The Chap-Book* appeared as a model artist because of his maleness and his youth, has slipped: "[H]is much praised technique is degenerating into a mere pyrotechnique" (CB 1.7: 165).

Throughout the review, the shortcomings of the magazine are linked to its modernity. *The Yellow Book* is "intensely modern" and "ultra-modern," but to be modern is no longer a good thing, as becomes evident when the claim that Beardsley's art is "morbid" is said to be nothing more than "a polite little modern way of saying 'nasty'" (CB 1.7: 163). Clearly, La Rose is reluctant to say anything good about *The Yellow Book* because that journal is now regarded as one of *The Chap-Book*'s major competitors. The move to Chicago involved a removal from *The Chap-Book*'s original cultural context, but it also gave Stone and Kimball a chance to assert their editorial independence from that context. The difference between the "old" Boston *Chap-Book* and the "new" Chicago version is made obvious by contrasting the 15 August 1894 number with the prior issue of 1 August—the last one edited out of Boston. The 1 August issue is replete with material reflecting the Jacobite politics so fashionable among the Visionists, Pewter Mugs, and other Boston cults of the early 1890s. The issue contains a Jacobite poem by Ralph Adams Cram that includes the refrain: "Ride on, ride on for the King!" (CB 1.6: 139). Immediately following this poem in the same issue is an account of "A Legitimist Kalendar," which lists "the festivals and days of mourning or rejoicing which Jacobites should bear in mind" (CB 1.6: 140). *The Chap-Book* was not completely free of reactionary ideology once it was moved to Chicago, but the cultural tone did shift away from the Jacobite, Anglophilic interests of the earliest issues.[31]

Once in Chicago, with *The Yellow Book* adjudged overly modern, and with a measure of both cultural and geographical distance between it and the medievalism of the Boston crowd, *The Chap-Book* settled into a largely Francophile but weirdly Americanized variety of decadence. This tendency was partly evident even before the break with Boston, as the fourth issue of *The Chap-Book* shows. This number contains a near-unreadable translation of Verlaine's "Clair de lune" and a translated review of "My Hospitals" by Anatole France. Taken together, the poem and the review suggest an oddly American version of Verlaine. The final quatrain of the translated poem illustrates how far removed from the decadent sensibility the verse really is; it reads more like the conventional, prettified poetry that appeared all too frequently in the magazine:

> The melancholy moonlight, sweet and lone,
> That makes to dream the birds upon the tree
> And in their polished basins of white stone
> The fountains tall to sob with ecstasy. (CB 1.4: 36)

France's review attributes a rather Whitmanesque character to Verlaine. He is said to be "a singularly robust old vagabond," "a superb and magnificent savage" (CB 1.4: 80, 81). True, one hospital room where he stays "is known as the Decadents' room," and journalists besiege the old poet with questions about "decadents and symbolists" (CB 1.4: 81). But France says that somewhere within "this bad fellow you find very soon the primitive, natural man" (CB 1.4: 84). Obviously, the observation is made by Anatole France and not by the editors of *The Chap-Book*, but the editorial choice to include the piece is consistent with the cultural combination of weariness and vigor, decadence and bohemianism, that one finds in the pages of the magazine.

Sometimes, *The Chap-Book* is overtly antidecadent, as in a rather amusing report of Verlaine's attendance at a *soirée* hosted by the arch-decadent Compte de Montesquiou himself. Concern is expressed that M. Verlaine's appearance at the event might have been too respectable. He is reported to have shown up "decked in all the luxury of a frock coat":

> dressed, in fact, like what Parisian journalism calls *"les plus élegants de nos club-men."* They even allege that he wore an opera hat, while the friendliest cliques in Paris were torn with dissensions as to whether or not he had really carried a monocle. This news is horrible. There was a bohemian sort of charm about the poverty of the poet—but the innocent, childlike Verlaine attired in tall hat and frock is very unpleasant: it suggests decline—or intoxication. (CB 1.10: 263–64)

This is a curious cultural turn, to say the least, despite the mild irony that figures respectability as a form of decline: Verlaine, author of the seminal decadent poem, "Langeur"; icon of Anatole Baju's *Décadisme* movement in Paris; and veteran of a notorious, disastrous affair with Arthur Rimbaud, suddenly becomes "innocent" and "childlike." The quality of Verlaine's childlike innocence, however, is open to question. As the report of Verlaine's adventure in high society continues, we are told that, after he acknowledges "his presentation to a certain high-born countess with a profound bow," he asks her, politely, for "un petite verre," that is, a glass of absinthe. The ambivalent attitude toward decadence seems to be resolved, temporarily at least, in favor of the neoromantic sentiment announced in an anonymous poem titled "The Decadents":

> All manikins. . . . Oh, is there left one wonder
> No roomy soul where primal Nature speaks,
> Where roll at times the ground-swell and the thunder
> Among sea-caves and the mountain peaks? (CB 1.10: 264)

Appropriately, the antidecadent wish for a "roomy soul" is granted, in a way, by the notice on the facing page of Richard Hovey and Bliss Carman's newly published *Songs of Vagabondia,* a bohemian, Whitmanesque collection of poetry also indebted to that Victorian best-seller, Edward Fitzgerald's *Rubaiyat of Omar Khayyam.*

If Verlaine's connection to decadence is treated with a degree of ambivalence, a similar mixture of appreciation and reservation attaches to *The Chap-Book's* treatment of Oscar Wilde. An early issue features Charles Rickett's striking *art nouveau* designs for *The Sphinx,* by Wilde (see figure 10), in an edition sold by Copeland and Day. Another early issue includes an exploration of Wilde's "admirable creed that nature as well as Life imitates Art." In this case the editors find, after looking at Monet's paintings, that "a strange alteration came over the face of nature" (CB 1.6: 144, 145). With the move to Chicago, *The Chap-Book* suddenly finds Wilde slightly less admirable. For example, the first Chicago number recounts an anecdote in which James Abbott McNeil

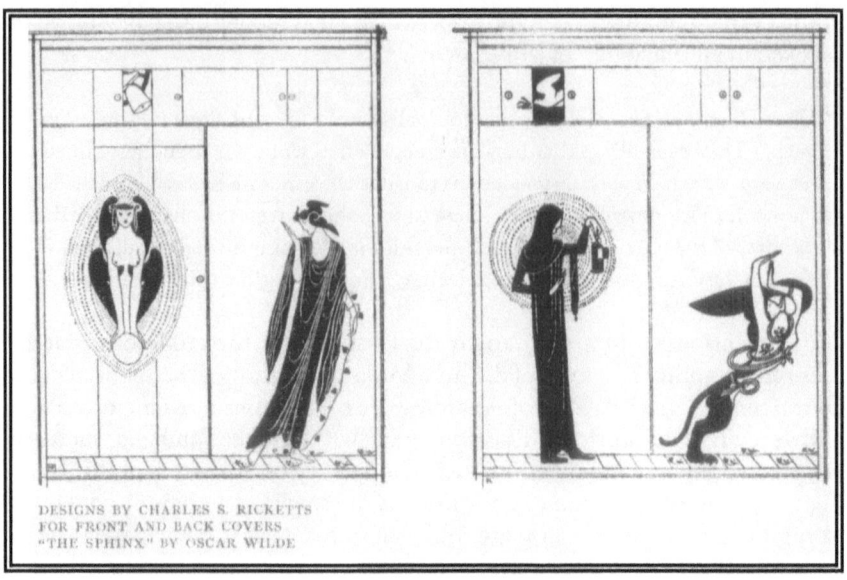

DESIGNS BY CHARLES S. RICKETTS
FOR FRONT AND BACK COVERS
"THE SPHINX" BY OSCAR WILDE

FIGURE 10   Charles Ricketts, designs for Oscar Wilde, *The Sphinx* (1894)

Whistler names a pet kitten "Oscar," after Wilde. When Oscar grows up and
has kittens of "his" own, Whistler refuses to believe the report of the blessed
feline event until his wife takes him to the place "where Oscar and the kittens
lay." Whistler stands "for a moment in amazement and dismay" and then remarks: "Never mind. . . ; they must be plagiarized" (*CB* 1.8: 201). In the same
number Wilde is criticized "for only following the French," and the editors also
note of the French edition of *Salome* "how much better it was in that musical,
suggestive tongue than in its translated English" (*CB* 1.8: 202).

The attitude here is consistent with Herbert Stone's general Francophilia
and may not reflect serious reservations about Wilde's artistic abilities. Still,
The Chap-Book's ambivalent position on Wilde after his conviction for gross
indecency is oddly in harmony with the editors' earlier reluctance to fully en-
dorse his work. Once the Wilde scandal broke, the editors condemned the
authorities of the British Museum for withdrawing "from circulation all books
written by Mr. Oscar Wilde." They argue "the necessity of disassociating the
man from his work. . . . Once and for all a book printed and given to the public has a life wholly its own and independent of the fortunes of its author"
(*CB* 2.12: 480, 481). At the same time, the editors comment that "[a]s to certain criminal proceedings not long past, fortunately there can be but one
opinion" (*CB* 2.12: 480). Moreover, the works that are singled out to show

that "Mr. Wilde's writing is immortal" are those "pure and charming" productions generally free of controversy and sexual innuendo: "the 'Poems,' 'The House of Pomegranates,' 'The Happy Prince and Other Tales.'" By contrast, "'The Picture of Dorian Gray,' 'The Sphinx,' and 'Salome' are bad books" (CB 2.12: 480). In separating the man from his work, the editors single out for praise those works most separate from the reality of the man himself. Surely there is more of Wilde in *The Picture of Dorian Gray* than in *The Happy Prince*. Clearly, more than one double-standard is at work in *The Chap-Book's* "defense" of Wilde's work against the actions of the British authorities, as there is in its general preference of Verlaine over Wilde. The editors, after all, remained silent on the moral implications of Verlaine's famous misadventures with Rimbaud.

The treatment of one decadent—Verlaine—in such antidecadent terms as *natural, primitive, childlike* and the ambivalent attitude toward another—Wilde—raise questions about *The Chap-Book's* relation to decadence generally. But we should not assume from the editorial attitude toward Verlaine and Wilde some kind of wholesale dissociation from the decadent sensibility. Although decadence and degeneration are not necessarily the same thing, *The Chap-Book* welcomed the designation *degenerate* as a culturally descriptive term and published the opinions of someone who identified himself (or herself) as "A Degenerate."[32] What seems to be at the core of *The Chap-Book's* strange relationship to decadence is an editorial policy that, on the one hand, tried to capture a feeling of youth and newness and, on the other hand, cultivated an awareness of belatedness and "age-end" sensitivities. This double sensibility comes through, for example, in *The Chap-Book's* presentation of John Sloan, known today as a realist painter of the Ash Can School but who began his artistic career in the 1890s as a practitioner of art nouveau (see figure 11). Sloan is described as a "new man" who "is capable of doing very excellent book work—as age-end art goes" (CB 2.1: 40). The issue that celebrates Sloan as a new age-end artist also contains a photograph of Louise Imogen Guiney, author of a notable essay on age-end art called "Willful Sadness in Literature." In that essay Guiney observes that "the pathos of the decadence . . . is the prevailing feature of current verse."[33]

The fin-de-siècle will to sadness is also evident in an assessment of "end-of-the-century" drama that lauds the "younger writers"—including Ibsen and Maeterlinck—for "keeping the tragic background of life in clear view" as "a departure from the conventional" (CB 2.9: 369–70). Tragic, youthful, unconventional: these are the age-end aesthetic qualities *The Chap-Book* valued so much that, sometimes, they are to be taken as a guide to life as well as to art. This sentiment is expressed in a comparison of the "popular" Maeterlinck and the more obscure Villiers de l'Isle Adam. The editor argues for the superiority of de l'Isle Adam by recounting the closing scene of *Axël* and noting its broader relevance to contemporary life:

> Axel has renounced the intellectual world, and Sara the religious world, each in
> the search for a hidden treasure. They meet, for the first time, in the crypt of an
> ancient castle. Life, at that moment, seems to offer them wealth, power, and,
> above all, a new birth of love. "We can now realize all our dreams," exclaims
> Sara. And Axel replies, summing up the thoughts of a whole generation in one
> illuminating sentence: "Why realize them? They are so splendid!" A deeper
> meaning, it seems to me, than any to be found in Maeterlinck's plays; it explains
> half the vagaries of the century's end. (CB 1.12: 355)

However vague this explanation of fin de siècle "vagaries," it does capture the
characteristic note of decadence as a form of youthful weariness and disillusion with the world.

Like *The Chap-Book* itself, the books published by Stone and Kimball reflect a mixture of American and European authors and a literary taste far
from uniform. Decadents and symbolists are well represented but by no
means comprise a majority of titles on the firm's list. Of the 106 titles published by Stone and Kimball, roughly half are books of poetry, short stories,
tales, and romances by authors who are largely forgotten today, with notable exceptions such as Hamlin Garland and Harold Frederic, whose *Damnation of Theron Ware* (1896) was the best-selling book published by the
firm.[34] That said, Stone and Kimball did direct substantial efforts to satisfy
the audience for decadent literature. The company published several special series, such as the Green Tree Library and the Carnation series that
were intended as contributions to what the publishers saw as a contemporary canon of literary decadence. The Green Tree Library, in fact, was advertised as: "A series of books representing what may be called the new
movement in literature. The intention is to publish uniformly the best of
the decadent writings of various countries done into English and consistently brought together for the first time."[35] The series included Richard
Hovey's translations of *The Plays of Maurice Maeterlinck* (two different collections, published 1894 and 1896); William Archer's versions of Ibsen's
Little Eyolf (1894) and *John Gabriel Borkman* (1896); Gertrude Hall's ren-
derings of Verlaine's *Poems* (1895); and Edith Wingate Ryder's treatment of
The Massacre of the Innocents and Other Tales by Belgian Writers (including
Maeterlinck). Titles in the Carnation series included Ralph Adams Cram's
Black Spirits and White (1895; see chapter 3) and a collection of "tales and
episodes" delightfully titled *The Sin Eater* by Fiona Macleod, pseudonym of
William Sharp, who also published in the Green Tree Library.[36] If the ten-
volume edition of *The Works of Edgar Allan Poe* (1895) is added to the list of
Carnation and Green Tree titles specifically identified as "decadent," and if
the poetry collections of decadent fellow travelers such as George Santayana, John Davidson, and William Butler Yeats are also included among "the
best of the decadent writings" in Stone and Kimball editions, then it may

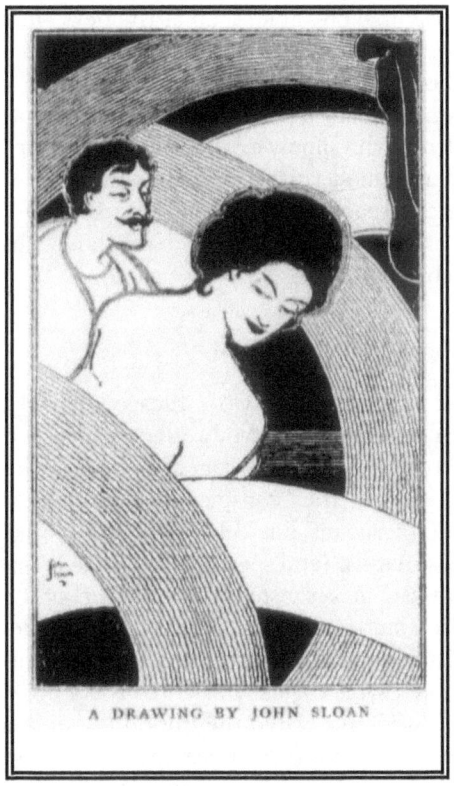

A DRAWING BY JOHN SLOAN

FIGURE 11   John Sloan, drawing (1894)

fairly be said that close to one-third of the company's publications contribute to the canon of literary decadence.

But Stone and Kimball did more than simply contribute to the canon of
decadence. With *The Chap-Book* as its house organ, the publishing house did
much to ameliorate and legitimate the idea of decadence. As the announcement for the Green Tree Library shows, to be decadent was to be part of a cultural vanguard. This seemingly paradoxical condition is consistent with the
notion of "age-end art"; that is, the cultural conditions that obtain during a
period of social decadence can only be expressed by new, unconventional
voices. This paradox was first described, and best described, by Théophile
Gautier in his review of the third edition of Baudelaire's *Les Fleurs du Mal*
(1868). According to Gautier, the poet must resort to "le style de décadence"—meaning, a style appropriate to conditions of decadence—in order to

express the previously inexpressible, such as the new, "unknown needs" that arise in a civilization in which "factitious life has replaced natural life."[37] This is the logic that allows Stone and Kimball to claim that "decadent writings" comprise "the new movement in literature." Thus, no opprobrium attaches to the writer *of* decadence who simply expresses the conditions of an artificial age in which the wonders of modernity produce "unknown needs" and new desires for things that, strictly speaking, are not at all necessary to life. But what of those who are not artists, and who actually have those "unknown needs" that the artist of decadence describes?

vii

In 1899, a professor at the University of Chicago published an analysis of the social class much in evidence in the Midwestern capitol at the turn of the century. To be sure, Thorstein Veblen's *Theory of the Leisure Class* was not intended solely as an excoriation of the "conspicuous consumption" and "pecuniary tastes" of his fellow Chicagoans, but Veblen had in Chicago exemplars aplenty to support his thesis that wasteful spending is a reliable marker of social prestige. The idea that waste makes taste is certainly part of the popular notion of social decadence in America. No doubt this notion has developed partly as a result of Veblen's famous argument, which can be read as the sociological corollary of Gautier's more psychologically oriented theory of decadence. Indeed, both Veblen and Gautier associated the notion of unnatural needs with the concept of decadence. In Veblen's America, the more one spends on the things one needs the least the more "decadent" one appears. The quotation marks around the epithet in this instance are intended to signify a critical difference between this type of American social "decadence" and its cultural counterpart in Europe. For one thing, the Continental counterpart is truly more cultural than consumerist: J.-K. Huysmans writes things; J. P. Morgan buys things (or, to more accurately reflect Veblen's thesis, J. P. Morgan's *wife* buys things).

American "decadence" in this social sense is above all inauthentic, and no where more so than in its relationship to the aristocracy. In terms of simple content, literary decadence in Europe is largely an artistic response to the actual existence of an aristocratic class. American "decadence," by contrast, is a response, not in art, but in reality, to an imagined ideal of an aristocratic class. In most cases, the best Americans can do, even today, is merely imitate whatever tastes the European aristocrat is imagined to exemplify (v. Donald Trump's Manhattan penthouse, with its gilded Louis *quinze* décor).[38] It is simply not possible for any American to *be* an actual, authentic member of the aristocratic class—not by birth, anyway. In the nineteenth century the only way for a leisure-class American to correct this stigma of inauthenticity was matrimony, and certainly there was no more complete indicator of social prestige than an American marriage—however loveless—to an English aristocrat, as happened occasionally with the odd Vanderbilt and the even odder Marlborough.

In Veblen's analysis, 'decadent' is rarely used to describe the social dynamics of the leisure class. In fact, the word does not appear until the chapter "Pecuniary Canons of Taste," almost half-way through the book. In this chapter Veblen explores the relation between aesthetic tastes and consumable goods, arguing that "[t]he requirement for conspicuous wastefulness is not commonly present, consciously, in our canons of taste, but it is none the less present as a constraining norm selectively shaping and sustaining our sense of what is beautiful, and guiding our discrimination with respect to what may legitimately be approved as beautiful and what may not."[39] Hence, our appreciation of beautiful objects is "in great measure a gratification of our sense of costliness masquerading under the name of beauty" (Veblen, 128). In Veblen's view, "the superior aesthetic value of the decadent book" (Veblen, 164) is an instance of the paradoxical preference for goods that are imperfect, crude, and handmade over machine-made goods that are "more perfect," because manufactured items "show a more perfect adaptation of means to end" (159). Here, then, is sociological validation for Wilde's dictum that "All art is quite useless."[40] As Veblen explains, "the visible imperfections of the hand-wrought goods, being honorific, are accounted marks of superiority in point of beauty, or serviceability, or both": "Hence has arisen that exaltation of the defective, of which John Ruskin and William Morris were such eager spokesmen in their time; and on this ground their propaganda of crudity and wasted effort has been taken up and carried forward since their time" (Veblen, 162). It is possible, and even probable, that Veblen has the Chicago firm of Stone and Kimball in mind when he says that what is true of Morris's Kelmscott Press also "holds true with but slightly abated force when applied to latter-day artistic book-making generally" (Veblen, 162). What Veblen calls "the decadent book," then, serves to illustrate the larger principle of conspicuous wastefulness. The decadent book is so called because of its defectiveness in relation to the superior serviceability of machine-made products. But it may be that Veblen's usage of 'decadent' was chosen precisely because the deliberate imperfection of the books he describes were often manifestly decadent in their cultural content. After all, Stone and Kimball published books that were decadent in both senses; that is, they were "defective" not only because their functionality was compromised but also because their literary standards departed from convention.

Whether Veblen actually looked to the relatively minor phenomenon of American literary decadence to complement his thinking about the social "decadence" of the American leisure class is hard to say. Veblen scholars identify his major influences as a mixture of the German "historical school" of economics and the tradition of American pragmatism, along with Kant's philosophical critiques and Herbert Spencer's adaptation of Darwinian thinking to the social sciences. Influences from literature are generally limited to radical, utopian works such as Edward Bellamy's enormously popular *Looking Backward* (1888) and the naturalistic school of fiction exemplified by the novelists Stephen Crane and Frank Norris.[41] Naturalism was shaped by some of the same Darwinian ideas that led Spencer to adapt natural selection to social relations, so there is a certain logic to the assumption that Veblen would have been attracted to the naturalists' insistence on "a pessimistic realism that sets man in a mechanical world."[42] But it seems much more reasonable to assume that Veblen would have taken interest in another kind of realism that was much closer to hand.

viii

The novels of Henry Blake Fuller anticipate Veblen's ideas about leisure class life so completely that it is remarkable that Veblen scholars have not counted the Chicago novelist among the sociologist's more pertinent predecessors. By contrast, Fuller scholars, though small in number, are almost unanimous in noting the general correspondence. Commenting on *The Cliff Dwellers*, Fuller's biographer says that "Veblen could have taught Fuller nothing about the mechanisms of conspicuous consumption," and he calls *With the Procession* (1895) "a novel that Thorstein Veblen might have written."[43] For now, the question remains open as to whether Fuller merely anticipates Veblen or whether in fact Veblen derived some of his more interesting ideas from Fuller. But the conjecture is sound, given that Fuller's literary reputation in the early 1890s was substantial, as a result of the widespread success of his first novel.

While *The Chevalier of Pensieri-Vani* does not deal so insistently with the dynamics of social class as do *The Cliff Dwellers* and *With the Procession*, even there Fuller sounds the basic theme that was subsequently taken up by Veblen: "Too much had been said about the dignity of labor and not enough about the preciousness of leisure. Civilization, in its last outcome, was heavily in the debt of leisure, and the success of any society worth considering was to be estimated largely by the use to which its *fortunati* had put their spare moments" (82). And one of the things that makes the kingdom of Arcopia such an ideal society is the freedom the nobles enjoy from the pressures of modern, metropolitan life. The members of the landed aristocracy, secure in their private estates, are "quite exempt from the sorry expedient to which heads of families in less happily organized states were forced—that of expressing their social importance through their wives and daughters" (92–93). Thus, as early as 1890 Fuller expresses in fairly exact terms one important aspect of the theory Veblen elaborated nine years later.

However much Fuller may have anticipated Veblen with his first novel, it is *With the Procession* that provides the most material for comparison with *The Theory of the Leisure Class*. In fact, the plot of the novel is almost exclusively concerned with the leisure class ambitions of Chicago's business community.

The focus is on the generational differences between the older and younger members of a long-established Chicago family, the Marshalls. David Marshall, the patriarch of the family, has made a fortune of some $3 million by dealing in wholesale groceries, yet he and his wife, Eliza, are content to remain in the modest house they built together when they were first married, sometime before the Civil War. Their children, by contrast, have social ambitions of various sorts, with the exception of the older brother, Roger, who has joined his father in business. The youngest daughter, Rosamund, or Rosie, means to use her beauty and vivaciousness (not to mention her father's vast wealth) to make a great *début* in Chicago society; her older, plainer sister, Jane, intends to make her mark by doing charity work on a grand scale; and Truesdale, the other brother, has wide-ranging artistic ambitions consistent with his abortive Ivy League education (he leaves Yale after his second year) and his European travels and studies. Of these three siblings, the most important is Jane, who sees in her sister's beauty and her brother's culture ample material to exploit in the service of her own social advancement.

Jane begins her charity campaign by courting the wealthy Mrs. Bates, who has understood early on that wasteful "show" is a social necessity to verify material wealth, especially self-made, middle-class wealth. When Jane calls on the woman she is struck first by the doorman's costume—"knee breeches and black stockings"—and quite disconcerted by it: "The splendor of the front that [the servant's] master had presented to the world had indeed intimidated poor Jane."[44] The reaction to the doorman's outfit is of a piece with Veblen's later observation that "the apparel . . . of domestic servants, especially liveried servants," as "a very elaborate show of unnecessary expensiveness" is often "the insignia of leisure" (Veblen, 182, 171). Additional insignia of leisure-class life await Jane once inside the Bates mansion, where she is treated to a succession of ostentatious displays. First she enters a music room furnished with an oversized, luxurious piano and a music stand to match, "laden with handsome bound scores of all the German classics and the usual operas of the French and Italian schools," but it is obvious that these scores "have not been disturbed for a year past" (56). Next she is ushered into a library that is a model of "latter-day magnificence," complete with Cordova leather lining the walls and lengthy stretches of "ornate bookcases" (59). When Mrs. Bates comments that she possesses some "twenty or thirty yards of Scott" (59), Jane realizes that all the books are "for show and display" only, "bought by the pound and stacked by the cord; doing nobody any good" (60). Finally, Jane is taken into a bedroom to view a "massive brass bedstead full panoplied in coverlet and pillow cases" (70) but hardly intended for sleep. Mrs. Bates explains that "it's for the women to lay their hats and cloaks on." Jane finds Mrs. Bates a "strange woman" and comments to herself on the lengths her wealthy hostess has gone to sustain a sense of "show": "'She doesn't get any music out of her piano; she doesn't get any reading out of her books; she doesn't even get any sleep out of her bed'" (71). But as Mrs. Bates explains, such displays are necessary to "keep up with the procession . . . , and head it if you can" (70). Although Jane, as Veblen would, finds the décor of Mrs. Bates's home "interesting from an historical and a sociological point of view" (67), sociological interest gives way to social ambition, and Jane resolves to use her newly formed connection with Mrs. Bates to join the procession herself.

In Fuller's novel social ambition is completely governed by the "laws" of conspicuous consumption later described by Veblen: the more ostentatious the display, the greater the social prestige attached to it. In *With the Procession*, this type of "decadence" is intertwined with progress: the city of Chicago was once an "Arcadia" (9), a place of "simple hopes and ideals" (245), a town that has grown "from an Indian village to a metropolis of two millions within the lifetime of a single individual" (335). This progression is common to America at large but is most noticeable in the western regions. One character asks where those "simple hopes and ideals" are today and observes: "What the country really celebrated at Philadelphia in 1876, however unconsciously, was the ending of its minority and the assumption of full manhood with all its perplexities and cares" (245). The proof of this assertion is the railroad riots that followed the nation's centennial by one year, the product, in part, of European immigrants who brought their radical politics with them from their various homelands. Another character says, showing off his knowledge of "social science" (Veblen's discipline), "[T]oday we have all the elements possessed by the old world itself, and we must take whatever they develop, as the old world does. We have the full working apparatus finally, with all its resultant noise, waste, stenches, stains, dangers, explosions" (245–46). Chicago, in short, has become "too urban" (21), but in a squalid sense, "disgusting rather than indecent": "all the unclassifiable riff-raff that is spawned by a great city leered from corners, or slouched along the edge of the gutters, or stood in dark doorways, or sold impossible rubbish in impossible dialects wherever the public indulgence permitted a foothold" (9). Thus, from the perspective of the leisure-class characters in Fuller's novel, the immigrant denizens of the Black City are the ones who make Chicago a site of urban decadence and decline—but paradoxically vibrant with mercantile energy.

The relationship of the Marshalls to this new world is ambiguous. Up until the "year of grace 1893" they feel that they are living under "a state of siege" (25). They are the "Old Guard," but, at the same time, David Marshall, founder of the firm, has become a member of the "advance guard," almost against his will, as the old family grocery business becomes a corporation and broadens its financial reach to include real estate and the stock market. This ambiguity is conveyed by the subject of a lecture for which Marshall's daughter Jane has acquired a modest reputation: "the Decadence of the Renaissance Forms" (66). The substance of this lecture is never laid out in detail, but Fuller's ironic point is clear. The rebirth of the new Chicago out of the old city destroyed by the great fire and symbolized by the White City of 1893 is at the same time something cheap and inferior in comparison to what has gone before. Jane's brother Truesdale does not return from Europe in time to visit the Exposition, but he goes to see "the great white shell" that remains in its aftermath. Truesdale does express the hope that "the spirit of the White City was but just transferred to the body of the great Black City close at hand" (87), but the description of the Black City that follows casts doubt on this possibility:

> The great town . . . sprawled and coiled about him like a hideous monster—a piteous, floundering monster, too. It almost called for tears. Nowhere a more tireless activity, nowhere a more profuse expenditure, nowhere a more determined striving after the ornate, nowhere a more undaunted endeavor towards the monumental expression of success, yet nowhere a result so pitifully grotesque, grewsome [sic], appalling. "So little taste," sighed Truesdale; "so little training, so little education, so total an absence of any collective sense of the fit and the proper! Who could believe, here, that there *are* cities elsewhere which fashioned themselves rightly almost by intuition—which took shape and reached harmony by an unreasoned instinct?" (87)

Hence the great Chicago renaissance is decadent, in part, because of a lack of organic form.

The basis for Truesdale's criticism of Chicago is his European sensibility, which other characters regard as decadent. Truesdale's brother Roger, for instance, resents his younger sibling's wastrel ways as a connoisseur of fine art and music, especially when Truesdale claims to have superior experience in the ways of the world. Roger's rejoinder is to defend the life of the Chicago businessman: "Who *are* the world if not my father and I and all the other earnest men who work to make the frame of things and to hold it together? We are the world, and you—you are only the rubbish strewn over the top of it!" (270). The accusation echoes the thoughts of Roger's father, the founder of the firm at which the son works as an attorney: "Art was not an integral part of the great frame of things; it was a mere surface decoration, and the artist was but for the adornment of the rich man's triumph" (141). What emerges is a symmetrical irony that pits the cultivated artist against the money-hungry business tycoon whose success requires the ostentatious display of culture that only the artist can supply. Each type has nothing but disdain for the other, no doubt because each is so vital to the other's needs. To the businessman, the artist is decadent because of his odd cultural habits; to the artist, the businessman is decadent because of his excessive materialism and lack of taste.

This twin dynamic depends on opposing values that allow one party to judge the other for the failure to live up to its standards: the artist is decadent because he lacks social respectability grounded in business success; the businessman is decadent because he lacks taste based on aesthetic judgment. In addition to these rather commonplace ideas of decadence, Fuller assigns certain characters, most notably Truesdale Marshall, an aesthetic sensibility that is consistent with a more nuanced sense of decadence as a cultural tradition. Truesdale comes to this sensibility by way of "the Romantic School—by 'Mademoiselle de Maupin,' in part; by the 'Vie de Boheme,' more largely; and this taste had taken a confirmed set through the perusal of other works of a like trend—more contemporaneous and therefore still more deleterious" (92). Truesdale is disappointed to discover that contemporary Parisian counterparts of Mimi and Mussette are "far, far from the *gracieuse* and *mignonne* creations of Murget and of 1830" (92). Truesdale is simply too educated, too wealthy to acquire, or even desire, membership in Bohemia as a social class, and he is disappointed to make this discovery: "And if disappointing in Paris, how much more so in Chicago?—where impropriety was still wholly incapable of presenting itself in a guise that could enlist the sympathies of the fastidious" (92). This formulation has a wider application and can almost serve as yet another definition of decadence: fastidious impropriety. Perhaps the problem with Chicago as Fuller presents it lies in the separation of these two qualities. The monied classes are fastidious about everything except impropriety; the immigrant classes do not lack for impropriety, but they lack refinement. Curiously, the bridge between the two classes is business. Truesdale observes of his father's partner: "Though Brower was out of Society, Truesdale did not find him on this account any more in Bohemia; he merely occupied the firm and definite middle-ground of business" (91).

Truesdale is a man of many talents: he sings, he writes, he paints. When his aunt asks him to paint a portrait of her daughter, she is shocked by what she sees, prompting Truesdale to ask if she "should prefer something a little less advanced" (225). His painting is evidently impressionist, or, possibly, pointillist. He explains: "I decompose what is before me into the primary colors. Now the thing for you to do is to step back ten or twelve feet and recompose them" (225-26). Whatever it is, Truesdale's method is said to comprise "the spirit of complete modernity" (226). He struggles to express this spirit in the culturally backward city of Chicago and longs for the company of like-minded individuals. He has the fantasy of a club where "a dozen agile wits had their own way with Monet and Bourget and Verlaine" (88). But Chicago, alas, lacks the cultural infrastructure necessary to the full expression of the decadent-aesthetic sensibility: "He deplored the absolute non-existence of the institution known as the café," the café, that is, in its European form, as "the crowning gem in the coronet of civilization" (140). The Chicago version of this necessary institution offers "[n]o journals . . . no demi-tasse, no clientèle, no leisure" (141). Truesdale, in fact, thinks of himself as living in a kind of cultural wilderness, "and being thus placed, what could he be but a pioneer—the pioneer of a leisure class" (86). Fuller's genius in this novel is to combine the frontier thesis and the theory of the leisure class.

But as Truesdale's cultural isolation shows, frontier decadence leaves a lot to be desired. Although Fuller himself may not have been quite so isolated in Chicago as his character was, Truesdale's solitary reflections suggest a more general lack of cultural community that seems particular to the decadent aesthete in fin de siècle America. At the same time, the fictional character's belief that he might establish an outpost of "advanced" culture in the United States is one that was taken up again and again by Americans with ties to European decadence. In New York, Boston, and Chicago the culture of decadence is set up as an alternative—often an antagonist—to some larger facet of the American scene. In New York, decadence emerges as a cultural counter to the mass of immigrants making their way in the great metropolis and also to the growing social role of women. In Boston, decadence is the negation of both the genteel tradition of arts and letters and the Puritan heritage of repressive morality. In Chicago, the culture of decadence is thoroughly at odds with the forces of business and commerce. Like James Huneker and Ralph Adams Cram, Henry Blake Fuller found in decadence something America was not. Fuller has in common with Huneker a taste for Continental literature, and he shares with Cram an aversion to modern architecture, but Fuller met with far less success than either Huneker or Cram in conveying his cultural vision to the public at large. All of them seemed to have been living at the wrong time, but Fuller was in the wrong place as well. In America at least, anyone who looks to the West will not find, paradoxically, the twilight sensibility so conducive to the crepuscular culture of decadence.

CHAPTER FIVE

San Francisco: The Seacoast of Decadence

By the time the 1890s arrived the golden age of San Francisco culture was long since gone. Between 1849 and 1869, between the Gold Rush and the completion of the transcontinental railroad, San Francisco was the capitol of the American West—almost an autonomous city-state because of its geographical isolation from the rest of the country. The city had grown from a village of only eight hundred residents in 1848 to a populous metropolis almost overnight. The Gold Rush of 1849 brought in would-be prospectors from across the nation as well as fresh immigrants from Europe and Asia. Indeed, until the opening of the Suez Canal in 1869, the port of San Francisco was the principal point of entry to the Western world, not only for Asian workers but also for Asian goods. When the Civil War broke out, the city's economy did not suffer as other American cities' did. On the contrary, tens of thousands of Americans, like Samuel Clemens, sought refuge from the war in San Francisco or in the Nevada Territory town of Virginia City. Clemens, who began to use the penname *Mark Twain* as a Virginia City newspaperman, was not the only literary pioneer in old San Francisco. Bret Harte came from New York, Ambrose Bierce from Ohio, and Joaquin Miller from Indiana. During its cultural heyday, San Franciscans boasted that the city published more newspapers than London. There was no shortage of literary journals, either; the *Hesperian*, the *Pioneer*, the *Californian*, the *Golden Era*, and, above all, the *Overland Monthly* rivaled the best magazines published on the East Coast. But for all this, San Francisco maintained its frontier identity as a hard-drinking mining town. As Franklin Walker, a pioneer himself of California literary history, puts it, "San Francisco remained rough and grew sophisticated at the same time. . . . While its editors, its publishers, and its writers were becoming socially mature enough to describe what they saw around them, a steady stream of frontiersmen was constantly being pumped in and out of the heart of the West."[1]

Despite some diminution of San Francisco's cultural prestige and economic power, in 1890 the city remained "the West Coast's answer—the West Coast's only answer—to all the cities east of the Rocky Mountains." With almost 300,000 inhabitants, San Francisco ranked eighth in population among the cities of the United States. [2] But San Francisco was no longer the self-contained cultural center it had been in the days before the railroad linked it to the rest of the nation. In 1872, when a group of artists and journalists founded the Bohemian Club, "they were hard pressed to find illustrious names for its roster, for surprisingly few of the writers from the golden fifties and silver sixties were left in the city."[3] One of the few who remained was Ambrose Bierce, a founding member of the Bohemian Club who had served as its secretary from 1876 through 1877. Bierce resigned when it became obvious to him that the club was anything but bohemian; in fact, he thought that its members were "too sycophantic to royal and noble visitors from overseas."[4] Eventually, the club came to be dominated by San Francisco's business and professional men, and, no less than in Chicago, culture lost out to commerce. Moreover, William Randolph Hearst's purchase of the San Francisco *Examiner* in 1887 ushered in the age of yellow journalism, and the jingoistic tone of the Hearst newspapers went hand-in-glove with the chauvinism and imperialism that took hold in fin-de-siècle America. In many ways, the conditions in San Francisco were ripe for decadent culture to counter the "Bohemian" establishment and the Hearst empire. There was ample grain to go against, but there were precious few first-rate writers, like Bierce, to go against it. And even Bierce was on the Hearst payroll.

i

Ambrose Bierce, like the San Francisco evoked by Walker, was "rough and . . . sophisticated at the same time." The roughness means that he had none of the true decadent's deliquescent taste, but he did have the decadent's affection for pessimism and a cynical confidence in cultural decline. The paradox in Bierce's case is that he encouraged outmoded forms of romantic art that wound up contributing to the very decline he hoped to reverse. The mistaken assumption that yesterday's taste might somehow raise the cultural level of the nation led him to encourage second-rate talents such as George Sterling, whose poetry failed to reflect the removal from convention that his bohemian existence entailed. Bierce's own removal from the pretend Bohemia of the official San Francisco scene evidently forced him to seek out an alterative, "authentic" bohemianism that was no less false than the official version but false in a different way. Bierce's proud outsider status, combined with his role as the most feared cultural arbiter of the West, put him in the ambiguous position of advancing literature by looking backward and of encouraging his acolytes to be wary of authority but not of convention. Bierce, then, aids in the formation of a new counterculture that has something in common with decadence but is socially removed from it. Bierce, in short, has a role in the modulation of decadence into bohemianism, a social shift of some significance because it ultimately leads to the dissipation of decadence altogether.

Bierce did not anticipate this type of dissipation exactly, but he did predict his own cultural destiny with a clever couplet: "My! how my fame rings out in every zone—/ A thousand critics shouting, 'He's unknown!'"[5] Just about every study of Bierce begins with an analysis of the author's undeserved obscurity (as here). It is as if the last thing Bierce is known to have written were prophetic not only of his still mysterious death but also of his as-yet unrealized reputation: "As for me, I leave here tomorrow for an unknown destination."[6] Critical uncertainty about Bierce's place in American letters since his death in 1914 (?) contrasts sharply with Percival Pollard's assessment of 1909 "that no other American book written in the last fifty years will survive so long" as *Tales of Soldiers and Civilians* (1892, expanded edition 1898), Bierce's collection of short stories based on his Civil War experiences (also published under the title *In the Midst of Life*). Pollard was of course writing at a time when the Civil War was still a living memory for many Americans, so the temptation is to say that Bierce's fame was generational, that the book about the war was gradually forgotten as the generation that fought the war passed away. But such a theory does not explain why *Tales of Soldiers and Civilians* has fallen into obscurity while Stephen Crane's *Red Badge of Courage* has not. Indeed, the likelihood is that Crane's book has survived because of Crane's connections to the naturalist movement and that this type of validation by an existing literary tradition is precisely what the versatile Bierce lacks. Those whose work is not readily categorized are not easily canonized, either. Indeed, *Tales of Soldiers and Civilians* is not fairly described by calling it a book of war stories since at least half the volume is made up of tales of the supernatural.

Bierce was a remarkably prolific writer who produced work in a variety of genres. In addition to his collection of Civil War stories and fantastic tales in the mode of Poe, he wrote verse satire, elegiac poetry, parodies (such as "The Perverted Village," a take-off on Goldsmith's "Deserted Village"), and even patriotic, occasional verse. The work for which he is best known today is *The Devil's Dictionary*, originally *The Cynic's Word Book*. In his lifetime he achieved considerable fame as a journalist, working under contract to William Randolph Hearst for twenty years. Carey McWilliams, Bierce's first biographer, says the author had "enormous power and fame . . . in the Bay District. He was a Titan and Cyclops in San Francisco for a quarter of a century . . . , the most original, forceful and important literary figure in the west."[7] McWilliams adds that, to fully appreciate Bierce's California fame, "it must be remembered that in the eighties and nineties, San Francisco was the only western city that made a pretense of culture" (McWilliams, 201). But by the mid-1890s, Bierce's reputation was not limited to the West. A portrait of the then-famous satirist painted by J. H. E. Partington won a gold medal at the 1893 World's Fair in Chicago. And his fame among the eastern literary establishment was secured when William

Dean Howells numbered Bierce "among our three greatest writers," to which Bierce responded, characteristically, "I am sure Mr. Howells is the other two" (McWilliams, 219). As the author of "Prattle," the signature column he took from *The Wasp* to the San Francisco *Examiner* when he went to work for Hearst, Bierce regularly skewered the rich, the powerful, and the pretentious with his clever invective. His two greatest successes as a journalist were his satiric campaign against the railroad lobby in Washington and his principled opposition to the Spanish-American War.

The railroad lobby was led by Collis Huntington, president of the Southern Pacific. At issue was the Funding Bill, which would have forgiven or postponed repayment of the railroad's $75 million debt to the U.S. government. Writing in the *Examiner* and the New York *Journal* (both Hearst papers), Bierce kept the pressure on Huntington and encouraged his nemesis, Senator Morgan from Alabama, to expose the self-serving machinations of the railroad magnate. "Huntington Lying in His Last Ditch" is the typically clever headline of one of Bierce's dispatches. His journalistic efforts were rewarded when the Funding Bill was defeated and the railroads were forced to repay their massive debt over a ten-year period.[8] In his efforts against the railroad barons Bierce had the full support of the Hearst empire but wrote against his employer's position when he turned his attention to the Spanish-American War. A recent critic says that "Bierce was probably the only journalist in America who would dare to regularly oppose Hearst's policies on the editorial page while remaining in his employ, and one of the extremely few Americans from any walk of life who risked public censure by conspicuously and continuously opposing war with Spain."[9] Like Henry Blake Fuller, who in 1899 published a collection of verse satire opposing American imperialism,[10] Bierce objected to the war on the basis of a general opposition to empire: "We are at war with Spain today merely in obedience to a suasion that has been gathering force from the beginning of our national existence. The passion for territory once roused rages like a lion; successive conquests only strengthen it. That is the fever that is now burning in the American blood."[11] Here, Bierce gives expression to Frederick Jackson Turner's frontier thesis, or something like it, but he obviously does not endorse that thesis.

Resistance to American expansionism chimes with the political culture of the Boston and Chicago decadents, but Bierce's connection to the aesthetic culture of those two groups is harder to discern, as his vitriolic excoriation of Oscar Wilde shows. On the occasion of Wilde's American lecture tour in 1882 Bierce published a diatribe against him in *The Wasp*, the San Francisco weekly. The invective runs from crude—"He has mounted his hind legs and blown crass vapidities through the bowel of his neck"—to clever: "this consummate and star-like youth, missing everywhere his heaven-appointed functions and offices, wanders about, posing as a statue of himself."[12] One of the things that set the satirist off was the way Wilde positioned himself as the heir of a tradition Bierce admired: "this gawky gowk has the divine effrontery to link his name with Swinburne, Rossetti, and Morris" (*SR*, 6). Later in his life Bierce moderated his view of Wilde. In a 1904 letter to his literary disciple George Sterling, he allowed that "Wilde's work is all right" but expressed moral reservations: "[W]hat can one do with the work of one whose name one cannot speak before women?" (*MMM*, 122). Despite Bierce's moralistic disapproval of Wilde, his respect for Swinburne, Rossetti, and Morris belied an interest in the very aestheticism that Wilde so famously advocated. The interest is also revealed in a letter to one of his few female confidants, Blanche Partington (daughter of the portrait painter), in which Bierce sets the art-for-art's-sake sensibility against the Christian socialism of Tolstoy: "[M]en holding Tolstoi's view are not properly literary men (that is to say, artists) at all. They are 'missionaries,' who, in their zeal to lay about them, do not scruple to seize any weapon they can lay their hands on; they would grab a crucifix to beat a dog."[13] The remark helps us to understand something important about Bierce's attitude toward his own art. Clearly, in his journalistic campaigns Bierce was capable of something very like the missionary zeal he finds so distasteful in Tolstoy and others who are not "properly" artistic. But that is what journalism is for; art is for something else. The biographer McWilliams is right to say that Bierce's theory of aesthetics was "highly artificial": "Art had nothing to do with reality; ergo, the more unreal a story was the better story it must be."[14] This formulation, derived from Poe, likely lies at the heart of Bierce's grudging acceptance of Wilde's work, since it can serve as an aesthetic criterion not only for *The Picture of Dorian Gray* but also for Bierce's ghost stories.

An insistence on the value of unreality in art made Bierce skeptical of any affiliation of art and politics, as in his criticism of Tolstoy as a "missionary" and also in his denunciation of Edwin Markam's once-famous "Man with the Hoe" (1899), a didactic paean to the worker that expressed the author's conversion to socialism. Bierce did not object to Markam's promotion of socialism per se, only to the use of poetic art for sentimental and propagandistic purposes. In fact, Bierce seems to have been highly sympathetic to socialist politics and favored policies that led eventually to the development of what was once called "the welfare state" (currently in process of disassembly). According to M. E. Grenander, Bierce "favored government ownership of railroads, public employment for the needy, and some form of inheritance and progressive income taxes. He also believed that private ownership of land, the importation of cheap labor, and competitive wage systems should all be abolished."[15] Bierce's progressive, egalitarian politics sets him apart from most of the American decadents, especially those in Boston who nurtured Jacobite fantasies and imagined a return to the days of monarchy. Bierce's politics is also at odds with those British and Continental decadents who cultivated an interest in anarchism for aesthetic reasons (as Wilde and Mirbeau did). Indeed, the Chicago Haymarket bombings of 1886 made it harder for an American of Bierce's generation to transpose anarchism from political to aesthetic terms. Bierce looked with extreme disfavor on anarchism and understood that ideology, along with plutocracy, as the principal threats to the Republic.[16]

Bierce's politics sets him apart from some American decadents (e.g., Cram) but connects him to others (e.g., Fuller); likewise, his art-for-art's-sake sensibility aligns him with American decadence in some ways, yet his romantic aesthetic seems a little old-fashioned beside the work of Saltus and Huneker, say, who made a point of sounding "the complex modern note."[17] But if Bierce's relation to decadence is ambiguous politically and aesthetically, no such ambiguity attaches to his philosophy, for he is one of the great pessimists of the American fin de siècle. Clifton Fadiman once called him "a pessimism machine,"[18] and, while the epithet is not completely fair to the private Bierce, it captures an important aspect of his public persona. And no doubt because Bierce is an American, his pessimism seems especially virulent, deliberately contrived to counter the forward-looking attitude of so many citizens of the progressive republic. To a female interviewer who asked him to recommend some ancient authority on the best method of child rearing, Bierce responded, "Study Herod, Madam, study Herod" (qtd. in McWilliams, 255). When a correspondent of 1905 announces the birth of a daughter Bierce responds by reminding the writer that he "believe[s] with Schopenhauer that it is a crime to bring a child" into the world but concedes that as long as "she's here I vote to let her remain; it would be hardly fair to put her to death."[19] The pessimism implicit in Bierce's grudging acceptance of the child's birth is matched or exceeded by an earlier journalistic report of infant mortality that has an almost gleeful tone: "Last week was the best week for dead babies we have ever had. Of the seventy-four deaths occurring in the city, more than half were infants under two years of age. Thirty were under one year. Whom the gods love die young, particularly if their parents get drunk and neglect them" (SR, 3).

In The Devil's Dictionary, Bierce defined "Birth" as "The first and direst of all disasters" (DD, 18). Like Edgar Saltus, Bierce was an admirer of Schopenhauer's pessimistic philosophy, and, like Schopenhauer's follower Eduard Von Hartmann, he was not particularly disturbed by the prospect of human extinction, as this "utilitarian" aphorism shows: "The greatest good to the greatest number: Death" (SR, 3). Bierce also found support in Schopenhauer for his extremely unforgiving attitude toward any sort of behavior in others that he perceived as a personal betrayal. When he broke with his disciple Herman Scheffauer (over Scheffauer's support of German nationalism), Bierce wrote his new disciple George Sterling: "Scheff is impossible—I deeply regret that I ever knew him. I regret also that I transiently forgot my Schopenhauer, who warns against condoning an infamy by a friend, for in similar circumstances he will surely repeat the offense."[20]

Bierce's thoroughgoing pessimism may account for his choice of the letter P as the starting point for what would eventually become known as The Devil's

Dictionary. In fact, *pessimism* does appear among the entries under *P*, with this definition: "A philosophy forced upon the convictions of the observer by the disheartening prevalence of the optimist with his scarecrow hope and his unsightly smile."[21] Such definitions began to appear in 1881 as a regular feature of his "Prattle" column in *The Wasp* and later in the *Examiner*. Published in book form in 1906 as *The Cynic's Word Book*, subsequent editions of the sardonic definitions have appropriated the title under which they originally appeared in the "Prattle" columns. *The Devil's Dictionary* helps to make the case that Bierce may have had more in common with his decadent Continental counterparts than with his all-American contemporaries. Being a writer, Bierce said, requires the maintenance of "an ever-present consciousness that this is a world of fools and rogues, blind with superstition, tormented with envy, consumed with vanity, selfish, false, cruel, cursed with illusions—frothing mad! He must be a sinner and in turn a saint, a hero, a wretch."[22]

This "job description" of the writer, observes Roy Morris Jr., has "more in common with Baudelaire's *poete maudit* than with such homegrown American humorists as Mark Twain [and] Artemus Ward." Moreover, "Bierce carefully cultivated a public image that, in keeping with the dictionary's title, was overtly satanic. He habitually dressed in black, carried a loaded revolver under his coat, and displayed a human skull and a box of ashes on his desk—the remains, he said, of former friends. His overall philosophy he summed up in two words, 'Nothing matters.'"[23] In thinking of Bierce as a kind of bayside Baudelaire or a frontier Flaubert, the recent critic Morris echoes the earlier opinion of Percival Pollard, once of Bierce's first admirers and an American decadent in his own right. Pollard appreciated the "pitiless perfection" of Bierce's style and detected in his work something akin to *l'art pour l'art*: "[I]n Bierce's stories you get no glimpse of a personality. This art, and this prose, was absolutely impersonal . . . as perfect and purposeless as the diamond."[24] Pollard was convinced that Bierce's short stories would assure his ultimate fame, "as certain as Flaubert and Baudelaire are famous" (Pollard, 256). This roundabout comparison has a reasonable basis because, like Baudelaire, Bierce rather starkly divided his imagination between romanticism—expressed in his stories of the supernatural—and realism, which found voice in his splenetic newspaper columns. Flaubert's imagination was similarly divided, and there is further basis for comparison to Bierce in his case. As "the Beau Brummel of syntax,"[25] Bierce follows Flaubert in the tradition of immaculate style, and, further, in the ironic effect achieved by casting an ordinary narrative in the dispassionate voice of an extraordinary narrator, as he does in his "Civilian" stories and as Flaubert did in *Madame Bovary*. In addition, this *frisson* between mundane matter and incisive style links Bierce's *Devil's Dictionary* and Flaubert's *Dictionnaire des Idées reçues*, even though there is no evidence of influence.

The critic Jacques Barzun calls *The Dictionary of Received Ideas* Flaubert's "great contribution to moral realism."[26] The same might be said on Bierce's behalf of *The Devil's Dictionary*, for the satirist no less than the ironist must possess a well-developed sense of personal morality to measure the failures of bourgeois convention and comment on them. Flaubert's dictionary was originally written as a supplement to *Bouvard et Pécuchet*, his final novel, unfinished at his death in 1880. The dictionary, like the novel, shows the absurdity of knowledge when it is reduced to routine. Barzun reminds us that, in printing, the word *cliché* refers to the clicking sound of a metal plate that reproduces "the same image mechanically without end" (Barzun, 4). *The Dictionary of Received Ideas* plays on the tradition of prescriptive lexicography by telling its readers how to think or what to say when, ironically, all the definitions reflect the unthinking conventions and automatic expressions of everyday nineteenth-century bourgeois life. Stylistically, then, Flaubert's dictionary is rather different from the one devised by Bierce, who expressed mock concern in 1906 that his publisher would turn down the book because, he said, it was "only sense, wit and good English" (McWilliams, 289). But the difference between good English and deliberately bad French is really only a surface distinction: Bierce and Flaubert are both out to expose the absurdity of mindless convention. If Flaubert gives us the cliché, Bierce exposes the "logic" underlying the cliché by providing a brilliant alternative to it.

A few examples will illustrate the point. In Flaubert, the entry for "Duties" reads: "Require them of others. Avoid them yourself. Others have duties towards us, not we toward them."[27] Bierce's definition of *Duty* follows: "That which sternly impels us in the direction of profit, along the line of desire" (*DD*, 42). Both writers "define" the concept in terms of self-serving bourgeois hypocrisy—Flaubert with ironic platitudes, Bierce with a pointed aphorism that exposes the motivation for the hypocrisy. Similarly, Flaubert on "Selfishness" instructs the reader to "[c]omplain of other people's; overlook your own" (77); in Bierce, to be "Selfish" is to be "[d]evoid of consideration for the selfishness of others" (*DD*, 182)—very near the same thought as Flaubert's. In *The Dictionary of Received Ideas*, bourgeois diffidence over "Justice" is captured in the cliché "Never worry about it" (51). Bierce's definition explains why such diffidence is understandable: because "Justice" is "[a] commodity which in a more or less adulterated condition the State sells to the citizen as a reward for his allegiance, taxes and personal service" (*DD*, 101).

Flaubert and Bierce bring to the definitions in their respective dictionaries a healthy disrespect for the machinations of government and politicians. Their mutual disillusion with democracy and party politics emerges in a number of definitions that expose the "false consciousness" of various ideologies. For example, Flaubert defines "Conservative" with an image and a hackneyed observation: "Politician with pot belly. 'A limited, conservative mind? Certainly! Limits keep fools from falling down wells'" (24). Under his heading for "Conservative," Bierce skewers two ideologies at once: "A statesman who is enamored of existing evils, as distinguished from the liberal, who wishes to replace

them with others" (*DD*, 28). "Radicalism" in Flaubert is "[a]ll the more dangerous because it is latent"; hence, "[t]he Republic is hurtling forward into radicalism" (71). A similar sense of political dynamism is archly expressed in Bierce's
definition: "The conservatism of to-morrow injected into the affairs of to-day"
(*DD*, 156). The sarcasm is obvious in Flaubert's succinct definition of "Minister of State" as "[t]he highest reach of human glory" (58). Bierce's cynicism is
more expansive; to him, a "Minister" is "an agent of a higher power with a lower
responsibility. In diplomacy an officer sent into a foreign country as the visible
embodiment of his sovereign's hostility. His principle qualification is a degree
of plausible inveracity next below that of an ambassador" (*DD*, 126). The absurdity of government leads both writers to emphasize warfare as the inevitable
outcome of politics. In Flaubert, a "Battle" is "[a]lways 'bloody,'" and the political dimension of bloody confrontation is expressed by the observation that in
any battle "[t]here are always two sets of victors: those who won and those who
lost" (17). Bierce tells us that a "Battle" is "[a] method of untying with the teeth
a political knot that would not yield to the tongue" (*DD*, 15). Surely Flaubert
brings to his definition of "Grapeshot" memories of the Commune: "The only
way to make the Parisians shut up" (41). Bierce, likewise, realizes the relation of
"Grapeshot" to radical politics when he defines it as: "An argument which the
future is preparing in answer to the demands of American socialism" (*DD*, 69).
Perhaps Flaubert's disillusion with the Third Republic is contained in the cliché saying that serves as the definition of "Monarchy": "'A constitutional monarchy is the best of republics'" (59). Bierce shows his exasperation with democratic processes and reveals himself to be momentarily akin to Ralph Adams
Cram and other Jacobite Bostonians when he defines "Monarchical Government" succinctly, and simply, as "Government" (*DD*, 128).

   This comparison of two of the nineteenth century's greatest misanthropes
is fanciful, to be sure, since they belonged to different cultures and different
generations (Flaubert was born in 1821, Bierce in 1842). What they have in
common is what Roger Williams calls "the horror of life"—a pessimism and a
distaste for humanity that runs so deep as to be pathological.[28] In both men
the horror of life was fueled by ill health: Flaubert suffered from epilepsy and
Bierce from asthma. Bierce also served as a Union soldier in the Civil War
and took a bullet to the head in the battle of Kenesaw Mountain, Georgia, in
1864; fragments of the bullet remained in his skull throughout his life. Flaubert did not suffer the horrors of the Franco-Prussian War firsthand, but he
grew up with dead bodies all about him because his father was a surgeon.
Bierce and Flaubert were both admirers, so to speak, of death, and they took
a dim view of birth. Both admired Malthus for his advocacy of limited population growth, and neither would have been upset at the cessation of population growth entirely. They also took the long view of human history and were
students of historical decline who understood the fall of Rome as a cautionary
tale for their own times.

Bierce regularly fulminated on the topic of national decline in his columns for *The Wasp* and other newspapers, often writing from the perspective of a future historian looking back on the disaster of American life (he assembled a collection of these satires in the mid-1890s and tried to get Stone and Kimball to publish it under the title *The Fall of the Republic and Other Satires*).[29] No topic brings out the fierceness of Bierce's invective so fully as the sorry state of the nation, as in this dispatch of 21 May 1881: "[W]e are hopelessly foundering and helplessly floundering in a sea of public and private corruption as offensive as that upon which the Ancient Mariner saw the shiny things that 'did crawl with legs'; . . . we are a laughing stock to Europe and a menace to civilization" (qtd. in McWilliams, 158). Things were no better for Bierce after the election of 1884, which brought Grover Cleveland's administration to power:

> Is this, then, the best that Civilization's centuries can show?—this devil's-work of moral desolation? Is Progress but a wisp, through penetrable brambles shimmering infeasible bogs, or burning inaccessible on heights of air beyond moonfrosted fens? Is Reason only a vain voice crying in the wilderness—calling vaguely to eternal, dead silences? Is religion a vagrant meteor freaking the mists that rise and reek in the Valley of Unfaith?
>
> Ugh! It is as if God had fallen dead from the steps of the great white throne, squandering the sweet angels like a flock of startled pigeons, and Mahound had reared the ugly horrors of his head in sable supremacy over a dead world! (*SR*, 48)

Bierce's jeremiad is oddly in harmony with the decadent formulation that sees the end of civilization ushered in by an invasion of barbarians. At the same time, however, no one would mistake Bierce's cynical rant over the decadence of civilization for Verlaine's melodious plaint that signals the acceptance of the empire's end. The radical difference in form between prose and poetry is the least of it: in Bierce the tone is wrong. He does not possess that delectation of decline that sets the decadent apart from the prophet of doom—not that Bierce is that, exactly, because his morality is too meticulous to allow vague, prophetic announcements about civilization's demise. Simply stated, however much Bierce may decry decline, he does not wish for the end; on the contrary, he resists it—actually, actively—as his campaign against the railroad barons shows.

For this reason, among others, Bierce's position in the decadent tradition is highly paradoxical. Unlike Edgar Saltus, Ralph Adams Cram, and Henry Blake Fuller, he was not an admirer of British or Continental decadents, and he made no attempt to emulate them. If anything, Bierce is at the head of a tradition of plain-spoken cynicism that leads in the direction of antidecadence, of a sort later represented by the work of H. L. Mencken (see chapter 6). But decadence is such a polyvalent, hybrid concept that characterizing Bierce as antidecadent does not seem quite right, either. Decadence, after all, is another name for transition, and it is possible to see more than one tradition leading up to Bierce and still others leading away from him. In San Francisco, Bierce was a powerful presence indeed—the "western literary czar" is a common epithet—and he truly was in a position to dictate cultural tastes. His hatred for middle-class values finds a fairly direct route of dissemination through his literary disciple George Sterling and on to Mencken, who was Sterling's friend and confidant. And no doubt Mencken would have approved of Bierce's epithet on that popular but pathetic alternative to alcohol: "Water has one merit—it is cheap; and one disadvantage—it is not good" (qtd. in McWilliams, 161). At the same time, Bierce's absolute intolerance for anything that smacked of fashion made impossible in San Francisco the cultivation of the kind of British decadent sensibility that flourished in Boston in the early 1890s. What was possible instead, at least for a time, was a form of bohemianism that was oddly in harmony with decadence, even though Bierce himself held bohemian pretensions in low esteem: a definition that could have appeared in *The Devil's Dictionary* but does not calls Bohemia "[a] taproom of a wayside inn on the road from BÆotia to Philistia" (qtd. in McWilliams, 204). But Bierce's self-positioning outside of "Philistia"—the normative world of middle-class social, moral, and material interests—made him a precursor of San Francisco's bohemian circles if not a participant in them. Hence Bierce contributes to the dissipation of decadence downward into bohemianism and, ultimately, into the various countercultures of the twentieth century. With his art-for-art's-sake sensibility, his virulent pessimism, and his cynical opposition to the rising class of American "Philistines," Bierce becomes an influential exemplar of a type of oppositional culture just shy of decadence but close enough to inspire others to go against the social and literary grain. In this respect George Sterling emerges as the official disciple who would eventually become "The King of Bohemia," but Gelett Burgess can also be seen as a figure whose cultural existence owes something to the great shadow cast by Bierce over the San Francisco literary scene. Burgess, like Sterling, had no choice but to be something Bierce inspired but that Bierce himself was not—something his invective had not yet touched. And Burgess no less than Sterling helped to shift decadence in the direction of Bohemia.

ii

Gelett Burgess (1866–1951), born in Boston, responded to the aestheticism and decadence of the Boston group by moving to San Francisco and writing verse parodies and satires of the movement. By the late 1890s Burgess had achieved considerable popular success as the author of nonsense verse, but critics have since regarded his work as "subliterary" at best, so his fame did not long survive the fin de siècle. Linguists know Burgess for at least two coinages now securely part of the English lexicon: *bromide*, meaning "a boring or platitudinous person," and *blurb*, the publishing term for the brief, laudatory remarks on a book jacket.[30] His best known work is the nonsense poem about a purple cow that many American children can recite to this day: "I never saw a purple cow, I never hope to see one; / But I can tell you anyhow, I'd rather see than be one!"[31] The poem appeared in the premier issue of *The Lark*, the little magazine loosely patterned after *The Chap-Book* that Burgess founded in San Francisco. Together with a group of friends who called themselves "Les Jeunes" (The Young), Burgess established the magazine, according to one commentator, in an attempt "to bring some of the wit and exhilaration of 1890s Paris to the West Coast."[32] Members of the group included the minor artist Ernest Peixotto, the minor poet Yone Noguchi (father of the famous sculptor), and Bruce Porter, whom Burgess called his "intellectual Mentor."[33] Porter, the coeditor of *The Lark*, was secretary of San Francisco's Guild of Arts and Crafts.[34] Burgess, Porter, and the rest disported themselves among the redwoods just north of San Francisco, calling the site of their festivities Camp Ha-Ha. Another commentator numbers the group among those with "an aesthetics of decadence that marked such figures as Oscar Wilde and Aubrey Beardsley in England, or Huneker and Edgar Saltus in New York. But the Bohemians of Camp Ha-Ha were light and gay, whimsical and raffish" (Hart, *BB*, vi). The latter part of this assessment will ring true to anyone who has perused the forgotten pages of *The Lark*, but the association with any form of bohemianism, let alone one that is "light and gay, whimsical and raffish," is bound to make any wholesale identification of the magazine with "an aesthetics of decadence" problematic. Indeed, the title of Burgess's magazine is a guide to its content, for its publication was mainly a means of pulling off literary larks or pranks.

In May 1897, Burgess described the cultural atmosphere that had led to the founding of *The Lark* only two years earlier:

> The success of the "Chap Book" incited the little riot of the Decadence, and there was a craze of odd sizes and shapes, freak illustrations, wide margins, uncut pages, Jenson types, scurrilous abuse and petty jealousies, impossible prose and doggerel rhyme. The movement asserted itself as a revolt against the commonplace; it aimed to overthrow the staid respectability of the larger magazines and to open to younger writers opportunities to be heard before they had obtained recognition from the autocratic editors. It was a wild, hap-hazard exploration in search of a short cut to fame; it proposed to carry Prestige by storm. . . .
>
> [W]hen the history of the Nineteenth Century is written, these tiny eruptions of revolt, these pamphleteering amateurs cannot remain unnoticed, for their outbreak was a symptom of the discontent of the times, a wide-felt protest of emancipation from the dictates of the old literary tribunals.[35]

As this quote makes clear, if Burgess is a decadent, he is one by virtue of his general identification with a type of fin-de-siècle culture that was the deliberate counter to not only the realist movement inspired by Howells but also to popular magazines such as *McClure's* and *The Century*. But what is most striking about Burgess's description of "the little riot of the Decadence" is his emphasis on the way any little publication associated with the Decadence had to be *designed:* he cares as much about the appearance of typeface and paper—the look of the page—as he does about whatever "impossible prose" or "doggerel rhyme" is actually printed on the page.

A good example of Burgess's fascination with the material aspects of publishing appears in the seventh number of *The Lark* (November 1895). A "Nocturnal Colloquy" is a humorous and highly imaginative conversation among a linotype machine, a lead pencil, and a typewriter. Each of the three writing media is personified and speaks in the style associated with the purposes to which each is normally put: the linotype speaks in the language of journalism, the pencil in everyday colloquialisms and hackneyed phrases, and the typewriter in business lingo. The linotype, "speaking" in newspaper columns, has trouble understanding words because "the variety of their meanings leads me astray," as in this passage:

I Was Once Wrecked

And cast upon a desert coast. After I had coasted for a considerable period, I changed the period into a dash. This last dash brought me to the very crest. The crest was, however, not as startling as the coat-of-arms—the arms were as yet unloaded; so we loaded the barrels with shot. This shot was heard for leagues—the leagues, however, gradually disbanded—the separate bands playing Yankee Doodle as they—

At this point the pencil interrupts, in cursive script: "Must have been rattled—when I try—get caught in just the other way Something of a rhymester myself—but when I get a couple good words cant shake 'em to save neck." A sample of the pencil's problem follows in the form of a poem about the sunset:

> I love to see the gorgeous purple glow
> That glows at evening when the sun sinks low
> Empurpling all the atmosphere, as slowly sinks
> The sun, bright glowing, till one really thinks
> The heavens one mass of gorgeous purple light
> as the bright sun sinks slowly out of sight

The typewriter replies to both the linotype machine and the pencil and offers a thoroughly businesslike solution:

Sirs: The misunderstanding of which you complain can, I think, be adjusted to our mutual satisfaction. If Mr. Faber finds it impossible to do without the stock of

words which he has on hand and Lino. has difficulty, as he says, in setting a precise valuation upon his goods, why cannot each manipulate the words with
which they are familiar, according to the phrases for which they are billed, thus
securing a net profit of economy and variety.[36]

The "Nocturnal Colloquy" is certainly interesting because of the playful way
in which Burgess melds form and content, or, rather, style and design. But despite Burgess's claim that design elements constitute a significant component
of literary decadence (and they do), it is clear that the lightness and whimsy
represented by the "Nocturnal Colloquy" represent a significant departure
from the decadent aesthetic.

During the two-year run of The Lark, Burgess published two additional little magazines that turned out to be even more ephemeral than The Lark itself
but are noteworthy for their design eccentricities and their problematic relationship to the Decadence. In 1896, Burgess started Le Petit Journal des Refusées, the purpose of which was to publish "contributions that had been refused
by at least three journals of repute" (Burgess, BB, 28). In this journal, Burgess
wanted to remove "all barriers of taste" in an attempt to "out-Lark The Lark"
by "send[ing] out a rollicking, whooping gabble of ultra-nonsensical verbiage,
eschewing seriousness in any form" (Burgess, BB, 25, 26). The cover of the
premier issue is striking because of its unusual trapezoidal shape (see figure 12),
featuring a central, circular design of grotesque male nudes with the following
words inscribed on their sides: "art, literature, counterpoint, vulgar fractions
[?], dress reform, yachting."[37] Presumably, these were to be the main concerns
of the journal, but it seems clear that Burgess's primary purpose was to raise
funds for himself. In the October 1895 issue of The Lark Burgess announced
that Le Petit Journal des Refusées would publish all submissions, provided they
were accompanied by "a letter of regret" from another publisher indicating
that the submission had been previously rejected—that and "cash, invariably
in advance." Publication rates were set at five dollars a page for prose and ten
dollars a page for poetry,[38] substantial amounts in 1895.

When Le Petit Journal des Refusées foundered, Burgess hit upon another idea
for raising cash by publishing Phyllida: or, the Milkmaid. Through this journal
Burgess hoped to find a society matron who would serve as an anonymous patroness and be known only by the name of the journal that she sponsored. The
appeal was made "in the manner of the old Tatler, printed in the typographical
style of 1702" (Burgess, BB, 33), as this sample address to the hoped-for patroness shows:

[Y]ou have the lighter Burden to bear in our Enterprise, P H Y L L I D A, for the Bills
you shall have to pay, will be neither so many, nor so important as the Persons it is
my Part to meet, that the name of C A L I F O R N I A may not be forever a By-Word
and a Hissing.—And while I have the Town by the Ears, if I fail, you shall rest

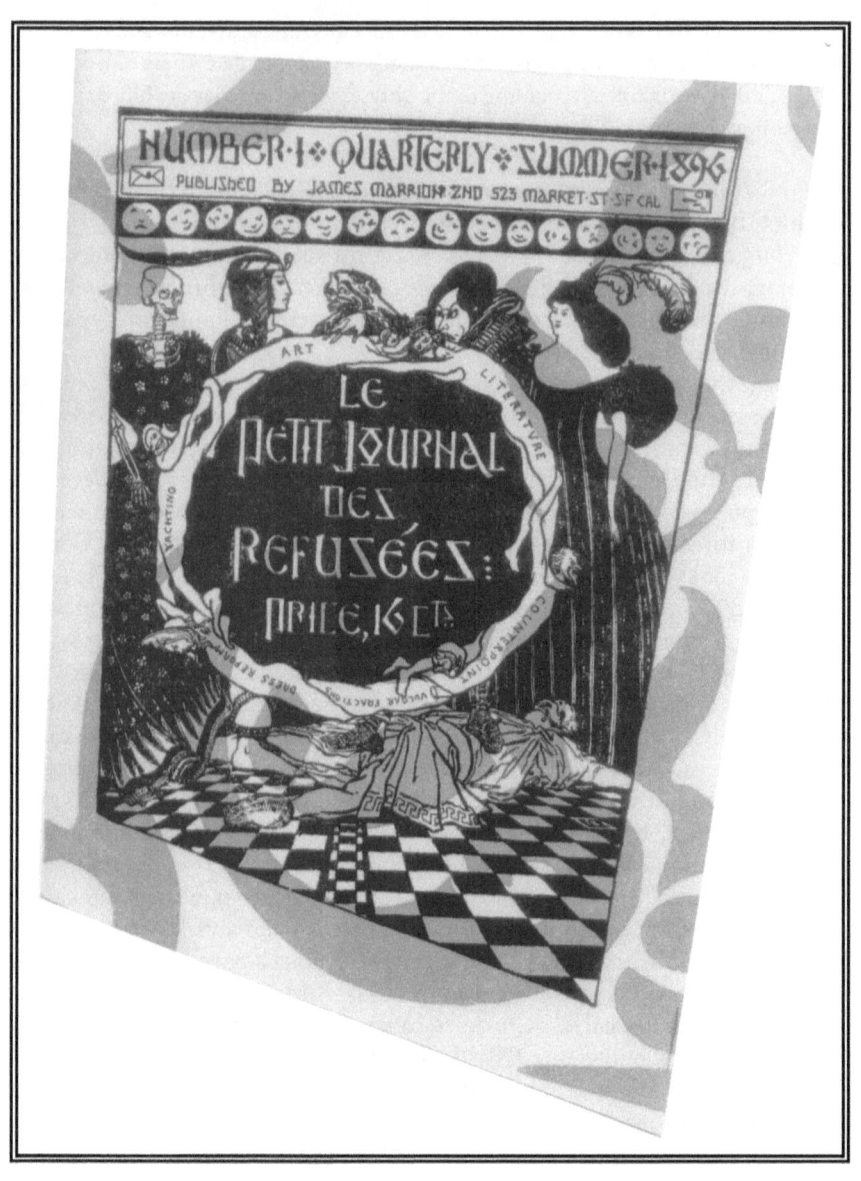

FIGURE 12   Gelett Burgess, cover design for *Le Petit Journal des Refusées* (1896)

Undiscover'd, & safe to twit me with my *Disrepute*. Yet if I should prove my Point,
I may not do the same by you, who shall then be magnify'd into a *Patroness* of the
A R T S!

Burgess later said that "*Phyllida* was an effort to give scope to literary ideas of
the more critical sort, which were too formal to be tolerated in" *The Lark*. He
added that in *Phyllida* "it was our dream to revive the art of the pleasant, personal 'short essay' of Addison and Steele" (Burgess, *BB*, 31). The venture did
not succeed—"after two numbers . . . *Phyllida* committed suicide" (Burgess,
BB, 34)—and a few months later *The Lark* folded as well. Burgess moved on to
write for *The Wave*, described as "out-and-out Society paper, chronicling all
the small-talk of the town" (Burgess, *BB*, 37). In *The Wave*, Burgess published
lightly satirical interviews and observations of vaudeville performers and burlesque dancers, as well as a few naturalistic sketches of immigrant workers in
seedy scenes, done in the manner of Frank Norris. He also offered a telling retrospective assessment of *The Lark*: "[I]t has stood for the reaction against decadence—and prophesied the renaissance."[39]

The reaction to decadence is clear enough, but it is hard to say what sort of
renaissance Burgess imagined his lighthearted *Lark* to be prophesying for, because so much of the writing in the magazine is simply silly—a joke, a lark.
Bad puns—verbal and visual—abound, as with the drawing of a roof of a
building surrounded by birds on the inside back cover of the January 1896
issue titled *Modern Larkitecture*.[40] The editors liked the joke enough to repeat
it in the next issue, this time in French as part of a bogus advertisement for a
new book, *L'Arkitecture Moderne*. The French theme continues with a drawing of a lark under an arch, captioned "L'Ark de Triompe," no less.[41] Given
this type of material, it is surprising that critics even consider *The Lark* as
somehow part of the same fin-de-siècle context that includes *The Chap-Book*
or even *The Yellow Book*. In fact, by the end of the magazine's first year the editors began to consciously distance themselves from the Decadence. "An Epi-
logue to Book the First" says that the audience for *The Lark* "are those who
prefer humor to satire, and relish both *finesse* and *naïveté*."[42] "An Essay on
Style" in the issue for July 1896 takes note of "a new school of Literature . . .
inaugurated by a few apostles of the modern" characterized by "the wedding of
Art and Decadence." It soon becomes clear that the analysis is satirical, since
"the chief characteristic of the latest style in letters is Vagueness and Vacu-
ity." The author adds that "it is extremely difficult to discriminate as to the
relative value of these two qualities, and the finer *fin-de-siècle* productions
partake largely of both. The most splendid vagueness is gotten by careful construction of sentences, which may be so involved as to cloud their meaning
beyond all hope of disentanglement."[43]

In *Le Petit Journal des Refusées*, *The Lark*'s sister magazine, the criticism of
the decadents was emphasized in one of Burgess's doggerel poems, which

has been described as "the standard alphabetical guide" [44] to the little magazine movement:

> A is for *Art* of the age-end variety;
> We *Decadents* simply can't get a satiety.
> B is for *Beardsley*, the idol supreme,
> Whose drawings are not half so bad as they seem.
> C is for *Chap-Book*, the pater familias
> Of magazines started by many a silly ass.[45]

Burgess also used his light, energetic verse to satirize the type of decadence practiced in Boston, which was much more in keeping with the British original. In "The Bohemians of Boston," Burgess turns his doggerel eye to the Jacobite gatherings that attracted Ralph Adams Cram and F. Holland Day:

> They formed a Cult, far subtler, brainier,
> Than ordinary Anglomania,
> For all as Jacobites were reckoned,
> And gaily toasted Charles the Second![46]

Though Burgess calls the group "Bohemian," the type of behavior of which they are guilty seems more typical of the British decadents: "The orchids went from bad to worse, / Made epigrams—attempted verse!" Indeed, the group is introduced as a burlesque version of English aesthetes:

> The "Orchids" were as tough a crowd
> As Boston anywhere allowed;
> It was a club of wicked men—
> The oldest twelve, the youngest, ten;
> They drank their soda colored green,
> They talked of "Art" and "Philistine,"
> They wore buff "wescoats" and their hair,
> It used to make the waiters stare!
> They were so shockingly behaved
> And Boston thought them so depraved,
> Policemen, stationed at the door,
> Would raid them every hour or more! (Foster, ed., 89–90)

The poem ends with a police raid that finds evidence of the Orchids' tendency to "make fun of Boston ways": the leader of the club has written a line of "shocking" graffiti—"*Beacon H—ll!*" (92).

Given this type of satire, it is surprising to find the odd piece of writing that seems genuinely inspired by the Decadence, as in this collection of epigrams

jointly authored by Carolyn Wells, Bruce Porter, and Gelett Burgess from October 1896, titled "Inexpensive Cynicisms":

A Profit is not without Honour save in Boston.
A Poet is not without Humour save in San Francisco.
A Lark in the Hand gathers no Moss.
Accessions will happen in the best regulated Families.
One touch of Nature makes the whole World blush.
The Course of true Love is the Route of all Evil.
Flirtation is the Thief of Time.
The Milk of human Kindness never did run smooth.
'Tis a mean Door that hath no Key Hole.
Poets are born not Maids.
Western communications corrupt good Manners.
Of two devils choose the Prettier.
It is always the Unexpensive that happens.
If a Man kiss thee on one Cheek, turn to him the Other also. So shines a
    good Deed in a naughty Girl.

The choice of title suggests that this brief list of "Inexpensive Cynicisms" may
owe some debt to Bierce's entries for *The Devil's Dictionary* in his "Prattle" columns, which Burgess was sure to have read in the *Examiner*. But the epigrams
also suggest Wilde's "Phrases and Philosophies for the Use of the Young." Either way, what makes the list of cynical epigrams stand out from so much of
The Lark's literary offerings is the attention to language, a certain care of style
not always evident in the little journal's pages. What the authors do in many
cases is freshen a familiar saying by the clever substitution of a word or phrase,
as with the replacement of "flirtation" for "procrastination" in "Flirtation is
the Thief of Time," or the punning combination of two shopworn axioms into
one to make something entirely new: "The Course of true Love is the Route of
all Evil."

As this epigram illustrates, the San Francisco group cultivated a kind of Bohemian naughtiness to counter whatever they imagined Philistine morality to
be. That Burgess and his friends were more bohemian than decadent is shown
not only by the deliberate distance they placed between themselves and the
Boston and Chicago groups but also by their removal from the middle class. Of
course, the Boston group removed themselves from the middle class as well, but
in their case the social trajectory of the removal was upward, fueled, in large
measure, by F. Holland Day's considerable fortune. The Norwood estate where
the Boston decadents gathered was a long way, geographically and socially,
from Camp Ha-Ha where the San Francisco bohemians disported themselves.

Burgess provided readers of *The Lark* with a fanciful map of his cultural explorations in the issue of 1 March 1896. "A Map of Bohemia" (see figure 13)

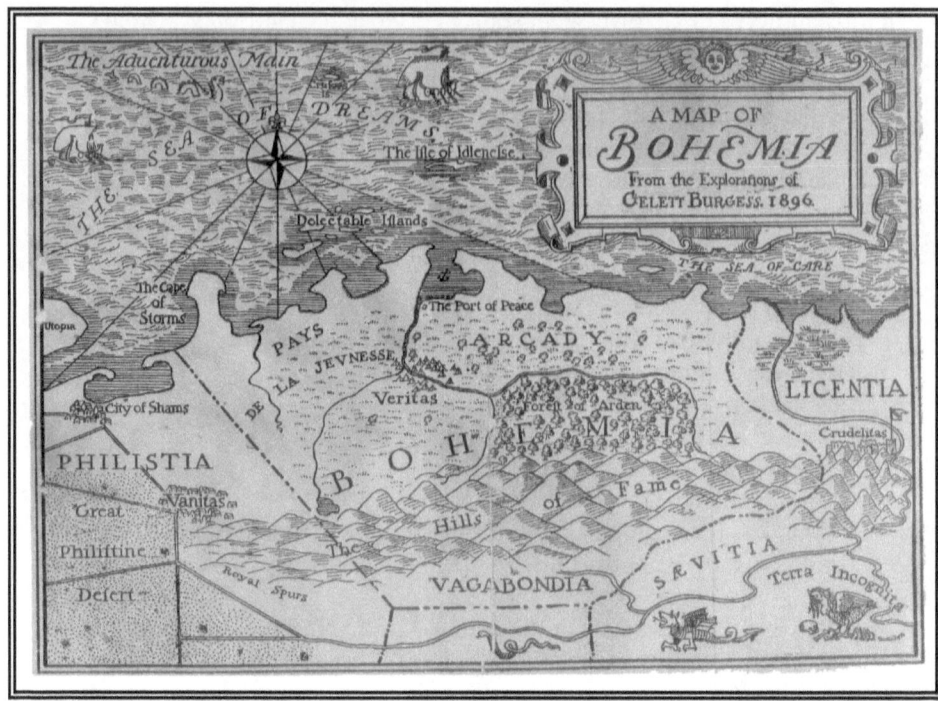

FIGURE 13   Gelett Burgess, *A Map of Bohemia* (1896)

makes clear Burgess's identification with one of the earliest of California's many countercultural movements. By Burgess's reckoning, "Bohemia" lies between the provinces of "Philistia" and "Licentia." Within Philistia and Licentia are, respectively, "Vanitas" and "Crudelitas," regions evidently intended to emphasize, allegorically, the dangerous extremes of each province. By contrast, Bohemia includes the "Pays de la Jeunesse" (Country of Youth), which leads to "Truth." Moreover, a river runs from the foothills of "Fame" and the "Forest of Arden" through the planes of "Arcady" to the "Port of Peace." Since Burgess has drawn stylized tents in the idealized landscape where youth, truth, and "Arcady" meet, most likely the place is meant as Camp Ha-Ha, and the Forest of Arden stands in for the redwood forests north of San Francisco. San Francisco itself is likely represented as the "City of Shams" in the province of Philistia, with routes leading (south?) to the great Philistine desert.

Despite the idealization of Bohemia in Burgess's fanciful map, and despite the antidecadent fulminations that occasionally appeared in *The Lark*, Burgess reconnected with the decadent movement not long after the little magazine expired when he published a slight but delightful novel, *Vivette, or The Memoirs of the Romance Association*, in 1897. Based on sketches that had originally appeared in *The Lark*, the book was published in a fine edition by Copeland and Day with gilt-lettered red boards embossed with the emblem of the fictional association. Especially notable are the endpapers, featuring a map drawn by Burgess himself of the fictional town of Millamours where the action of the novel takes place (see figure 14). A more urban version of the "Map of Bohemia" that appeared in *The Lark*, the Millamours map is likewise allegorical but tuned to a gentler register of romanticism than the earlier exercise in imaginative cartography: street names include "Moonlight Row," "Valentine Quay," "Maiden Lane," and the like. The plan of the fictional city might be intended to suggest the San Francisco of Burgess's recent imaginative experience; a major thoroughfare is "Lark Street," which runs from "Joyeuse Road" through "Trysting Corners" to "Gallant Street." One episode in the novel is set in the "Lark café," and another recounts the hero and heroine's adventures in the publishing trade when they decide to bring out an extremely *Lark*-like journal. The little magazine achieves renown for its "subtle vagaries and high-flown humor," its "sense in the guise of absurdity, and non-sense masquerading as reason."[47] The magazine is called *Phyllida, or the Milkmaid*, the name, of course, of one of *The Lark*'s short-lived sister publications. The resemblance of the "Phyllida" of the novel to *The Lark* is certified by one of the many amusing running heads in the book: "Erratum. . . : for 'Milkmaid,' read 'Lark'" (V 84). In the novel, when *Phyllida* ceases publication it is replaced by *La Revue Jeune*, which is printed "in that fascinating 8 X 12 size of 'The Tatler,' with square wood-cut initials and double columns, the proper names in small caps" (V 84). And this, of course, is a description of the real-life *Phyllida, or the Milkmaid*, but the name of the fictional journal also alludes to "Les Jeunes," the designation Burgess and his fellow San Franciscans used for their bohemian group. Moreover, the new magazine is advertised with a doggerel poem that recalls the rhythms of the already-famous "Purple Cow," which appeared in the first issue of *The Lark*:

> I never read the 'Revue Jeune,'
>   I never care to read it;
> But if I live its wit to learn,
>   Then, Lord, how I shall need it!

What happens in Millamours, in short, bears more than a slight resemblance to occurrences in the city of Burgess's first—and only—success.

The novel is replete with the sort of self-conscious—and somewhat self-congratulatory—in-jokes described above, but the main action of the narrative concerns the love affair of the narrator, Richard (Robin) Redforth, and Vivette, one of the principals of the Romance Association. As the novel begins,

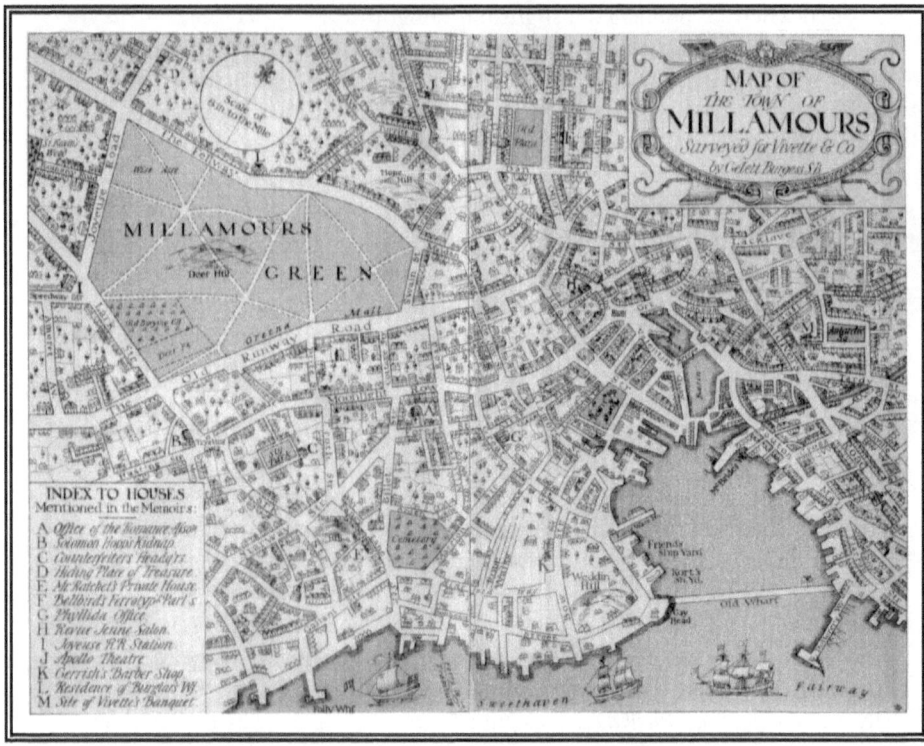

FIGURE 14   Gelett Burgess, *Map of Millamours* (1897)

Robin applies for a job with the association on the basis of his past experience as an actor and author. These two professions perfectly qualify the narrator for the association, the purpose of which, as the director explains, is to provide to a paying clientele real-life experiences of activities normally limited to the pages of romance novels: "We are, in a way, in the enterprise of retailing romance—or wholesaling it, for that matter—we force Fate; we make interesting things happen. And what, after all, is our Association but the true *Theatre Libre?* Instead of set scenes and painted flats, we perform on the picturesque stage of Life" (V, 7–8). The allusion to André Antoine's Théâtre Libre, the avant-garde company that premiered Ibsen's *Ghosts* in Paris, suggests a fin-de-siècle interest in mixing the aesthetic modes of naturalism and symbolism. Such a mixture is consistent with the device that drives the novel throughout, a device perfected, if not pioneered, by Oscar Wilde: the use of art as a superior substitute for life.

After testing Robin's abilities to improvise romantic adventures in reality, the director assigns him to his first case: the task is to enliven the humdrum existence of one Solomon Hopp, who calls on the Romance Association "as a last resort" because he has "lived five and forty years without having been rejuvenated by anything worth being called an adventure" (V, 11). Armed with the information that Hopp's library is "stocked to a plethora with the novels of . . . [the] less subtle disciples of Poe," Robin and Vivette together contrive to entangle the client in a web of criminal intrigue that is so verisimilar Hopp has no inkling of the artifice. In fact, so convinced is he that his adventures are the real thing he visits the association to cancel his one-month trial subscription after only two weeks or so: "'The fact is,' said Hopp, 'that I have had such surprising adventures with a gang of criminals this month, that I hardly need make use of the company's assistance'" (V, 15). When the director presents the client with irrefutable evidence that the reality he has experienced was contrived by the association—that is, that what he thought was real was really art—Hopp awakens from his "happy dream" and demands an annual subscription on the spot (V, 16). The evidence that convinces him that what he thought was real is artificial after all is a receipt for $287, itemizing one of the association's expenses in the perpetuation of the ruse. The figure matches the amount of "counterfeit" bills Hopp has received from the gang of "criminals" with whom he has so recently cavorted. The Romance Association has pulled off the artifice of reality by substituting actual banknotes for fake currency.

In the course of working together on such dizzying assignments, Robin and Vivette fall in love. Their courtship consists of an elaborate game of mutual seduction in which Vivette pretends to be an anonymous client whom Robin courts over the telephone, in a kind of modern embodiment of a highly condensed epistolary novel. The epistolary form, so seminal to the romance genre, resurfaces after the couple have been married for a while and come to realize that their romance has been too romantic. Vivette concludes that "the only correct diversion for such a romantic couple" has to be "the most commonplace Realism" (V, 65). To experience ordinary, realistic love, husband and wife advertise for partners in the *Matrimonial Times*. Vivette describes herself as "[a] sparkling, gracile brunette of twenty-three, who might be the daughter of D'Artagnan and Little Dorit" (V, 67–68), the allusions to Dumas and Dickens being sure to attract the most pedestrian or "realistic" correspondents. Likewise, Robin's advertisement is in the style of a popular novelist which makes him out to be "a slashing hero of the Ouida sort" (V, 68). When the letters arrive in reply to the couple's *Matrimonial Times* announcements, Robin and Vivette spend many happy hours pairing up the correspondents and readdressing envelopes to complete the process of epistolary match-making as far as they can take it. But they reserve the two most "realistic" correspondents for themselves: Miss Alicia Featherbone and Mr. Arthur Ragelsburg Rachet. Robin and Vivette pretend affection for their respective "mates" and succeed in making each other mildly jealous. The exercise in "realism" ends when Vivette sets up an assignation with Mr. Rachet and Robin arranges a tryst with Miss Feather-bone, at an address on "Fancy Lane" (V, 73), no less. But the couple, after all, are a pair of master manipulators with the Romance Association, so the plot has a double twist: when Robin calls on Miss Featherbone he does so in the pose of Mr. Rachet, and Vivette receives him in the role of Miss Featherbone, each lover having anticipated the other's deceptive fidelity.

One of Burgess's running heads in *Vivette* might be used to characterize the aesthetic that seems to have guided the author: "I Juggle with Feathers" (V, 57). Indeed, the combination of stylistic dexterity and thematic lightness re-minds the reader of Aubrey Beardsley's *Under the Hill*, but without the rococo sexuality. Certainly Beardsley must be counted as an influence on Burgess, whose line drawings for *The Lark* occasionally suggest his British counterpart's work for *The Yellow Book*. In *Vivette*, the only outright allusion to Beardsley comes when the heroine takes up photography and fashions "*outré* wall-paper costumes for Beardsley poses" (V, 75), but there is a more general sense of play-ful naughtiness about the novel that suggests Beardsley. The epigrams of Wilde are also suggested at times, as in this exchange of cynical witticisms:

> "Truly, it is only the luxuries that are necessary," mused Vivette.
> "And necessity knows no law," replied [a minor character].
> "The gods give nuts to those that have no teeth," said [Robin].
> "Then they should get false ones!" (V, 126–27)

All of these minor stylistic flourishes—together with the clever conflation of art and life—ally Burgess's bagatelle of a book with decadence, but a deca-dence so airy and light as to almost belie the alliance. As a stylist, Burgess has something in common with his heroine; when Vivette writes, she produces "pastel[s] in prose" (V, 81). The phrase alludes to a book by the American ex-patriate poet Stuart Merrill (1863–1915), whose *Pastels in Prose* (1890) intro-duced Americans to French decadent-symbolist writers, but it may also stand as a description of *Vivette* itself. Self-conscious; playful; whimsical; somehow subtle and silly at the same time, *Vivette, or The Memoirs of the Romance Asso-ciation* might inspire some critics to call it "postmodernist" were it not so com-pletely pre-. And how does the novel end? With the heroine Vivette becom-ing a mere dot in the sky—aboard a balloon disappearing into the blue: the perfect ending for a work of fiction lighter than air.

iii

Even though Burgess's sunny nonsense is the obverse of Bierce's dark cyni-cism, Burgess occupies a cultural space in fin-de-siècle San Francisco that would have been nigh impossible without Bierce's example. Burgess operated in an artistic realm that Bierce himself neither claimed nor condemned. Had he attempted a psychological novel in the manner of James or tried a realist work in the style of Howells, Burgess would surely have drawn critical fire from the great Bierce in his role as Western literary czar. In a way, Burgess resembles Bierce in that both men set themselves against the genteel tradition and the cultural hegemony of the magazine-publishing house establishment, albeit in rather different ways. The cynical wit attacked that establishment, while the genial humorist provided a light-hearted alternative to it. And if Bierce took no notice of Burgess, the reason most likely lies in the kind of literature that Burgess produced, which Bierce, like most critics since, would hardly consider literature at all. For Bierce, the cultural hierarchy of the arts endorsed by Hegel still obtained: poetry was queen over all, the highest of the arts. Moreover, poetry held a special place in Bierce's aesthetic understanding as a marker of a nation's maturity. Bierce himself had tried and, he thought, failed to raise the nation's cultural prestige by means of poetry, but he thought the project essential to make America the equal of Europe: "What makes a nation mature? Its trippers gaping at the arts of other nations? Its commercially-minded politicians? Its politically-minded shopkeepers? No, its poets. Beyond question it would be a brave undertaking to place American poetry on a level with the poetry of the mature nations of Europe. A few among us have thought they could do it, and failed. Some day someone is going to succeed."[48] In 1892, Bierce was introduced to George Sterling, newly arrived in the Bay Area from the East Coast to work in his uncle's real estate office in Oakland. The two men—one fifty, the other twenty-three—developed one of those master-disciple relationships so important to Bierce, who began to groom the younger man to become the great American poet who would make the nation mature. Significantly, Bierce was instrumental in placing Sterling's "Memorial Day, 1901" ode in the *Washington Post* and commented that the younger poet's verses recalled his own "Invocation" ode written for Independence Day (MMM, 78–79). The two odes were obviously paired in Bierce's mind as dual efforts toward the establishment of the elusive maturity that America lacked. But Sterling turned out to be a bad choice for any mission to maturity, let alone a national one. Certainly the bohemian, hedonistic Sterling seems an odd choice of disciple for the man who defined "Once" as an adverb meaning "Enough" (*DD*, 136).

If George Sterling is known at all today, it is not so much for his poetry as for his role as the leader of the San Francisco bohemian community in the early twentieth century. Dubbed the "King of Bohemia" by the newspaperman Idwal Jones,[49] Sterling founded an artist's colony at Carmel-by-the-Sea south of San Francisco after the earthquake of 1906 destroyed most of the city's bohemian haunts.[50] Sterling's involvement with bohemianism complicates his relationship to decadence and begs the question of the difference between the two cultural phenomena. While it would be wrong to insist on hard-and-fast distinctions, the bohemian normally cultivates class associations in the lower reaches of society in an effort to form a communal alternative to bourgeois life, whereas the decadent aims for aristocratic isolation from society altogether. Sterling's own explanation of Bohemianism shows an understanding of this class distinction: "There are two elements, at least, that are essential to Bohemianism. The first is devotion or addiction to one or more of the Seven Arts; the other is poverty. Other factors suggest themselves: for instance, I like to think of my Bohemians as young, as radical in their outlook on art and life, as unconventional, and, though this is debatable, as dwellers in a city large enough to have the somewhat cruel atmosphere of all great cities."[51] The last "debatable" point about the cruelty of great cities might be taken as a point in favor of decadence rather than bohemianism, but for the most part Sterling's definition will serve. In San Francisco, however, the social factor of poverty is rendered problematic by the exclusive nature of the Bohemian Club, founded in 1872 and still in existence today. The club owns close to 2,500 acres of redwood forest near Monte Rio known as the "Bohemian Grove," where every year since 1879 an all-male, members-only celebration takes place known as the "High-Jinks"; the festivities feature the presentation of plays in an outdoor theater.[52] In 1907 Sterling's verse drama *The Triumph of Bohemia* was presented at the grove theater during the midsummer Jinks, acted by members of the club, described by one commentator as the "fat businessmen of San Francisco out on a Summer picnic."[53] In 1903 Bierce warned against membership in the Bohemian Club, saying he had known it "to be the ruin of many a promising youngster" (*MMM*, 105). But Sterling evidently saw no need to separate himself from the bourgeois Bohemian Club, whose exclusive membership included the city's business and political leaders, in order to keep up the artist's colony at Carmel, which included, at one time or another, such luminaries of American literature as Jack London, Sinclair Lewis, Upton Sinclair, and Robinson Jeffers.

The social confusion of the San Francisco bohemian scene is matched by a number of cultural contradictions that make the California variant harder to reconcile with traditional notions of bohemianism. Usually, it is fairly easy to distinguish between the types of culture that the bohemian and the decadent either produce or appropriate. The fiction of *La Bohême*, either in the form of Murget's novel or Puccini's opera, more or less dooms the eponymous bohemian to repeat *ad nauseam* the conflict between a romantic, liberating lifestyle and the repressive demands of bourgeois society. In Sterling's verse drama *The Triumph of Bohemia* the contest takes the form of the personified figures of "Mammon" and the "Spirit of Bohemia." Mammon and Bohemia wage deadly rhetorical warfare over the souls of the woodmen who populate the grove, asking them to choose between money and all that money makes possible—"The wild wine singing madly in your veins! / The white, permissive breasts!"—and the "lasting happiness" that comes with the adoration of Nature: "Great Nature, refuge of the weary heart, / And only balm to breasts that have been bruised!" Asked to make a choice, the woodmen opt for the simple pleasures of Bohemia, whereupon the wisdom of their choice is revealed when an *"immense owl"* descends and attacks Mammon, who, *"hearing the rush of its wings, turns and dies at its touch."*[54] As this painful example illustrates, the bohemian experiences the conflict of materialism and happiness as a life-or-death *agon* that he—or, in this case, the reader—must suffer through.

The decadent, by contrast, avoids the *agon* altogether by casting the conflict as one between art and life and then by simply substituting one for the other. To live life as art, to render the natural as artificial as possible, is the goal of the decadent imagination. The bohemian thinks of art as the natural expression of a life that he must struggle to maintain, while the decadent imagines art as the artificial alternative to a life that is too boring to contemplate. But again, these distinctions are too pat and simplistic to describe the San Francisco bohemians of the fin de siècle. One of Sterling's contemporaries says that sometimes the group would set decadent lyrics to music and sing them around the campfire, as was the case with Arthur Symond's "Ode to a Greek Girl."[55] The odd association of decadent-aesthetic culture and the great outdoors probably owes something to Joaquin Miller, the frontier poet who became a sensation in the London of the 1870s and was much admired by Oscar Wilde and Dante Gabriel Rossetti. Sometime after 1901 Sterling and Jack London visited Miller at his home in the Piedmont hills and heard the old poet share his memories of Wilde. He was especially sympathetic in his assessment of *De Profundis,* Wilde's self-flagellating account of his affair with Lord Alfred Douglas, only recently published in America. London called *De Profundis* "a Salvation Army tract," but Sterling, according to the first-hand account of his friend Joseph Noel, "was less critical of the book's message or lack of it, arguing that the beauty of the writing justified everything Wilde said."[56] This is a telling comment, given Wilde's deep sense of guilt and degradation over the affair with Douglas, and looks forward to Sterling's own capacity for degradation and self-destruction.

One of the few book-length studies of Sterling characterizes him as "An American Decadent," to give the chapter title of Thomas E. Benedicktsson's assessment of the poet's mature work. For Benedicktsson, Sterling's poetry "exploit[s] the Decadent interest in neurosis and the Decadent impulse for personal degradation."[57] To my mind, Sterling is less interested in *la nevrose,* at least as one finds it depicted in Baudelaire and Huysmans, and more involved with degradation, as described by Wilde and Ernest Dowson. Also, one might question whether mere descriptions of degradation (as in *Dorian Gray* or "Cynara") merit the name of decadence, which implies an abstruse refinement of pleasure that seems the obverse of the excesses that degradation demands. But Benedicktsson is on much firmer ground when he claims to find "nearly every characteristic of Decadence" in Sterling's poems: "the search for novelty, the interest in the exotic and the unnatural, the aesthetic assumption that poetry is a means of enchantment, with a concurrent emphasis on language as an evocative and connotative instrument, the rhetorical ornamentation (resting at times in a disintegration of artistic unity), the scorn of contemporary society, and the many allusions to an exotic past."[58] To this list, cribbed from *The Princeton Encyclopedia of Poetry and Poetics*,[59] I would add the characteristic note of pessimism that Sterling derived, at least in part, from Bierce. Joseph Noel records that Sterling "was sure that the universe . . . was a monstrous invention of some malignant spirit who hated mankind" (Noel, 99).

In some ways Sterling goes further in his pessimism than Bierce does, as Sterling's centenary ode on the birth of Robert Browning suggests. In this poem, published first in the *Boston Transcript* in 1912, Sterling compares the great Victorian poet to his American contemporaries and of course finds the latter lacking, not to mention the shortcomings of his own pathetic self:

> But who am I to speak,
> Far down the mountain, of its altar-peak,
>   Or cross on feeble wings,
> Adventurous, the oceans in thy mind?
> We of a wider day's bewilderings
>   For very light seem blind,
> And fearful of the gods our hands have formed.
>   Some lift their eyes and seem
> To see at last the lofty human scheme
> Fading and toppling as a sunset stormed
> By wind and evening, with the stars in doubt.[60]

The pessimistic sentiment expressed here is typical of one type of decadent mind: cultural decline is a harbinger of a more general, even apocalyptic ruin. Now that Browning is gone, Sterling says, the end of civilization cannot be far behind. At the same time, Sterling's poetry forces consideration of another type of decadence. In addition to the various "positive" markers of decadence that Benedicktsson enumerates (search for novelty, rhetorical ornamentation, and so on), the negative feature of outworn conventionality is also much in evidence in Sterling's poetry. As Jack London's daughter Joan observed, even though Sterling "wrote continuously through the first two decades of the twentieth century he gave back no echo of the new tempos and themes so clearly caught by those after 1912 who brought about the renascence of American verse."[61] The imagist revolution in poetry was well underway when Sterling wrote his Browning ode, Ezra Pound having published *Personae* in 1909. Yet Sterling continued to write in conventional verse forms, no doubt because of the early influence of Bierce, a master of prosody. Ironically, Bierce was one of the first American critics to admire

Pound (MMM, 199, 201), but Sterling took no notice of the literary innovations going on about him.[62]

Sterling's masterwork is generally taken to be "A Wine of Wizardry," first published in *Cosmopolitan* in 1907 with an introduction by Bierce full of ostentatious praise for his protégé's poetic achievement. "Whatever length of days may be accorded to this magazine," Bierce wrote, "it is not likely to do anything more notable in literature than it accomplished in this issue by the publication of Mr. George Sterling's poem, 'A Wine of Wizardry.'"[63] In addition to the introduction, Bierce also provided an essay, "A Poet and His Poem," that can be used to argue that Bierce had at last found the poet who would usher America into the ranks of "mature" nations: "I steadfastly believe and heartily affirm that George Sterling is a very great poet—incomparably the greatest that we have on this side of the Atlantic. And of this particular poem, I hold that not in a lifetime, has our literature had any new thing of equal length containing so much poetry and so little else. . . . It has all the imagination of 'Comus' and all the fancy of 'The Fairie Queene.'"[64] These remarks show that Bierce had found in Sterling's poem something true to the aesthetic that guided his own pen when he wrote his *Tales of Soldiers and Civilians*: the farther removed from reality a work of literature was the better it was. In March 1902 Bierce wrote Sterling on the importance of poetry's removal from reality: "[I]f poets saw things as they are they would write no more poetry" (MMM, 83). "A Wine of Wizardry" is nothing if not fantastic, as the first mention of the poem in the Bierce-Sterling correspondence shows. In a letter of 8 January 1904 Bierce quotes with admiration the sensational lines—"The blue-eyed vampire, sated at her feast, / Smiles bloodily against the leprous moon"—and says they "give me the shivers. Gee! they're awful!" (MMM, 116), meaning "full of awe." But Bierce's romantic-sublime aesthetic is not fully adequate to describe the poem, and Benedicktsson is right to place the poem in the fin-de-siècle decadent-symbolist tradition, however belated and conventional that tradition becomes in the mannered hands of Sterling.

"A Wine of Wizardry" is a fairly straightforward exercise in poetic imagination, personified as Fancy. At the opening of the poem, the first-person narrator, presumably the poet, pours himself a glass of wine and "observes" his fancy take flight, aided not only by the wine but also by opium: "Now Fancy, empress of a purpled realm, / Awakes with brow caressed by poppy-bloom, / And wings in sudden dalliance her flight" (ll. 7–8). The first part of the poem charts the flight of Fancy using the points of the compass: she first "wanders to an iceberg oriflammed / With rayed, auroral guidons of the North"; then "hastens . . . to a lone, / Immortal garden of the eastern hours" (ll. 34–35); next "seeks a stainéd twilight of the South" (l. 68); and finally "Flies to a violet headland of the West" (l. 90). Each quarter of the globe is rife with fantastic, directionally appropriate imagery. In the North, Fancy encounters "artic elves" who "have hidden wintry gems / And treasuries of frozen anadems, / Alight with timid

sapphires of the snow" (ll. 23–25). In the East, or, more specifically, "in a Syrian treasure-house," Fancy "pours, / From caskets rich and amethysine urns, /
Dull fires of dusty jewels" (ll. 48–51). The South boasts "tiger-lilies known to
silent ghouls, / Whose king has digged a somber carcanet / And necklaces with
fevered opals set" (ll. 86–88). The West, in keeping with the crepuscular quality of decadence, is ariot with rich, synaesthetic imagery, especially in the
"deep-hued ocean" of that region:

> The tiny twilight in the jacinth set,
> The wintry orb the moonstone crystal holds.
> Snapt coral twigs and winy agates wet,
> Translucencies of jasper, and the folds
> Of banded onyx, and vermilion breast
> Of cinnabar. (ll. 95–100)

The first part of the poem ends with Fancy completing her underwater exploration of "the ocean's phosphorescent caves" (l. 110) in some hitherto uncharted
region of the West. Thus far, the poet's imagination has been limited, more or
less, to a phantasmagoric vision of the real world, despite the odd reference to
elves and gnomes that give the poem a slightly overwrought Wagnerian feel.

    Roughly midway through "A Wine of Wizardry" the poem becomes overtly
otherworldly and diabolic in a way that seems calculated to shock. Fancy first
"smiles to see / Black incense glow, and scarlet bellied snakes / Sway to the
tawny flutes of sorcery" (ll. 114–16). Soon she is entertained by "priestesses in
purple robes" (l. 117) and then by the great Circe herself, queen of all the sor-
ceresses, who regards the suffering of the men she poisons with great delectation, as she "listens to her victim's moan, and sips / Her darkest wine, and
smiles with wicked lips" (ll. 145–46). The sadism of this scene is amplified in
the next, when "Fancy . . . turns / To caverns where a demon altar burns, / And
Satan, yawning on his brazen seat, / Fondles a screaming thing his fiends have
flayed" (ll. 155–58). "But Fancy is unsatisfied" with this diabolic demonstra-
tion of sadism and seeks for visions somehow more destructive and intense.
"The sins of demons" (l. 190) culminate in the lines about the "blue-eyed
vampire" that so thrilled Ambrose Bierce, and the adventures of Fancy are
stilled for the evening. "A Wine of Wizardry" ends when the poet contem-
plates an old saying about vipers lurking in wine-cups and meditates on the
exotic exploits of Fancy he has witnessed: "And I . . . / Gaze pensively upon
the way she went, / Drink at her font, and smile as one content" (ll. 206–07).

    The poem is "decadent" insofar as it recapitulates much of the imagery and
some of the themes of an earlier literature that had become known by that epithet by the time Sterling wrote the poem. The style might fairly be called "jeweled," not only because of the many images of gems and minerals that recall
such lists as the one in Wilde's *Picture of Dorian Gray* but also because of the

self-conscious effort at florid, ornamental diction. The general conceit that posits the entire poem as a literary record of the effects of drugs and alcohol of course has precedence in Thomas de Quincey's *Confessions of an English Opium Eater,* although that work is less important to the decadent canon in itself than it is to the works it inspired, notably Baudelaire's prose poems about the experience of hashish. Indeed, "A Wine of Wizardry" might fairly be described as a versified prose poem on a common theme of decadence. Likewise, the jaded references to Satanism and sadism seem a versified version of the fuller exploration of diabolism that Huysmans set down in *Là Bas.* In Baudelaire and Huysmans, however, the unconventional themes are presented in the form of avant-garde art, and there is a sense of harmony and consistency between the authors' formal experimentation and the novel experiences their literature recounts. Sterling, by contrast, is adamantly and deliberately old-fashioned: "A Wine of Wizardry" is that odd work that is simultaneously prodecadent and antimodernist. Another way of understanding the difference between Baudelaire and Sterling is to say that Baudelaire writes, as Gautier first observed, in the style of decadence; that is, in a style appropriate to the cultural upheaval of the late stages of empire. Sterling, by contrast, writes in a decadent style; that is, in a derivative style that reveals the poet's reliance on cultural convention rather than imaginative invention.

The retrograde aesthetic that guided Sterling through "A Wine of Wizardry" might have been forgiven in 1904 when the poem was composed, but it became rapidly antiquated with the rise of the imagist-modernist renaissance in poetry. In 1916 Harriet Monroe, despite having accepted a handful of Sterling's work when she founded *Poetry* in 1912, made the critical judgment that separated Sterling once and for all from his modernist contemporaries. Of his overwrought imagery and inflated diction, Monroe observed: "The truth is, this sort of pomposity has died the death. If the imagists have done nothing else, they have punctured the gas bag—English poetry will henceforth be more compact and stern—'as simple as prose,' perhaps. . . . When Mr. Sterling learns to avoid the 'luscious tongue' and the 'honeyed vine,' he may become the poet he was meant to be."[65] Sterling, of course, had been encouraged to uphold the grand manner in poetry by Bierce, who found intolerable any kind of experimentation, including free verse, which he termed "Whitmaniacal" (MMM, 154).

When Bierce vanished into the Mexican Revolution in 1913, he and Sterling were no longer on familiar terms, in part because of Bierce's moral objections to Sterling's adolescent womanizing. Although Sterling continued to enjoy the prestige conferred on him by the great man's enthusiastic approval, his star had set by the time the modernists arrived, more or less around the same time that Bierce disappeared. Fortunately for Sterling, he gained the support of the most influential critic after Bierce, and the man who was probably more like Bierce than anyone since: H. L. Mencken. As S. T. Joshi observes,

"Mencken is . . . in many ways a twentieth-century Bierce: his tartly satiric journalism bears numerous similarities with Bierce's long-running 'Prattle' column in the *San Francisco Examiner*, and Mencken's brief collection of satirical definitions, 'The Jazz Webster,' is nothing more than a compressed *Devil's Dictionary*."[66] Indeed, Mencken admired the *Devil's Dictionary*, as well as *Tales of Soldiers and Civilians*, and had a good deal of respect for the man himself, having "enjoyed the curious experience of going to a funeral with him." On this macabre occasion, Bierce delighted Mencken with "a long series of gruesome but highly amusing witticisms," including the suggestion that the dead man's ashes—probably Percival Pollard's—"be molded into bullets and shot at publishers." Mencken was especially fond of Bierce's epigrams and said of one— "Ah, that we could fall into women's arms without falling into their hands"— "it is hard to find a match for that in Oscar himself."[67] Hence Mencken, for one, found in Bierce a link to the Decadence, even as he found in Sterling an ally against modernism. Mencken was also on the scene in San Francisco when George Sterling died, a suicide by cyanide, in a room at the Bohemian Club. Thomas Beer was also on hand that night, drinking with Mencken in the Club as Sterling lay dead or dying in a room upstairs.[68] It is an odd concurrence: Bierce's disciple, Bierce's twentieth-century avatar, and the chronicler of Bierce's decade, at the same place, at the same time. The year was 1926; Beer had just published *The Mauve Decade*, the first-ever account of American decadence, a book that not only reflects on decadence but also contributes to its revival.

CHAPTER SIX

The Decadent Revival

Shortly before the United States entered World War I different groups of Americans began to renew the interest in the culture of decadence that had circulated among artistic circles in the late nineteenth century. The conclusion follows that America's literary tastes might be related, in some measure, to the ideological inclinations of the nation's political leaders. Continental, "feminine" decadence did not survive the muscular imperialism and jingoism of the Roosevelt era, even though a few isolated decadents, such as Henry Blake Fuller, made ineffectual protest against the extension of the American frontier and the expansion of American values that occurred as the nation entered the twentieth century. A decade or so later, the idealism and internationalism of Woodrow Wilson's administration (1913–1921) perhaps made it easier for American intellectuals and artists to cultivate Continental culture on native ground. Also, the disillusion and despair that followed the Great War, as registered in works such as T. S. Eliot's *Waste Land*, added the qualities of pessimism and disaffection so crucial to decadent culture. Whatever the causes, there is no question that just before World War I a fair number of American writers and critics began to take an interest in decadence, again. The reasons for this interest vary from group to group and add up to a rather complex cultural phenomenon with several lines of development, some of them overlapping.

First, and most familiar, are the expatriate writers now known as High Modernists, such as Ezra Pound and Eliot, who drew inspiration for their own work from the French decadent tradition, Baudelaire especially. Second, and less well known, are the journalists and publishers who understood Continental decadence as a form of high culture expressive of a "modern," revolutionary sensibility that broke with the past and was experienced as liberating and new. Of course, the "modern" culture that journalists such as James Huneker celebrated was not at all new but belonged to the fin de siècle. Yet it was new to most Americans, and Huneker made a career of introducing these "moderns" as iconoclasts, without taking a great deal of care to distinguish the finer points of culture and politics they represented (figures as dissimilar as Huysmans, Ibsen, Nietzsche, and Mirbeau were all presented as if cut from the same "iconoclastic" cloth). Along with this spirited dissemination of decadence on the part of journalists, book publishers eager to capitalize on new "modern" tastes built up their lists by reprinting works from the decadent tradition. For example, Boni and Liveright's Modern Library imprint relied almost exclusively on fin-de-siècle authors in its first year of business (1917). In this context the death of William Dean Howells in 1920 was opportune, since he symbolized—fairly or not—an older tradition of genteel realism no longer felt to be relevant to the new tastes of a rapidly changing America. Likewise, the Pulitzer Prize awarded posthumously in 1919 to Henry Adams for *The Education of Henry Adams* is a telling sign of shifting tastes.

A third development in the decadent revival is the reappearance, in print, of some of the original American decadents of the fin de siècle. Huneker and Fuller, both in their late fifties when the revival began, contributed to the renewal by publishing novels that drew on their earlier experience of cultural and social decadence in New York and Chicago. Finally, the effort to popularize decadence as something new and "modern" inevitably led to the production of some literature that was decadent in more traditional senses: it was outworn, belated, moribund, mannered. A prime example of this decadent decadence is *The Prophet* by Kahlil Gibran. Hence the decadent revival is also a decline of decadence, but only partly. Decadence anew in the teens and twenties involves many paradoxes, not the least of which was a kind of counterrevival, a tendency to treat decadence itself *à rebours*. Strangely, during the revival it was possible to take decadent and antidecadent positions simultaneously, as the career of H. L. Mencken shows. As the dominant literary and social critic in America during the 1920s, Mencken had the power to make or break any writer affiliated with decadence; and that is exactly what he did—he made some and broke others.

i

H. L. Mencken is too vigorous a writer for the decadent tradition, yet his career was shaped by that tradition in curious and paradoxical ways. His lifelong campaign against Puritanism and his insistence that art and morality remain separate sectors of human endeavor put him in the company of such decadent-aesthetic authors as Walter Pater and George Moore, even though he did not take either author as a model for his own style.[1] Likewise, Oscar Wilde is another writer for whom the removal of morality from art was of critical importance, and Mencken was one of the earliest to argue for a resuscitation of Wilde's reputation solely on the basis of his work, despite whatever reservations he might have had about the man's sexuality. Mencken urged the public to forget that Wilde had been "careless of the decencies" and to remember instead his contributions to literature: "He restored wit to the English drama. . . ; he made sound and permanent contributions to English criticism; and he left behind him more than one example of inspired English verse."[2] In 1916 Mencken tried his hand at fin-de-siècle style himself with *A Little Book in C Major,* a collection of epigrams indebted to Wilde, Bierce, Twain, and Nietzsche.[3] Appropriately, the publisher was John Lane, who continued to offer editions of *The Yellow Book, Salome,* and other staples of the decadent canon well into the twentieth century. Mencken's interest in Wilde was driven in part by what he saw as a shared antagonism to "[o]ur depressing Puritan philosophy," which "distrusts the artist with a great distrust; it sees in him a prophet of that innocent gusto, that pagan joy in life, which is its chief abomination."[4] The pagan joy of life that Mencken sets against Puritanism here recalls Nietzsche's notion of Dionysianism—more complex than simple joy, to be sure—but Nietzsche is just as surely one of Mencken's culture heroes and a model for his own robust anti-Puritan morality. What Mencken wrote of Nietzsche can easily be applied to Mencken himself: "The proper thing for a man to do, he decided, was to formulate his own morality as he progressed from lower to higher things. He should reject the old conceptions of good and evil and substitute for them the human valuations, good and bad."[5]

In 1908 Mencken published *The Philosophy of Freidrich Nietzsche,* a wide-ranging study intended "to make Nietzsche comprehensible to the general reader" (*N*, xli). Vincent Fitzpatrick calls the book "a seminal text for an understanding of Mencken's thought" because it emphasizes the commonalities of the critic and the philosopher, presenting "their mutual opponents in clear fashion: altruism, democracy, the gullibility of the masses, and universal manhood sufferance." Fitzpatrick summarizes "the German's gospel according to the Baltimoran" as follows:

> Mencken draws Nietzsche as an iconoclast stridently endorsing individualism. Ineffectual people, Mencken explains through his subject, use religion to protect themselves from their superiors; an enervating force, religion impedes progress. Life proceeds by the harsh lessons of loss and gain: the strong can succeed only at the expense of the weak. The culture that seeks equality sickens itself, and charity, at best a temporary palliative, ultimately makes the weak even less efficient in the battle for life. An advanced culture endorses aristocracy, not of blood or money but of intellect and expertise. Perhaps most important, the ideal government has the good sense to leave its citizens alone.[6]

Mencken's Nietzsche is a Darwinist, and in Mencken's world the survival of the culturally strong finds its corollary in the decline of the socially weak, as represented in the narratives of the naturalist novel. Indeed, Mencken's aesthetic preference for naturalist works of fiction likely has some basis in the antinaturalist strivings of Nietzsche.

Mencken's deep interest in both Nietzsche and naturalism would seem to pave the way for a parallel or ancillary interest in decadence, but one looks in vain through Mencken's study of Nietzsche for any analysis of decadence, in either a social or a literary sense, which is somewhat surprising given the importance that Nietzsche himself placed on decadence in its various nineteenth-century manifestations. In *The Case of Wagner*, Nietzsche says that "[n]o problem has occupied me more profoundly than the problem of decadence."[7] And that type of life-negating morality Mencken called "Puritanism" Nietzsche sometimes refers to as "decadence."[8] But the only point at which the topic of decadence comes up for Mencken is in connection with Max Nordau's criticism of Nietzsche as a "degenerate," which is taken as the equivalent of "decadent" (*N*, 269–70). In other words, Mencken places no positive valuation on decadence as a cultural designation. On the contrary, Mencken treats Nietzsche as antidecadent, insofar as he follows Nietzsche in understanding Christianity, or Puritanism, as "the morality of decadence."[9] Mencken also follows Nietzsche in thinking of decadence as somehow "feminine." This usage emerges a few years after the Nietzsche study in a review of Ezra Pound's *Provença*, a collection of poetry inspired by the medieval lyrics of Provencal. Mencken sides with Pound—another early reader of Nietzsche—in the assessment of "latter day English poetry" as an art form too much the province of female writers. These "lady poets," Mencken avers, are "the bards of our decadence." Pound's poems, by contrast, "are rough, uncouth, hairy, barbarous, wild," that is, masculine and Nietzschean. Mencken says "a sort of stark, heathenish music emerges" from Pound's verses: "Dionysos and his rogues are at their profane prancing." [10]

Despite the antidecadent, Nietzschean tone that Mencken often assumes, it is not quite accurate to say that he abandoned altogether the aesthetic values of the Decadence. He seems, instead, to have "masculinized" those values, as becomes evident in his enthusiastic appreciation of James Huneker. In a 1920 review of *Steeplejack*, Huneker's autobiography, Mencken credits Huneker with delivering "the national letters from the old camorra of schoolmarms, male and female."[11] In Mencken's first important work of criticism, *A Book of Prefaces* (1917), Huneker is one of three seminal figures in modern literature singled out for analysis, along with Joseph Conrad and Theodore Dreiser. Mencken was one of the first American critics to recognize Conrad as a major author, and he was perhaps the one critic most responsible early on for establishing Dreiser's reputation. No one today doubts that Mencken was discerning in his judgment of these two writers, but Huneker has fallen into obscurity, and it is difficult to understand why Mencken would group him with Conrad and Dreiser. Evidently he did so because Huneker is one of Mencken's models and mentors in the art of criticism, especially because of the older critic's lively style of writing and his obsessive concern with the state of current literature: both Huneker and Mencken fashioned themselves as *introducteurs*, and both used the medium of journalism to keep the public up-to-date on the latest developments in arts and letters.

As we have seen, Huneker was thoroughly saturated in the literature of the decadence, but he did not convey his delight in decadence in a decadent way: not for him the weary, diffident tone or the fading notes of Walter Pater, but a vigorous style that borders on boosterism. It is precisely this style that Mencken finds so attractive. Indeed, Mencken identifies Huneker as "the only critic among us whose vision sweeps the whole field of beauty, and whose reports of what he sees there show any genuine gusto."[12] At the same time, Huneker is said to be "something of an epicure" whose essays "show some reflection" of "the symbolism madness" of the nineteenth century. Nonetheless, Huneker emerges in Mencken's essay as one of the few legitimate fin-de-siècle figures, a man who "gave some semblance of reality in the United States, after other men had tried and failed, to that great but ill-starred revolt against Victorian pedantry, formalism and sentimentality which began in the 90s" (*BP*, 163). Huneker is especially valued for being "a true cosmopolitan": "His world is not America, nor Europe, nor Christendom, but the whole universe of beauty" (*BP*, 161). Although Huneker is praised chiefly as a critic, Mencken also has kind words to say about his short stories, which are soundly rooted in the fin-de-siècle traditions of decadence, aestheticism, and diabolism. As Mencken says, the "point of view" of Huneker's stories "is essentially the aesthetic one; the overwhelming importance of beauty is never in doubt" (*BP*, 188). The decadent pedigree of this beauty is obvious when it is described as "highly artificial," possessing the "tone-colours" of "the second act of 'Tristan und Isolde.'" Huneker also "riots in . . . aesthetic occultism" that "slides into diabolism." One of Huneker's stories, "The Eighth Deadly Sin," is "a paean to perfume—the only one, so far as I know, in English," which implies that Mencken knows of others in French (most likely, he is thinking of the tenth chapter of Huysmans's *À Rebours*). In short, Mencken finds Huneker's stories "[s]trangely flavoured, unearthly, perhaps unhealthy stuff" (*BP*, 189). To validate Huneker's work in such terms is to validate the decadent tradition that Huneker himself so energetically defended.

Given Mencken's great influence on American letters throughout the 1920s, his enthusiastic support of Huneker's work cannot be overestimated and must be counted among the possible reasons for the decadent revival that occurred in that decade. In a long appreciation of Huneker published in *Prejudices: Third Series* (1922) after his death in 1921, Mencken singles out *Painted Veils* (1920), Huneker's only novel, as a book that might be said to "contain the man himself."[13] In particular, Mencken calls attention to "the chapter in which the hero soliloquizes on art, life, morality, and women" (*PS*, 130). The degree of Huneker's debt to decadence in *Painted Veils* is so extensive that the book has to be read to be believed. The then-scandalous novel had to be published privately to avoid certain censorship and criminal prosecution by the

New York Society for the Suppression of Vice, and no doubt Huneker's ability to outmaneuver the Puritans was an additional reason for Mencken's admiration. There is plenty to offend the Puritan reader of *Painted Veils* in the occasional lesbian adventure and the odd suggestion of sadomasochism, but what truly distinguishes the novel as "decadent" are the cultural tastes of its disaffected hero, Ulick Invern. The novel is chock-full of adulatory allusions to such authors as Huysmans, Pater, Paul Bourget, and Gabriele D'Annunzio, to name only a few. Moreover, the decadentism of such authors is insistently held up as something "new" and "modern." Huneker's sensitivity to the latest cultural developments in art and literature, his ability to "sort . . . out the newcomers with sharp eyes" (*PS*, 133), is one of the more abiding reasons for Mencken's admiration. In retrospect, Mencken's sense of Huneker's avant-garde sensibility is somewhat paradoxical because of Mencken's own aversion to much that was truly new in his own times. Indeed, the modernist authors that Mencken rejected are in many ways the heirs of the decadent tradition Huneker so tirelessly promoted in his essays and represented so fully in his novel.

Another paradox involved in Mencken's admiration of Huneker is his corresponding distaste for Edgar Saltus. Saltus and Huneker are both thoroughly rooted in the Parisian milieu of decadence and symbolism circa 1880, and Saltus anticipates Huneker as an *introducteur* of modern European authors. In other words, the things that Mencken found to admire in Huneker also resided in Saltus; moreover, Saltus is superior to Huneker in some ways, certainly as a novelist. Yet Mencken finds Saltus's novels "facile improvisations, full of satanic melodrama and wooden marionettes."[14] In truth, these faults are better represented by *Painted Veils* and Huneker's short stories than by the fiction of Edgar Saltus. The only book by Saltus that still "holds up," according to Mencken, is *Imperial Purple*: "A certain fine glow is still in it; it has gusto if not profundity" (*PF*, 282). "Gusto" in one book implies a paucity in the others, and "gusto" is, for Mencken, a marker of that vigorous, "masculine" style he found in Huneker and in Ezra Pound and that he thought was necessary to overthrow the literary dominance of Puritan "schoolmarms" and foppish professors. Saltus, in short, differs from Huneker in that his brand of decadence is too "feminine," an opinion Mencken formed by taking Marie Saltus's dubious account of her husband's life as a truthful biography.

Marie Saltus published her biography in 1925 in an attempt to capitalize on the Saltus revival that was beginning to stir, shortly before his death in 1921. It is a measure of Mencken's power as a critic that he was able to put an end to this revival with one damning essay, provoked by Mrs. Saltus's biography, and, as a result, Edgar Saltus is all but unknown today. And it is certainly ironic that Mrs. Saltus's efforts to exploit her husband's reputation wound up as the impetus to its destruction. That Saltus's reputation was on the rise in the 1920s is not in doubt. The revival was prepared by Carl Van Vechten's appreciation in *The Merry-go-round*, published in 1918. A review of this book in

Current Opinion understands Van Vechten to be "displaying a new type of patriotism" by "discovering, since the outbreak of the war, that America has actually produced writers of genius and originality."[15] Van Vechten encourages this strange patriotic appreciation of the disaffected Saltus by saying that his style "may be said to possess American characteristics." In fact, his sentences are said to "explode like so many firecrackers and remind one of the great national holiday!" Nonetheless, Van Vechten says Saltus should "have been born in France" and compares him favorably to European authors: "Page after page that Walter Pater, Oscar Wilde, or J. K. Huysmans might have been glad to sign might be set before you."[16] The reviewer of Van Vechten's book likewise has an appreciation of "the great decadent stylists of France" and numbers Saltus among them (*CU*, 255).

This sense of Saltus as the equal of the better-known decadents continues after Saltus's death in 1921 with an appreciation by Carl Van Doren, who says that Saltus "stood out conspicuously as a *fin de siècle* man . . . in a country which the *fin de siècle* scarcely touched at all with its graceful, graceless maladies."[17] No doubt thinking of *Imperial Purple*, Van Doren sums up Saltus in a way that might be taken as an explanation for the writer's limited early success and the revival of interest in this work in the 1920s: "What especially touched his imagination was the spectacle of Imperial Rome, as interpreted to him by French decadence: that lust for power and sensation; those incredible temples, palaces, feasts, revelries, blasphemies, butcheries. Dreaming of them he let his imagination brood until he became the Satanist of America" (Van Doren, 45). The earlier context of American literature that provided no place for a decadent of Saltus's dimensions forms the basis of another positive reassessment, also from 1922, by Gorham B. Munson. Munson aims to rescue Saltus from the limbo of literature to which he has been consigned by the "professor-preachers" who prefer morality and realism over originality and talent.[18] "Today he is still submerged because our aggressive seekers for a virile American literature find him too exotic, too Gallic, let us say" (Munson, 258). Although stylistic excesses mean that Saltus is guilty of "Swinburne's fault committed in prose," his "wit and epigrammatic quality" compare to Wilde's (Munson, 256). Munson sums up by saying "we have in him a temperament saturated with pessimism which expresses itself by the beautiful decoration of sinister themes"; indeed, "[t]o read Saltus is to take a showerbath of jewels" (Munson, 258, 259).

Saltus's status in the 1920s as a full-fledged decadent is certified by no less an authority than Arthur Symons, whose 1893 essay, "The Decadent Movement in Literature," did much to form the notion of decadence as an alternative to more typical forms of late Victorian literature.[19] Symons describes Saltus as an "unholy genius" who "writes with his nerves."[20] For Symons, Saltus's decadence is validated by his style or rather by the features of that style that are akin to a more widely recognized style of Continental decadence. This style is said to include "a kind of decadent French fashion of transposing words" (Symons, 267–68), by which he seems to mean a habit of coining new words by blending old ones, as well as irregularities of syntax. On this latter point he quotes Oscar Wilde—"In Edgar Saltus's work passion struggles with grammar on every page"—and applies to Saltus "Léon Bloy's admirable phrase on Huysmans: 'That he drags his images by the heels or the hair upside down the worm-eaten staircase of terrified syntax'" (Symons, 268).

If Symons certifies Saltus as a decadent by virtue of his literary style, Sadakichi Hartmann provides a similar kind of certification of Saltus's decadence on the basis of his personal behavior. In "The Edgar Saltus I Knew," Hartmann offers this sketch of a visit to the author in the last decade of his life, probably around 1915:

> One felt a little foolish, shy and embarrassed as one entered the spacious library, dimly lit and cluttered with books and *objects d'art*, Chinese hangings, Japanese screens, East Indian statuary. And there Edgar Saltus would sit on a sort of baldachined throne, much higher than the divans of his guests, dispense cigarettes ten inches long, read Chinese poetry and lecture, learnedly and enthusiastically, on the art ideals of the far Orient. . . . In dress he was neither loud nor eccentric, but rather up to date with the latest fashion, tailormade, immaculate. With his *boutonnière* and the traditional triangle of a silk handkerchief always visible, with white socks, gloves, stovepipe, and walking stick, he impressed one as a dandy of the MacAllister era.[21]

Symons's literary appreciation and Hartmann's fantastical personal account were both published in 1923. Despite the admixture of fiction to Hartmann's reminiscence, or, rather, because of it, it is clear that something close to a Saltus cult was forming in the early 1920s. Boni and Liveright were publishing reprint editions of Saltus's works in New York, and Pascal Covici was doing the same in Chicago. In sum, critical and popular opinion were combining to restore a neglected genius of American literature to his rightful place. Then came Mencken.

Mencken's 1926 sketch of Saltus leads the reader to believe that the author of *Imperial Purple* continues to languish in the obscurity that enveloped him at the turn of the century. As we have seen, nothing could be further from the truth. Yet Mencken insists that Saltus's cultural eclipse is total: "I can recall . . . no more complete collapse. Saltus plunged from the top of the world to the bottom of the sea" (PF, 277). The reason for this collapse is largely Saltus's practice of *le style de décadence*—"the gaudy glittering phrase" (PF, 277), the very quality Arthur Symons singled out as Saltus's great distinction. Mencken cites his late friend Percival Pollard to support his criticism of Saltus's style, claiming that Saltus, in Pollard's view, "was simply a bright young fellow who succumbed to his own cleverness" (PF, 277). In fact, Pollard's assessment of

Saltus is more nuanced than Mencken allows. In *Their Day in Court* (1909), Pollard places Saltus in a group of "feminist" writers (by "feminist" Pollard means "erotic") that includes Pierre Loüys, Gabriele D'Annunzio, and Richard Le Galliene. Saltus, Pollard says, is "the only American among these feminists who has deserved well of us by having had care of literary style."[22] But Pollard goes on to say that in his last books Saltus's style was "too exclusively his preoccupation," to the point that the author "became the slave of his own syllables" (Pollard, 82, 84). Mencken's emphasis is on this later Saltus, "drunk on words" (*PF, 278*) and on the sensational creature of Marie Saltus's biography who goes by the same name as her late husband. What Mencken finds most damning in this biography is Saltus's alleged cultivation of theosophy, more than likely an interest of his wife's that she rather gratuitously imputed to him for sensational effect; in any case, Mencken takes Marie Saltus at her word: "In the end poor old Schopenhauer lost a customer and the art of epigram a gifted and diligent practitioner. Saltus passed into senility with his thoughts concentrated powerfully upon Higher Things" (*PF, 281*). In sum, Mencken makes Saltus out to be a substanceless stylist and an empty-headed mystic, lacking in "dignity, information, sense" (*PF, 282*). These supposed virtues seem better suited to the journalist than the literary artist, which may account for Mencken's preference for his fellow newspaperman Huneker over the similarly minded Saltus, for Huneker is something like an information machine. Still, the fact remains that both Huneker and Saltus are decadent writers, with the signal difference that Saltus is slightly less belated in his relations to Continental decadence, which places him closer to the origins of the movement in America.

For Mencken, Saltus's prior position as an American decadent of some distinction in both a literary and a critical sense must have made it harder for him to present Huneker as the cultural trailblazer he said he was. Saltus was not quite the popularizer of decadence that Huneker was, but he was a popular author for a time, and he was well ahead of Huneker in introducing European aesthetic values into the cultural backwater of Puritan America. Also, had Saltus been allowed to occupy the position in American letters that other critics were advocating in the early 1920s, the latter-day decadents of that decade—authors such as James Branch Cabell and Joseph Hergesheimer—might have appeared less original than Mencken made them out to be. For these were the authors that Mencken promoted not as the derivative decadents they were, but as original artists: Cabell was called "a man of novel and ingenious ideas,"[23] and Hergesheimer's novel *Cytherea* was said to treat "old material" with "a new illumination" (*PF, 44*).

The collapse of the reputations of these two authors is every bit as complete today as the obscurity Mencken claimed for Saltus in the twenties, but Cabell's fall from the cultural firmament seems especially meteoric—not least because of a Cabell revival circa 1970 that figured him as a "fantasy" writer. By contrast, Mencken's reviews of Cabell's work create the impression of a writer thoroughly within the decadent-aesthetic tradition. He calls an early novel one "that has, from first to last, a French smack; one constantly hears overtones that suggest Anatole France and J. K. Huysmans."[24] What Mencken admires in Cabell's work is a "fastidiousness," an "ironical detachment," that shows forth the conviction "that artificiality is the only true reality" (*MAL*, 97, 99). Stylistically, Mencken finds in Cabell a "Paterism somehow humanized and made expansive," and, indeed, the critic's summary of Cabell's virtues could well stand as a description of Pater at his best: "In brief, excellent reading—shy, insinuating learning; heterodoxy infinitely gilded; facts rolled out in fragile thinness and cut into pretty figures; above all, a sure and delicate sense of words, a style at once exact and undulate, very caressing writing" (*MAL*, 99).

To turn from breathless encomia such as these to Cabell's actual writing is a bit of a shock, for the author seems about as far removed from the aesthetic style of Pater or the refined corruption of Huysmans as it is possible for a writer to be, and nowhere more so than in *Jurgen*, the novel that brought Cabell great fame and notoriety after its publication in 1919. Like most of his fiction, *Jurgen* is a romance drawn from the fictional folklore of Poictesme, a medieval realm of Cabell's invention. Today, it is fairly easy to see *Jurgen* as the product of the widespread influence of Sir James Frazer's *Golden Bough* (1890–1915) and the fertility-myth mania that ensued. In fact, Cabell begins *Jurgen* with a tongue-in-cheek foreword that alludes to "the esoteric meaning of these folk-stories and their bearing upon questions to which the 'solar theory' of myth explanation has given rise."[25] The romance also includes a surfeit of "Freudian" imagery that makes the novel read like highbrow pornography and was the reason for Cabell's run-in with the New York Society for the Suppression of Vice.[26] To give one of many possible examples of this "pornographic" quality, in one extended episode a lady admires "the avenging sword of Jurgen" as a "very large" instrument. The hero assures her that because his sword "is the comfort of all pretty women" she should allow him to satisfy the "legacy" of her dead husband. When she acknowledges "[t]hat there is something in what you advance," he assures her that his "logic" is of "the most natural and penetrating kind" for he wishes merely to "discharge his duty," whereupon the lady exclaims, "Oh what is anybody to do with you! Here is the sheath for your sword" (125).

It is easy to see how Mencken would find such passages satisfying because they are so obviously calculated to offend the Puritan tastes the Baltimorean abhorred. *Jurgen*, he said, was "brilliantly written, . . . full of racy and mirthful ideas": "Such a book simply refuses to fit into the decorous mid-Victorian pattern of American literature" (*MAL*, 101). Briefly, *Jurgen* recounts the hero's erotic adventures in the storied world of medieval romance. Part Faust, part Don Juan, Jurgen is a middle-aged pawnbroker and part-time poet who nonchalantly "speaks a kind word for evil" (11) and thereby ingratiates himself with a diabolic figure who restores his youth, dispenses with his aged wife, and

allows him to experience love affairs with such fabled women as Lady Guene-
vere, the amorous moon goddess, Anaïtis (the name is an anagram of *insatia*),
and a female vampire named Florimel, among others. The affair with Florimel
is set in Hell, which provides occasion for some political satire that even
Mencken finds heavy-handed, however consonant with his own ideology:

> The religion of Hell is patriotism, and the government is an enlightened democ-
> racy. This contented the devils, and Jurgen had learned long ago never to fall out
> with either of these codes, without which, as the devils were fond of observing,
> Hell would not be what it is. . . .
>
> "It is a comfort . . . ," said Jurgen, "to discover who originated the theory of
> democratic government. I have long wondered who started the notion that the
> way to get a wise decision on any conceivable question was to submit it to popu-
> lar vote. Now I know." (277, 286)[27]

Mencken finds this kind of thing "outlandish" (*MAL*, 101), but even though
Jurgen is mildly diabolic, it is hardly decadent, except in some superficial, adolescent sense suggested by the hero's erotic adventures. And even this type of
"decadence" is negated when, at the end of the novel, Jurgen opts for middle-
aged normality and returns to Lady Lisa, his broken-down but devoted wife. In
retrospect, the novel seems especially reactionary and politically decadent
when contrasted with the social realism of the 1930s. As Leslie Fiedler puts it,
Cabell and other twenties writers, "like Joseph Hergesheimer, came to be considered in the gray days of the depression too effete, elegant, involuted, affected, and 'decadent' to be endured."[28]

Fiedler also comments on a surprising turn in Cabell's reputation that suggests another vector of American decadence. Clearly, Cabell's erudite romances mean to impress as "great literature" but fall short of the mark, partly
because they suffer in comparison to the modernist works that Cabell—like
Mencken—dismissed (he described Gertrude Stein and James Joyce as the authors of nothing more than "sad twaddle").[29] But Cabell, also like Mencken,
dismissed the popular literature of his age as well and felt an elitist disdain for
anything that appealed to a mass audience (for example, he rejected Margaret
Mitchell's *Gone with the Wind* as unreadable).[30] In Cabell's case, Fiedler says,
"time has proved the mass audience right":

> *Jurgen* (contrary to what Cabell himself thought) *is* the best of his novels—not
> despite its pornographic passages and because of its "fine writing," but despite its
> "fine writing" and because of its appeal to prurience. Had Cabell or any of the
> critics who first touted him understood as much, they would have been able to
> surmise what they did not in fact foresee: that his work was ironically destined to
> survive not as "high literature," belles lettres, "serious art"—but as a kind of
> "pop" appealing to adolescents of all ages. (Fiedler, 134)

Proof of this assertion comes in the form of the mass-market repackaging of Cabell's Poictesme romances as a form of fantasy writing along the lines of, say, J. R. R. Tolkein's *Ring* trilogy. In fact, the introduction to a 1970 Ballantine Books reprint of *The High Place* (1923) makes the astonishing claim that Cabell is "probably the only American fantasy writer of genius."[31] As we shall see, this will not be the only instance of an author identified with the decadent revival of the 1920s making an ironic entrance into American popular culture later on.

The distinction of latter-day popularity has thus far been denied to Joseph Hergesheimer, another Mencken favorite, and for this reason his cultural eclipse now appears more complete than Cabell's. The absence of the kind of posthumous popularity that Cabell underwent is paradoxical given the trajectory of Hergesheimer's literary career, since the author deliberately adjusted his style to appeal more to a popular audience in the mid-1920s—this after an earlier, more aesthetic period directly indebted to the British Decadence. The shift is surprising in view of the success that Hergesheimer was experiencing at the time: in 1922 a *Literary Digest* poll ranked him first among living American novelists.[32] The following year his good friend Mencken expressed disappointment when Hergesheimer failed to take advantage of the "almost complete freedom" that "now prevails for the serious artist" by choosing instead to write "novelettes for the *Saturday Evening Post*."[33] Mencken often used Hergesheimer's earlier novels, usually paired with Cabell's, to set the aesthetic standard he used to estimate the worth of other writers. Sherwood Anderson, Willa Cather, and the Jewish Lithuanian immigrant author Abraham Cahan are all judged against Hergesheimer's "elaborate preciosities," his "high seriousness," and his ability to write "like a gentleman" (*MAL*, 81, 94, 162). Not all of these qualities necessarily derive from decadence, but Hergesheimer himself records the influence of such decadent authors as Ernest Dowson, Arthur Symons, and Paul Verlaine and recalls an adolescent interest in *The Yellow Book* and *The Savoy*.[34] We would do well to remember that these two publications, though hardly intended for a mass audience, enjoyed a measure of popular success, so perhaps the appearance of Hergesheimer's aesthetic fiction in the *Saturday Evening Post* and *Redbook* follows a cultural logic after all, but one that Mencken could never understand.

The popular and the precious come together in *The Bright Shawl*, "the most purely aesthetic of Hergesheimer's novels,"[35] originally published in *Redbook* from June to September 1922. The narrative takes the form of a melancholy reverie on the part of the middle-aged Charles Abbot, who begins to reminisce about his idealistic youth when he is confronted with the "satirical bitterness" of his nephew Howard Gage, recently returned from the Great War.[36] The nephew's mocking "references to the 'glorious victory in France'" give Abbot the impression of "bestiality choked in mud" (10). The older man is struck by "the common decline" of the present age and contrasts its decadence with the period of his youth, the mid-1890s. Abbot, it turns out, spent much of the fin de siècle in Havana, having been sent to breathe the Cuban air because of "the delicacy of his lungs" (17). The sound of Liszt's *Spanish Rhapsody* triggers the Cuban reverie, which is dominated by two figures: Andrés Escobar, a young Cuban patriot working underground for the insurgency, and La Clavel, an Andalusian dancer who aids the rebels by gathering information from the Spanish officers whose patronage she enjoys. Having met Andrés Escobar's father on the steamer from New York and experienced a political conversion en route, Charles arrives in Havana eager to see "Cuba liberated from a bloody and intolerable tyranny" (18).

Despite his ardent opposition to Spanish oppression, Charles Abbot could never be mistaken for one of the Rough Riders of 1898. On the contrary, he imagines himself making the ultimate sacrifice for Cuba only under the most refined conditions: "His, Charles Abbot's, would be a select, an aristocratic, fate; the end, when it overtook him, would find him in beautiful snowy linens, dignified, exclusive, to the last. His would be no pot-house brawling. That was his double necessity, the highest form of good in circumstances of the first breeding. One, perhaps, to his aesthetic fibre, was as important as the other. And, dressing for dinner, he spoiled three shirts in the exact right fixing of his studs" (42). Abbot's fellow revolutionaries are also dandies: Andrés Escobar cuts "an impressive figure of the best fashion," dressed "in immaculately ironed linen, a lavender tie and sprig of mimosa" (37); another, Jaime Quintara, is "even more an exquisite than Andrés," not least because he wears "lemon-colored gloves [imported] by the box from Paris . . . made to his measure" (52).

As for the dancer, La Clavel, she is admired by Abbot and the other dandy insurrectionists "as a symbol of beauty," something "aesthetic rather than social" (90), despite the fact that she puts herself at great personal risk in the service of the revolution. The *mantón* La Clavel wears as she dances—the "bright shawl" (96) of the title—first functions to give symbolic expression to "her feelings" only: "[T]he scarlet and magenta and burning orange and blue were her visible moods, her capriciousness and contempt and variability and searing passion" (55). Later, the shawl assumes much greater symbolic weight in a passage doubtlessly inspired by Flaubert's descriptions of the veil of Tanit in *Salammbô*. Here, the shawl ceases to stand for La Clavel's "grace and perversity and stark passion" and signifies, instead, "the revealed outspread pattern of [Abbot's] own existence" (167):

> The shawl was a map, a representation, of the country of the spirit through which he had passed; such emotions, such heat, and such golden roses, all had been, were, his against that background of perilous endeavor. It seemed to float up from the bed and to reach from coast to coast, from end to end, of Cuba; its flowers took root and grew, casting about splendor and perfume; the

blue widened into the sky, the tenderness of the clasping sea; the dark greens were the shadows of the great ceiba trees, the gloom of the jungles, the massed royal palms of the plains. (168)

In a way, this extended pictorial passage forms the climax of the novel, for here the subordination of political meaning to aesthetic effect is most complete. Indeed, the novel ends with Abbot's failure to make the glorious, linen-clad sacrifice he imagined; worse, he indirectly contributes to the death of his friend Andrés and is deported to New York by the Spanish authorities, without accomplishing much of anything. When Abbot awakens from his reverie he seems, at first, on the verge of some larger realization: "His sympathies were, by birth, aristocratic rather than humane; he preferred strength to acquiescence; but there were times now, perhaps, when he was aging, when there was a relief in sinking into the sea of humility" (216). But at the very end of the novel this newfound humility seems indistinguishable from simple futility—"If liberty, justice, were to come, one life, two, could make no difference"—and the value of subjective aesthetic satisfaction is affirmed: "Perhaps what [he and Andrés] had found was, after all, within them, that for which they had swept the sky" (220).

Because of their extreme aestheticism and social detachment, Cabell and Hergesheimer were later classed as "exquisites" by Alfred Kazin, members of a group of authors representative of the "new decadence" of the 1920s. These exquisites were felt to be "the very concentration of all the elusiveness and poise, the self-conscious civilization that the modern emancipation demanded."[37] Interestingly, Kazin numbers George Jean Nathan, Mencken's co-editor on The American Mercury and sometime collaborator on literary projects (they coauthored the play Heliogabalus), among these new decadents, and credits him with one of the seminal "testaments of the Exquisites, 'The Code of the Critic'" (Kazin, 229). Mencken's critical and personal friendship with Huneker, Cabell, Hergesheimer, and Nathan shows that the culture of decadence, however masculinized and Americanized as "anti-Puritanism," was very much a part of his critical tastes, even though Mencken did his best to erase one of the true introducteurs of that taste—Edgar Saltus—from American cultural history.

ii

H. L. Mencken's attempt to rewrite the cultural history of the 1890s in favor of the masculine, anti-Puritan values he so admired is all the more interesting in view of the work of Thomas Beer (1889–1940), one of Mencken's friends and admirers best known today for The Mauve Decade: American Life at the End of the Nineteenth Century.[38] Published in 1926, the book is the first thorough account of American culture during the 1890s to include serious consideration of decadence in the United States. Beer follows Mencken in excoriating the hypocrisy of Puritan America, but, unlike Mencken, he enlists decadents such as Edgar Saltus, circa 1890, to make the critique: "someone mentioned Christianity and Saltus slowly said, 'Has it appeared in America?'"[39] Beer claims that one of the last observations Saltus made before his death was something to the effect "that America was the hypocrite of nations" (103). Beer also relies on Ambrose Bierce, another fin-de-siècle writer Mencken sometimes slighted, to elaborate the shallowness and depravity of the age. Calling him "death's dilettante" (96), Beer notes Bierce's ironic disappointment with the shabby state of murder in the Bay Area and opines that "[i]f the high quality of slaughter had been maintained, Bierce would never have left San Francisco" (85). The point here is that Beer writes some of the same figures into his account of the fin de siècle that Mencken wrote out of it, yet they both write to the same purpose in pointing out the shallowness and hypocrisy of American life.

Beer also follows Mencken in celebrating the "masculine" values of Nietzsche and evokes them to show, by contrast, just how "feminine" America had become by the end of the nineteenth century. While Americans "share . . . the depravity of an extreme softness," Nietzsche is said to have "rebounded from study of his own nature into exaggerations and harsh yells in praise of strength, building out of his weakness a philosophic concept of persistent honour" (115). Quite possibly, Beer might have intended The Mauve Decade to be a study of the nature of Americans that would allow them to "rebound," Nietzschelike, from softness to strength. In any event, the American failure to measure up to other nations informs much of Beer's analysis and, indirectly, supplies him with the title for his book. The inspiration for the title is a remark by Whistler that serves as the book's epitaph: "Mauve? Mauve is just pink trying to be purple."[40] The context suggests a doomed attempt on the part of Americans (pink) to achieve the cultural status (purple) of some other group, without worrying too much over what that other group might be—could be German Volk, could be British aristocracy. Regardless, the color mauve connotes the kind of mixture that comes with the transition from one cultural condition to another, a transition commonly called "decadence." The Mauve Decade is a baggy, slippery book, and the same meanings are not carried consistently from chapter to chapter or even from page to page. But Beer clearly understands America to have undergone a cultural transition from a greater period to a lesser one.

The past greatness of "American thought" is located in the strong individualism of "the Boston tradition" as represented by Emerson; the decay of that tradition is represented by the Alcotts, namely Bronson and his sister Louisa Mae. The first chapter of Beer's book is titled "The Titaness," a term that captures what is, for him, the true sign of declining times: the growth and even dominance of the role of women in American life, in politics no less than literature. Strangely, a reformer such as Jane Addams is partnered with Louisa Mae Alcott in a general scenario of feminized decay, as if the founder of Hull House and the

author of *Little Women* are equally to blame for the degeneration of the Emersonian ideal. The following passage from the first chapter is key:

> [T]he Middle Western woman had quietly become a fixture on the American so-
> cial chart, a shadowy Titaness, a terror to editors, the hope of missionary soci-
> eties, and the prey of lecturers. . . . Was she fabulous? No, but she existed rather
> as a symptom of America's increasing cheapness than as an attitude of woman-
> hood. . . . The collapse of American thought excused her forays; all that had
> been finely stalwart in the Bostonian age had vanished, the reckless courage and
> self-willed individualism of Emerson [and] Thoreau . . . , the deliberate cultiva-
> tion of research into the motives, not the manners of human action. The confu-
> sion of morals with manners . . . had helped the mental lassitude of the Ameri-
> cans to destroy what was honourable in the Boston tradition, and from the
> remains of that tradition welled a perfume of decay, cants and meaningless
> phrases: "the nobility of democracy," "social purity," and the like. In the weak
> hands of the Alcotts individualism ceased to be a sacred burden. (36)

Beer is not the first author in the tradition of American decadence to regard
political reform as a paradoxical indicator of social decline. In *The Decadent*,
Ralph Adams Cram likewise expressed anxiety over socialist politics and
sought refuge in aesthetic individualism. But the kind of individualism that is
the object of Beer's nostalgia is not aesthetic, but "manly." No doubt there is
more than a hint of the "masculine" culture his friend Mencken promoted in
Beer's formulations.

The "perfume of decay" that emanates from the Alcotts also permeates the
later age of Mencken that Beer inhabits as he writes. In another chapter Beer
alludes to "the Bostonian age" as "the tag end of an intellectual stir that died
out in the rank commerce of the collapsing dignity of the '70's and '80's"
(139). The object of the author's rancor here is the oppression of personal freedom by religious orthodoxy, another topic favored by Mencken. In one of the
many highly poetic passages in this odd book, Beer compares that earlier con-
strained age with his own:

> There were cool, gloomy academies of sophisticated discourse up any alley in
> those days, deep livery stables where the voices of Negro hostlers mixed an oily
> languor with the harsh drawl of grooms as harness was polished on sunny after-
> noons; the adolescent of the succeeding time has found freedom in the smell of
> gasoline and wayward gin; in the '90's freedom was perfumed with saddle-soap
> and leather, with rotted straw and dung. (139–40)

The twenties, then, represent a recrudescence of the rankness of the nineties,
but the quality of decay has coarsened somehow, and Beer (who was born in

1889) seems genuinely nostalgic for "the haunts of the vulgar and displaced" (139) that evidently formed his childhood memories.

A similar kind of nostalgia permeates Beer's presentation of the literary culture of the fin de siècle, and he makes any number of links between that earlier era and his own. "The cleverness of the '90s," he says, "was very much the cleverness of our moment" (97). The remark is made in the context of commentary about Gelett Burgess's Lark and The Chap-Book and could well apply, though Beer does not make the link, to those latter-day decadents who formed the Algonquin Round Table and wrote for The New Yorker. After all, the magazine borrowed the emblem of a dandified aesthete peering through a monocle from The Chap-Book (see figure 15), adding a butterfly design derived from Whistler by way of Beardsley. Certainly the wits of this group, such as Alexander Wolcott and Dorothy Parker, seem to have stepped out of a play by Oscar Wilde. For Beer, however, Wilde is of interest only as a case study in the cultural myopia of Puritan America. According to Beer, there was little interest in Wilde prior to the scandal of 1895: "Unless there was a private cult of admirers in the county, Wilde cannot have been a great figure to Americans in the early '90's" (129). As we now know, there was a cult of Wilde admirers in Boston in the early 1890s, but Beer may be excused for neglecting to mention the group associated with The Mahogany Tree. His larger point is doubtless true: that the sodomy case brought Wilde before the American public not as a sophisticated author but as a great sinner. Beer says that "the president of Princeton told the undergraduates that Oscar Wilde was the vilest sinner since Nero," and that he "was mentioned in at least nine hundred known sermons between 1895 and 1900" (129).

Although Beer thinks "Wilde's art becomes too dusty," his "standing as a great sinner" will keep his memory alive among the American public. Beer has greater admiration for the art of "another set of decadents" who succeeded Wilde and allows that "[s]ome of these men were talented." These include Arthur Symons and Lionel Johnson, though the latter's talent turns out to be flawed—"an admirable critic up to the point of his rigid intellectual dishonesty." Symons, however, is adjudged a fine "specimen of thermal conductivity in letters, through which the ideas of French artists passed into English perception with little damage." But Beer reserves his highest praise for Aubrey Beardsley, "a decorator so superior that his 'Salomé' convinced people that Oscar Wilde had written a tragedy of the same" (179). These British figures, along with a number of American writers, contribute to the decadent revival in the United States, which Beer dates from 1916. He provides a succinct account of the American precursors to the "exquisites" of his own generation, noting that his contemporaries have yet to acknowledge the debt to their cultural forebears:

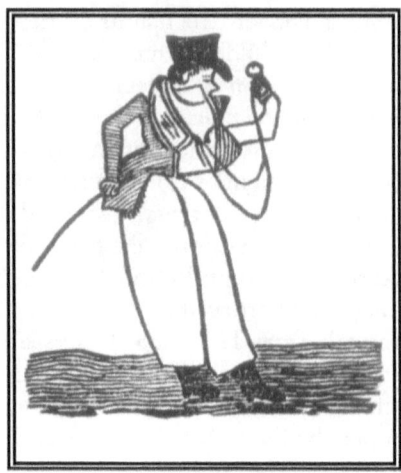

FIGURE 15   Design of monocled figure
from *The Chap-Book* (1894)

There was in the '90's a distinguished but scattering and, of course, ineffective effort toward a primary sophistication in American letters. Survivors of the movement, such as Vance Thompson, John Barry and the publisher of the *Chap Book* must have grinned, and James Huneker groaned aloud, when the new sophisticates of 1916 solemnly disclosed the works of Rimbaud, Laforgue, Vielé-Griffin . . . to a renovated public. . . . [W]holesale thefts from Peck's paper on Stephane Mallarmé and quotations from Richard Hovey's translation of "Herodiade," without mention of Hovey, figured in the revival. (192)

What Beer most admires in these fin-de-siècle writers is their independence from the "Titaness" of female taste: "In the last decade of the nineteenth century there had been a very plain tendency, not at all unhealthy, to cut across the maternal intervention and to take ideas undiluted from Paris without awaiting the passage through an intermediary province" (193).

The men of the nineties who negotiated a way around "maternal intervention" are still admired as models and mentors because the Titaness continues to cast her shadow over Beer's own age:

It is not alleged against the women of the Mauve Decade that they invented cheap cruelty and low social pressures, but they erected these basenesses into virtues of some defensive sense of rectitude, and a generation of sons was reared in the shadow of the Titaness, aware of her power, protected by nothing from her shrill admonitions. Is it a matter for such wonder among critics that only satire can describe this American of our time who drifts toward middle age without valor, charm or honour? (60–61)

Beer's rhetoric here smacks of the cultural wish for a return to medieval values— valor, charm, honor—that was part of the reaction to American materialism that the Adams brothers and Ralph Adams Cram had voiced thirty years earlier. But Beer's complaint also points to an unease with his own masculinity that has to be a reflection of the closeted conditions under which the man was compelled to live. The biographer John Clendenning speculates that the writer committed suicide because of anguish over his homosexuality.[41] At the very least, Beer's nostalgia for a culture grounded in "masculine" values suggests a level of anxiety not uncommon among men with same-sex desires who construe those desires as a diminution of the manliness mainstream society requires.

Aside from Beer's excursus on Wilde as the "great sinner" of the fin de siècle—which includes a lengthy account of the last days of Wilde's Paris exile—the author of *The Mauve Decade* has little to say about the homophilic nature of decadence, American or otherwise. At the same time, Beer discusses in some detail the Petronius craze of the mid-1890s, after "Wilde had crashed" (229). One of Beer's obvious points is the hypocrisy of the American fascination with Petronius at a time when Wilde was being denounced by college presidents and firebrand preachers. But Beer also implies, perhaps unconsciously, that the sudden fashion for Petronius represents a sublimated, culturally acceptable means of exploring the "sinful" sexuality Wilde represented. This possibility is heightened when Beer, ventriloquizing the voice of a modern-day Petronius, surveys the culture of the Mauve Decade for positive signs. Among the items that meet with the approval of "Petronius" is Henry Blake Fuller's first novel: "Neither is this image of the Chevalier of Pensieri Vanni [sic] despicable with its air of joking softly at respectabilities and its unstressed narrative grace" (231). As we have seen, marriage and heterosexual relations were among the "respectabilities" that Fuller quietly undermined in his genteel travel romance. Beer, of course, could not be too direct in suggesting to his readers that "masculine" culture might not be the only way to challenge the dominance of the Titaness, either in the late nineteenth century or in his own age. Fuller, however, did just that with *The Chevalier of Penseri-Vani*; he waited almost thirty years before doing it again, but the second time around the homosexual theme was not obscured by aesthetic ambiguities.

iii

The publication in 1919 of *Bertram Cope's Year* by Henry Blake Fuller was hardly a literary event. H. L. Mencken expressed surprise that the author who had satirized the Chicago social scene in the 1890s was still alive,[42] but he gave the novel a favorable albeit tepid review anyway: "A very fair piece of writing, as novels go. A bit sly and *pizzicato;* even a bit distinguished."[43] The reason for Mencken's reserve is no doubt Fuller's forthright treatment of ho-mosexual relations: in *Bertram Cope's Year* Fuller returns to the topic of same-sex love hinted at in *The Chevalier of Pensieri-Vani* and directly addressed in "At Saint Judas's," the symbolist drama published in *The Puppet-Booth* of 1896. Mencken, at least, went further than most critics of the time, who refused to acknowledge the novel at all. The lack of critical response mirrored the diffi-culties Fuller had encountered when he tried to find a publisher for the book. He spent many months in New York City shopping the manuscript around to various publishers, but without success. In the end the novel was published privately at Fuller's expense by Ralph Fletcher Seymour, a friend who handled the printing of Harriet Monroe's *Poetry* magazine, whose advisory board in-cluded Fuller. As Kenneth Scambray notes, the trials undergone by *Bertram Cope's Year* were "not unusual for a homosexual novel in America. The private publication of homosexual literature had become standard practice in societies that branded homosexuals as moral deviates and criminals."[44] Sadly, this be-nighted attitude toward homosexuality, even after decriminalization, contin-ued to dog Fuller's reputation as recently as the 1970s. One critic of that decade chides Fuller for "his failure to deal adequately with the impact of sex-ual abnormality [!] upon the lives of his characters."[45] Another remarks that "At Saint Judas's" "foreshadows the novel *Bertram Cope's Year* . . . in its indi-rect presentation of a perverse relationship."[46]

In truth, the homosexual relationship that Fuller examines in *Bertram Cope's Year* is far from "perverse," and his treatment of that relationship is not indirect at all. The author is quite straightforward in describing the title character's preference for same-sex associations: "[H]e had developed no par-ticular dexterity in dealing with the younger members of the opposite sex."[47] The meaning of *dexterity* here is elaborated later in the novel when Cope and Basil Randolph, an older man, have a conversation about women after skinny-dipping together in Lake Michigan:

> "Each woman according to her powers and gifts. Varying degrees of desire, of de-termination, of dexterity. To be just, I might add a fourth *d*—*devotion.*"
>
> "You've run the gauntlet," said Cope, "You seem to have come through all right."
>
> "Well," Randolph returned deprecatingly, "I can't really claim ever to have enlisted any woman's best endeavors."
>
> "I hope I shall have the same good luck. Of your four *d*'s, it's the dexterity that gives me the most dread." (76–77)

Both men are careful to avoid any direct reference to their own homosexual feelings as they express their mutual wish to avoid female intimacy, settling instead on a kind of genial bachelor solidarity that might, conceivably, be interpreted as a desire for heterosexual freedom. Such an interpretation is gainsaid, however, by Cope's many overt expressions of tenderness toward Arthur Lemoyne, the man he loves. Their life together consists of a kind of decorous affection that cannot be termed "perverse" in any sense, despite the claims of those critics from the 1970s.

The genteel sexuality so modestly displayed in *Bertram Cope's Year* might well be read as fairly typical of same-sex relations among the decadents and aesthetes of the fin de siècle, even though the novel appeared in 1919. In fact, despite the odd reference to motorcars, gramophones, and other trappings of modernity more pervasive at the time of the novel's publication than in the 1890s, the novel seems to belong to an earlier time. Fuller makes no reference to more recent historical events—like World War I, for example—so while the novel is not specifically set in the fin de siècle, it does not seem to belong especially to the period of its publication. If we are to take *Bertram Cope's Year* as a window into the world of homosexual relations in the 1890s, we must remember that the vision is, after all, that of one rather unhappy and dispirited man, whose point of view is colored by his own experiences and disappointments. At the same time, it would be a mistake to assume that homosexual men and women of the fin de siècle were not beset by the same Victorian mores and Puritan inhibitions as were their heterosexual counterparts. More than one critic has claimed that *Bertram Cope's Year* is a "weak" or "unsuccessful" novel because of Fuller's narrative reserve: "Fuller's efforts to soften the impact of his [homosexual] theme serve only to weaken his main character."[48] But it may very well be that Fuller's tempered treatment of the homosexual theme is reflective of the care and caution needed to live a homosexual life in the 1890s.

This sense of discretion is conveyed by an early scene when the musically talented Bertram Cope is asked to sing before a group of young women at the home of Medora Phillips, a matronly widow who frequently entertains members of the academic community in Churchton, the small Midwestern university where Cope works as an English instructor. Fuller's description of Cope's singing on this occasion seems deliberately calculated to convey an important aspect of the author's attitude toward his own literary career, and, perhaps, to his own sexuality: "He sang with care rather than with volume, with discretion rather than with abandon. . . . Possibly Cope gave too great heed to his hostess's caution; but it seemed as if a voice essentially promising had slipped through some teacher's none too competent hands, or—what was quite as serious—as if some temperamental brake were operating to prevent the complete expression of the singer's nature" (24). Metaphorically, the "temperamental brake" that works against "complete expression" here inhibits much more than Cope's singing. The character is placed in a social environment that involves expectations of heterosexual behavior of one kind or another, from harmless flirtation to serious courtship. Not surprisingly, the second time Cope is asked to sing before a similar audience in the same house, he faints. But on a later occasion, when Cope sings a duet with his partner, Lemoyne, Mrs. Phillips is struck by the passion in his voice: she "had never heard Cope sing like that before; had never seen so much animation in his singing face" (193).

The plot of *Bertram Cope's Year* concerns a gentle rivalry between various parties for the title character's affections. Were it not for the reader's access to Cope's consciousness, the book would seem not unlike a typical romance novel of the period. Even as Medora Phillips plays matchmaker and tries to set the young man up with one of her female boarders, Cope composes a letter in his head to Arthur Lemoyne, who has yet to join him at Churchton: "I miss you— even more than I thought I should" (26). The principal rivals for Cope's atten- tion are Amy Leffingwell, one of Mrs. Phillips's boarders, and Basil Randolph, a Chicago stockbroker and art collector who fancies himself a member of the uni- versity community because of his elevated aesthetic tastes—that, and the pres- ence of a brother-in-law on the university's board of trustees. He is described as a "scholar *manqué*"—a "haunter of academic shades or its intermittent dabbler in their charms.... No alumnus himself, he viewed, year after year, the passing procession of undergraduates who possessed in their young present so much that he had left behind or never had at all" (6). While Randolph makes plans to find a larger apartment so he can ask Cope to move in with him, Miss Leffing- well, with Mrs. Phillips's aid, traps the young man into an engagement. Both see their designs frustrated when Arthur Lemoyne finally comes to town to live with Cope. Lemoyne is an actor who has performed in amateur theatricals, so when Cope secures a university position for him—with Randolph's aid—he ap- pears in a campus production. The role he chooses for himself requires that he wear a female costume. The night of the performance, dressed as a woman, Le- moyne makes inappropriate advances to a male student, and scandal ensues. Lemoyne is forced to leave the university—and the town—and Cope leaves with him. A letter from Cope to another of Mrs. Phillips's female boarders leaves open the possibility that he and Lemoyne have broken off their relation- ship, but the ending is ambiguous. Cope may simply have avoided mentioning Lemoyne in his letter because of the less-than-decorous conditions of his depar- ture from the town of Churchton.

Throughout the novel, fin-de-siècle culture is evoked as a point of contact between the younger generation represented by Cope and the older generation represented by Mrs. Phillips and Basil Randolph. For example, on a visit to Mrs. Phillips's country house on the shores of Lake Michigan, Cope charms his host- ess by renaming a pair of pine trees, formerly known as "Paolo and Francesca," "Pelleas and Melisande," after the names of the lovers in Debussy's opera (or in the play by Maeterlinck on which the opera is based). Cope avers that, given the static nature of the trees and the tumultuous conditions under which Dante's lovers suffer, "[i]t might be less violent and more modern to call your trees Pel- leas and Melisande" (85). The allusion to a fin-de-siècle drama with a plot driven by amorous rivalry is mildly suggestive of the plot of *Bertram Cope's*

Year—for two reasons: the novel involves romantic competition for Cope's attention, and it is also rather static, like a symbolist play without the symbolism. Fuller also alludes to the plot of his own fin-de-siècle novel *The Chevalier of Pensieri-Vani* when he has Randolph present Cope with "his latest acquisition—a volume of Bembo's 'Le Prose,'" lately arrived from Venice—"'*in Venetia al segno de Pozzo*, MDLVII,' said the title page" (154). In this case, the resort to the kind of connoisseurship the Chevalier might have used to ingratiate himself with a younger man falls flat, since Cope has no idea who Pietro Bembo was.

The fin-de-siècle sensibility comes into clearer focus in Fuller's description of the homosocial and homophilic relationships in the novel. Randolph's fantasy of the kind of evening he would like to spend with Bertram Cope is especially telling. He imagines inviting the young man into his bedroom "perhaps after an informal smoke in pajamas among the curios ranged round the small den" (153). This fantasy makes its appearance before Randolph learns of Cope's attachment to Lemoyne, which also finds expression through the ritual of cigarette smoking; at a moment when Cope is caught in a mesh of social obligations to Mrs. Phillips and her "gifted girls," he wishes "he were back home, smoking a quiet cigarette with Arthur Lemoyne" (224). As we have seen, cigarette smoking was especially valued among the more advanced, artistic, and "queer" types of the fin de siècle, and the addition of this detail helps to certify the proclivities of the male characters in the novel. The clearest indication, however, that Bertram Cope and Arthur Lemoyne are representative of same-sex love during the fin de siècle comes when the two men return to their apartment after learning that Amy Leffingwell has broken off her engagement to Cope (because of Cope's inattentiveness and emotional distance): "They spent ten minutes in the clear winter air. As Cope, on their return, stooped to put his latch-key to use, Lemoyne impulsively threw an arm across his shoulder. 'Everything is all right, now,' he said, in a tone of high gratification; and Urania, through the whole width of the starry firmament, looked down kindly upon a happier household" (211). The meaning of "Urania" here is not limited to the mythic epithet for "the heavens" but alludes to one of the more favored terms for homosexual love during the fin de siècle. The utopian socialist Edward Carpenter, among others, used the word *Uranian*, as in the phrase "Uranian temperament," to suggest that same-sex attachments involved a "higher" form of love than heterosexual unions because of the impossibility of biological reproduction among homosexuals. Instead, Uranian couples, so Carpenter argued, were likely to be more artistic than their heterosexual counterparts, reproducing themselves in art and song instead of flesh and blood.[49]

The Uranian context, in fact, provides the basis for the decisive action in the novel, in that Arthur Lemoyne behaves in such a way as to compromise the ideal or higher form of homosexual love so necessary to same-sex relationships in an age of sodomy laws. At least one critic sees a parallel in the action at the close of *Bertram Cope's Year* and in "At Saint Judas's": in both the novel and the play, "Fuller is acknowledging the moral impropriety and 'sinfulness' of homosexuality and is attempting to redeem the two men."[50] The impropriety in *Bertram Cope's Year*, however, seems to lie in the risk of exposure caused by Lemoyne's performance as a female character in "The Antics of Annabella," a musical comedy that features numerous female roles for male actors. Unlike the other actors, Lemoyne does not play his character for laughs: "It was Arthur Lemoyne's fortune—or misfortune—to do his work all too well" (268). Some members of the audience are disconcerted at his "light tenor tones and mincing ways" and his refusal to exploit the comic possibilities of performing in drag: "Of course the right sort of fellow, even if he had to sing his solo in the lightest of light tenors, would still, on lapsing into dialogue, reinstate himself apologetically by using as rough and gruff a voice as he could summon. Not so Lemoyne: he was doing a consistent piece of 'characterization,' and he was feminine, even overfeminine, throughout" (268). But the real trouble comes when Lemoyne stays in character after the play has ended and flirts with another male performer: "He continued to act off-stage; and in his general state of ebulliency he endeavored to bestow a measure of upwelling femininity upon another performer who was in the dress of his own sex. This downright fellow, in cutaway and silk hat, did not understand,—or at least had no patience with a rôle carried too far" (271). Both the on-stage and off-stage performances meet with "distaste and disapproval," and Lemoyne is forced to leave the university. For his part, Cope feels "a personal chagrin," not so much because Lemoyne has shown an interest in another man, but because he has put their relationship at risk by revealing too much about his own sexuality. "Truly, the art of human intercourse was an art that called for some care" (271). It is not clear if these are Cope's thoughts or the author's commentary, but Fuller, discreet as always, leaves it to the reader to riddle through the ambiguities of the phrase "human intercourse."

Fuller's reserve and discretion had long been admired by James Huneker, who singled out "At Saint Judas's" for praise in a letter to Fuller of 1902: "It is always the disciple addressing the master when I write you. I realized this but an hour ago, when I read your magnificently subtle 'At Saint Judas.'"[51] And in 1920, when Huneker was the grand old man of American decadence, he wrote to Fuller to express his admiration for *Bertram Cope's Year*: "I can't help telling you that after 'The Chevalier,' which was a marking-stone in my development, nothing you have written has so stirred me as 'Bertram Cope's Year.' . . . Its portraiture and psychological strokes fill me with envy and also joy."[52] Huneker's private recognition of the worth of Fuller's novel, of course, did nothing to rescue the book from the obscurity that enveloped it so rapidly after publication. Another fifty years would elapse before *Bertram Cope's Year* received any serious critical attention at all. In 1970, on the occasion of the republication of *With the Procession*, Edmund Wilson published a long appreciation of Fuller's career in *The New Yorker*. Wilson devotes more attention to *Bertram Cope's*

Year than to any of the author's other volumes, calling the "curious book . . . perhaps Fuller's best."[53] He finds in the novel "a kind of philosophic theme, which seems to raise it well above the fiction of social surfaces of the school of William Dean Howells" (Wilson, 40).

Strangely, Wilson says that even though the novel "involves homosexual situations," it "is not really a book about homosexuality" (Wilson, 40). Even more remarkable, he asserts that "[a]t no point has the reader been given any clue as to Bertram's sexual inclinations" (Wilson, 43). This is an astonishing comment in view of the Uranian reference, discussed above, not to mention the many other scenes where Cope's relationship to Lemoyne is quite overtly represented as sexual in nature. For example, one character compares the two friends to "a young married couple" and complains, albeit indirectly, "that they brought the manners of the bed-chamber into the drawing room" (200). No doubt Wilson failed to notice Cope's "sexual inclinations" because they are so discreetly handled. Indeed, more recent readings of Fuller's novel emphasize how routine and ordinary Cope's relationship to Lemoyne seems to be. Andrew Solomon observes that *Bertram Cope's Year* "portrays what would now be called normative homosexuality—discreet, occasional, often unfulfilled, neither delirious nor unbearable."[54] The description will stand as one perspective on same-sex relations in the fin de siècle at least as valid as more sensational representations, of a sort found, say, in the erotic novel *Teleny*, attributed partly to Oscar Wilde, or in *De Profundis*, Wilde's self-flagellating confession of the nature of his affair with Lord Alfred Douglas. *Bertram Cope's Year* helps us to understand that the Mauve Decade could also be mundane.

iv

To shift from Henry Blake Fuller to Kahlil Gibran is to show just how varied the decadent revival of the 1920s really was. Yet Fuller and Gibran, different as they are, have something in common in that they both preserve for us aspects of American decadence otherwise hidden from view. Through *Bertram Cope's Year* Fuller allows us to see into the furtive world of same-sex relations among aesthetes and decadents at the turn of the century. In *The Prophet*, Gibran gives us a sense of just how amorphous and overheated those fin-de-siècle mystical cults must have been. But the celebrated case of Kahlil Gibran can also be used to show the relevance of one of the more traditional conceptions of decadence to the American context. The negative meaning of decadence as a type of secondhand culture overwrought into mannered, conventional form surely applies to the mystical prose poetry that Gibran produced more than to most of the literature that emerged from the decadent milieu of fin-de-siècle America. In Gibran's case, calling his work secondhand is really quite generous, since to consider his work closely is to enter a *mise en abîme* of belatedness almost comic in its ramifications.

As we have seen, Gibran's intellectual development started when F. Holland Day began to tutor him in the literature of decadence he so admired. Day's choice of Maeterlinck's *Treasure of the Humble* to provide instruction to the young Gibran was doubtless the result of his close association with Richard Hovey, whose *Rubaiyat*-like collection of poetry, *Songs from Vagabondia* (coauthored with Bliss Carman), Day had published in 1894. Hovey had traveled to Europe and gotten to know Verlaine, Mallarmé, and Maeterlinck, eventually becoming Maeterlinck's principal English translator.[55] In 1895 Hovey translated an edition of Maeterlinck's plays and wrote an introduction titled, "Modern Symbolism and Maurice Maeterlinck." In this introduction Hovey set symbolism against morality by arguing that literature "lives for itself and produces no impression of being a masquerade of moralities; but behind every incident, almost behind every phrase, one is aware of a lurking universality, an adumbration of greater things" (qtd. in Foster, 28). While Hovey was not the translator of the version of *The Treasure of the Humble* that Day read to Gibran, Hovey more than anyone else was responsible for the American fascination with the Belgian symbolist that led to additional translations of Maeterlinck's work.

Even though the book is saturated with symbolist thought, *Le Tresór des humbles* marked a new phase in Maeterlinck's career. By 1896 the decadent influence of Verlaine and Villiers de l'Isle Adam that Maeterlinck had undergone was receding in favor of a kind of mystical optimism that owes its general outlines to the transcendental philosophy of Ralph Waldo Emerson.[56] Comparisons of Emerson and Maeterlinck were being made as early as 1896,[57] and with good reason: some elements of the symbolist aesthetic are due to the influence of the eighteenth-century mystic Emanuel Swedenborg, whom Emerson appreciated early on in his career.[58] In 1912, at the apex of the Belgian's celebrity (the year after he received the Nobel Prize for literature), the translator of Maeterlinck's essay on Emerson noted "how completely and how unconsciously Emerson's thoughts have been assimilated by Maeterlinck. In his essay there are many echoes of 'The Oversoul' and 'Spiritual Laws.'"[59] The English translation of *The Treasure of the Humble* omits an early version of Maeterlinck's Emerson essay included in the French original, but even without it the book shows abundant evidence of the great transcendentalist's influence,[60] as the following chapter titles suggest: "The Awakening of the Soul," "Mystic Morality," "The Invisible Goodness," "The Deeper Life." In sum, there are large cultural ironies at work in Day's choice of Maeterlinck as Gibran's introduction to fin-de-siècle European literature, because *The Treasure of the Humble* owes more to the everyday streets of Concord than to the rarefied salons of Paris.

An appreciation of Maeterlinck published in 1915 describes the *Treasure of the Humble* as the contribution to "a theory . . . of metaphysical idealism coloured by an imaginative intellectuality and an aesthetic emotionalism, a theory too vague to be named a system, too restrictedly personal, perhaps, to impose itself as a doctrine."[61] This assessment might stand equally well as a description of Gibran's *Prophet*, the world-renowned collection of mystical aphorisms published in 1923 that continues to be a best-seller. In fact, passages from Maeterlinck and Gibran can be set side-by-side to show the debt the younger mystic owes to the elder. The 1897 translation of Maeterlinck's *Treasure of the Humble* opens with the chapter "Silence," where we are told straight off that "[i]t is idle to think that, by means of words, any real communication can ever pass from one man to another" because "the true life, the only life that leaves a trace behind, is made up of silence alone."[62] Gibran opines that "there are those who have the truth within them, but they tell it not in words," because, after all, "[i]n the bosom of such as these the spirit dwells in rhythmic silence."[63] The two writers are perhaps most alike on the subject of beauty, which, as the title of Maeterlinck's final chapter in *The Treasure of the Humble* makes clear, is a purely internal affair. "The Inner Beauty" resides somewhere in the soul and is evidently the soul's lone activity: "For beauty is the only language of our soul; none other is known to it. It has no other life, it can produce nothing else, in nothing else can it take interest" (*Treasure*, 219). Gibran says that beauty is apparent only to "the soul enchanted," whereupon it becomes "an image you see though you close your eyes and a song you hear though you shut your ears" (*Prophet*, 101).

It is almost too easy to tag Gibran "decadent" in the negative sense of someone so unknowingly belated in his artistic efforts as to give decadence a name worse than it deserves. The example of Gibran's shallow profundities illustrates the decay of the tradition of philosophical idealism into something so mannered and conventional, so belated and secondhand, as to approach absurdity. If Gibran is secondhand Maeterlinck, that means he is really thirdhand Emerson; and if Emerson is really secondhand Hegel (or secondhand Hinduism), that means Gibran is so far removed from anything like originality he appears, paradoxically, original—at least to those with no awareness of the outworn tradition from which he emerged. This point is borne out by Gibran's critic-proof reputation and the impressive sales record of his books. One source claims that *The Prophet* remains "the all-time best selling book in America,"[64] while another states that it was still selling in the millions of copies in the 1990s.[65] In America, yesterday's decadence is often today's popular commercial culture.

Gibran's popular success would have been hard to predict on the basis of the critical reception of his books when they appeared in the 1920s. *The Prophet* was his third book in English, and like the previous two it was reviewed in Harriet Monroe's *Poetry: A Magazine of Verse*. Reviews of Gibran's books in this journal help to show his relationship to modernism and, perhaps, allow us to say something about the relationship of decadence to modernist culture. After all, Gibran, born in 1883, belongs to the first generation of modernists and was subject to many of the same European influences that they were. Like

Yeats, he admired Blake; like Joyce, he read Maeterlinck; like Eliot, he was attracted to "Oriental" traditions. Yet no one today would dare to place Gibran's work in an anthology of modernist authors. Why not? The question is larger than it seems and has some surprising ramifications, not all of them pleasant.

In her review of Gibran's first book, *The Madman* (1918), Harriet Monroe offered an assessment that most academic readers today would likely echo: "[T]he symbolism is too expository, and its high-sounding easy wisdom ultimately boils down into platitudes. The book annoys by its prosy and somewhat pompous triteness."[66] Another *Poetry* reviewer said much the same things about Gibran's second book, *The Forerunner* (1920): "There is in this book neither the stark authenticity of prophecy, nor the beautiful crystallizations of a creative imagination. What we have here is only pompous dramatizations of only half-individualized platitudes."[67] The review from which this comment is taken is titled "One Poet," meaning that of five poets reviewed only one has written a book "worth any serious consideration" (Schneider, 39). The one true poet is Ben Hecht's friend Maxwell Bodenheim, himself—like Hecht—a product of one strain of the decadent tradition, who in the reviewer's estimation has an abundance of what Gibran lacks utterly: newness. Bodenheim, we are told, "has found new themes, going to neglected or forbidden realms to find them. And he has come to them with a new attitude, enabling him to equip his foundry with new molds" (Schneider, 42). All told, the reviewer uses the word *new* at least twenty-three times in her review of Bodenheim's *Advice*, eight times in one sentence.

The qualities of staleness and pomposity emphasized in *Poetry*'s reviews of Gibran's work and the contrasting newness of Maxwell Bodenheim make an obvious point about modernism—that the single-minded search for newness might have occasionally clouded critical judgment. So, too, does the fact of Bodenheim's contemporary obscurity and Gibran's enormous popularity. This contrast between the moribund newness of Bodenheim's poetry and the deathless staleness of Gibran's philosophy perhaps reveals some unintended truths about the opposition of "new art" and "popular art" in classic analyses of the avant-garde. Ortega y Gasset observed that "the new art . . . helps the elite to recognize themselves and one another in the drab mass of society and to learn their mission which consists in being few and holding their own against many."[68] In Gibran's case, the masses seem to be behaving like the elite in holding their own against the few, perhaps because Gibran embodies not so much the newness that modernist taste preferred, but the fashion for newness that modernism inadvertently promulgated. What fashion does, according to Renato Poggioli, is put some "rarity or novelty into general or universal use."[69] Gibran himself seems to have quite shrewdly inserted himself into the dual cults of genius and newness that modernism encouraged. To validate himself as the sort of artist-genius the age demanded, Gibran produced a blurb for *The Madman* from Auguste Rodin in which the celebrated sculptor

named the Syrian mystic "the William Blake of the Twentieth Century."
Even the sympathetic authors of Gibran's biography acknowledge that "[i]t is
probable that the quotation was invented" by Gibran himself (Gibran and
Gibran, 325). Interestingly, in her review of *The Madman*, Harriet Monroe
expresses a good deal of skepticism about the Rodin remark, which only
shows that she too believed that genius and newness were prerequisites for inclusion in the emerging modernist canon she was helping to form.

The review of *The Prophet* in *Poetry* begins with an explicit recognition of
the split between the literature of the masses and another type of literature
more suited to the sophisticate: Gibran's book "will have a deep appeal for
some readers and leave many others cold."[70] The appeal is said to reside in the
way the book succeeds in "the linking of man to a *subjective* universe by thread
after thread of gossamer speculation"; those readers who are left cold by this
gossamer quality want instead something "from the actual world of sharp *objective* reality" (Seiffert, 216). What is most interesting about the review is how
secure the reviewer is of a readership for actuality, sharpness, objectivity, and
"vigor" (217)—aesthetic features that might be used to imply a male gender-
ing of modernism after the fashion of H. L. Mencken (in the tradition, say, of
the poet Louis Zukovsky, whose work appears for the first time in the issue of
Poetry in which *The Prophet* is reviewed). But the critic's disapproval of *The
Prophet* is not grounded so much in masculinist aesthetics as in a rather xeno-
phobic attitude that makes Gibran's work "Foreign Food" (the title of the review) to an emerging audience for modernist literature. This audience finds
value in the aforementioned actuality, sharpness, objectivity, and vigor.

One way of explaining this taste is to say that it arises as a reaction against
the belated Emersonian mysticism represented by Maeterlinck's philosophical
writings that animates—if that is the word—the witless wisdom of Gibran.
But there is another, more disturbing taste at work in the review, namely, that
the literature we now call "modernist" has a particular racial appeal. Gibran's
book is called "a bit of Syrian philosophy, a mode alien to our culture," which
makes its acceptance by "a people essentially Nordic" all the more "puzzling"
(216). Though *The Prophet* expresses a form of "inward-gazing speculation"
that is "the legitimate heritage of the Oriental" (216), "it could never be a satisfying interpretation of our world" (217). In short, "the essence of the book,
which is its spiritual significance, cannot satisfy the robust hunger of the occi-
dental spirit" (218). These remarks appear even more wrong-headed when the
origins of Gibran's "Oriental" heritage are revealed to owe so much to
Maeterlinck's reworking of Emersonian idealism.

Despite its rather convoluted belatedness, *The Prophet* offers special insight
into both the fin de siècle and the modernist period. Gibran's mystical out-
pourings help us to understand, albeit at some remove, what those theosophi-
cal evenings might have been like in the late nineteenth-century. As Cram's
biographer Shand-Tucci remarks, "*The Prophet*, whatever its shortcomings,

does preserve a sense of the mystical vapors that pervaded Boston's Bohemia and found its focus in the Order of the Visionists."[71] *The Prophet* is also useful to discussions of modernism because it can be used in a kind of definition exercise to highlight certain literary elements that have value in being what modernism is not. At the same time, the decadent legacy of modernism is revealed in those fin-de-siècle elements that Gibran and more canonical authors share, including that most canonical of modernist authors, T. S. Eliot. The decadent legacy is obviously evident in Eliot's high regard for French poets such as Baudelaire and Jules Laforgue, who belong to a tradition of European decadence. Less obvious is the debt he owes to American decadence. Among many possible connections that might be made, there is Eliot's reference to the German immigrant writer George Sylvester Viereck (1884–1962), whose 1907 novel, *The House of the Vampire*, inspired one of the poet's more memorable allusions in *The Waste Land*. Viereck's line, "They called me Betsy, the Hyacinth Girl," gets into Eliot's poem virtually unchanged.[72] But this kind of isolated borrowing is less important than the more general relation, still not fully recognized, between Eliot and the High Anglican, royalist subculture of fin-de-siècle Boston.[73]

Eliot's debt to American decadence remains largely unexamined because Eliot went to considerable pains to obscure it, mainly by remaking himself into a British modernist. But the modernist distance from decadence now seems far less than it once was, a point that can be made by examining one of the authors whom Eliot himself put before the public as someone who shared his aesthetic preoccupations: Djuna Barnes. Interestingly, Eliot introduced Barnes's novel *Nightwood* in terms borrowed, conceptually at least, from Oscar Wilde. Writing in 1937, when social realism was in fashion, Eliot complains that "most contemporary novels . . . obtain what reality they have largely from an accurate rendering of the noises that human beings currently make in their daily simple needs of communication."[74] The elevation of accuracy and realism in fiction was precisely what Wilde objected to in "The Decay of Lying." Thus, if Kahlil Gibran represents the decadent legacy at its worst, Barnes suggests how essential that legacy is to the best of modernist literature.

v

Any account of Djuna Barnes's career has to acknowledge the writer's multiple connections to various avant-garde literary and artistic groups and individuals now associated with modernism: the Provincetown Players (best known for staging Eugene O'Neill's work); Greenwich Village bohemians prior to World War I; the postwar avant-garde journal *transition*; Natalie Barney's largely lesbian Paris salon; Peggy Guggenheim, James Joyce, T. S. Eliot, and so on. Her high modernist pedigree notwithstanding, Barnes's biography also supports arguments in favor of her belated relation to fin-de-siècle decadence. In this connection an important early influence is the now-forgotten Greenwich Village publisher Guido Bruno (1884–1942), described as "an extreme case" of someone "wholly committed to the *fin de siècle*."[75] Born Curt Josef Kisch in Bohemia, Bruno immigrated to New York in 1906 and settled in Chicago in 1911. The next year he started up *The Lantern*, a monthly magazine dedicated to publishing "discarded truth and rejected fiction."[76] Under the literary pseudonym derived from the first names of his two younger brothers, Guido Bruno promoted the work of Edgar Allan Poe and Oscar Wilde. When *The Lantern* folded in 1913 he moved back to New York and set up a new publishing venture on Washington Square South in Greenwich Village. Living in Yonkers with his wife and adopted daughter, Bruno commuted to the Village and became a kind of professional bohemian catering to the tourist trade. From mid-1914 to May 1916 Bruno published two periodicals, *Greenwich Village* and *Bruno's Bohemia*, plus a series titled *Bruno Chap Books*, all "edited by Guido Bruno in his garret on Washington Square"—a certification of bohemian authenticity printed on the title page of each volume. The first number in this series was a reprint of Oscar Wilde's poem "The Harlot's House"; another number was devoted to a defense of Wilde's *Salome* by Lord Alfred Douglas.[77] Djuna Barnes's *Book of Repulsive Women*, a collection of poetry, appeared as one of the *Bruno Chap Books* in 1915, and the slight volume is certainly reflective of Bruno's posture as "a champion of the aestheticism and decadence of the 1890s and its leading figures—Oscar Wilde, Arthur Symons, Frank Harris, Aubrey Beardsley."[78]

The Beardsley connection is especially relevant to Barnes's early career. The eight poems (or "Rhythms," as the pieces are called) published in *The Book of Repulsive Women* are followed by five drawings that show a debt to Beardsley's style while also departing from it. An image of one presumably repulsive woman, for instance, employs Beardsley's stippled line to decorative effect but reverses the use of black typical of Beardsley in the figure-ground relationship (figure 16). The poems themselves conform to Guido Bruno's scheme to promote "the risqué image of Greenwich Village for the bourgeois tourist, consolidating and overtly advertising the notion of decadent Village bohemianism." Greenwich Village therefore becomes a kind of lesbian Babylon, with Barnes presenting her "repulsive" women "as spectacles of a male-oriented viewpoint,"[79] as in the following verse:

> See you sagging down with bulging
> Hair to sip,
> The dappled damp from some vague
> Under lip.
> Your soft saliva, loosed
> With orgy, drip.[80]

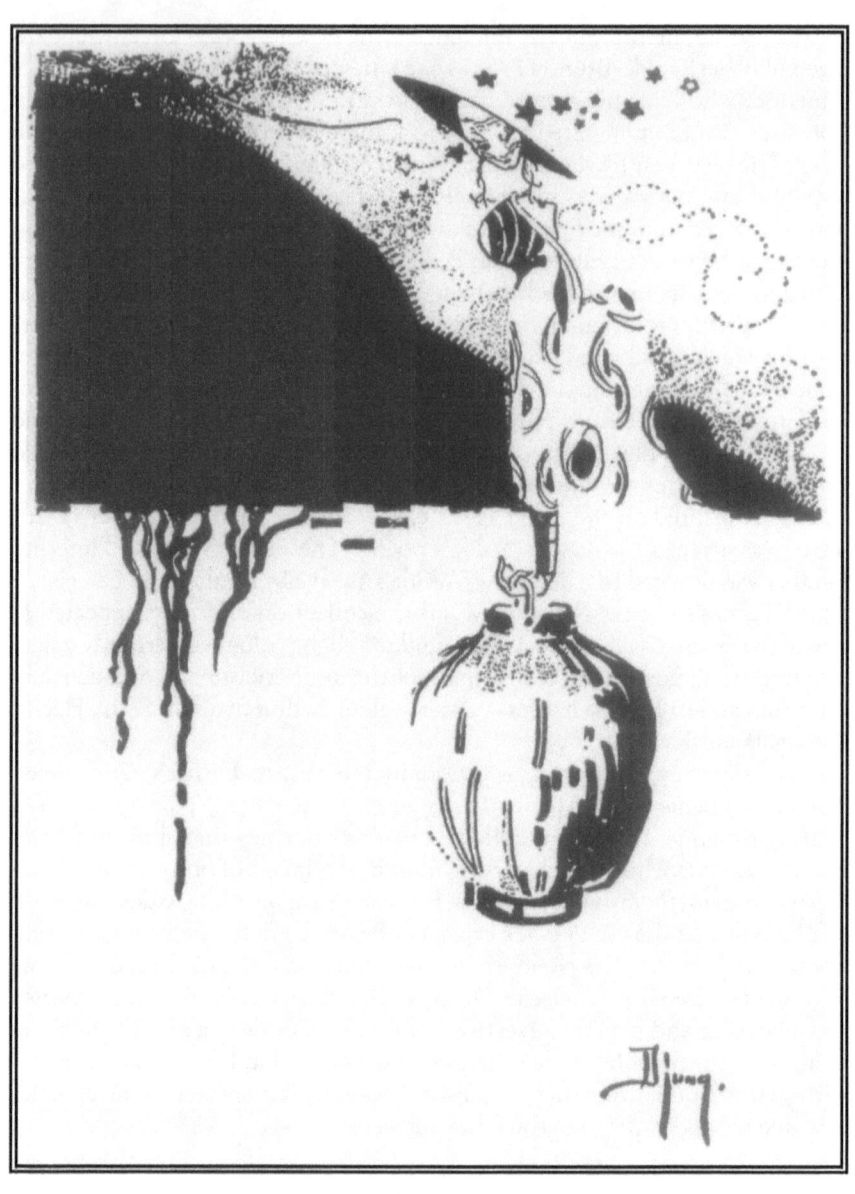

FIGURE 16 Djuna Barnes, drawing from *The Book of Repulsive Women* (1915)

Another poem, "The Twilight of the Illicit," describes a kind of female arche-
type of sin, a Lilith figure whose exhausted condition prompts the poet-
narrator to express melancholy admiration mixed with regret:

> One sees you sitting in the sun
> Asleep;
> With the sweeter gifts you had
> And didn't keep,
> One grieves that the altars of
> Your vice lie deep.
>
> You, the twilight powder of
> A fire-wet dawn;
> You, the massive mother of
> Illicit spawn;
> While the others shrink in virtue
> You have borne.[81]

As these passages show, *The Book of Repulsive Women* suggests the "fatal
woman" theme of decadent literature, but the shift to the female point of view
renders that "fatality" desirable in a different way from the more familiar mas-
ochistic male narratives of female dominance during the fin de siècle.

Barnes's appropriation of this classic decadent narrative for the purpose of
exploring female pleasure takes form in her drama and fiction as well. The
best-known nineteenth-century narrative of female fatality is the Salomé
story, variously rendered into poetry or prose by Flaubert, Mallarmé, Huysmans, Laforgue, and, of course, Wilde, whose one-act tragedy evidently had
the most influence on Barnes. Phillip Herring says that Barnes most likely
owned the American edition of *Salome* published in 1906 and claims that "the
curiously stilted dialogue of many of Barnes's plays point[s] with certainty to
the Wilde drama as a very important early influence."[82] The influence is
played out in some of Barnes's early short stories, notably "What Do You See,
Madam?" (1915) and "The Head of Babylon" (1917). The first of these stories
is a slight, amusing piece about a music hall dancer named Mamie Saloam
whose long-standing admiration for Oscar Wilde (whom she "learned to inter-
pret . . . [a]t the age of ten") inspires her to raise her cultural status from burlesque performer to *artiste* by working a scene from *Salome* into her act.[83] Her
ambition "to kiss the lips of John the Baptist" comes into conflict with the affection her stage manager, Billy, has for her (he wants her to give up "this ambition stuff") and also with a ladies' antivice society known as the "P.I.B.,"
which stands for "the Prevention of Impurities upon the Boards" (57, 60).
Both the ladies of the P.I.B. and Billy are satisfied, more or less, when Mamie
performs and kisses the lips of the prophet "with perfect impartiality" (62), not

knowing that the stage manager has replaced the Baptist's plaster head with his own by standing beneath the boards.

The second Salomé story, "The Head of Babylon," does not allude to Wilde's play directly, and the "Babylon" of the title likely refers to the town in Long Island, not Mesopotamia.[84] The "Head" of the title belongs to a young Polish woman named Theeg, who is paralyzed from the waist down. She is the favorite child of her father, Pontos, who has succeeded in marrying off his disabled daughter to his neighbor Slavin, another farmer. Slavin "had fallen in love with Theeg at first sight; she seemed like something newer and stranger and more desirable because of her oddity" (127). A similar reason might be advanced for Salome's attraction to John the Baptist in Wilde's play, and the gender reversal is confirmed when Theeg speaks on her wedding day, sounding the notes of biblical prophecy: "Yes, the land and the moving things thereon, and all the young year that has begun, are theirs. All the grass that has found renewal, all the flowers that bloom, all the old hopes and the old manner—but this, then, is mine. This new man and this new day are mine, and mine the task to make this lonely head a wild, grand thing upon its helpless pedestal" (131). Herring comments that "The Head of Babylon" is "a bit enigmatic" for a newspaper story (it was originally published in the Sunday magazine supplement of the New York *Morning Telegraph*) and says that "the main point of the story seems to be that the rewards of imagination are to be preferred to the physical labor and conventional prosperity that farmers prize."[85] Perhaps, but given the perverse sexual subtext of Wilde's play—not to mention the explicit treatment of a quadriplegic woman as both a sexual object and a desiring subject in the story itself—other meanings are set in motion more consistent with Barnes's avant-garde art and her bohemian life. In the story, Theeg's mother offers words of advice to her daughter on her wedding day that surely resonate with Barnes's heterodox existence as a lesbian woman: "You will find it difficult. You will have to invent a way of living" (131).

With the bizarre character Theeg and her mannered way of speaking, "The Head of Babylon" looks forward to the narrative eccentricities of *Nightwood*, a novel generally described in literary-historical terms as a work of high modernism. Indeed, the novel does have many features associated with the modernist literary aesthetic: it is complex, difficult, and stylistically opaque; it is antirealistic or expressionistic; and it has a narrative that is chronologically discontinuous. At the same time, the work seems thematically grounded in the literature of decadence: degeneration is a recurrent theme, expressed through the rather compromised "aristocratic" Volkbein lineage that culminates in the sick child, Guido (named, perhaps, after the publisher Bruno); most of the characters are homosexual, bisexual, or transvestite, and some combine all these conditions, as in the notable case of Dr. Matthew O'Connor; marginal, less-than-normative lifestyles of degradation and hedonism are celebrated and given a positive valuation throughout the book.

Perhaps it can be said that the novel is a kind of modernization of decadence in which decadent material is subjected to the narrative and stylistic procedures of modernist fiction.

The title *Nightwood* seems to allude to the "dark wood" (*una selva oscura*) that Dante encounters "mid-way in [his] life's journey."[86] If so, Barnes's novel does not treat the theme of sin or error in a negative way, but, rather, elevates the darkness and degradation conventionally associated with sin and error through a positive valorization of various negatives. Stated more simply, *Nightwood* affirms negation, and this affirmation takes the oxymoronic form of decadent figuration whereby metaphors and other figures of speech combine both positive and negative terms. Kenneth Burke's phrase for this rhetorical maneuver is "transcendence downward," that is, "a perverse 'ascent' in terms of decay where corruption and distinction become interchangeable terms."[87] Examples of this sort of affirmative negation can be enumerated at some length, especially in such oxymoronic phrases as these: "good dirt," "damned upward," "holy decay," "dire happiness."[88] A more discursive example of the pattern is the description of French priests as typically Catholic "composite[s] of husband and wife in conjunction with original sin, carrying with them good and evil in constantly quantitative ascent and descent" (108). Another instance of this type of figuration is Dr. O'Connor's observation that Felix Volkbein's son Guido is "'maladjusted'"—a word that is not used "in the derogatory sense at all" (116).

Théophile Gautier's influential explanation of "le style de décadence" in his preface to the third edition of Baudelaire's *Les Fleurs du mal* (1868) uses the organic metaphor of physical decomposition to liken disintegrating language to a decaying body. As extended by Bourget, Nietzsche, and other writers, the theoretical paradigm of decadent style has come to describe a manner of writing that places the greatest degree of artistic emphasis on the smallest unit of literary composition: hence the word or phrase is polished to a point that the reader's attention is attracted to such smaller units at the expense of the whole. In his introduction to *Nightwood*, T. S. Eliot says that the novel will "appeal primarily to readers of poetry" (xi). In the nineteenth century, the critic Sainte-Beauve said something similar about Flaubert's novel *Salammbô*, a narrative about the decline and fall of ancient Carthage, calling it "[une] espèce de poëme en prose," one of the markers, in this critic's view, of a kind of decadence.[89] Eliot goes on to say that what he means is that "most contemporary novels are not really 'written'"; rather, they consist of "a prose which is no more alive than that of a competent newspaper writer or government official. A prose that is altogether alive demands something of the reader that the ordinary novel reader is not prepared to give" (xii). As noted, Eliot appears to be making an objection to realist fiction not unlike the one that Oscar Wilde makes in "The Decay of Lying." Thus, both of these stylistic points—that the novel is stylistically similar to poetry and is written in antirealist prose—are recognizable as attributes of decadent literature. It is also telling that Eliot thinks that good literature must make demands of the reader, that it must be difficult. The larger point here is that *Nightwood* can be used to illustrate the emergence of a modernist literary aesthetic out of the style of decadence.

Although not so discontinuous and fragmented as some other, better-known modernist novels (Joyce's *Ulysses*, Faulkner's *Sound and the Fury*), Djuna Barnes's *Nightwood* can hardly be described as a straightforward, chronologically ordered narrative. The novel begins conventionally enough by giving the "biographical" background of Felix Volkbein, one of the major characters, who is born in 1880. As Des Esseintes does in Huysmans's *À Rebours*, Felix Volkbein considers his lineage as represented in old portraits, and we are told that, at a certain point, "exact history stopped" (7). History, in other words, is exhausted as the novel begins, a situation similar to that in *À Rebours*, which likewise presents a narrative in sections that might, conceivably, appear in a different order. Hence the reader encounters episodes more than once, and it is not unusual for narrative chronology to be reversed or skewed, as in, for example, the moment when Robin Vote leaves Felix Volkbein after the birth of their child for Nora Flood (49), even though Robin and Nora do not meet until several pages later, "in the fall of 1923" (53). Although the novel cannot be called atemporal, it is still true that the work's coherence derives more from reiterated images than from plot connections. For example, the doctor says he's "an angel on all fours" (95), a clever phrase that is realized at the end of the novel in the image of Robin Vote behaving like a dog: "And down she went, until her head swung against his [the dog's]; on all fours now, dragging her knees" (169). Also, the phrase "down she went"—and various conceptual echoes thereof—functions like a leitmotif throughout the novel, as in the chapter titles "Bow Down," "Where the Tree Falls," and "Go Down, Matthew." This last title refers at once to the uplifting spiritual "Go Down, Moses" and to the common idiom for the performance of oral sex. Indeed, the basic thematic sense of "going down" that emerges from the novel is never far from sexual meanings.

Along these lines, *Nightwood* presents the reader with varieties of sexuality that can be called "decadent" because they are all at some remove from heterosexual "norms." The trapeze artist aptly named Frau Mann, for example, suggests the American circus performer Miss Urania in *À Rebours*. Frau Mann's leotards are so tight that the cloth crotch seems "so much her own flesh that she was as unsexed as a doll" (13). Nineteenth-century models of sexual types are in evidence in Nora's sexual preferences: "And I, who want power, choose a girl who resembles a boy," whereupon the doctor asks, "[W]hat is this love we have for the invert, boy or girl?" (136)—using the old sexologist's term "invert" as a synonym for "homosexual." A darker form of sexuality is explored as Robin Vote falls asleep reading "the memoirs of the Marquis de Sade" (47) then later falls into an abusive lesbian relationship with Jenny Petherbridge:

"Then Jenny struck Robin, scratching and tearing in hysteria, striking, clutching and crying. Slowly the blood began to run down Robin's cheeks, and as Jenny struck repeatedly Robin began to go forward as if brought to the movement by the very blows themselves" (76). Transvestitism is represented by the recollection of Nora's grandmother, "who, for some unknown reason, was dressed as a man, wearing a billycock [i.e., a derby hat] and a corked moustache, ridiculous and plump in tight trousers and a red waistcoat" (63). The doctor is an even more spectacular transvestite, equipped with "laces, ribands, stockings, ladies' underclothing and an abdominal brace, which gave the impression that the feminine finery had suffered venery" (78–79). Finally, the male doctor's desire to bear children is one of the more endearing expressions of perversion in the book: "God, I never asked better than to boil some good man's potatoes and toss up a child for him every nine months by the calendar" (91). One suspects that some sort of euphemism is at work in the expression "boil [a] good man's potatoes," as there is in this account of Nora and Robin breakfasting in bed: "She sat up in bed and ate eggs and called me, 'Angel! Angel!' and ate my eggs too" (144).

Strictly speaking, Djuna Barnes's *Nightwood*, first published in 1937, does not belong to the decadent revival in the same sense that Huneker's *Painted Veils*, Fuller's *Bertram Cope's Year*, or even Gibran's *Prophet* do. But in a way it does, because Barnes herself is a product of that revival. Moreover, the novel is set in the 1920s, and, as such, it captures, in modernist form, the tastes and sensibilities of those latter-day decadents whose ideas of culture were shaped largely by fin-de-siècle authors. Like many modernist authors, Barnes appropriated that culture and made it new through the deployment of narrative and poetic devices, which, curiously enough, also have their origins in the literature of decadence. But literary modernism is not the only legacy of decadence in the United States. Indeed, the original literature of decadence continues to be very much a part of the American cultural scene.

Decadent literature is kept alive today by many of the same American publishers who found—or created—a market for once-controversial modernists such as Barnes and Joyce in the 1920s and 1930s. Barnes's *Nightwood* was published in affordable paperback format by New Directions, a press that has kept Baudelaire's *Les Fleurs du Mal*, that ur-text of decadence, on its list to the present day. New Directions also keeps an edition of Mallarmé's poetry on its list, as well as Edouard Roditi's *Oscar Wilde*. But no publisher did more, in its day, to keep decadent culture alive for modern readers than Boni and Liveright, and, later, Random House, through the Modern Library imprint. Indeed, Wilde's *Picture of Dorian Gray* was the premier publication of the firm that Albert Boni and Horace Liveright formed in 1917 to bring high culture to a mass audience. Interestingly, the date of the Modern Library's inception coincides almost exactly with Thomas Beer's reckoning of the beginning of the decadent revival, and with good reason. Of the Modern Library's initial run of twelve titles, all reflected fin-de-siècle tastes, including, in addition to Wilde's novel, a play by Maeterlinck, fiction by Anatole France, and a volume of Schopenhauer, *Studies in Pessimism*. The initial list of twelve Modern Library titles was quickly followed by more books in the decadent-aesthetic tradition, notably a volume of Wilde's poetry and an edition of George Moore's *Confessions of a Young Man*.[90]

All of the Modern Library's offerings included introductions by respected critics. Floyd Dell's preface to Moore's *Confessions* is especially noteworthy because it shows how thoroughly intertwined decadent culture was with the "modern" spirit:

> These "Confessions of a Young Man" constitute one of the most significant documents of the passionate revolt of English literature against the Victorian tradition. It is significant because it reveals so clearly the sources of that revolt. It is in a sense the history of an epoch—an epoch that is just closing. It represents one of the great discoveries of English literature: a discovery that had been made from time to time before, and that is now being made anew in our own generation—the discovery of human nature.[91]

In Dell's view, the discovery involves the revelation that human nature "is much more selfish, brutal, and lascivious than we care to admit" (vii). His linkage of the decadents and contemporary moderns could not be clearer and provides evidence for Thomas Beer's claim that Moore was an "idol of American writers" (119). Beer, of course, refers to writers of the Mauve Decade, but the point here is that decadence was new again in the 1920s, and Floyd Dell's preface to Moore's *Confessions* makes that point insistently. Moore's rebellious "discovery" is completely grounded in the literature of decadence (Dell names Gautier, Baudelaire, Swinburne, and "the Parisian diabolists" [xi] among Moore's precursors), a literature that is of value because it offers "a truly revolutionary conception of life," one that "has begun to obtain acceptance in our day" (viii).

Decadence today is no longer so closely intertwined with modernist literature or the kind of "modern" lifestyle Dell required, and this detachment from modernism may be one explanation for its continuing appeal. While the postmodernist critique of modernism has mostly run its course, one result of the various feminist, postcolonial, and queer treatments of modernism that have taken place in recent years is a heightened appreciation of the cultural worth of the literature just prior to modernism. Not all of this literature can be characterized as "decadent," but much of it can. In the 1920s, as the decadent revival developed, critics such as Dell were in no position to distinguish the "moderns" from the modernists. Indeed, the necessity of the designation *modernist* only became evident later on, as a way of describing something in addition to the "modern" spirit that decadent culture captured.[92] As we have seen, the work of an author such as Djuna Barnes is modernist and "modern" at the same time, and *Nightwood* is noteworthy not only because of its innovative style but also because of its narrative of elevated degradation. The passion for self-destruction is a creative passion, too, or so the decadent would have us believe. In a way, the modernist complexities of *Nightwood* reflect the difficulties of maintaining, in America, the refinements of corruption that true decadence demands. But there is no denying that the culture of corruption and the literature that celebrates it have their appeal. Modern but not modernist, popular (now) but not populist, decadent literature, at its best, is pleasantly offensive in its heightened treatment of perversity, sickness, degradation, and decay. And while the American decadents will never rank with their British and Continental counterparts, perhaps one day some future "Petronius" will survey the modest accomplishments of the Mauve Decade and appreciate the lesser delights of Edgar Saltus, F. Holland Day, Henry Blake Fuller, Gelett Burgess, and other masters of the age-end art that is American Decadence.

Afterword

Sometime in 1926 a newspaper reporter and illustrator named Wallace Smith, who had come to Hollywood from Chicago, presented the silent film star Rod La Rocque with a copy of *Fantazius Mallare* (1922), a decadent novel written by Ben Hecht, Smith's friend and fellow newspaperman at the Chicago *Daily News*. In the early 1920s, Hecht was widely known as the author of the realist novel *Eric Dorn* (1921), a book that, despite its straightforward style, prompted the critic Burton Rascoe to call its creator a "reincarnation" of Joris-Karl Huysmans.[1] Hecht is known today not as the author of precious novels in the manner of Huysmans and Mirbeau but as one of the greatest screenwriters of the twentieth century.[2] But Smith knew Hecht as a decadent novelist, and he knew *Fantazius Mallare* especially well because he had illustrated Hecht's depraved tale with ten fantastic, Beardsleyesque drawings, several of them depicting the sterile orgies of the novel's deluded, reclusive hero (figure 17). Rod La Rocque must have meant a lot to Wallace Smith, as the inscription he wrote to the star implies: "For Rod La Rocque—who has a thousand masks for his face—but, thank Christ, never an one for his heart."[3] As further token of his admiration, Smith hand-colored a number of the drawings in the book he gave to the celebrated screen idol, who had more than two dozen pictures to his credit in 1926, including a role in Cecil B. DeMille's *Ten Commandments* (1923).[4] But like many other stars of Hollywood's silent era, Rod La Rocque is all but unknown today. His name lives on, however ironically, because of a film about the forgotten stars of the silent screen: Billy Wilder's *Sunset Boulevard* (1950). In a critical scene from this famous film about the loss of fame, the luckless screenwriter Joe Gillis (William Holden) looks down from his garage apartment window into the empty swimming pool of the crumbling Hollywood mansion owned by Norma Desmond (Gloria Swanson), the deranged former star who is planning her comeback—or "return," as she puts it—in a film about Salomé. Gazing at the empty pool swept with leaves in the late evening, Gillis thinks: "And of course she had a pool. Who didn't then? Mabel

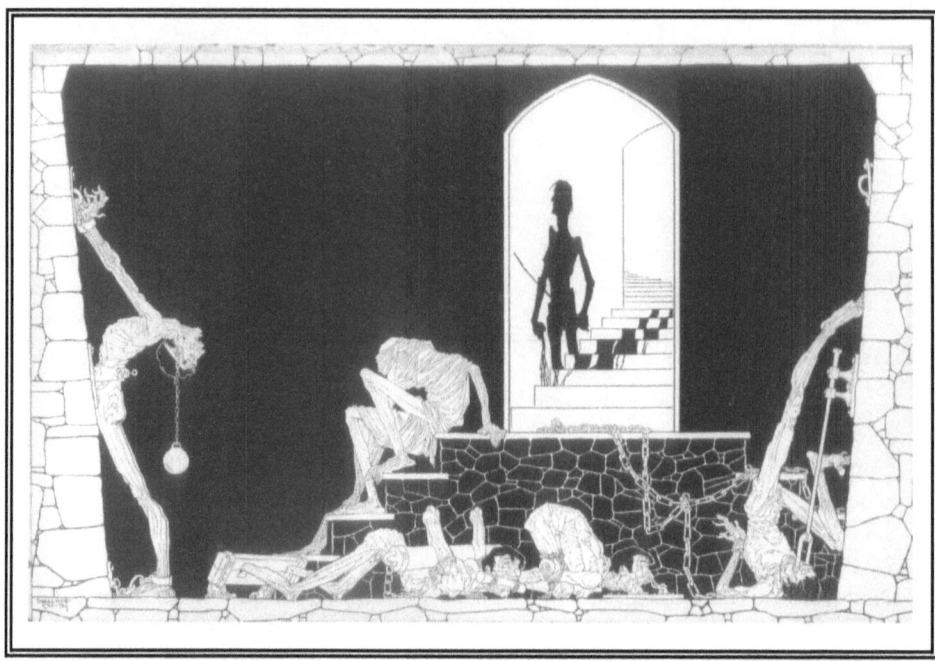

FIGURE 17   Wallace Smith, drawing from Ben Hecht, *Fantazius Mallare* (1922)

Norman and John Gilbert must have swum in it ten thousand midnights ago, and Vilma Banky and Rod La Rocque. It was empty now. Or was it?" A close-up reveals that the pool is full of rats.[5]

Wallace Smith's gift to Rod La Rocque in 1926 can stand as a symbol of a larger cultural transfer that occurred in the 1920s: the passage of decadence from literature to film. Despite the revival of the 1920s, decadence did not survive in literary form because of competition from two considerable cultural fronts: modernism and social realism. Artistically, American avatars of the fin de siècle could not match the growing cultural prestige of Continental modernist authors such as Joyce, Mann, and Proust (all of whom also owe a dept to decadence) during the interwar period, nor were they the equal of their expatriate contemporaries Hemingway and Eliot. And if Huneker, Hecht, and the rest—including Hergesheimer and Cabell—appeared aesthetically retrograde by comparison with the great modernist authors, after the Wall Street Crash of 1929 their precious fiction seemed downright substanceless next to the work of a socially engaged realist such as John Steinbeck. But even before the Great Depression did decadence in as a literary culture another kind of decadent culture had begun to emerge through the powerful new medium of the motion picture. Decadence, however, did not survive the transfer intact; indeed, the popular, commercial style of the cinema guaranteed a radical transformation of whatever cultural material the new medium adapted for its mass audience. What happened when decadence went to the movies, however, was not so much a transformation as a deformation: decadence disseminated into the broader culture was also decadence dissipated.

Still, the dissipation of decadence into popular culture through the new cultural form made a certain amount of sense, given the decadent pedigree of the early screenwriters, many of whom—like Hecht—had started out as news-papermen steeped in fin de siècle literature. As Mencken had been before him, Hecht was a protégé of James Huneker, whose journalism had already aided the entrance of decadence into American popular culture well before the younger generation of pressmen made the career shift to Hollywood.[6] Huneker's prolific endorsements of decadent authors at odds with Puritanism and Main-Street respectability likely contributed to the fashion for silent screen scenarios derived from fin-de-siècle literature in the early years of Hol-lywood. Certainly the presence of decadence in popular culture over the first decade of the twentieth century is not in doubt, as the "Salome craze" shows. In May 1905, Wilde's play was revived by the New Stage Club of London and presented in England for the first time; in December of the same year the play premiered in Dresden in the form of an expressionist opera by Richard Strauss.[7] The craze was fueled by music hall performances circa 1907–1908 by the Canadian dancer Maud Allan and a *Salomé* ballet by the Russian actress Ida Rubenstein. American interest became so intense that the popular actress Marie Cahill "pleaded with Teddy Roosevelt to stop the Salome craze in the United States."[8] The 1918 silent screen version of *Salome* starring Theda Bara no doubt capitalized on continuing popular fascination with the famous temp-tress. Indeed, this actress's celebrated vamp persona (the screen name *Theda Bara* is an anagram of "Arab Death") draws on a popular version of the "fatal woman" theme in decadent literature. Another silent *Salome*, this one star-ring Alla Nazimova in 1922, proved fatal in more than one sense, for it fol-lowed the Wilde-Beardsley text a little too closely for film audiences to appre-ciate and bombed at the box office. No doubt the full census of silent-screen Salomés and related, "fatal" types—such as Cleopatra—would run in the doz-ens or possibly the hundreds, so the cultural logic that Wilder uses in *Sunset Boulevard* is solid: of course Norma Desmond would use *Salome* as the vehicle for her return to the silver screen. What else?

But decadence in the context of American film has another meaning unre-lated to the fin-de-siècle subject matter of some of the early silents: Hollywood is also the playground of depraved celebrities whose behavior is both admired and condemned as wildly out of line with the middle-class mores of the film audience. Celebrity decadence is another pop-culture field into which deca-dence dissipates, one that has been lovingly documented by the independent filmmaker Kenneth Anger in his two sensational *Hollywood Babylon* books. As the back-cover blurb of a recent reprint of the first of these books has it, *Hollywood Babylon* is "brimming with detail and decadence,"[9] and there is no mistaking the type of decadence on display: celebrity excess, moral depravity, self-destructive hedonism. Anger takes inspiration for his title from a 1915 film by D. W. Griffith set in Babylonian times and uses the Mesopotamian reference to make Hollywood "a synonym of sin": "a New Babylon whose evil influence rivaled the legendary depravity of the old" (Anger, 15). A celebrated example of New Babylon depravity is the story of Fatty Arbuckle's notorious gin party on Labor Day weekend, 1921, at the Hotel St. Francis in San Francisco. As Anger tells it, on the second full day of the party, Arbuckle, then at the height of his fame as a slapstick actor with Paramount Studios, took a pretty bit player named Virginia Rappe into a hotel bedroom and performed some sort of perverted sex act—possibly involving a champagne bottle—on the hapless actress. Whatever Arbuckle did ruptured the girl's bladder and caused her to die of peritonitis five days later. After three well-publicized trials, Arbuckle was acquitted of any wrongdoing because of confused eye-witness testimony (everyone was drunk at the time of the incident) "and lack of specific evidence (such as a bloody bottle)" (Anger, 42). Nonetheless, the scandal was so sensational that Paramount cancelled Arbuckle's $3 million contract, and the man never worked as an actor again. One of Virginia Rappe's former boyfriends moralized that "this is what comes of taking vulgarians from the gutter and giving them enormous salaries and making idols of them. . . . They are the ones who participate in orgies that surpass the orgies of degenerate Rome" (qtd. in Anger, 44).

Anger, however, has no wish to give degeneracy or depravity a bad name. What he exposes is not so much the decadence of the stars (though he does do that) but the hypocrisy of the Hollywood publicity machine, the rapacity of the studio moguls, the viciousness of the gossip columnists, and the goof-ball naïveté of the "gee-whiz public" (Anger, 189). As often as not the glamorous pleasure-hungry movie stars, who are simply doing what comes unnaturally, end up looking weirdly innocent—the victims of the various powers of industry and audience they are contracted to satisfy. Anger manages the trick by using a gossipy tabloid style of writing to incriminate the gossip columnists and the tabloid mongers, as in this virtuoso debunking of Louella Parsons, "the Paganini of Piffle," and the New York *GraphiC*:

> Lumpen-Pate Louella! Lollipop's daily morning prattle column told the breakfasting nation the scoop-by-scoop Hollywood Score, the Who's-Fucking-Who-Stakes-Out-West Where Fortunes Grow. Lolly called it "going out" together but the flappers knew what *that* naughty-naughty meant. . . .
>   While pushy L. O. P. and her legion of copycat peddlers teased the newsprint nationwide, the smart-ass big-city tabs offered ranker meat: for the *GraphiC* &

Co there was No Badder Place than Hollywood—Reborn BABYLON, with Santa Monica-Sodom and Glendale-Gomorrah for suburbs. The tattlemen luridly depicted the Stars as glittering soulless women wandering from wicked to wanton orgy on the tuxed arms of vainglorious males of malevolent beauty, in a moneyed, perfumed world haunted by the specters of Drink, Dope and Debauchery, Insanity, Suicide and Murder. While in the Sodom-Gomorrah suburbs, the Lavender Swamp, ways of sinning took place that were certainly weirder, it was hinted, than fornication and adultery. (Anger, 189, 191)

One of Anger's tales of lavender depravity has considerable relevance to the filmmaker's own career. His account of Rudolph Valentino's failed marriages and premature death includes a 1926 Chicago *Tribune* screed that holds Valentino responsible for a nationwide "degeneration into effeminacy" and asks, quite reasonably, if the new breed of feminine man "is a cognate reaction with pacifism to the virilities and realities of the war" (qtd. in Anger, 157–58). Anger locates the cause of the journalist's attack in the screen idol's dandyism, his "well-known taste for sartorial extravagance, . . . his gold jewelry and preference for heavy perfumes"—that, and his habit of wedding lesbians who later testified in divorce proceedings that their marriage to the Sheik had gone unconsummated (158, 163). According to Anger, both of Valentino's wives, Jean Acker and Natacha Rambova, were "'protégées' of the exotic and equally lesbian actress Alla Nazimova," the woman who had produced and starred in the silent *Salome* of 1922. Nazimova's production featured costumes designed by Rambova based on Beardsley's drawings for the lead role (Anger, 163), while the "supporting male actors [were] decked out in spangled tights, heavy makeup, and pasties."[10] Anger adds that Nazimova "employed only homosexual actors as 'homage' to Wilde" (Anger, 163).

The box-office failure of Nazimova's feature does not deter the admiration of Anger, never a friend of the Hollywood establishment. On the contrary, in an essay effectively titled "Diva de la décadence: Salomé," he praises Nazimova "as the female Orson Welles of her time" because of the creative control she exercised over her own films in the face of the studio system.[11] More important, Anger took inspiration from Nazimova and other female stars of Hollywood's silent era for one of his earliest independent film projects, *Puce Women*. Planned as a feature-length film but never completed, *Puce Women* was intended as a tribute to the women of 1920s Hollywood—"a study of their lifestyles, their clothes, their cars, their houses, their social patterns, with an all women cast" (Hutchinson, 41). Anger called the film "my love affair with mythological Hollywood. A straight, heterosexual love affair . . . with all the great goddesses of the silent screen" (qtd. in Hutchinson, 41). All that survives of Anger's original 1949 project is six minutes of footage edited in 1970, with a pop music soundtrack added. Retitled *Puce Moment*, the film is Anger's own camp contribution to the tradition he documents in the *Hollywood Babylon* books.

The opening sequence of *Puce Moment* features a series of shimmering, se-quined evening gowns shimmying flapper-style toward the camera. The seg-ment is followed by shots of a deliriously narcissistic screen goddess (Yvonne Marquis) getting dressed, applying perfume, and lounging about. The short film ends with the woman following her four wolfhounds down the steps of her Hollywood Hills mansion. With its evocation of self-absorbed but forgotten stardom, the film anticipates by one year Wilder's narrative treatment of the same theme in *Sunset Boulevard*. The critic Alice C. Hutchinson, however, does not look to the cinematic past of Nazimova's *Salome* or the future of Wilder's film for explanation of Anger's homage to a by-gone Hollywood but to the decadent literary tradition. She finds in the "Rococo clutter of *Puce Moment*'s style of decadence" something "luxurious and glamorous, capturing Baudelaire's 'phosphorescence of decay.'" She also resorts to a scholarly study of French decadent literature to describe the "introspective microcosm" of the film "as a self-preoccupied attempt to create another world through the cult of sensationalism."[12] Here, the dissipation of decadence into cinema could not be clearer. Less clear, however, is how decadence is modified in the process of moving from literature to film.

Hutchinson is not alone in using the discourse of decadence to characterize Anger's avant-garde cinema, and for this reason the filmmaker can serve as a kind of case study in the dissipation of decadence into various forms of Ameri-can culture. Another critic locates a "decadent occult Eucharist" (whatever that is) in Anger's phantasmagoric *Inauguration of the Pleasure Dome* (1954/ 1966) and observes that "the lavish costumes, elaborate sets and gorgeously jeweled colours create the effect of stasis and a decadence turned in upon it-self."[13] One reason for the critical alignment of this lusciously visual artist with the decadent literary tradition evidently lies in Anger's own affection for that tradition. In his biography of the filmmaker, Bill Landis records Anger's early interest in Beardsley and the French decadent writers, especially Huysmans, whose work he introduced to fellow filmmaker Curtis Harrington.[14] But Anger was more interested in the diabolic Huysmans of *Là Bas* than in the decadent Huysmans of *À Rebours*. This interest illustrates yet another way that deca-dence has dissipated since the nineteenth century, for decadence and diabo-lism are hardly the same thing: one deals with aesthetic tastes and the other concerns religious (albeit Satanic) beliefs. True, during the fin de siècle some decadents were also interested in Satanism (as Huysmans was), but a whole-sale identification of decadence and diabolism does not follow from this histor-ical fact. Nevertheless, Kenneth Anger is often accounted "decadent" because of his fascination with occult traditions.

Anger's interest in the occult, which started in the mid-1940s when he was still a high school student, developed into one of the most important ele-ments of his film aesthetic. Anger ultimately regarded himself as an outright disciple of Aleister Crowley (1875–1947), the British occultist who claimed to actually *be* the Great Beast of Revelations 13:18, whose mystical number is 666.[15] As Lawrence Sutin explains, when Crowley identified himself with the Beast of the Apocalypse he became, in his mind, "no less than the Prophet of a New Aeon that would supplant the Christian Era and bring on the reign of the Crowned and Conquering Child, embodiment of a guiltless, liberated humanity that had, at last, chosen to *become* the gods it had merely worshiped in the past."[16] Crowley's influence on Anger's career is all-pervasive; indeed, this least commercial of artists once claimed that "[t]he one product I'm trying to sell is Aleister Crowley."[17]

Crowley's neopaganism is prominently displayed in *Inauguration of the Pleasure Dome*, which features cryptic performances by Marjorie Cameron and Samson DeBrier as, respectively, the Scarlet Woman and the Great Beast 666. Anger frequently reedited and otherwise manipulated his films to suit the occasion of their presentation, but *Inauguration of the Pleasure Dome* exists in a more-or-less official version known as "The Sacred Mushroom Edition," which is accompanied by the following synopsis and dedication:

> Lord Shiva, The Magician, wakes. A convocation of Theurgists in the guise of figures from mythology bearing gifts: The Scarlet Woman, Whore of Heaven, smokes a big fat joint; Astarte of the Moon brings the wings of snow; Pan bestows the grapes of Bacchus; Hecate offers the sacred mushroom, yagé, wormwood brew. The vintage of Hecate is poured. Pan's cup is poisoned by Lord Shiva. The orgy ensues—a magick masquerade at which Pan is the prize. Lady Kali blesses the rites of the children of light as Lord Shiva invokes the godhead with the formula "Force and Fire." Dedicated to the few; and to Aleister Crowley, and the crowned and conquering child.[18]

No synopsis, however, can do justice to the orgiastic riot of Ecktachrome color; the cascading montage of exotic, superimposed images; and the magisterial music of Janáček's *Glagolithic Mass* on the soundtrack: these elements have rightly earned the film the epithet "psychedelic."[19] Hence there is ample justification for reading the film as an example of "counterculture aesthetics" (Hutchinson, 7), but do such aesthetics qualify as decadence?

The question becomes more complicated with *Scorpio Rising* (1963), the film for which Anger is perhaps best known. Shot in Brooklyn in 1962 and completed in San Francisco the following year, the film explores "the cult of the motorcycle" as a prescient instance of the youth culture that flowered more fully later in the decade.[20] The title refers at once to Anger's astrological birth sign and to the character Scorpio, the leader of the pack of cultists who ride their machines to a climactic Walpurgisnacht orgy. Each of the film's thirteen segments is scored to a different pop song of the day, and the juxtaposition of music and image is often ironic, amusing, or irreverent. For example, one sequence cross-cuts shots of the antihero, Scorpio, stepping out into the night with old silent film footage of Jesus walking with his disciples and then healing the blind (when the blind man is healed, an erotic image flashes briefly on the screen)—all to the music of the Crystals' "He's a Rebel." More interesting are the gender and cultural reversals set in motion by the juxtaposition of Bobby Vinton's saccharine teen ballad "Blue Velvet" with highly homoerotic shots of the biker-dandies donning their leather and chains for the sadomasochistic scenes to come. The segment has the effect of an ornately descriptive passage in a decadent novel (such as Flaubert's *Salammbô*) in that it arrests the narrative flow to allow the viewer to luxuriate in the images of bodies and objects on the screen. As Juan A. Suárez observes, in *Inauguration of the Pleasure Dome* this kind of fetishistic delectation and "theatrical excess" is traceable to "high culture traditions, such as fin de siècle decadentism," whereas in *Scorpio Rising* the effect derives "from popular sources."[21]

Although Suárez rightly understands *Inauguration of the Pleasure Dome* as a film that belongs more "fully in the tradition of decadentism and aestheticism" than does *Scorpio Rising* (Suárez, 146), he still locates Anger's work generally in the tradition of decadence, as do a number of other critics.[22] In film studies as well as in literary studies, 'decadence' is never so clear and self-evident as those who use the term assume, but the word seems especially fraught in Anger's case. Formally, Anger's cinematic art might be likened to *le style de décadence* in literature because of its emphasis on the smaller units of filmic composition at the expense of the whole. Anger once said that "the pivotal thing" about *Inauguration of the Pleasure Dome* is "the legend of Bacchus": the film ends "with the God being torn to pieces by the Bacchantes."[23] But surely the ritual *sparagmos* Anger imagines is not represented so much as enacted by the filmmaking process itself, which is already a form of fragmentation. Quick cuts and close-ups are especially well-suited to suggest the fetishistic fragmentation of the body of Bacchus Anger describes, or, for that matter, any body at all. Anger's camera seeks out fetish objects and body parts in *Scorpio Rising,* also. Here the objection might be made that the fragmentary, fetishistic aspect of Anger's films—which we are aligning with *le style de décadence*—is common to *all* films and therefore should not be taken as a formal marker of the cinematic decadence of a particular filmmaker. But the epithet 'decadent' might be easier to justify in Anger's case because of the alliance of the formal marker with certain topoi typical of the decadent tradition, such as the combination of morbidity and eroticism. Indeed, Suárez points to Anger's "unsettling mixture of desire and death" as a common feature of both his films and the *Hollywood Babylon* books. This quality comes through in a line from Anger's own synopsis of *Scorpio Rising*: "Thanatos in chrome and black leather and bursting jeans."[24]

Another traditional meaning of decadence that is relevant to Anger's films concerns that quality of cultural mixture typical of periods of transition. The filmmaker's career begins, more or less, at a key transitional moment, when the button-down conformity of the 1950s starts to come apart. He manages to do much more, however, than simply capture moments of social disintegration on film; rather, Anger relates these moments of transition by connecting—cinematically—one period of cultural decadence with another. *Puce Moment,* for example, is ostensibly "about" a movie goddess of the 1920s, but the film also looks forward to the Technicolor decadence of the 1950s (the "star" Yvonne Marquis could almost pass for the young Elizabeth Taylor). At the same time, the late-sixties pop music on the soundtrack connects these earlier moments of social transition to a later one. The twenties, fifties, and sixties—not to mention the 1890s—are also simultaneously evoked by *Inauguration of the Pleasure Dome.* Originally shot in 1954, the 1966 version also includes the superimposed images of most of *Puce Moment.* By quoting his earlier film in this way, Anger connects 1920s decadence to a later California counterculture. Add the *Pleasure Dome* titles in the style of Beardsley (which partially reappear near the end of the film), and the transitional pastiche is complete. Another example of this sort of diachronic decadence involves a character in *Pleasure Dome* derived from the silent cinema of the Weimar period in Germany: Cesare the Somnambulist from Robert Wiene's classic expressionist silent, *The Cabinet of Dr. Caligari* (1919). In Anger's film, the Somnambulist enters a door "created" by an image of Aleister Crowley and goes on to pour a magic elixir for the Roman Caesar Nero. This transaction between Cesare and Caesar forms another link between a prior and a later decadence (Rome and Weimar), both of which are connected to the countercultural present. If decadence and transition are equivalent, as Flaubert and Baudelaire said, then Anger makes the most of this equivalency.

Even though it might be possible to reconcile the stylistic and thematic preoccupations of Anger's films with the decadent tradition, the fact remains that that tradition is mainly literary—and, more important, mainly nineteenth century. Clearly, then, those who would situate a filmmaker such as Anger in this tradition must have something more in mind, because Anger's films are not notably "literary," nor do they seem to belong to the world of the nineteenth century. On the contrary, Anger's films seem most closely connected to various twentieth-century counterculture movements, and therein lies the reason for his presumed inclusion in the decadent tradition. The original decadents of the nineteenth century in both Europe and the United States might be called "counterculture" artists, but the culture their work countered was significantly different from the commercial culture Anger's independent art opposes. Also, nineteenth-century literary decadence is largely aristocratic in spirit if not in fact; the social trajectory of the decadent is always upward, away from the democratic masses of the bourgeois world: his is a counterculture of elites. By contrast, Anger's counterculture "decadence" separates itself from the bourgeoisie by moving down the social scale into an alternative, bohemian world that is not antidemocratic or elitist at all. Obviously, this critical social distinction between nineteenth-century decadence and twentieth-century "decadence" has some important aesthetic ramifications. For example, there are more consistencies than contradictions in the relation of fin-de-siècle literary decadence to high modernism: Proust follows logically from Huysmans, just as Joyce depends from Pater. Hence decadence in the literary context is tantamount to avant-gardism. Anger's "decadence" is likewise in the aesthetic vanguard, but his social position as a bohemian artist means that his influence has been registered mainly in the realm of popular culture. For example, *Scorpio Rising* anticipates the biker films of the mid-to-late 1960s—*The Wild Angels* (1966), *Hells Angels on Wheels* (1967), and the more estimable *Easy Rider* (1969). The film also looks forward to the music video, as does *Kustom Kar Kommandos* (1965), a three-minute film about customized hot-rods scored to the Parris Sisters' "Dream Lover." The point here is that Anger's "decadent" posture outside the mainstream puts him, paradoxically, in the avant-garde of the very commercial culture he opposes. If Anger's aesthetic innovations do derive from nineteenth-century decadence, as so many commentators claim, then those innovations are culturally belated, and the moment these belated innovations enter the mainstream of popular culture they become decadent in another sense: as cultural formulae available for commercial exploitation (e.g., music videos, exploitation films, and so on).

Although Anger can hardly be held accountable for the commercial appropriation of his work by others, he is exemplary of contemporary American "decadence" in a larger sense, which can only be explained by bringing the quotation marks out of the closet. As this last phrase suggests, one of the ways in which "decadence" differs from decadence is in the area of same-sex relations. The social implications of homosexuality are vastly different now than at the end of the nineteenth century. Then, F. Holland Day and Ralph Adams Cram called themselves "decadent" partly because they were "queer": they had no choice but to accept the judgment of abnormality, deviance, or decadence placed on them by medical and legal authority. Today, gay artists and writers are not decadent in this nineteenth-century sense, but some of them might choose to be "decadent" in another sense—by adopting the pose, say, of the Wildean dandy, as Quentin Crisp (1908–1999) did not so long ago in New York City.[25] In different ways, Anger participates in and explores this "decadent" pose in his films, perhaps most interestingly in *Scorpio Rising*. The "decadent" sexuality of this film is bound up with another distinction between the old decadence and the new. "Decadence" today differs from its fin-de-siècle cousin in its affection for popular culture, which can be endlessly appropriated and reworked for ironic effect: pop songs and Jesus films get this treatment in *Scorpio Rising*. Finally, "decadence" is not so refined as decadence and requires a special sensibility for its appreciation. Though readily accessible, "decadence" is not to everyone's taste; even though the film can hardly be called "elitist," *Inauguration of the Pleasure Dome* is, after all, dedicated "to the few."

"Decadence" in this sense is hardly distinguishable from camp, the "good taste of bad taste," in Susan Sontag's celebrated phrase. What Sontag says of camp might also be said of *Inauguration of the Pleasure Dome*: "It incarnates a victory of 'style' over 'content,' 'aesthetics' over 'morality,' of irony over tragedy."[26] Sontag's "Notes on Camp" (1964), dedicated to Oscar Wilde, makes abundantly clear that the sensibility she describes descends in large measure from fin-de-siècle decadence.

So "decadent" sexuality, "decadent" culture, and "decadent" taste all derive from decadence, but, at the same time, this new dissipated "decadence" cannot quite replace the fin-de-siècle original. And even though American cinema did take over the cultural space occupied by decadent literature, all Hollywood was able to do with decadence, in the end, was what Hollywood always does: commodify, popularize, debase. Not even the "magic hour," it seems, can adequately capture the crepuscular world of decadence, which gets its weary energy by going against the grain of some dominant cultural form. Perhaps we should not expect the mass-market medium that *was* the dominant cultural form of the twentieth century (but may not hold that position in the twenty-first) to go against the grain of anything at all or to do much more than simply offer the age the images it demands. The social dissipation of decadence into bohemianism, on the one hand, and into the leisure or celebrity classes, on the other, means that the only cultural forms that decadence can take today are either camp or commercial, and of course these two categories may sometimes combine. Perhaps the continuing appeal of fin-de-siècle decadence lies in the knowledge that its like will never be seen again. The decorous dandies and refined aesthetes, actual or fictional, who took art as a guide to life in the nineteenth century are no more. Looking backward now, we can only be nostalgic for that vanished age when depravity and corruption actually meant something, when excess needed careful calculation and perversion required discipline and discretion. Today, of course, America offers no shortage of depravity, corruption, excess, and possibly even perversion, but never decadence: it is too late for that.

Notes

PREFACE

1. J.-K. Huysmans, *Against Nature*, trans. Robert Baldick (London: Penguin, 2003), 203. Further references to this edition are cited parenthetically in the text.

2. Edith Wharton, *"Madame de Treymes" and Three Novellas* (New York: Simon & Schuster, 1995), 216. Further references to this edition are cited parenthetically in the text.

3. Brian Stableford, introduction to *The Dedalus Book of Decadence (Moral Ruins)* (Cambs: Dedalus, 1990), 75.

4. For a survey of definitions, see "The Definition of Decadence," chapter 1 of David Weir, *Decadence and the Making of Modernism* (Amherst: University of Massachusetts Press, 1995), 1–21.

5. William Blake, *The Marriage of Heaven and Hell* (London: Oxford University Press, 1975), xvii.

6. For Gautier's description of Baudelaire as a practitioner of *"le style de décadence,"* see Claude-Marie Senninger, ed., *Baudelaire par Théophile Gautier* (Paris: Klincksieck, 1986), 124. For the elaboration of *le style de décadence* by Paul Bourget and Friedrich Nietzsche, see Matei Calinescu, *Five Faces of Modernity: Modernism, Avant-Garde, Decadence, Kitsch, Postmodernism* (Durham: Duke University Press, 1987), 157–71, 186–87.

7. One of the more celebrated accounts of this dimension of decadence is Elaine Showalter's *Sexual Anarchy: Gender and Culture at the Fin de Siècle* (New York: Penguin, 1990).

8. The synonymous usage appears in Baudelaire's remarks on Victor Hugo as a "compositeur de décadence ou transition." See *Curiosités esthétiques* (Paris: Conard, 1923), 105–106.

9. I am indebted to my student Michaelanthony Mitchell for this felicitous formulation.

10. I refer to William Carlos Williams's *In the American Grain* (New York: Albert & Charles Boni, 1925) and to Dwight Macdonald's *Against the American Grain* (New York: Random House, 1962). I should add Vera M. Kutzinski's *Against the American Grain: Myth and History in William Carlos Williams, Jay Wright, and Nicolás Guillén* (Baltimore and London: Johns Hopkins University Press, 1987) to the list of titles that, despite the evident similarity to mine, are irrelevant to it.

11. See Showalter, *Sexual Anarchy*; Murray Pittock, *Spectrum of Decadence: The Literature of the 1890s* (London: Routledge, 1993); Ellis Hanson, *Decadence and Catholicism* (Cambridge: Harvard University Press, 1998); and Weir, *Decadence and the Making of Modernism*.

12. George C. Schoolfield, *A Baedeker of Decadence: Charting a Literary Fashion, 1884–1927* (New Haven and London: Yale University Press, 2003), 372.

CHAPTER ONE

1. For Couture, see the painting *Les Romains de la décadence* (1847), now in the Musée d'Orsay; for Nisard, see *Études de moeurs et de critique sur les poètes latin de la décadence*, 5th ed. (Paris: Hachette, 1888).

2. Max Nordau, *Degeneration* (1895; New York: Fertig, 1968), 27: "The degenerate artist who suffers from *nystagmus*, or trembling of the eyeball, will, in fact, perceive the phenomena of nature trembling, restless, devoid of firm outline."

3. Théophile Gautier, *Baudelaire par Théophile Gautier*, ed. Claude-Marie Senninger (Paris: Klincksieck, 1986), 124: "Le poète des *Fleurs du mal* aimait ce qu'on appelle improprement le style de décadence."

4. For a brief history of the development of the Marxist idea of cultural decadence, see Matei Calinescu, "The Concept of Decadence in Marxist Criticism," *Five Faces of Modernity: Modernism, Avant-Garde, Decadence, Kitsch, Postmodernism* (Durham: Duke University Press, 1987), 195–211.

5. In Spengler's view, America's republican political system was "untenable" and must one day "make way for formless powers such as those with which Mexico and South America have long been familiar." Oswald Spengler, *The Decline of the West: Perspectives of World History*, trans. Charles Francis Atkinson (New York: Knopf, 1950), 2: 416.

6. Douglass Shand-Tucci, *Boston Bohemia, 1881–1900: Ralph Adams Cram: Life and Architecture* (Amherst: University of Massachusetts Press, 1995), 13, 16.

7. *Harper's Bazaar*, 18 Feb. 1882: 98; *Boston Evening Transcript*, 30 January 1882: 4; 1 February 1882: 2; 2 February 1882: 4; *Buffalo Commercial Advertiser*, 2 February 1882: 2. Quoted by Mary Warner Blanchard, *Oscar Wilde's America: Counterculture in the Gilded Age* (New Haven and London: Yale University Press, 1998), 18. Further references are cited parenthetically in the text as "Blanchard."

8. Quoted by Richard Ellmann, *Oscar Wilde* (New York: Knopf, 1998), 183. Further references are cited parenthetically in the text as "Ellmann."

9. Washington Gladden, "Christianity and Aestheticism," *Andover Review* 1.1 (January 1884): 16, 18–19. Gladden does not offer a wholesale endorsement of aestheticism, however, and cautions against the aesthetic excesses of Oscar Wilde's religion of art.

10. H. W. Brands, *The Reckless Decade: America in the 1890s* (Chicago and London: University of Chicago Press, 1995), 27.

11. Quoted by Brands, *The Reckless Decade*, 22.

12. Frederick Jackson Turner, "The Problem of the West," in Susan Harris Smith and Melanie Dawson, eds., *The American 1890s: A Cultural Reader* (Durham and London: Duke University Press, 2000), 397. Further references to material in this reader are cited parenthetically in the text as "Smith and Dawson."

13. T. J. Jackson Lears, *No Place of Grace: Antimodernism and the Transformation of American Culture, 1880–1920* (1983; Chicago and London: University of Chicago Press, 1994), 49–50.

14. George M. Beard, *American Nervousness: Its Causes and Consequences* (New York: Putnam's, 1881), vi. Further references cited parenthetically in the text.

15. Tom Lutz, *American Nervousness, 1903: An Anecdotal History* (Ithaca and London: Cornell University Press, 1991), 6.

16. Henry Childs Merwin, "On Being Civilized Too Much," *Atlantic Monthly* 79 (June 1897): 839. Quoted by Lears, *No Place of Grace*, 47.

17. Max Nordau, "Degeneration and Evolution: A Reply to My Critics," *North American Review* 161 (July 1895): 90. Further references cited parenthetically in the text as "Nordau."

18. S. Weir Mitchell, *Wear and Tear, or, Hints for the Overworked*, 5th ed. (Philadelphia: Lippincott, 1887), 62. Further references are cited parenthetically in the text as "Mitchell."

19. Mayo W. Hazeltine, "Nordau's Theory of Degeneration," *North American Review* 160 (July 1895): 735–52. For a discussion of militaristic responses to Nordau by Hazeltine and others, see Lears, *No Place of Grace*, 112–17.

20. A signal event in the Pre-Raphaelite movement in the United States was the appearance of the *Crayon*, the first Pre-Raphaelite journal in the nation, which began publication in New York City in 1855. See David Howard Dickason, *The Daring Young Men: The Story of the American Pre-Raphaelites* (Bloomington: Indiana University Press, 1953), 47–64.

21. Lears, *No Place of Grace*, 133.

22. Quoted by Ernest Samuels, *Henry Adams: The Major Phase* (Cambridge: Harvard University Press, 1964), 130.

23. Stephen G. Brush, *The Temperature of History: Phases of Science and Culture in the Nineteenth Century* (New York: Franklin, 1978), 122.

24. Quoted by Samuels, *Henry Adams*, 167.

25. Brush, *The Temperature of History*, 30–31.

26. Brooks Adams, *The Law of Civilization and Decay: An Essay on History* (1916; rpt. Honolulu: University Press of the Pacific, 2002), viii–ix. Further references are cited parenthetically in the text.

27. James Buchan, *Frozen Desire: The Meaning of Money* (New York: Farrar, Straus and Giroux, 1997), 163.

28. Lears, *No Place of Grace*, 30.

29. Mark Sullivan, *Our Times: The United States, 1900–1925* (New York and London: Scribner's, 1926), 1: 289–90, 289n.1.

30. Owen Wister, *Roosevelt: The Story of a Friendship, 1880–1919* (New York: Macmillan, 1930), 22. Further references are cited parenthetically in the text.

31. William Taylor Marrs, M.D., *Confessions of a Neurasthenic* (Philadelphia: Davis, 1908). Although this work is sometimes regarded as a straightforward medical account of a nervous condition, the book in fact is quite humorous. One sign that the author should not be identified with the first-person narrator is the M.D. degree that Marrs evidently holds. In the course of the narration we learn that the narrator attends medical school but does not complete his degree (107).

32. Quoted in Edmund Morris, *The Rise of Theodore Roosevelt* (New York: Coward, McCann & Geoghegan, 1979), 126.

33. Morris, *The Rise of Theodore Roosevelt*, 162; Sullivan, *Our Times*, 2: 215.

34. Morris, *The Rise of Theodore Roosevelt*, 162.

35. Quoted by Sullivan, *Our Times*, 2: 217.

36. Morris, *The Rise of Theodore Roosevelt*, 131.

37. Thomas Beer, *The Mauve Decade: American Life at the End of the Nineteenth Century* (1926; New York: Knopf, 1937), 192.

38. William Dean Howells, "Editor's Study," *Harper's New Monthly Magazine* 73 (September 1886): 641.

39. W[illiam] D[ean] Howells, *"Criticism and Fiction" and Other Essays*, ed. Clara Marburg Kirk and Rudolf Kirk (New York: New York University Press, 1959), 62, 85.

40. Howells, *"Criticism and Fiction" and Other Essays*, 87.

41. Howells, *"Criticism and Fiction" and Other Essays*, 87.

CHAPTER TWO

1. Stuart Merrill, trans., *Pastels in Prose*, W[illiam] D[ean] Howells, intro. (New York and London: Harper & Brothers, 1890), 189-90, v.

2. Oscar Wilde to Edgar Saltus, September 1890. *The Letters of Oscar Wilde*, ed. Rupert Hart-Davis (New York: Harcourt, Brace & World, 1962), 275.

3. Edgar Saltus was born in New York City on 8 October 1855, to parents of Dutch ancestry with a measure of wealth (his grandfather had acquired a vast area of iron-rich land around Lake Placid). Saltus completed two semesters at Yale, the last in 1873, and entered Columbia Law School in 1878. In the period between he traveled in Europe and came into contact with a number of leading figures in literature and philosophy. While in Paris studying at the Sorbonne, Saltus met writers who played a major role in three major schools of French literature: Victor Hugo (Romanticism), Leconte de Lisle (Parnassianism), and Paul Verlaine (Symbolism). While in Germany he became an avid follower of Schopenhauer and met Eduard von Hartmann, from whom he derived his own philosophic pessimism. In England Saltus met Oscar Wilde, just as Wilde was building the celebrity that would make him the central figure of the Decadence in England. After Saltus returned from Europe, he did complete his law degree, but determined on a career in literature instead. With the encouragement of his brother Frank, a prolific poet well-regarded in bohemian circles in New York and Paris, Saltus embarked on a biography of Balzac, which was published in 1884. Saltus likely saw in Balzac a model for his own ambitions, since the French author also endured a legal apprenticeship early in his career. In the biography Saltus writes that Balzac "felt . . . that his vocation was not such as is found in courts, and expressed a preference for a purely literary life" (see *Balzac* [Boston: Houghton, Mifflin, 1884], 10). In Saltus's case, "purely literary" interests were put aside for the study of pessimism in *The Philosophy of Disenchantment*, published in 1885. His first novel, *Mr. Incoul's Misadventure*, followed in 1887. His brother Frank died in 1889, and though they had grown close, Saltus's productivity was not affected; he published *A Transaction in Hearts* that year. But his literary success was dogged by personal misfortune when, in 1891, he divorced his first wife amid scandalous newspaper reports that exploited his reputation as an erotic novelist (a fictionalized version of the marriage's deterioration appears in *Madam Sapphira* [1893]). *Imperial Purple* (1892) can be regarded as the culmination of Saltus's artistic career. His creative decline begins in 1893 with the shift to journalism, which he pursued by writing articles for newspapers in San Francisco and Los Angeles and for magazines such as *Harper's Bazaar* and *Smart Set*. By most accounts his effort to revive the

earlier success of *Imperial Purple* with *Imperial Orgy* in 1920 was a failure. He died in the city of his birth on 31 July 1921. This sketch of Edgar Saltus's career is based on Claire Sprague, *Edgar Saltus* (New York: Twayne, 1968).

4. H. L. Mencken, *Prejudices: Fifth Series* (New York: Knopf, 1926), 278. Further references are cited parenthetically in the text.

5. Percival Pollard, *Their Day in Court* (New York and Washington: Neale, 1909), 47. Pollard alludes to both the title and subtitle of Walter Pater's *Marius the Epicurean: His Sensations and Ideas*.

6. Alfred Kazin, *On Native Grounds: An Interpretation of Modern American Prose Literature* (1942; New York: Harcourt Brace Jovanovich, 1982), 66.

7. Van Wyck Brooks, *The Confident Years: 1885–1915* (New York: Dutton, 1952), 114.

8. Harry Levin, "The Discovery of Bohemia," *Literary History of the United States*, 3d ed., ed. Robert E. Spiller et al. (New York: Macmillan, 1963), 1073.

9. See Larzer Ziff, *The American 1890s: Life and Times of a Lost Generation* (New York: Viking, 1966).

10. Edgar Saltus, *The Philosophy of Disenchantment* (1885; New York: AMS, 1970), 5–6. Further references to this edition are cited parenthetically in the text.

11. Edgar Saltus, *Mr. Incoul's Misadventure* (New York: Benjamin & Bell, 1887), 23–24. Further references are cited parenthetically in the text as *MIM*.

12. Edgar Saltus, *Balzac* (Boston: Houghton, Mifflin, 1884), 55.

13. Edgar Saltus, *The Anatomy of Negation* (1925; New York: Ams, 1968), 10. Further references are cited parenthetically in the text as *AN*.

14. Edgar Saltus, *The Truth about Tristrem Varick* (Chicago and New York: Belford, Clark, 1888), 15. Further references to this edition are cited parenthetically in the text.

15. It is not quite accurate to say that after he got his law degree from Columbia University in 1880 Saltus never practiced law. He put much of what he learned of the law into practice in the writing of his second novel—the accumulation of legal details that attach to the overturning of the will, to Tristrem's criminal defense, and even to the lack of an international copyright law to protect American authors is indeed impressive. Certainly the legal details impart a degree of realism into the sensational story, and in this respect Saltus was doubtless inspired by a similar density of legal detail in Balzac's *Eugenie Grandet*.

16. Joris-Karl Huysmans, *Against Nature*, trans. Robert Baldick (New York: Penguin, 2003), 89. Further references to this edition are cited parenthetically in the text as *AR*.

17. Leon Edel, introduction to *We'll to the Woods No More*, trans. Stuart Gilbert (New York: New Directions, 1957), viii.

18. Claire Sprague, *Edgar Saltus* (New York: Twayne, 1968), 72.

19. Edgar Saltus, *Imperial Purple* (Chicago: Higgins, 1892), 162. Further references to this edition are cited parenthetically in the text.

20. Quoted by Sprague, *Edgar Saltus*, 49.

21. James Gibbons Huneker, *Steeplejack* (New York: Scribners, 1922), 2: 190. Further references are cited parenthetically in the text with the abbreviation *SJ*.

22. Brooks, *The Confident Years*, 155.

23. *M'lle New York* 1.6 (October 1895), [7]. The pages of the magazine are unnumbered, and many articles do not have titles; not all of them are signed. Further references to this issue are designated parenthetically as *MNY* 1.6., with the page number following in brackets.

24. Edward Foster, ed., *Decadents, Symbolists, & Aesthetes in America: Fin de Siècle American Poetry: An Anthology* (Jersey City: Talisman, 2000), 30n. Quotations from Huneker's story are cited parenthetically from this anthology with the abbreviation *DSA*.

25. *M'lle New York*, new series, 1 (November 1898): n.p.

26. *M'lle New York*, new series, 2 (December 1898): n.p.

27. Ziff, *American 1890s*, 144.

28. Ziff, *American 1890s*, 144.

29. Vance Thompson, *French Portraits: Appreciations of the Writers of Young France* (Boston: Badger, 1899), vii–viii. Further references to this edition are cited parenthetically in the text.

30. Vance Thompson, *Eat and Grow Thin: The Mahdah Menus* (New York: Dutton, 1914), 16. Further references are cited parenthetically in the text.

CHAPTER THREE

1. Van Wyck Brooks, *New England: Indian Summer 1865–1915* ([New York:] Dutton, 1940), 146.

2. Henry Adams, *The Education of Henry Adams* (Mineola, NY: Dover, 2002), 265.

3. Quoted by Stephen Maxfield Parrish, *Currents of the Nineties in Boston and London: Fred Holland Day, Louise Imogen Guiney, and Their Circle* (New York and London: Garland, 1987), 265. The phrase "willful sadness" comes from Guiney's essay, "Willful Sadness in Literature," *Decadents, Symbolists, & Aesthetes in America*, ed. Foster, 33–36.

4. "The Quest: Being an Apology for the Existence of the Review Called The Knight Errant," *The Knight Errant* 1 (1892): 1. Further references to this issue are cited parenthetically with the abbreviation *KE* 1.

5. "Round the Mahogany Tree," *The Mahogany Tree* 26 (9 July 1892): 411.

6. "Round the Mahogany Tree," *The Mahogany Tree* 22 (28 May 1892): 346.

7. See citation in note 3 in this chapter.

8. Brooks, *New England Summer*, 150.

9. According to Douglass Shand-Tucci, *Boston Bohemia 1881–1900: Ralph Adams Cram: Life and Architecture* (Amherst: University of Massachusetts Press, 1995), Cram somehow gained entry to Norton's Shady Hill salon; his diary from the early 1880s shows that he read Ruskin and William Morris and came to "worship Art as the highest development of man, especially the Pre-Raphaelites" (22, 32). Almost certainly, Cram was in the audience for Wilde's January 1882 lecture on the Pre-Raphaelites and may even have met the great man himself. By the mid-1880s, Cram had established himself as the art critic for the Boston *Evening Transcript* and wrote frequently about the Pre-Raphaelites. In one dispatch, written on his first trip to Europe, he said of Dante-Gabriel Rossetti that the artist "seems to enter of a sudden into the consciousness of all the magic and mystery of life, love and passion, the intense and beautiful ardor of the middle ages" (59). Further references to this biography of Cram are cited parenthetically in the text as "Shand-Tucci."

10. Ralph Adams Cram, *My Life in Architecture* (Boston: Little, Brown, 1936), 91–92. Further references are cited parenthetically in the text.

11. Estelle Jussim, *Slave to Beauty: The Eccentric Life and Controversial Career of F. Holland Day* (Boston: Godine, 1981), 51. Further references are cited parenthetically in the text as "Jussim."

12. Thayer Lincoln to Ralph Adams Cram, letter of 8 January 1935. Quoted by Shand-Tucci, *Boston Bohemia*, 374.

13. In fact there is a historical connection between Anglicanism and Theosophy, since Madame Blavatsky's *Isis Unveiled* draws on the copious writings of Thomas Maurice, an Anglican churchman who published several accounts of Hindu mythology in the late eighteenth century.

14. According to T. J. Jackson Lears, *No Place of Grace: Antimodernism and the Transformation of American Culture* (Chicago: University of Chicago Press, 1981), in Boston at the turn of the century, the Catholic Church would have been socially *déclassé* for someone of Day's wealth and social standing. As Lears says of Ralph Adams Cram's conversion, Cram was "unwilling to embrace Roman Catholicism, the church of the immigrant," choosing instead "the more fashionable solution of High Church Anglicanism" (204).

15. Willa Cather, "Peter," *The Mahogany Tree* 1.21 (21 May 1892): 323–24.

16. In truth the second volume of the journal continued publication beyond the six-month period of the first volume but under different editorship. The second volume is a more conventional review of theater and music with far less emphasis on decadence.

17. Editorial, *The Mahogany Tree* 1.1 (1892): 3. Further references to the journal are cited parenthetically in the text as *MT*, plus volume number and issue number, followed by page number (e.g., *MT* 1.1: 3).

18. Oscar Wilde, *Complete Works* (New York: Harper & Row, 1966), 70.

19. Jussim, *Slave to Beauty*, says that Louise Guiney "was able to bring Fred along to Yeats's newly formed Rhymers' Club in London, where they met . . . a frequent guest, Oscar Wilde" (48), but she gives no source for the information.

20. Walter Crane, *An Artist's Reminiscences* (London: Methuen, 1907), 365. Further references are cited parenthetically in the text as "Crane."

21. Aurelian Blake concludes the conversation with this remark: "Go your ways, and leave me to mine" (24). The whole encounter between Cram's aesthete and a socialist named McCann anticipates a similar encounter in James Joyce's *Portrait of the Artist as a Young Man*—when another aesthete and another socialist named MacCann end their argument when Stephen Dedalus says: "You are right to go your way. Leave me to go mine." See James Joyce, *A Portrait of the Artist as a Young Man* (New York: Viking, 1964), 198. In *Stephen Hero*, the early draft of *A Portrait*, the socialist's name is not spelled "MacCann" but "McCann," as in Cram's novel.

22. Letter from Day to an unidentified correspondent, 21 November 1893. Quoted in Jussim, *Slave to Beauty*, 58.

23. Shand-Tucci, *Boston Bohemia*, 362. Shand-Tucci quotes Jeffrey Weeks, *Sex, Politics and Society* (New York and London: Longmans, 1981), 103.

24. Elaine Showalter, *Sexual Anarchy: Gender and Culture at the Fin de Siècle* (New York: Penguin, 1990), 15. Showalter's formulation employs terminology derived from Jonathan Dollimore, "Homophobia and Sexual Difference," *Oxford Literary Review* 8 (1986): 7.

25. Sidney Kramer, *A History of Stone & Kimball and Herbert S. Stone & Co.* (Chicago: University of Chicago Press, 1940), 229.

26. Wilde, *Complete Works*, 996.

27. Wilde, *Complete Works*, 558, 557.

28. Cram, *My Life in Architecture*, 84.

29. Ralph Adams Cram, *Black Sprits and White: A Book of Ghost Stories* (Chicago: Stone & Kimball, 1895), 80. Further references to this edition are cited parenthetically in the text.

30. Eve Kosofsky Sedgwick, *Between Men* (New York: Columbia University Press, 1985), 90. Quoted by Shand-Tucci, *Boston Bohemia*, 359.

31. Day was on personal terms with Morris, having secured the great man's services in the production of "a leaflet of invitation to the unveiling of the American memorial to Keats at Hampstead." F. H[olland] D[ay], "William Morris," *The Book Buyer* 12.10 (November 1895): 545–49. Quoted in *F. Holland Day: Selected Texts and Bibliography*, ed. Verna Posever Curtis and Jane Van Nimmen (Oxford: Clio, 1995), 40. The American memorial to Keats was a project that Day completed with his friend Louise Imogen Guiney in 1894. See Parrish, *Currents of the Nineties in Boston and London*, 96–209.

32. Jussim, *Slave to Beauty*, 61–62; Shand-Tucci, *Boston Bohemia*, 355–56.

33. Joe W. Krauss, *Messrs. Copeland and Day: 69 Cornhill, Boston, 1893–1899* (Philadelphia: MacManus, 1979), 16. Further references are cited parenthetically in the text.

34. *Critic* 24, n.s. 21 (26 May 1894): 360. Quoted by Krauss, *Messrs. Copeland and Day*, 21.

35. *Literary World* 25 (16 June 1894): 188. Quoted by Krauss, *Messrs. Copeland and Day*, 21–22.

36. *Critic* 27, n.s. 24 (30 November 1895): 371. Quoted by Krauss, *Messrs. Copeland and Day*, 23.

37. "The Passing of the Decadent," *Publishers' Weekly* 47 (13 April 1895): 630–31. Quoted by Krauss, *Messrs. Copeland and Day*, 22.

38. James Crump, *F. Holland Day: Suffering the Ideal* (Santa Fe: Twin Palms, 1995), 9.

39. Edward Foster, ed., *Decadence, Symbolists, & Aesthetes in America: Fin-de-Siècle American Poetry: An Anthology* (Jersey City, NJ: Talisman House, 2000), 159. Further references cited parenthetically in the text.

40. Richard Hovey, trans., *The Plays of Maurice Maeterlinck* (Chicago: Stone & Kimball, 1895). Quoted by Foster, ed., *Decadence, Symbolists, & Aesthetes in America*, 28.

41. Quoted by Verna Posever Curtis, "F. Holland Day: The Poetry of Photography," *History of Photography* 18.4 (Winter 1994): 299. Further references to this essay are cited parenthetically in the text as "Curtis."

42. F. Holland Day, "Is Photography an Art?" *F. Holland Day: Selected Texts and Bibliography*, ed. Curtis and Van Nimmen, 80.

43. Walter Pater, *The Renaissance: Studies in Art and Poetry* (Oxford: Oxford University Press, 1986), 123.

44. Jussim, *Slave to Beauty*, 121–22.

45. Jonathan Katz, *Gay American History: Lesbians and Gay Men in the USA* (New York: Crowell, 1976), 49–51. Quoted by James Crump, "F. Holland Day: 'Sacred' Subjects and 'Greek Love,'" *History of Photography* 18.4 (Winter 1994): 331.

46. Crump, "F. Holland Day: 'Sacred' Subjects and 'Greek Love,'" 329.

47. John Addington Symonds, *Male Love: A Problem in Greek Ethics and Other Writings* (New York: Pagan, 1983), 8.

48. Jean Gibran and Kahlil Gibran, *Kahlil Gibran: His Life and World* (New York: Interlink, 1998), 36–37. Further references are cited parenthetically in the text as "Gibran and Gibran."

49. Jessie Fremont Beale to F. Holland Day, 25 November 1896. Quoted in Gibran and Gibran, *Kahlil Gibran*, 37–38.

50. Estelle Jussim, *Slave to Beauty*, dates a picture of "Kahlil Gibran in costume" "about 1896" (116).

CHAPTER FOUR

1. Henry B. Fuller, *The Cliff-Dwellers* (1893; Ridgewood, NJ: Gregg, 1968), 240, 241.

2. The full-page advertisement for *The Chevalier of Pensieri-Vani* appears as part of the back matter of the second edition of the novel published in Boston by J. G. Cupples.

3. *The Chevalier of Pensieri-Vani*, 2d ed. (Boston: Cupples, 1890), 32, 160.

4. David Reisman, *Thorstein Veblen: A Critical Interpretation* (New York: Seabury, 1975), x.

5. Kenneth Scambray, *A Varied Harvest: The Life and Works of Henry Blake Fuller* (Pittsburgh: University of Pittsburgh Press, 1987), 75.

6. Joris-Karl Huysmans, *Against Nature*, trans. Robert Baldick (London: Penguin, 2003), 171. Further references to this edition are cited parenthetically in the text.

7. Darrel Abel, "Expatriation and Realism in American Fiction in the 1880's: Henry Blake Fuller," *American Literary Realism: 1870–1910* 3 (Summer 1970): 245.

8. Henry Blake Fuller, "The American School of Fiction," ed. Darrel Abel, *American Literary Realism: 1870–1910* 3 (Summer 1970): 249.

9. Fuller, "The American School of Fiction," 255 n.11.

10. Darrel Abel assigns the date 1885 to "Howells or James?" See the introductory note to "'Howells or James?'—An Essay by Henry Blake Fuller," *Modern Fiction Studies* 3 (Summer 1957): 159.

11. "'Howells or James?'—An Essay by Henry Blake Fuller," *Modern Fiction Studies*, 161. Further references are cited in the text as "H or J."

12. Quoted by John Pilkington, Jr., *Henry Blake Fuller* (New York: Twayne, 1970), 82.

13. *Atlantic Monthly* 80 (October 1897): 541. Quoted by Pilkington, *Henry Blake Fuller*, 84.

14. Stephen G. Brush, *The Temperature of History: Phases of Science and Culture in the Nineteenth Century* (New York: Franklin, 1978), 14.

15. Kenneth Scambray, *A Varied Harvest: The Life and Works of Henry Blake Fuller* (Pittsburgh: University of Pittsburgh Press, 1987), 103.

16. Henry Blake Fuller to Charles Eliot Norton, 8 April 1898. Quoted by Scambray, *A Varied Harvest*, 102.

17. This account of the Olmstead affair is taken from Laurence Senelick, *Lovesick: Modernist Plays of Same-Sex Love 1894–1925* (London and New York: Routledge, 1999), 65.

18. Letter of 19 March 1894, in Havelock Ellis, *Studies in the Psychology of Sex* (New York: Random House, 1936), 2: 171.

19. Senelick, *Lovesick*, 65.

20. Henry B. Fuller, *The Puppet-Booth: Twelve Plays* (New York: Century Company, 1896), 89. Further references are cited parenthetically in the text as *PB*.

21. Scambray, *A Varied Harvest*, 103.

22. Senelick, *Lovesick*, 61.

23. "Notes," *The Chap-Book* 5.3 (1896): 142.

24. "Notes," *The Chap-Book* 2.4 (1 January 1895): 193.

25. Although *The Chap-Book* is sometimes thought to be "inspired" by *The Yellow Book*, Sidney Kramer, *A History of Stone & Kimball and Herbert S. Stone & Co.* (Chicago: University of Chicago Press, 1940), 31, observes that "the correspondence in time of issue is too close, and the difference in content too great, to permit *The Chap-Book* to be called a mere reflection of *The Yellow Book*." Kramer, 31 n.10, also notes that "[t]he first number of *The Yellow Book* is dated April 1894, and, according to a note in *The Bookman* of September 1896, reached America on April 12th, 1894. *The Chap-Book*'s issue of May 15, 1894 was made up during April and was available in May."

26. The March 1894 announcement for *The Yellow Book* touted the forthcoming journal as "popular in the better sense of the word" and promised "no advertisements other than publishers' lists." Quoted in Fraser Harrison, introduction to *The Yellow Book* (1914; Woodbridge, Suffolk: Boydell Press, 1982), 7, 8.

27. Kramer, *A History of Stone & Kimball*, 1, 2.

28. In May 1894, when the first issue of *The Chap-Book* was published, Herbert Stone explained the purpose of the magazine to his family: "To speak plainly the *Chap-Book* is no more nor less than a semi-monthly advertisement and regular prospectus for Stone & Kimball." Quoted by Kramer, *A History of Stone & Kimball*, 25.

29. "A Bitter Complaint of the Ungentle Reader," *The Chap-Book* 1.1 (15 May 1894): 9–10. Further references to the journal are cited parenthetically in the text as *CB*, followed by volume and issue number, followed by page number (e.g., *CB* 1.1: 9–10).

30. Kramer, *A History of Stone & Kimball*, says that the Beardsley illustrations that appeared in the early issues of *The Chap-Book* were "intended for Stone & Kimball's edition of Poe" (31).

31. Another sample of the reactionary, Jacobite-inspired politics from an early issue is a piece titled "Concerning Me and the Metropolis." In it, the author details how miserable he is in Paris, as a "misanthrope [and] a royalist," especially when he is forced to look at cabbies and other workers. Such sights cause him to "grind my teeth at them and the whole incarnate Revolution" (*CB* 1.2: 36).

32. In the course of reviewing Max Nordau's *Degeneration*, the reviewer concludes that he or she must be a degenerate and so signs the review "A Degenerate" (*CB* 3.4: 147–51). "A Degenerate" later authored "The Pleasures of Historiography" (*CB* 5.2: 58–63) and "The Bureau of Literary Revision" (*CB* 5.4: 177–79).

33. Louise Imogen Guiney, "From 'Willful Sadness in Literature,'" *Decadents, Symbolists, & Aesthetes in America: Fin de Siècle American Poetry: An Anthology*, ed. Edward Foster (Jersey City: Talisman, 2000), 36. It should be noted that in this essay Guiney expresses hope that the prevailing mood of sadness in literature is about to end: "Change is at hand. The Maypole is up in Bookland" (36).

34. Kramer, *A History of Stone & Kimball*, 236.

35. Kramer, *A History of Stone & Kimball*, 218.

36. Despite the sensational title, *The Sin-Eater* is a fairly conventional collection of stories of the supernatural, set in the Irish countryside. With his occasional use of Gaelic in the dialogue, the author may be attempting to capitalize on the "Celtic Twilight" of the late nineteenth century. See Fiona Macleod [William Sharp], *The Sin Eater and Other Tales* (Chicago: Stone & Kimball, 1895).

37. Claude-Marie Senninger, ed., *Baudelaire par Théophile Gautier* (Paris: Klincksieck, 1986), 125.

38. Along these lines, it is worth remarking that upscale hotels and gambling casinos in the United States are often "palaces," as in the Helmsley Palace Hotel in New York City and Caesar's Palace in Atlantic City and Las Vegas.

39. Thorstein Veblen, *The Theory of the Leisure Class* (1899; New York: Penguin, 1979), 128. Further references are cited parenthetically in the text as "Veblen."

40. Oscar Wilde, preface to *The Picture of Dorian Gray, Complete Works* (New York: Harper & Row, 1966), 17.

41. For a general indication of Veblen's influences, see Joseph Dorfman, "Background of Veblen's Thought," *Thorstein Veblen*, ed. Carlton C. Qualey (New York: Columbia University Press, 1968), 106–30, and the preface to the paperback edition of David Riesman, *Thorstein Veblen: A Critical Interpretation* (New York: Seabury, 1960), vii–xvi. For specific reference to literary influences, see Dorfman, "Background," 122–23, and Riesman, *Thorstein Veblen*, xii.

42. Vernon Louis Parrington, *Main Currents in American Thought* (New York: Harcourt Brace, 1930), 3: xii. Quoted by Riesman, *Thorstein Veblen*, xii.

43. Bernard R. Brown, Jr., *Henry B. Fuller of Chicago: The Ordeal of a Genteel Realist in Ungenteel America* (Westport, CT: Greenwood, 1974), 135, xix.

44. Henry B. Fuller, *With the Procession* (New York: Harper & Brothers, 1895), 49. Further references are cited parenthetically in the text.

CHAPTER FIVE

1. Franklin Walker, *San Francisco's Literary Frontier* (New York: Knopf, 1939), 11. The account of San Francisco circa 1849–1869 in this paragraph is derived from Franklin, chapter 1, 3–16.

2. Donald T. Blume, introduction to Ambrose Bierce, *Tales of Soldiers and Civilians* (Kent: Kent State University Press, 2004), ix.

3. Walker, *San Francisco's Literary Frontier*, 352.

4. S. T. Joshi and David E. Schultz, eds., *A Much Misunderstood Man: Selected Letters of Ambrose Bierce* (Columbus: Ohio State University Press, 2003), 9n.6. Further references are cited parenthetically in the text as MMM.

5. Quoted by Lawrence I. Berkove, *A Prescription for Adversity: The Moral Art of Ambrose Bierce* (Columbus: Ohio State University Press, 2002), xi.

6. Letter to Blanche Partington, 26 December 1913, MMM, 246.

7. Carey McWilliams, *Ambrose Bierce: A Biography* (New York: Albert and Charles Boni, 1929), 179, 190. Further references are cited parenthetically in the text as "McWilliams."

8. For an account of Bierce's campaign against the Funding Bill, see McWilliams, 236–46; M. E. Grenander, *Ambrose Bierce* (New York: Twayne Publishers, 1971), 55–58; and Ernest Jerome Hopkins, ed., *The Ambrose Bierce Satanic Reader: Selections from the Invective Journalism of the Great Satirist* (Garden City, NY: Doubleday, 1968), 210–22.

9. Berkove, *A Prescription for Adversity*, 26.

10. See Henry Blake Fuller, *The New Flag: Satires* (Chicago, 1899). For discussion, see Kenneth Scambray, *A Varied Harvest: The Life and Works of Henry Blake Fuller* (Pittsburgh: University of Pittsburgh Press, 1987), 113–17.

11. *The Examiner*, 31 July 1898; quoted by McWilliams, 248.

12. "Greetings to an Aesthetic Visitor" (1882), *The Ambrose Bierce Satanic Reader: Selections from the Invective Journalism of the Great Satirist*, ed. Ernest Jerome Hopkins (Garden City, NY: Doubleday, 1968), 5–6. Originally published in *The Wasp* 296 (31 March 1882): 198. Further references to *The Ambrose Bierce Satanic Reader* are cited parenthetically in the text as SR.

13. Letter to Blanche Partington, 15 August 1892, MMM, 24.

14. McWilliams, *Ambrose Bierce*, 184.

15. M. E. Grenander, *Ambrose Bierce* (New York: Twayne Publishers, 1971), 163.

16. In his patriotic "Invocation," an ode to liberty read on Independence Day, 1888, in San Francisco, Bierce worries prophetically over the day when "Majorities in passion draw / Insurgent swords to murder Law" but is more anxious about the "nearer menace" when "the band / Of feeble spirits cringe and plead / To the gigantic strength of Greed." *Poems of Ambrose Bierce*, ed. M. E. Grenander (Lincoln and London: University of Nebraska Press, 1995), 16. Of Bierce's "Invocation" McWilliams observes: "Much of its tone of dire foreboding and its prescience of dark times ahead may be attributed to the fact that the famous anarchist bombing in Chicago occurred in 1886." McWilliams, 181.

17. The phrase is Huneker's, from *Bedouins* (1920; New York: Scribner, 1926), 10.

18. Clifton P. Fadiman, "Portrait of a Misanthrope," *Saturday Review* (12 October 1946): 12. Quoted by Joshi and Schultz, introduction to MMM, xv.

19. Letter to Myles Walsh, 6 June 1905, MMM, 136.

20. Letter to George Sterling, 8 May 1908, MMM, 179.

21. *The Devil's Dictionary* (New York: Oxford University Press, 1999), 144. Further references to this edition are cited parenthetically in the text as *DD*. For the observation that the definitions originally began with the letter *P*, see McWilliams, *Ambrose Bierce*, 155.

22. Quoted by Roy Morris, Jr., introduction to *The Devil's Dictionary* (New York: Oxford University Press, 1999), xxii.

23. Morris, introduction to *The Devil's Dictionary*, xxii.

24. Percival Pollard, *Their Day in Court* (New York: Neal, 1909), 261, 262. Further references are cited parenthetically in the text as "Pollard."

25. Joseph Noel, *Footloose in Arcadia: A Personal Record of Jack London, George Sterling, Ambrose Bierce* (New York: Carrick & Evans, 1940), 44.

26. Jacques Barzun, introduction to *The Dictionary of Accepted Ideas* (New York: New Directions, 1954), 2. Further references are cited parenthetically in the text as "Barzun."

27. Gustave Flaubert, *The Dictionary of Accepted Ideas*, trans. Jacques Barzun (New York: New Directions, 1954), 31. Further references are cited parenthetically in the text.

28. For this discussion, see the chapter on Flaubert in Roger L. Williams, *The Horror of Life* (Chicago: University of Chicago Press, 1980), 111–216.

29. S. T. Joshi and David E. Schultz, introduction to Ambrose Bierce, *The Fall of the Republic and Other Satires* (Knoxville: University of Tennessee Press, 2000), xi. The book edited by Joshi and Schultz uses Bierce's original title from the 1890s but is not identical with the volume Bierce shopped to Stone and Kimball.

30. John Wenke, "Gelett Burgess," *American Humorists, 1800–1950*, ed. Stanley Trachtenberg, vol. 11 of *Dictionary of Literary Biography* (Detroit: Gale Research, 1982), 72, 75, 76.

31. *The Lark* (May 1895): n.p. The pages of *The Lark*, printed on one side of the paper only, are unnumbered for all issues.

32. Edward Foster, ed., *Decadents, Symbolists, & Aesthetes in America: Fin de Siècle American Poetry: An Anthology* (Jersey City, NJ: Talisman, 2000), 157.

33. Gelett Burgess, *Bayside Bohemia: Fin de Siècle San Francisco and Its Little Magazines*, intro. James D. Hart (San Francisco: Book Club of California, 1954), 19. Further references are cited parenthetically in the text as *BB*.

34. Joseph M. Backus, *Behind the Scenes: Glimpses of Fin de Siècle San Francisco* (San Francisco: Book Club of California, 1968), 11.

35. *The Epilark* (1 May 1897): 9.

36. *The Lark* (November 1895): n.p.

37. A reproduction of this cover appears between pages 24 and 25 of *BB*.

38. *The Lark* (October 1895): n.p.

39. Quoted by Backus, *Behind the Scenes*, 13.

40. *The Lark* (January 1896): n.p.

41. *The Lark* (February 1896): n.p.

42. *The Lark* (April 1896): n.p.

43. *The Lark* (July 1896): n.p.

44. Larzer Ziff, *The American 1890s: Life and Times of a Lost Generation* (New York: Viking, 1966), 140.

45. Anne Southampton Bliss [Gelett Burgess], "Our Clubbing List," *Le Petit Journal des Refusées* (Summer 1896): n.p. Quoted by Ziff, *American 1890s*, 140.

46. Quoted by Foster, ed., *Decadents, Symbolists, & Aesthetes in America*, 90.

47. Gelett Burgess, *Vivette, or The Memoirs of the Romance Association* (Boston: Copeland and Day, 1897), 83. Further references to this edition are indicated parenthetically as "V."

48. Quoted by Noel, *Footloose in Arcadia*, 76–77.

49. Albert Parry, *Garrets and Pretenders: A History of Bohemianism in America* (New York: Covici, Fried, 1933), 238.

50. For a full account of the Carmel colony, see Franklin Walker, *The Seacoast of Bohemia* (Santa Barbara and Salt Lake City: Peregrine Smith, 1973).

51. Quoted in Parry, *Garrets and Pretenders*, 238; also in Walker, *Seacoast of Bohemia*, 10.

52. W. J. Burke and Will D. Howe, *American Authors and Books: 1640 to the Present Day*, revised by Irving Weiss and Anne Weiss (New York: Crown, 1972), 63.

53. Parry, *Garrets and Pretenders*, 238–39.

54. George Sterling, *A Wine of Wizardry and Other Poems* (San Francisco: Robertson, 1907), 131, 132, 135.

55. Noel, *Footloose in Arcadia*, 45.

56. Noel, *Footloose in Arcadia*, 100.

57. Thomas E. Benedicktsson, *George Sterling* (Boston: Twayne, 1980), 86.

58. Benedicktsson, *George Sterling*, 87.

59. See the entry for "Decadence," *Princeton Encyclopedia of Poetry and Poetics*, enlarged edition, ed. Alex Preminger (Princeton: Princeton University Press, 1974), 185–86.

60. George Sterling, "Ode on the Centenary of the Birth of Robert Browning," *Selected Poems* (New York: Holt, 1923), 171–72.

61. Joan London, *Jack London and His Times: An Unconventional Biography* (Seattle and London: University of Washington Press, 1968), 258.

62. This observation must be qualified by Sterling's appreciation of the modernist poet Robinson Jeffers, published the year of his death: *Robinson Jeffers: The Man and the Artist* (New York: Boni and Liveright, 1926).

63. Ambrose Bierce, "A Poet and His Poem," *Cosmopolitan* 43 (September 1907): 551. Quoted by Noel, *Footloose in Arcadia*, 165.

64. Ambrose Bierce, "A Poet and His Poem," *Cosmopolitan* 43 (September 1907): 576. Quoted by Benedicktsson, *George Sterling*, 38.

65. H[arriet] M[onroe], "The Poetry of George Sterling," *Poetry* 7.6 (March 1916): 310–11. Quoted by S. T. Joshi, introduction to *From Baltimore to Bohemia: The Letters of H. L. Mencken and George Sterling* (Madison, NJ: Fairleigh Dickinson University Press, 2001), 8.

66. Joshi, introduction to *From Baltimore to Bohemia*, 9.

67. H. L. Mencken, "Ambrose Bierce," *Prejudices: Sixth Series* (New York: Knopf, 1927), 263, 264.

68. Letter from H. L. Mencken to John Cowper Powys, 11 December 1926. S. T. Joshi, ed., *From Baltimore to Bohemia*, 248.

CHAPTER SIX

1. "From the beginning Mencken saw clarity as the hallmark of good prose. Revealingly, he took Thomas Henry Huxley's style, rather than the more Byzantine constructions of a John Ruskin or a Walter Pater, as his model." Vincent Fitzpatrick, *H. L. Mencken* (New York: Continuum, 1989), 22.

2. H. L. Mencken, "Portrait of a Tragic Comedian," *H. L. Mencken's "Smart Set" Criticism*, ed. William H. Nolte (Washington, DC: Gateway, 1987), 207. Originally published September 1916.

3. H. L. Mencken, *A Little Book in C Major* (New York: Lane, 1916).

4. H. L. Mencken, "A Note on Oscar Wilde," *H. L. Mencken's "Smart Set" Criticism*, ed. Nolte, 217. Originally published January 1910.

5. H. L. Mencken, *The Philosophy of Friedrich Nietzsche*, 3d ed. (1913; New Brunswick: Transaction, 1993), 92–93. Further references to this edition are cited parenthetically in the text as "N."

6. Fitzpatrick, *H. L. Mencken*, 20–21.

7. Friedrich Nietzsche, *The Birth of Tragedy and the Case of Wagner*, trans. Walter Kaufman (New York: Random House, 1967), 155. Further references are cited parenthetically in the text as *CW*.

8. For Nietzsche's use of 'decadence' to mean life-negating moralism, see *CW*, 155, and also *Ecce Homo*, where morality is called "the idiosyncrasy of decadents." *On the Genealogy of Morals and Ecce Homo*, trans. Walter Kaufmann (New York: Random House, 1967), 333. Further references to this edition are cited parenthetically in the text as *EH*.

9. Nietzsche defines "*Christian* morality" as "the morality of decadence" in *EH*, 328. Again, Mencken does not follow Nietzsche in his language, but he does in his thinking, when he treats Puritanism as something that robs life of its "gusto," to use one of Mencken's favorite words.

10. H. L. Mencken, "Ezra Pound," *H. L. Mencken's "Smart Set" Criticism*, ed. Nolte, 77. Originally published April 1911.

11. H. L. Mencken, "Huneker's Confessions," *H. L. Mencken's "Smart Set" Criticism*, ed. Nolte, 204. Originally published December 1920.

12. H. L. Mencken, *A Book of Prefaces* (1917; New York: Garden City, 1927), 159. Further references are cited parenthetically in the text as *BP*.

13. H. L. Mencken, *Prejudices: A Selection* (Baltimore and London: Johns Hopkins, 1996), 129. Further references to this edition are cited parenthetically in the text as *PS*.

14. H. L. Mencken, *Prejudices: Fifth Series* (New York: Knopf, 1926), 281–82. Further references to this edition are cited parenthetically in the text as *PF*.

15. "The Stylist Who Created a Mythology of Manhattan," *Current Opinion* 65.4 (October 1918): 254. Further references are cited parenthetically in the text as *CU*.

16. Carl Van Vechten, *The Merry-Go-Round* (New York: Knopf, 1918), 45, 70.

17. Carl Van Doren, "The Roving Critic," *The Nation* 114 (11 January 1922): 45.

18. Gorham B. Munson, "The Limbo of American Literature," *Broom* 2 (1922): 251. Further references are cited parenthetically in the text.

19. See Arthur Symons, "The Decadent Movement in Literature," *Harper's New Monthly Magazine* 67 (November 1893): 858–67.

20. Arthur Symons, *Dramatis Personae* (Indianapolis: Bobbs-Merrill, 1923), 263, 267. Further references to this edition are cited parenthetically in the text.

21. Sadakichi Hartmann, "The Edgar Saltus I Knew," *The Bookman* 58.1 (September 1923): 17.

22. Percival Pollard, *Their Day in Court* (New York and Washington: Neale, 1909), 71. Further references are cited parenthetically in the text as "Pollard."

23. H. L. Mencken, "James Branch Cabell," *H. L. Mencken on American Literature*, ed. S. T. Joshi (Athens: Ohio University Press, 2002), 96. Originally published August 1918.

24. S. T. Joshi, ed., *H. L. Mencken on American Literature* (Athens: Ohio University Press, 2002), 98. Further references are cited parenthetically in the text as MAL.

25. James Branch Cabell, *Jurgen: A Comedy of Justice* (1919; New York: McBride, 1922), 3. Further references are cited parenthetically in the text.

26. For a brief account of the *Jurgen* controversy, see Ritchie D. Watson Jr., "James Branch Cabell: A Bibliographical Essay," *James Branch Cabell: Centennial Essays*, ed. M. Thomas Inge and Edgar E. MacDonald (Baton Rouge: Louisiana State University Press, 1983), 153.

27. In his *Smart Set* review of January 1920, Mencken makes the point that "[t]he satire here ceases to be light-fingered and becomes heavy handed" (MAL, 103). But in another *Smart Set* review of another Cabell book, *Figures of Earth*, from May 1921, Mencken quotes the same passage he had earlier called "heavy-handed" but calls it "memorable buffoonery" (MAL, 105).

28. Leslie A. Fiedler, "The Return of James Branch Cabell," *James Branch Cabell: Centennial Essays*, ed. M. Thomas Inge and Edgar E. MacDonald (Baton Rouge: Louisiana State University Press, 1983), 135. Further references to this essay are cited parenthetically in the text as "Fiedler."

29. James Branch Cabell, *Quiet Please* (Gainesville: University of Florida Press, 1952), 27.

30. Edward Wagenknecht, ed., *The Letters of James Branch Cabell* (Norman: University of Oklahoma Press, 1975), 103: "I did not find *Gone with the Wind* to be even readable, far less a masterpiece."

31. Lin Carter, "About *The High Place* and James Branch Cabell," introduction to *The High Place* (New York: Ballantine Books, 1970), xi.

32. Victor E. Gimmestad, *Joseph Hergesheimer* (Boston: Twayne, 1984), 99.

33. H. L. Mencken, *H. L. Mencken's "Smart Set" Criticism*, ed. William H. Nolte (Washington: Gateway, 1987), 330.

34. Gimmestad, *Joseph Hergesheimer*, 6.

35. Gimmestad, *Joseph Hergesheimer*, 69.

36. Joseph Hergesheimer, *The Bright Shawl* (Garden City, NY: Garden City Publishing, 1922), 9. Further references to this edition are cited parenthetically in the text.

37. Alfred Kazin, *On Native Grounds: An Interpretation of Modern American Literature* (1942; New York: Harcourt Brace Jovanovich, 1982), 228. Further references are cited parenthetically in the text as "Kazin."

38. At midcentury Thomas Beer was sufficiently remembered for Van Wyck Brooks to include him among the young writers of the 1920s who were "in revolt against an aesthetically joyless American scene" and against "the colorless 'genteel tradition.'" Brooks groups Beer with the all-but-forgotten James Branch Cabell and Joseph Hergesheimer as practitioners of an "artificial style and vision[,] tokens in various ways of the 'golden boom, the gaudiest spree in history,' as Fitzgerald called it." Van Wyck Brooks, *The Confident Years: 1885–1915* (New York: Dutton, 1952), 560.

39. Thomas Beer, *The Mauve Decade: American Life at the End of the Nineteenth Century* (1926; New York: Knopf, 1937), 103. Further references to this edition are cited parenthetically in the text.

40. Strictly speaking, the epitaph reads: "Mr. Whistler said: 'Mauve? Mauve is just pink trying to be purple.'" I have not identified Beer's source for Whistler's remark.

41. John Clendenning, "Stephen Crane and His Biographers: Beer, Berryman, Schoberlin, and Stallman," *American Literary Realism* 28.1 (Fall 1995), 25, 26, 31.

42. Bernard R. Bowron Jr., *Henry B. Fuller of Chicago: The Ordeal of a Genteel Realist in Ungenteel America* (Westport, CT: Greenwood, 1974), 170.

43. Quoted by Kenneth Scambray, *A Varied Harvest: The Life and Work of Henry Blake Fuller* (Pittsburgh: University of Pittsburgh Press, 1987), 153.

44. Scambray, *A Varied Harvest*, 149.

45. John Pilkington Jr., *Henry Blake Fuller* (New York: Twayne, 1970), 151.

46. Bowron, *Henry B. Fuller of Chicago*, 174.

47. Henry Blake Fuller, *Bertram Cope's Year* (New York: Turtle Point, 1998), 25. Further references to this edition are cited parenthetically in the text.

48. Scambray, *A Varied Harvest*, 151–52.

49. In *The Intermediate Sex: A Study of Some Transitional Types of Men and Women* (New York: Kennerly, 1912), Edward Carpenter argues that "Uranian love [is] of a higher order than the ordinary attachment" (20 n.) and names Sappho, Michelangelo, Shakespeare, and Marlowe, among others, to support his claim that the "greatest . . . artists have been dowered either wholly or in part with the Uranian temperament" (36).

50. Scambray, *A Varied Harvest*, 103.

51. James Huneker to Henry B. Fuller, 11 May 1902. *Intimate Letters of James Gibbons Huneker*, ed. Josephine Huneker ([New York:] Boni and Liveright, 1924), 23.

52. James Huneker to Henry B. Fuller, 19 December 1920. *Intimate Letters of James Gibbons Huneker*, ed. Josephine Huneker, 310.

53. Edmund Wilson, *The Devils and Canon Barham: Ten Essays on Poets, Novelists and Monsters* (New York: Farrar, Straus and Giroux, 1973), 41. Further references are cited parenthetically in the text as "Wilson."

54. Andrew Solomon, afterword to *Bertram Cope's Year* (New York: Turtle Point, 1998), 290.

55. Edward Foster, ed., *Decadence, Symbolists, & Aesthetes in America: Fin-de-Siècle American Poetry: An Anthology* (Jersey City: Talisman House, 2000), 159. Further references cited parenthetically in the text as "Foster."

56. W. D. Halls, *Maurice Maeterlinck: A Study of His Life and Thought* (1960; Westport, CT: Greenwood, 1978), observes: "Perhaps it was through Carlyle that Maeterlinck came . . . to appreciate Emerson. Many essays of *Le Tresór des humbles* bear the stamp of the 'pastor of Concord'" (126).

57. See Hamilton Osgood, "Maeterlinck and Emerson," *Arena* 15 (March, 1896): 563–73.

58. Anna Balakian, *The Symbolist Movement: A Critical Heritage* (New York: New York University Press, 1977), 14–15.

59. Montrose J. Moses, foreword to Maurice Maeterlinck, *On Emerson and Other Essays* (New York: Dodd, Mead, 1912), 11.

60. For example, in the essay "The Inner Beauty," Maeterlinck speaks of "the great reservoir of truth and beauty" that provides the basis for "the shallower reservoir of true or beautiful thoughts." Although absolute access to the "great reservoir" is denied us, "Emerson tells us that there is not an act or event in our life but, sooner or later, casts off its outer shell, and bewilders us by its sudden flight, from the very depths of us, on high into the empyrean." *The Treasure of the Humble*, trans. Alfred Sutro (New York: Dodd, Mead, [1897]), 236. Further references to this edition are cited parenthetically in the text as *Treasure*.

61. Una Taylor, *Maurice Maeterlinck: A Critical Study* (1915; Port Washington, NY: Kennicat, 1968), 141.

62. Maeterlinck, *Treasure*, 20, 22.

63. Kahlil Gibran, *The Prophet* (London: Pan, 1991), 82. Further references cited parenthetically in the text as *Prophet*.

64. Jean Gibran and Kahlil Gibran, *Kahlil Gibran: His Life and World* (New York: Interlink, 1998), 371. Further references cited as "Gibran and Gibran."

65. Douglass Shand-Tucci, *Boston Bohemia 1881–1900: Ralph Adams Cram: Life and Architecture* (Amherst: University of Massachusetts Press, 1995), 43.

66. Harriet Monroe, "Journeyman Poets," *Poetry: A Magazine of Verse* 14 (August 1919): 278.

67. Isidor Schneider, "One Poet," *Poetry: A Magazine of Verse* 28 (April 1921): 41. Further references cited parenthetically in the text as "Schneider."

68. José Ortega y Gasset, *The Dehumanization of Art and Other Essays on Art, Culture, and Literature* (1925; Princeton: Princeton University Press, 1968), 7.

69. Renato Poggioli, *The Theory of the Avant-Garde*, trans. Gerald Fitzgerald (1962; Cambridge: Harvard University Press, 1968), 79.

70. Marjorie Allen Seiffert, "Foreign Food," *Poetry: A Magazine of Verse* 23 (January 1924): 216. Further references are cited parenthetically in the text as "Seiffert."

71. Shand-Tucci, *Boston Bohemia*, 373.

72. Foster, introduction to *Decadence, Symbolists, & Aesthetes in America*, 12n. Foster adds that the line occurs in *The House of the Vampire* when "a former vaudeville singer remembers the time when 'They called me Betsy, the Hyacinth Girl.' The vampire in Viereck's novel steals from people their most arresting qualities (in the case of the Hyacinth Girl, it is the melancholy sweetness in her otherwise undistinguished voice). Eliot's method in 'The Waste Land,' incorporating lines from other texts, is in effect the same" (12n).

73. See Shand-Tucci, *Boston Bohemia*, 70–71. Shand-Tucci quotes these lines to help explain Cram's conversion to the Church of England: "American Protestantism . . . had satisfied him neither intellectually nor emotionally. Yet the Christian patrimony he inherited from generations of upright New Englanders lay at the heart of his tradition. . . . In the Church of England, with its grand liturgy, its ancient intellectual power, its splendid churches of every period, its virtual identity with English culture, he came to discover what he had found wanting . . . in the latter day sectarianism of Beacon Hill." The explanation is taken from a biography of T. S. Eliot by Russell Kirk, *Eliot and His Age* (La Salle, IL: Sherwood, Sugden, 1971), 138–39, 144.

74. T. S. Eliot, introduction to Djuna Barnes, *Nightwood* (New York: New Directions, 1937), xii.

75. Frederick J. Hoffmann, *The Twenties: American Writing in the Postwar Decade*, rev. ed. (New York: Free Press, 1966), 38.

76. Alfred I. Kisch, *The Romantic Ghost of Greenwich Village: Guido Bruno in his Garret* (Frankfurt: Lang, 1976), 13, 17, 22.

77. Kisch, *The Romantic Ghost of Greenwich Village*, 23, 29, 31–32.

78. Louis F. Kannenstine, *The Art of Djuna Barnes: Duality and Damnation* (New York: New York University Press, 1977), 19–20.

79. Deborah Parsons, *Djuna Barnes* (Tavistock, Devon: Northcote House, 2003), 15, 16.

80. Djuna Barnes, "From Fifth Avenue Up," *The Book of Repulsive Women: Eight Rhythms and Five Drawings* (1915; Los Angeles: Sun & Moon, 1989), n.p.

81. Barnes, *The Book of Repulsive Women*, n.p.

82. Phillip Herring, *Djuna: The Life and Work of Djuna Barnes* (New York: Viking Penguin, 1995), 122.

83. Djuna Barnes, *Collected Stories*, ed. Phillip Herring (Los Angeles: Sun & Moon, 1996), 56, 57. Further references are cited parenthetically in the text.

84. Herring, *Djuna Barnes*, says the title "refers to Babylon, Long Island, just south of the Barnes's Huntington farm" (85), but the story itself does not make the setting clear.

85. Herring, *Djuna Barnes*, 85–86.

86. Dante Alighieri, *The Inferno*, trans. Robert M. Durling (New York: Oxford University Press, 1996), 26.

87. Kenneth Burke, "Version, Con-, Per-, and In-: Thoughts on Djuna Barnes's Novel, *Nightwood*," *The Southern Review* 2 (April 1966): 335, 336.

88. Djuna Barnes, *Nightwood* (New York: New Directions, 1937), 84, 95, 107, 117. Further references to this edition are cited parenthetically in the text.

89. Charles-Augustine Sainte-Beuve, *Nouveaux Lundis* (Paris: Lévy, 1881), 4: 35.

90. For an account of the early history of the Modern Library, see Jay Satterfield, *The World's Best Books: Taste, Culture, and the Modern Library* (Amherst and Boston: University of Massachusetts Press, 2002), 10–37.

91. Floyd Dell, introduction to George Moore, *Confessions of a Young Man* (New York: Modern Library, [1917]), vii. Further references to Dell's introduction are cited parenthetically in the text.

92. Matei Calinescu, *Five Faces of Modernity: Modernism, Avant-Garde, Decadence, Kitsch, Postmodernism* (Durham: Duke University Press, 1987), 69, notes that *modernism*, as a positive term descriptive of a particular type of culture (mainly literary), gained "acceptance and legitimacy only after the 1920s."

AFTERWORD

1. Burton Rascoe, introduction to Ben Hecht, *Eric Dorn* (New York: Modern Library, n.d.), vii: "If I were disposed to credit the theory of reincarnation . . . I should say that Ben Hecht has inherited the soul which Joris-Karl Huysmans relinquished when he commended himself to the Trappists and to God."

2. Pauline Kael made the claim that Hecht wrote "half the most entertaining movies to come out of Hollywood." Quoted by Doug Fetherling, *The Five Lives of Ben Hecht* (Toronto: Lester and Orpen, 1977), 87.

3. The inscription appears in Smith's presentation copy to La Rocque (in my collection) of Ben Hecht, *Fantazius Mallare: A Mysterious Oath* (Chicago: Covici-McGee, 1922), [3].

4. Ephraim Katz, *The Film Encyclopedia* (New York: HarperCollins, 1994), 791.

5. *Sunset Boulevard*, dir. Billy Wilder, 110 min., Paramount Pictures Corp., 1950, videocassette.

6. For a discussion of Hecht's career as a decadent author and his admiration of Huneker, see David Weir, *Decadence and the Making of Modernism* (Amherst: University of Massachusetts Press, 1995), 175–91.

7. Oscar Wilde, *Salome: A Tragedy in One Act* (London and New York: Lane, 1926), x–xii.

8. Elaine Showalter, *Sexual Anarchy: Gender and Culture at the Fin de Siècle* (New York: Penguin, 1990), 160–61.

9. The blurb by Rex Reed appears on the back cover of the December 1981 reprint of Kenneth Anger, *Hollywood Babylon* (New York: Dell, 1975). Further references to this edition are cited parenthetically in the text as "Anger."

10. Showalter, *Sexual Anarchy*, 163.

11. Alice L. Hutchinson, *Kenneth Anger: A Demonic Visionary* (London: Black Dog, 2004), 242 n.45. Further references are cited parenthetically in the text as "Hutchinson."

12. Charles Ross Ridge, *The Hero in French Decadent Literature* (Athens: University of Georgia Press, 1961), 57. Quoted by Hutchinson, 242 n.46.

13. Anna Powell, "The Occult: A Torch for Lucifer," *Moonchild: The Films of Kenneth Anger*, ed. Jack Hunter (New York: Creation Books, 2002), 65, 73.

14. Bill Landis, *Anger: The Unauthorized Biography of Kenneth Anger* (New York: HarperCollins, 1995), 25.

15. For Crowley's influence on Anger, see Landis, *Anger*, 25–34 and passim.

16. Lawrence Sutin, *Do What Thou Wilt: A Life of Aleister Crowley* (New York: St. Martin's, 2000), 2.

17. Quoted by Gerald Suster, *The Legacy of the Beast: The Life, Work and Influence of Aleister Crowley* (York Beach, Maine: Weiser, 1989), 226.

18. This synopsis appears in the filmography of Hutchinson's *Kenneth Anger: A Demonic Visionary*, 225; in the filmography of *Moonchild*, ed. Hunter, 109–10, the synopsis is essentially the same but with minor variations; the synopsis on the back cover of the Mystic Fire Video VHS recording of the film (1986), credited to Anger, is likewise the same in all important particulars, except that this synopsis begins: "A convocation of magicians assume the identity of gods and goddesses in a Dionysian revel."

19. Hutchinson mentions that the film was "[c]alculated by the filmmaker to be experienced under the effects of LSD" (91).

20. In 1962 Anger wrote from Brooklyn to Henri Langlois of the Cinémathèque Française in Paris: "I've started a film here in color, on the cult of the motorcyclist. But not at all 'The Wild One'!!" Quoted by Hutchinson, 121.

21. Juan A. Suárez, *Bike Boys, Drag Queens, and Superstars: Avant-Garde, Mass Culture, and Gay Identities in the 1960s Underground Cinema* (Bloomington and Indianapolis: Indiana University Press, 1996), 148. Further references are cited parenthetically in the text as "Suárez."

22. See references to Anger's decadentism by Hutchinson, Powell, and Landis, in earlier notes.

23. Quoted by Anna Powell, *Moonchild*, 69.

24. Quoted in the filmography of Hunter, ed., *Moonchild*, 111.

25. Quintin Crisp was best known as the author of *The Naked Civil Servant* (1968) and for his extremely dandified appearance. Appropriately, he wrote a preface to an edition of Jules Barbey D'Aurevilly's *Dandyism* (New York: PAJ, 1988).

26. Susan Sontag, "Notes on Camp," *Against Interpretation and Other Essays* (New York: Farrar, Strauss, and Giroux, 1966), 291, 287. Sontag does not include Anger in her "canon of Camp" (278) but she does list "many of the works of Jean Cocteau" (278). Cocteau was an important influence on Anger who participates in the "decadence" I am attempting to describe. For the record, in *Bike Boys* Suárez comments that Anger's "movies . . . show a self-conscious camp irony, present mainly in the excessive mise-en-scène, which undermines any pretense of seriousness" (146).

Index

www.ingramcontent.com/pod-product-compliance
Lightning Source LLC
Chambersburg PA
CBHW032341200526
45163CB00018BA/291